Language

Heidegger characterizes the relationship between language and Being as "language is the house of Being", negating the idea that language is merely a tool ready to be used at hand.

Drawing on this idea, as well as ideas from anthropology, pragmatics, and folklore studies, the author argues that "language is the last homestead of human beings", meaning that mankind lives within language, has to live within language, and lives in formulaic speech events. The author takes Western classic works on the philosophy of language and his own insights of language use, rooted in traditional Chinese culture, in order to develop his own localized theory. In this title, the author explores the philosophical aspect of man's survival by presenting day-to-day exchange routines such as weddings and fortune-telling dialogues in the Chinese context.

Awarded the first prize for Academic Excellence in Philosophy and Social Sciences in Guangdong Province, and second prize in the second Xu Guozhang Award for Foreign Language Studies, this is a must-read for researchers interested in the philosophy of language and pragmatics.

Guanlian Qian is a professor at Guangdong University of Foreign Studies. His research interests are the philosophy of language and pragmatics.

Chinese Linguistics

Chinese Linguistics series selects representative and frontier works in linguistic disciplines including lexicology, grammar, phonetics, dialectology, philology and rhetoric. Mostly published in Chinese before, the selection has had far-reaching influence on China's linguistics and offered inspiration and reference for the world's linguistics. The aim of this series is to reflect the general level and latest development of Chinese linguistics from an overall and objective view.

Titles in this series currently include:

Practical Grammar of Modern Chinese I
Overview and Notional Words
Liu Yuehua, Pan Wenyu and Gu Wei

Practical Grammar of Modern Chinese II
Function Words
Liu Yuehua, Pan Wenyu and Gu Wei

Practical Grammar of Modern Chinese III
Sentence Constituents
Liu Yuehua, Pan Wenyu and Gu Wei

Practical Grammar of Modern Chinese IV
Simple Sentence, Compound Sentence and Discourse
Liu Yuehua, Pan Wenyu and Gu Wei

Loanwords in the Chinese Language
Shi Youwei

For more information, please visit https://www.routledge.com/Chinese-Linguistics/book-series/CL

Language
The Last Homestead of Human Beings

Guanlian Qian

LONDON AND NEW YORK

This book is published with financial support from the Chinese Fund for the Humanities and Social Sciences.

First edition in English 2021
by Routledge
2 Park Square, Milton Park, Abingdon, Oxon OX14 4RN

and by Routledge
605 Third Avenue, New York, NY 10158

Routledge is an imprint of the Taylor & Francis Group, an informa business

© 2021 Guanlian Qian

Translated by Xiuwei Chu, Yongshou Huo, Ruiqing Liang, Shuang Liang

The right of Guanlian Qian to be identified as author of this work has been asserted by him in accordance with sections 77 and 78 of the Copyright, Designs and Patents Act 1988.

All rights reserved. No part of this book may be reprinted or reproduced or utilised in any form or by any electronic, mechanical, or other means, now known or hereafter invented, including photocopying and recording, or in any information storage or retrieval system, without permission in writing from the publishers.

Trademark notice: Product or corporate names may be trademarks or registered trademarks, and are used only for identification and explanation without intent to infringe.

English version by permission of The Commercial Press.

British Library Cataloguing-in-Publication Data
A catalogue record for this book is available from the British Library

Library of Congress Cataloging-in-Publication Data
A catalog record has been requested for this book

ISBN: 978-0-367-52878-2 (hbk)
ISBN: 978-0-367-52882-9 (pbk)
ISBN: 978-1-003-07970-5 (ebk)

Typeset in Times New Roman
by Newgen Publishing UK

Contents

Preamble	vi
Preface 1: Grabbing a language means grabbing its thoughts	vii
Preface 2	xi
Preface 3	xiv
Preface 4: Finally, I'm back home!	xvi
Preface for the English edition	xxiii

1 Introduction	1
2 Philosophical and pragmatic perspectives	13
3 Language: Mankind's last homestead	65
4 Language betraying human beings: The paradox of "language being mankind's last homestead"	263
5 Choosing not to speak	277
Postscript: Picking the grapes within my reach	282
References	305
Index	313

Preamble

Just as a snail stays in its shell, a human being dwells in his own homestead of language. Just as a snail carries its shell on its back forever, a human being carries on himself his own house of language forever.

The author

As one of the basic facets of human existence, mankind has to depend on language for every single moment of existence; we live in language, we have to live in language, and we live in formulaic verbal behavior. It is in such a basic state of Being that we live as we do and we are as we are. Especially when we, by speaking, make a thing (actual or virtual) in the world present, we also make ourselves present in the world. There is no presence of mankind where the word is lacking. The presence of human beings in the world is of greater significance than that of things, for it is human presence that makes possible the presence of things.

The author (summary in Section 3.4.2)

Preface 1

Grabbing a language means grabbing its thoughts

Yi Jiang[1]

I feel greatly honored to write this Preface to *Language: The Last Homestead of Human Beings*, a seminal book by Professor Guanlian Qian as part of his 2001 key research project funded by the Ministry of Education of China. It was not until about a year ago that I came to know Professor Qian by email and the Internet as an eminent linguist pioneering the research and teaching of the philosophy of language in the field of linguistics in China, and we cemented our friendship during my academic visit to Guangzhou last November, despite our age difference. Whether as a scholar or as a person, Professor Qian is inspiring indeed. His philosophical understanding of the relationship between language and human existence, I should say, renders his overall research more significant.

It is well known that the twentieth century witnessed a "linguistic turn" in Western philosophy, which of course did not signal a turn of philosophy to linguistics, but a closer relationship than ever before between philosophy and linguistics, so much so that more and more linguists took philosophy as the "cradle" or "foundation" for their linguistic research. For philosophers, however, the "linguistic turn" does not merely mean a shift of research objects and themes from thoughts or rational contents to language that expresses them. More importantly, this indicates that there might be no so-called rational contents at all beneath language. Or rather, language itself embodies such contents, so studying language is studying thoughts themselves. Admittedly, Anglo-American and Continental philosophers have different understandings of language; the former tend to regard language as the logical form of thoughts or the ordinary language in the empirical world, while the latter attach more importance to the ontological implications of language for human existence. Nevertheless, both camps of philosophers, no matter how they understand language, agree that language influences or even determines thoughts and, as a result, the states of existence of human beings. Their concerns over and reflections on language find eloquent expressions in Wittgenstein's dictum that "All philosophy is a 'critique of language'", or in Heidegger's statement that "language is the house of Being".

viii   *Preface 1*

Such concerns and reflections are entertained not only by philosophers. Scholars from various disciplines, linguists included, have also shed new light on the functions of language. For instance, Noam Chomsky proposed a purely rationalist theory of universal grammar and linguistic competence by elaborating on Leibniz's idea of "universal language". Patrick Gardiner initiated the "linguistic turn" in modern historical research with his reinterpretation of historical language. Richard M. Hare, with his detailed analysis of the language of morals, turned modern ethics from normativism to a metaethical approach. Moreover, religious scholars' interpretation of religious language has brought about a dramatic change in the methodology of modern religious studies, or rather a change in the way of religious communication, so much so that "the Word", as in "In the beginning was the Word", is now widely interpreted as representing the laws of development of things manifested by language. Besides, the relationship between computational linguistics and human mental activities has been a hot topic in modern computer science and artificial intelligence research. All these demonstrate that the study of language is assuming an increasingly important role in tapping the human mind.

Although traditional philosophers were fully aware of the importance of language and past linguists even took study of language as their vocation, they shared a belief that the importance of language is based on the thoughts it expresses, namely, language is important only if it expresses important ideas. Obviously, here language merely serves as a thought-expressing tool or means, and the meaning of language is to be clarified only for better expressing human thoughts. However, with the linguistic turn in philosophy, philosophers' conception of language has undergone unprecedented changes. In their eyes, language is not merely (or not primarily) a tool or means to express thoughts. It is thoughts themselves. There are no hidden thoughts beneath language waiting to be expressed. Our understanding of thoughts is accomplished in language use, so the process of understanding thoughts is exactly the process of understanding language. In other words, language does not only represent human thoughts, but also constitutes the way of human existence. As Professor Qian argues, language is the last homestead of humankind. Western philosophers, be they Anglo-American analytical philosophers or Continental existentialists and phenomenological philosophers, all consider language the last territory of human existence, despite the dramatic difference in their attitudes towards this territory and their ways of dealing with it.

As Anglo-American philosophers see it, language is both an end product and an object of human intellectual activities, and for this reason language is independent from human beings themselves, and thus objective. Only when language is regarded as something objective shared by the human community can we understand the true nature and functioning of language. Meanwhile, it is the misunderstanding or misuse of language in the past that has led us astray, so it is safe to say that language itself is the root of, or rather the last shelter for, philosophical confusion. For these philosophers, the task

Preface 1   ix

of philosophy is to reveal the objectivity and independence of language in clarifying the meaning and use of language so that philosophy becomes as strict and precise as natural sciences. From the perspective of Continental philosophers, however, language is not the object of philosophical research, but the foundation on which philosophy rests, and the basis for human existence, or the last factor that manipulates and determines what humans think. In this regard, Continental philosophers never think they are doing linguistic research while doing philosophy. But they take what they think of as a self-revelation of language – that is, it is their belief that language speaks itself, not that we are using language. In other words, language speaks by using the human body. In the process of speaking, the human body is the tool or bearer, while thoughts reveal in the form of language. It can be found that, despite their different understandings of language, both Anglo-American and Continental philosophers combine language and thought as closely as possible, emphasizing that thought is dependent on and undetachable from language, and even arguing that the two are one and the same.

Obviously, the construal of language, whether as thought itself or as the last homestead of human existence, is a brand-new conception of the nature of language, quite unlike the understanding of language in traditional philosophy or traditional way of thinking. If observed from a mere empirical perspective, language seems dominantly instrumental in nature. A closer analysis, however, reveals that the language activities we can observe do not represent or convey something else, but actually a kind of human activity, or rather an instinctive activity that has been socially transformed. Just as Professor Qian spells out in this seminal book, "Mankind lives in language, mankind has to live in language, and mankind lives in formulaic verbal behavior."

When we use language in our everyday lives, we are *prima facie* expressing our thoughts. However, in order for the hearer to properly understand our ideas, or make expected responses to our utterances, it depends on whether the utterances themselves can be accepted by the hearer. Here, whether and how our utterances are accepted by the hearer are crucial for us to express our thoughts successfully. It can be further argued that whether and how the hearer understands and accepts our ideas depends on his understanding and accepting the utterances we produce. Put differently, language itself is not only our way of expressing thoughts, but the only way for the hearer to understand and accept our thoughts couched in terms of language. Nevertheless, if what the hearer is able to understand and accept is merely our language, we need not weigh and consider how to express thoughts, but whether and how language can accurately represent what we think. Therefore, what matters is language, not "thought", because "language itself is thought". From the perspective of communication, the purpose of verbal communication is for the hearer to understand and accept the speaker's thought, but the object of this kind of understanding and acceptance is not "thought", but language. In other words, "grabbing language means grabbing thoughts".

x *Preface 1*

Moreover, the structure of language immediately constitutes or determines the structure of thought. This means that the structure of our ordinary language represents the general structure of our thought; in order for the hearer to understand our utterances, they should, first and foremost, comply with grammatical and logical requirements, which are nothing but constituents of our mental structure. Meanwhile, grammar and logic, as a mirror of the structure of thought, have a direct impact on the formation and change of mental contents. As already evidenced by modern linguistics and cognitive science, the mode of thinking is determined by the logic of language, which is further determined by the kind of grammar we have. A change in the structure of language often entails a change in the structure of thought. Sometimes, lexical changes also reflect a change in one's way of thinking. That is what Professor Qian reveals by his term "the formulaicity of verbal behavior". Indeed, just as people often say, "lexical changes reflect the vicissitudes of an era". It can be further argued that lexical changes themselves are just part of the change of times. As a matter of fact, we are living in an era that has undergone massive changes in words and expressions.

Note

1 Yi Jiang was a Research Fellow and Professor at the Chinese Academy of Social Sciences when this Preface was written in 2004. He is now Professor of Philosophy at Shanxi University, and also serves as Honorary President of the China Association for Modern Foreign Philosophy. Mainly interested in contemporary Anglo-American philosophy, the philosophy of language, and Wittgensteinian philosophy, he has authored over 300 journal articles and books, including *Wittgenstein: A Post-philosophy Culture* (1996) and *Wittgenstein* (1999), and edited *Western Philosophy Approaching the New Century* (as a main contributor, 1998).

Preface 2

Chuming Wang[1]

When asked by Professor Qian to write this Preface to his new book *Language: The Last Homestead of Human Beings* (hereinafter referred to as *Language*), I felt a little uncertain. My first response was: In the academic realm, with an established pecking order, is it really appropriate for a younger scholar to write a preface for an intellectual elder? Also, I take it as a taboo to speak like a layperson. Now that neither the philosophy of language nor pragmatics was familiar to me, I was afraid that talking nonsense would only stain the fruits of his years of hard work. But Professor Qian sincerely insisted that a preface might have more than one function, and that I might well write a commemoratory preface even if I cannot fully understand the book. On a second thought, I agreed to have a try. To me, a preface has many functions, for instance, as a propellant for younger scholars, as an illuminating commentary, or as a concise summary for the readers. To fulfill all such functions, it is a generally accepted practice for the author to invite a reverend elder scholar, or at least an experienced one, to glorify his book. Professor Qian, however, made an unusual decision against this practice, and added a new "commemoratory" function to prefaces, which I believe serves as a proof of not only his modesty but also his originality.

That a preface can be "commemoratory" in Professor Qian's opinion evokes my memories of some past interactions with Professor Qian. It was during the time when the Center for Linguistics and Applied Linguistics of Guangdong University of Foreign Studies was ranked as one of the top 100 national key research bases that I came into more personal contacts with Professor Qian. In this relatively well-equipped center, we worked for the primary purpose of undertaking key research projects and producing key research results. But how to measure the value of research? Among the many aspects measured, originality emerged as the core and essence of scientific research because, without originality, there would be no key achievements and, as a result, the research base would be useless. As a veteran researcher, Professor Qian never shirked his responsibility and kept reiterating the importance of creativity. As a matter of fact, he has been not merely an advocate, but also a zealous practitioner. A lesson we can learn from Professor Qian's academic experience is that a creative mind coupled with persistence makes success possible – that

xii *Preface 2*

is, set up an original goal, persist in probing, exploring, and analyzing one's research questions with fresh eyes, and then we will be able to succeed someday in the end. The publication of the present book is exactly a mirror of his continuous commitment to creativity.

In what sense is *Language* creative? The creativity lies first in the theme of the whole book – "Mankind lives in language, mankind has to live in language, and mankind lives in formulaic verbal behavior." This bold statement, at first thought, is dumbfounding. Is language really so magical? This is probably the initial astonishment that comes hand-in-hand with any new idea. Yet, after reading the whole book, you will have to buy the argument that mankind lives in language because it is really valid to a large extent. Professor Qian cites a huge variety of literature both at home and abroad to support his argument. A human being lives in many things, but not all of them are essential. Language, however, is essential to human existence as an indispensable cognitive and communicative tool by which humans survive and develop. It is just like air in the sense that we are so accustomed to it that we hardly recognize its existence. Who dares to say that we are not living in the air, or we can live without air? Imagine what would happen to human beings in a world without language. Would we have memories? Would human history be recorded? Would we live in a harmonious society? Would we enjoy the invaluable spiritual or cultural treasuries, say, literature and arts? Could we cooperate and develop sophisticated technologies and build a cultural edifice? What would be left behind if we lost all of these? What difference could then be made between humans and animals? *Language* provokes thoughts about our own existence, impresses us with the greatness of the speaking primate species, and makes known to us what language can do in addition to its basic communicative function.

Reading the book, you will get a feeling that the author has a keen awareness of creativity. In *Language*, Professor Qian draws on numerous works by foreign authors, but he refuses to parrot others' ideas, never satisfied with mere introduction or literature review. Instead, he prefers to come up with his own ideas, and he excels in doing so. He has tried hard to sow the seeds of wisdom in the fertile land of China in the hope of producing rich fruits. Based on his absorption of foreign philosophical and pragmatic theories, he keeps forging ahead and dares to build his own theories, always eager to say something that has never been said before, often in a witty and terse way. For fear of lack of evidence, he went with his students to remote areas where ethnic minorities reside to observe, to investigate, to collect first-hand data, and to verify his theories. *Language* is full of down-to-earth folk utterances with convincing analyses that are fresh to ears, having added a strong local flavor to the domestic linguistic research and set an example of research with global visions while rooted in China.

Professor Qian is not only a creative researcher, but also a prolific writer. Actually, he was the most productive professor in the first three years after the said research base was established. In addition to translated works, he completed two monographs during that period and published more than ten papers in a single year, all with numerous reprints and many citations. His dedicated pursuit of truth as well as his seemingly boundless energy often makes me wonder whether he has ever felt tired of research. To this, he replied, "One will lose interest and become definitely exhausted if he keeps copying and echoing and takes research as a burden. But when he sets foot on a path of discoveries, he will only feel being continuously amazed and find pleasure in any new proposition he makes, or any new concept or category he creates, and he will never feel sick and tired." Creative research, or research that contributes to mankind, brings endless pleasure, which is a reward to the brave and can only be tasted by those in courageous pursuit of truth, not to be experienced by those eager for instant successes.

Now, after finishing this Preface, I still cannot put my mind in peace, for leaving my name in such an original work makes me feel guilty. Many thanks to Professor Qian for having given me the opportunity.

Note

1 Chuming Wang is Professor of Linguistics at the National Key Humanities & Social Sciences Research Base, Guangdong University of Foreign Studies. His main research fields include second-language acquisition and foreign-language education. He was serving as a member of the subject consultative group of the Academic Degree Commission of the State Council of China when this Preface was written in 2004.

Preface 3

Jiaying Chen[1]

As a researcher in linguistics for over 20 years, Professor Guanlian Qian is brilliantly productive, having written three books and numerous papers. In recent years, he has been interested in the philosophy of language, reading extensively in this field. This is a natural development, since he has concentrated his academic efforts primarily on pragmatics, a new subject area inextricably tied up with philosophy.

Professor Qian has apparently been most deeply influenced by Martin Heidegger, among other Western philosophers, and this book of his begins with the statement "Die Sprache ist das Haus des Seins". But Professor Qian is not just copying Heidegger's sayings, nor is he confined to interpreting Heidegger's ideas. Rather, he has his own theoretical understanding and advances. This is evidenced by the following statement in his Introduction: "In the mind of Heidegger, it is thinkers and poets who dwell in the house of Being, namely, language. Unlike Heidegger, we propose that those who have language as their last homestead are all ordinary human beings, who live in behavior, in verbal behavior, and in formulaic verbal behavior."

The phrase "formulaic verbal behavior" in the last sentence is one of the key concepts in this book, characterized by: "1) A relatively fixed set of utterances; 2) a relatively fixed set of actions in relatively fixed move orders; and 3) a relatively fixed co-occurrence of the above two" (3.3.1.1). Since there have been few studies on formulaic verbal behavior, this section (3.3) of the book, I think, should be regarded as the unique contribution Professor Qian makes.

I always feel it a weakness in our theoretical creativity that scholars in China seldom read genuine philosophical works. It is a fact that Chinese scholars have made outstanding achievements but proposed few theories of universal significance in their respective areas of study. For this reason, Professor Qian's approach to academic pursuit is all the more recommendable. Of course, Professor Qian is basically a linguist, though well-versed in the philosophical way of thinking, and this book of his shows that for him philosophy is more of a spirit and a guide than of metaphysical speculation *per se*, as the conclusions arrived at in the book are concrete. For many years, he has attached great importance to language data collection and survey, which is reflected in this book by the citation of many real-life cases of speech, such as the procedural speeches in the process of fortune-telling, on the cattle market, and so on. His research starts from reality and is supported by living examples, thus providing a reliable basis for further inquiry, whether the readers might agree with the conclusions or not. This approach certainly has more merits than that of a mere deduction from one concept to another.

In his academic inquiries, Professor Qian has indeed developed his own methodological ideas on the basis of his experiences, one of which is his insistence on the three "footings": Theoretical construction, mother-tongue corpus, and originality. Using these three criteria to assess my own work in these years, I feel I am left far behind.

In terms of the themes that I am concerned with, I do feel unsatisfactory with a few points, after reading this book, especially with the last chapter, Chapter 5, entitled "Choosing not to speak". It follows from Chapter 4, "Language betraying human beings", which discusses "betrayals", such as the release of false and particularly harmful information, lies, illusory talks, and so on. What Chapter 5 seeks is the way of returning to the true homestead of language through saving oneself from the state of degeneration. This chapter has referred to ideas of Zen Buddhism, Wittgenstein, and Heidegger, but does not seem to be really new, since the old paradox of "voicing the wordless" is still left unsettled, as is what impressed me.

Of Professor Qian's previous works, I have read only *The Theory of Language Holography*, which makes me admire his courage and ability in theoretical innovation. Now I have the honor of reading his *Language: The Last Homestead of Human Beings* before it is officially published. I think the ideas expressed in this book cannot be apprehended just by skimming it over once, because his system is more grandly constructed and his scope of thought much wider than before. Therefore, I cannot say what I have written above is a preface at the request of Professor Qian; it is only a record of my experience of reading this book for the first time.

Note

1 Jiaying Chen was Professor of Philosophy at both Beijing University and East China Normal University in Shanghai when he wrote the Preface in 2004. He is now Professor at Capital Normal University, China.

Preface 4
Finally, I'm back home!

Guanlian Qian

The book before me is my first foray with "philosophy" embedded in its title.[1]

In my memory, the year of 1998 is unforgettable. When July arrived that year, Guangzhou entered a sizzling hot season, with sweltering wind and a steady temperature of up to 35 degrees centigrade. Nevertheless, a human being is a strange animal, which does not stop thinking, even in an extremely unfavorable condition. It was really bad for me because that was exactly the time when I needed to focus my attention on the writing of the third chapter, also the centerpiece, of the book – "Language is the last homestead of human beings". However, those words, propositions, and statements, as well as real and pseudo problems in the first two underpinning chapters, namely Chapter 1 ("Background: The linguistic turn in Western philosophy") and Chapter 2 ("A philosophical inquiry into language: Three reflections"), both no longer a part of the book for reasons to be revealed later, kept reoccurring to my mind and dragging me back to reread and revise them. My body was cooled down by showering, electric fans, and watermelon, but my mind boggled at the entanglement of such terms as "Being" (*Sein*), "speaking", and "homestead".

A note in passing is that, in the unforgettable days when the present book was being written that summer, the whole Yangtze River region was stalked by constant devastating floods, the most serious since 1931.

Let us turn back to the book-writing itself. Doubts and confusions compel reading, and reading breeds inspirations and revisions. Then, a new cycle begins. One should hold one's thoughts using one's words, for thoughts are often locked in words. The writer, as a being himself, resides firmly in his own language. Of course, one may think without words, say, by looking up at the ceiling or looking at a lamp or a meadow, but such thoughts, as I see it, are often primitive, fragmentary, and broken, and will never shape into a complete chain of thoughts. It is a mere illusion "to say something clearly after thinking it over clearly", because it is almost impossible to speak or write it out after everything is thought fully and clearly. Even Confucius' *Analects*, which were published posthumously by his students, were initially a record of his fragmentary comments on various issues. In other words, his thoughts were fragmented pieces and primitive (and of course real) before

Preface 4   xvii

they were compiled into *The Analects*. The same is true of Plato's *Republic* and Aristotle's *Metaphysics*, each of which might not have come into being as a ready-made dish after they had clear ideas of what they were going to discuss. Perhaps not. The reverse is probably true: *One's ideas take shape and surface gradually only when one speaks or writes*. It is in this "gradual" process that language straightens up and anchors one's thoughts, and builds a home for Being. It is not that clear speaking or writing comes only after clear thinking, but that speaking or writing makes thoughts gradually crystal clear. Supposedly, quite a few people might disagree, but my own experience has strengthened this belief of mine.

I had never anticipated writing a book to conduct philosophical and pragmatic investigations into the basic behaviors of human beings. Unlike *Pragmatics in Chinese Culture*, another book of mine finished with ten years' preparation, the present book, *Language: The Last Homestead of Human Beings*, has been written with no special preparatory phase. Admittedly, writing the book is not a mere coincidence, nor an unexpected hard journey on a passive bandwagon, but an imperative call for philosophical meditations in the gradual process of my deepening pragmatic studies.

Before doing pragmatics, I had little knowledge of philosophy except the life-and-death struggle between idealism and materialism, plus Maoist theories on practice and contradiction acquired during the Cultural Revolution and some fragmentary philosophical ideas that I had learned from ancient Chinese philosophical literature (definitely not in the sense of Western philosophy). My audacity to rise to the challenge of writing the present book, or, rather, my willingness to become involved in this research endeavor despite my weak background in philosophy, was perhaps exactly owing to my ignorance of how deep the philosophical sea is. It is a truism that knowledge fuels courage, but there is also undeniable truth in the saying that ignorance summons bravery.

In the early 1980s when I turned to pragmatics, I happened to find that a substantial amount of work in it was derived from Anglo-American analytic philosophy (or philosophy of language). The most obvious examples were John Langshaw Austin and Paul Grice. This puzzled me a lot; why have philosophers become the founding fathers of pragmatics? To solve this puzzle, I started mining Western philosophy with a shovel in the east and a hammer in the west. On the spur of the moment, an idea flashed into my mind that to deepen pragmatic studies required "tracing back" to Western philosophy. Fortunately, the flash of idea did not die out, and the flame of tracing stayed alive. This is what I mean by saying above that the gradual process of deepening pragmatic studies has initiated an imperative call for my involvement with philosophy.

After *Pragmatics in Chinese Culture* was published, I fended off all distractions and, starting from 1998, delved into the origins of Western philosophy of language at a time when my colleagues and friends retired, one after another. This switch to philosophy, which came not at the halfway point xviii *Preface 4*

but almost at the end of my academic career, neither ensured the right path of research, nor guaranteed any foreseeable success. However, it was perhaps not my last academic adventure yet. For me, it was a victory to stride a big step forward in the rational understanding of the world, even if I could not grow into a philosopher eventually. I guess I might have also been guided by Zhenning Yang, who said, "I entered the philosophical domain when I went beyond the limits of physics". If pragmatics originates from philosophy of language, I thought, why don't I venture into Western philosophy? At the start of my adventure, I conjured up a proposition that "language is the homestead of human beings", inspired by Heidegger's (1982, p. 63) claim that "language is the house of Being". It was a move from a theoretical premise to a new theoretical conjecture, a typical case of falsificationism. It takes only one step to develop a proposition or hypothesis, but such a proposition might be false. To avoid obvious fallacies requires the support of a few facts. I obtained – and I only needed – a few facts to support my proposition because my investigation into the said proposition was not verificationist, but speculative, inductive, and conjectural. What was required after I made the proposition (or hypothesis) was to await falsification. This is what Popper (1968b) called "conjectures and refutations".

In handling research materials, I kept asking myself, to what extent do human beings rely on language? During the preliminary stage of this project, I mainly referred to the 37 articles in *The Philosophy of Language* (second edition),[2] edited by A. P. Martinich, plus some works by contemporary Chinese philosophers like Youyu Xu, Guoping Zhou, Jiaying Chen, and Jie Shang. Of course, there were also inquiries into language in Chinese philosophy, so I read some books written by Youlan Feng and Shi Hu. Chapter 1 of the first manuscript of the present book was entitled "Background: The linguistic turn in Western philosophy", and was basically full of citations. To cite is to study and think, and in thinking arise doubts and curiosities. My first doubt, and curiosity, was whether during the three stages (with two turns) of Western philosophers' investigations of Being, only the way of asking their fundamental questions had changed, or, to be more specific, only the way of inquiring into Being had changed. A second curiosity (discussed in Chapter 2 of the first manuscript) was aroused after I came to know the linguistic turn and compared the linguistic research at home and abroad. I made three reflections, respectively on: 1) Whether language is a mere instrument from a philosophical perspective; 2) whether different languages generate different philosophies; and 3) why it is necessary to spell out the philosophical origins when introducing foreign linguistic theories and to do linguistic research on the philosophical track. Am I doing philosophy by voicing my own doubts and curiosities based on others' conclusions? I am not sure.

However, I did not anticipate a long disruption in the writing of *Language*. The unforeseen break was briefly reminded in the postscript ("Awakening") to *The Theory of Language Holography*.

Preface 4   xix

After the publication of *Pragmatics in Chinese Culture* in 1997, I started deliberating on a new book to be entitled *Language: The Last Homestead of Human Beings* (hereafter referred to as *Language*), based on some of my papers about the analytic philosophy or philosophy of language, the third stage of Western philosophy. But when I began writing the book, I found it difficult to include the theory of language holography as one of the chapters of *Language* because the two seemed not to fit each other. In the terminology of cognitive linguistics, something went wrong with categorization or conceptualization. I then came to realize that the theory of language holography, which is based on the law of biological holography, the law of cosmological holography and systems theory, and *Language*, which investigates language and human existence, were completely different, just like apples and oranges. Finally, I decided to spin off the theory of language holography into a separate system...

This being the case, I channeled all my energies into the unanticipated pursuit of *The Theory of Language Holography* before 2002 and, as a natural result, *Language* was deferred till an unpredictable date. This is the reason why I could not respond to readers who kept asking me when *Language* was due to be published.

Nevertheless, things happened. March 2000 marked a turning point in my own academic experience. Early that year, I was transferred to the Center for Linguistics and Applied Linguistics, the only key national-level social sciences research base in China in the field of linguistics and applied linguistics, and gained access to its extensive library of Anglo-American philosophical literature. In September, I was assigned to teach *Introduction to Western Philosophy of Language*, a compulsory course for PhD candidates. While preparing lessons, I was both gladdened and exhausted at the large number of clues about the analytic philosophy or philosophy of language whenever I did keyword-based search on the website of the said library or other search engines like Yahoo.com and Google.com. All this facilitated my writing of *Language*. I had believed that history advanced at the sacrifice of individual beings, but now I came to know that *the development of history might also bring about twists and turns for the better in the fate of the individual. This might be pleasant uncertainty of life as a result of historical changes*. Be it individual sacrifice or a twist of fate, I did not regret my dive into history, nor would I decline any hug given to me by history.

Another critical change in the writing of the present book was my successful application for a key research grant in 2001, shortly after I spared the time to pen *Language* while awaiting the publication of *The Theory of Language Holography*. The project, funded by the Ministry of Education, was about formulaic events and their corresponding utterance patterns, which I found could serve as a solid argument in support of my belief that language is the last homestead of human beings. Naturally, it became a third section, "Mankind lives in formulaic verbal behavior", of Chapter 3, the core part of the present

xx   *Preface 4*

book. In fact, the core of the book was composed of three sub-propositions, each of them discussed in a separate section. In addition to the statement that a human being lives in formulaic verbal behavior (3.3), the other two are, respectively, "mankind lives in language" (3.1) and "mankind has to live in language" (3.2). This change, I should say, was a significant gain for the whole book, but not without a cost. I had to discard (but with no reluctance) the previously planned first chapter, "Background: The linguistic turn in Western philosophy", and the resulting second chapter, "A philosophical inquiry into language: Three reflections", because both of them now seemed unwanted and detached from a philosophical and pragmatic investigation into the basic behaviors of human beings.

After the disastrous attack of SARS in spring, the year of 2003 saw the approach of a surprisingly hot summer, hotter than that of 1998. In the unprecedented burning-hot days, I was still putting the finishing touches to *Language* while advising a PhD student on his dissertation. Finally, my cool mind overcame the hot weather, just as my nation notched up the first victory against SARS. It turned out that fragile people might grow into a strong nation, but something must be done to stop this country from harming and destroying our ecological environment.

Finally, I was back home from a long journey, which began on February 10, 1998, interrupted midway by the writing and publication of another book, *The Theory of Language Holography*, then turned back to *Language* and came to an end in early 2004, when the last word was written. The whole project spanned six years, or seven years if calculated in terms of the date of publication. To put it differently, as a freshman in philosophy, I finished two assignments over a span of seven years.

The student has finally finished his tough task, and come back home from school.

As Schopenhauer (2010, pp. 54–55) argues, "Anyone who becomes a philosopher does so because of a perplexity that he is trying to tear himself away from. Perplexity is Plato's 'bewilderment.'" "To tear myself away from a perplexity" or "to observe the world in a non-stereotypical way out of curiosity" roughly describes my mentality when I ventured into the door of philosophy. It is in the process of writing this book that I have come to truly understand what Robins says in *A Short History of Linguistics* (1969, p. 88), that "philosophy [in its widest sense] had been the cradle of linguistics...". I have had a roll in this cradle, I should say.

A recollection of the research methodology I have used in writing my four monographs might be of some help to young scholars. *Aesthetic Linguistics*, *prima facie*, seems to be an inductive study based on abundant linguistic data, but its major theory-building argument that linguistic structures are beautiful, unknowingly to my then self, actually derives straight from another theoretical premise – beauty exists in science (J. Xu, 1987). The last part of the book – the linguistic microcosm is in perfect harmony with the natural macrocosm and linguistic structures correspond with cosmological structures

Preface 4 xxi

(G. Qian, 1993, p. 381) – is obviously conjectural. Those linguistic data only serve as factual evidences, which need to be falsified in the end. In a similar fashion, *Pragmatics in Chinese Culture* appears to be an inductive and empirical study because all the pragmatic strategies, as discussed in its fifth chapter, are generalized from exemplar utterances. However, again, its entire theoretical system – pragmatics is nothing but speechology in humanistic networks – does not depend on enumeration of facts, let alone any experimental result, but comes from speculations. My third book, *The Theory of Language Holography*, is basically deductive, for the theory of language holography is simply a one-move conjecture from the law of biological holography (and the law of cosmological holography). The present book is also deductive and speculative. Its theoretical framework goes like this: "As one of the basic facets of human existence, mankind has to depend on language for every single moment of existence; we live in language, we have to live in language, and we live in formulaic verbal behavior. It is in such a basic state of Being that we live as we do and we are as we are. Especially when we, by speaking, make a thing (actual or virtual) in the world present, we also make ourselves present in the world." Although some case studies can be found in this book, they are only instrumental in building the whole theory. Empirical sciences such as physics, chemistry, and biology, and even linguistics (say, psycholinguistics and second-language acquisition), which lie between social sciences and natural sciences, require not only patient experiments, meticulous investigations, exact numbers, and clear facts, but also abstraction of some metaphysical ideas from the objective world. This last step, that is, abstraction, is certainly speculative. However, mere speculation over empirical facts is not necessarily doing philosophy. In my humble opinion, philosophizing also requires speculating on one's speculations as well as staying vigilant about and reflecting on the existing truths. No wonder Zhenning Yang said, "I entered the philosophical domain when I went beyond the limits of physics". This suggests that a philosopher should transcend empirical speculations and proceed to speculate on his own speculations. Just as the contemporary Chinese philosopher Youlan Feng (1996, p. 1) puts it, "Philosophy is systematic reflective thoughts about life", that is, thought about thoughts. In addition, Karl Jaspers (1954, p. 12) argues, "The essence of philosophy is not the possession of truth but the search for truth ... Philosophy means to be on the way. Its questions are more essential than its answers, and every answer becomes a new question."

Dr Yongshou Huo, my first PhD student, collected all the cases of medical diagnoses and civil mediations for the present research, and drafted Section 2.2, "Pragmatic involvement", which was revised and finalized by myself. Xiuwei Chu, another PhD student of mine, gathered all the linguistic data concerning food markets, cattle markets, street fortune-tellers, Chinese New Year's Eve dinners and banquet drink persuaders, and he also formulated a complete theoretical framework for me to write Section 3.3, "Living in formulaic verbal behavior". Aihua Wang, Ruiqing Liang, and Shuang Liang, all PhD students of mine, offered some useful suggestions for me to revise

xxii   *Preface 4*

the manuscript, and Shuang Liang further helped me handle some format problems. I would like to thank them all here.

Thanks also go to GDUFS Office of Academic Research and Center for Linguistics and Applied Linguistics, the key social sciences research base where I am working, for its warm support for the publication of this book. I will be unable to repay the kindness unless I bear it in mind and produce more mature works in the future.

Churning up two books, i.e., the present book and *The Theory of Language Holography*, within six years – from the early spring of 1998 to the early spring of 2004 – makes me feel a little bit uneasy because there might be a quality problem. I have considered more revisions before publication, but have been urged to finish the research project before the deadline as stipulated by the domestic project closing system. This system, although it guarantees a publication fund, is problematic to the extent that each task is due to be fulfilled within a time limit. Setting a time limit may spur slackers or procrastinators, but may be at the cost of quality, so it seems to me not a practical solution. If urged to finish his work before a strict deadline, Qian Sima would not have been able to write *Shih Chi* (aka *Records of the Grand Historian*), a historic masterpiece in Chinese literature. For this reason, my concerns about the present book cannot be eased even if, to my surprise and relief, *The Theory of Language Holography* – my purely theoretical monograph also published by the Commercial Press – sold out within one-and-a-half years after its initial publication.

After this book was published, I planned to stop writing Chinese monographs, at least in the coming five years. I will spare more time reading Western philosophical literature and devote more efforts to instructing PhD students. This will of mine was strengthened after I read *Jiaohu Lake Poems* by Shen Huang, one of the eight reclusive Yangzhou-based unconventional painters in the prime of the Qing Dynasty. In one of his poems, he wrote, "This spring I idled away with no poem, to the disappointment of the plum tree overhanging the east wall". If this line is intended to push us ahead, then the following line – "At dusk I returned to my lodge in the depth of the bamboo forest, ready to read an unfinished book in the lamplight" – is obviously advising us to read more books, which is exactly my own intention.

What a happy coincidence! Now that I'm back home, I can finally calm down and "read my unfinished books in the lamplight".

February 2004

Notes

1 The author is referring here to the title of the Chinese edition of this book, *Language: The Last Homestead of Human Beings: A Philosophical and Pragmatic Probe into the Basic State of Human Existence*.
2 The fourth edition of the book on hand now includes 41 articles.

Preface for the English edition

Guanlian Qian

"Don't be eager to be famous. Don't write any book impetuously. Don't take out any book of yours in which there is no fresh idea at all. Don't represent any works that do not touch even yourself." This is what I said to a group of young colleagues in 2017 shortly after the Chinese version of this book won the Xu Guozhang Award for Foreign Language Studies.

In fact, it was by following the four don'ts that I finished this book and the other nine books of mine. And I, at the age of 81, am determined to write in the same way in the years to come. Philosophy may not help us make money, but it makes our whole life.

For the publication of this English edition, I would like to thank the following six individuals who helped with the English translation: Xiuwei Chu, Yongshou Huo, Ruiqing Liang, Shuang Liang, Limin Liu, and Aihua Wang. They were all PhD students whom I supervised at Guangdong University of Foreign Studies and from whom I have also learned. Each of them took an equal share of the translation work. Dr Xiuwei Chu was responsible for the editing and revising of the completed English manuscript. He worked diligently to ensure consistency in language style, format, and the use of terminology.

We would like to thank Dr Mike Opper, who taught in the College of International Studies at Southwest University, China, for his review of the early drafts of the English version. Our special thanks go to Dr Dilin Liu, Professor of Linguistics in the English Department at the University of Alabama, who was kind enough to read and comment on the entire final English draft, sentence by sentence. With his excellence in both Chinese and English, Professor Liu made an extremely valuable contribution to the clarity of thought, flow of text, and the overall readability of the book. Likewise, the Routledge copy-editor Mr Dan Shutt did an excellent job in helping to improve the formatting, language quality, and overall readability of the book. We would also like to express our appreciation to the staff, especially, Ms Lian Sun and Ms Ying Jing of Routledge, and Ms Xiaolu An and Dr Huaying Feng of the Commercial Press, for their help with the publication of this book. Special thanks also go to China's National Office for Philosophy and Social Sciences and the College of International Studies, Southwest University, China, for their financial support.

August 26, 2020

1 Introduction

Although verbal behavior is not the entirety of human existence, it constitutes one of the basic facets of human existence, that is, the "three livings": We live in language, we have to live in language, and we live in formulaic verbal behavior (see 1.3, "The three livings and the basic state of human existence"). Moreover, formulaic verbal behavior is the core of verbal behavior. It is thus held that a probe into formulaic verbal behavior is basically a study of verbal behavior and of the basic state of human existence as well. Hence the subtitle of the Chinese version of this book, *A Philosophical and Pragmatic Probe into the Basic State of Human Existence*.

In what sense do the three livings constitute one of the basic facets of human existence? Section 1.3 and the entirety of Chapter 3 (the core chapter of this book) are dedicated to this question.

In what sense can it be said that given that formulaic verbal behavior is the core of verbal behavior, a probe into formulaic verbal behavior is basically a study of verbal behavior? The answer is to come in the last paragraph of Section 1.2.

1.1 "Language is the house of Being" versus "language is the last homestead of human beings"

The proposition that "language is the house of Being" was raised by Martin Heidegger in his *Letter on Humanism* (1993, p. 217).

> Thinking accomplishes the relation of Being to the essence of man. It does not make or cause the relation. Thinking brings this relation to Being solely as something handed over to it from Being. Such offering consists in the fact that in thinking Being comes to language. *Language is the house of Being*. In its home man dwells. *Those who think [the thinkers] and those who create with words [the poets] are the guardians of this home*. Their guardianship accomplishes the manifestation of Being insofar as they bring the manifestation to language and maintain it in language through their speech.
>
> (Emphasis added)

2 *Introduction*

Heidegger restated the proposition in *A Dialogue on Language* (1982, p. 5): "some time ago I called language, clumsily enough, the house of Being".

In addition to claiming that "language is the house of Being", Heidegger also points out that "in its home [i.e., language] man dwells". Then, a question may arise: Isn't the present book repeating, at least in part, what Heidegger has argued, since it claims to probe into "language as the last homestead of human beings"?

The answer is no.

This is because the proposition that language is the last homestead of human beings differs from Heidegger's claim that mankind dwells in language in the following three respects.

The first difference between them lies in their ultimate goals. Heidegger's claim that mankind dwells in language only acts as a supporting argument of his proposition that language is the house of Being. It might be noted that "[human beings] bring this manifestation to language and maintain it in language through their speech" comes after "[t]hose who think and those who create with words are the guardians of this home" (Heidegger, 1982). This means that what the guardians do is to "bring the manifestation [of Being] to language and maintain it in language", and what they accomplish, which is the ultimate goal of Heidegger's discussion, is "the manifestation of Being". In a word, the guardians' central concern is about Being, which is an age-old problem in Western philosophy. It is for this reason that the advocator of such a proposition can be no one else but a philosopher in the Western tradition, which cherishes a long history of studying the problem of Being. By contrast, my proposition is not intended to solve the antiquated problem of Western philosophy. Instead, it is intended to answer the following question: How and why is mankind so dependent on language? As a result, the present research departs from the above ancient problem in Western philosophy, and proceeds along the track from human behaviors through speech acts to formulaic verbal behaviors. Therefore, interested readers, and critics, of this book can be philosophers, pragmaticians, sociolinguists, praxeologists, and communication researchers, and, I hope, they will be rewarded after digging the garden of the three livings.

Second, *they unfold along different threads.* Heidegger expounds his thought by making Being manifest through language, whereas I present my theme by elaborating step by step that mankind lives in language, that mankind has to live in language, and that mankind lives in formulaic verbal behavior.

Last but not least, *Heidegger's view and mine feature different residents in the home of language.* Special attention should be drawn to the fact that the residents in Heidegger's home of language are "those who think [the thinkers] and those who create with words [the poets]". Whenever he claims that man dwells in language, he repeatedly reminds us that the guardians in this home are thinkers and poets.

Here are some pieces of evidence. In *Poetry, Language, Thought*, Heidegger (1975) devotes much space to tamping down the above argument of his,

Introduction 3

respectively in "The Thinker as Poet", "What are Poets For?", and "... Poetically Man Dwells ...". Heidegger went on at great length about this in "Language in the Poem", the fifth chapter of *On the Way to Language*, insisting that "[t]he dialogue of thinking with poetry aims to call forth the nature of language, so that mortals may learn again to live within language" (1982, p. 161).

Similar ideas find expression in many of his works (the following quotes are accompanied with my brief expositions at the risk of criticism because Heidegger is well known for his obscure use of language). Take, for example, "Words", the fourth chapter of *On the Way to Language*. This piece of writing alone abounds in talks about poetry and poets.

"What is spoken purely is the poem" (Heidegger (1975, p. 192)). In order to illustrate that Being reveals itself and maintains in language, Heidegger tries to seek long and hard for the proper genre of language. He finally finds "a true friend" (as chanted in a Chinese nursery rhyme in the 1950s and 1960s). The true friend turns out to be poetry. So, according to Heidegger, poetic language is pure speech.

"We are now seeking the speaking of language in the poem. Accordingly, what we seek lies in the poetry of the spoken word" (*ibid.*, p. 194). Again, Heidegger stresses that what he has long sought after resides in the poems, which are composed of speaking words. In his writings, Heidegger sometimes writes that "man speaks", and sometimes claims that "language speaks" (i.e., the so-called speaking of language). In other words, it is language itself, not man, that is speaking. This is a prominent view held by Heidegger, who also observes,

> In the poem's speaking the poetic imagination gives itself utterance. What is spoken in the poem is what the poet enunciates out of himself. What is thus spoken out, speaks by enunciating its content. The language of the poem is a manifold enunciating.
>
> (*Ibid.*, p. 195)

"The first stanza speaks by bidding the things to come" (*ibid.*, p. 200). Then, how does poetry speak? It speaks "by bidding the things to come". This idea constitutes an essential part of Heidegger's philosophy. The function of language is to make the things come into being. Therefore, we come back to the point of departure: Language reveals Being and brings Being to language and preserves it in language. Things manifest themselves only after language speaks, and the pure speaking of language can only be found in poems (see the first quote above).

"The speaking of the first two stanzas speaks by bidding things to come to world, and world to things" (*ibid.*, p. 202). It is easy to understand "bidding things to come to world", which means that language makes Being manifest and maintains it in language itself. But how should we explain "bidding world to things"? Perhaps it means that the world and things are an organic whole, and that their coming to each other is accomplished in the speaking of poems.

4   *Introduction*

"Speaking occurs in what is spoken in the poem" (*ibid.*, p. 206). As the purpose of speaking is to bring Being to prominence, poems make Being manifest.

In the mind of Heidegger, it is thinkers and poets who dwell in the house of Being, namely, language. Unlike Heidegger, we propose that those who have language as their last homestead are all ordinary human beings, who live in behavior, in verbal behavior, and in formulaic verbal behavior. Therefore, Heidegger and we have different residents in the home of language.

1.2 Behavior, verbal behavior, formulaic verbal behavior

Mankind behaves as long as he is a rational animal.

All behaviors fall into four categories in terms of their relationship with language. One of them is spontaneous physiological behaviors (e.g., metabolism), which occur and can be accomplished independently of language.

A second category includes behaviors that can be carried out either with words or without words. Behaviors such as producing (products or commodities), constructing, and destroying are basically coordinated and performed with language. Other behaviors such as opening/closing, screwing/unscrewing, locking/unlocking, messing/cleaning, moving/restoring, and assembling/disassembling can be conducted without saying a word, but may also involve language if needs be, especially when they are to be done by more than one person or collectively.

A third category is what the philosopher John Langshaw Austin (1962a) and his followers call speech acts. For example, "I warn you that ..." is an act of warning, and "I announce that ..." an act of announcing. These behaviors, needless to say, are performed through language.

The fourth category is of purely mental behaviors. Such behaviors seem to require no language, but without language there would be no effective mental behaviors at all. For example, behaviors like conceiving, conceptualizing, categorizing, reflecting, contemplating, and meditating all come into existence only with recourse to language. In a word, *purely mental behaviors can crystalize truly scrutable ideas only through language.*

There are of course other kinds of behaviors, but all of them are subsets of the aforementioned four categories. More importantly, *among these four broad categories, except that a small proportion of spontaneous physiological behaviors can be divorced from language, other behaviors, like those of doing things and spiritual activities, especially those performed with words, are in the ultimate analysis parasitic on verbal behaviors.* That is why Heidegger (1975a, p. 205) argues that "the human is indeed in its nature given to speech – it is linguistic".

In the Anglo-American world there are "15 Golden Rules for Living", which seem to have been randomly pieced together as follows (Canfield & Hansen, 1996, p. 326).

(1) If you open it, close it. (2) If you turn it on, turn it off. (3) If you unlock it, lock it up. (4) If you break it, admit it. (5) If you can't fix it, call in someone who can. (6) If you borrow it, return it. (7) If you value it, take care of it. (8) If you make a mess, clean it up. (9) If you move it, put it back. (10) If it belongs to someone else and you want to use it, get permission. (11) If you don't know how to operate it, leave it alone. (12) If it's none of your business, don't ask questions. (13) If it ain't broke, don't fix it. (14) If it will brighten someone's day, say it. (15) If it will tarnish someone's reputation, please keep it to yourself.

Undoubtedly, there are of course more than fifteen golden rules in life, but, anyway, let us leave them aside for the time being. What interests us is that how many of these rules cannot work without language. As can be seen, behaviors to be performed with direct use of language include Rule (4), Rule (5) (you make a request with words), Rule (10) (you need ask someone before permitted), and Rule (14). Related to verbal behaviors (but with a warning of not using language) are Rule (12) (you are reminded not to use language) and Rule (15) (you are advised not to mention it or speak it out to the person involved, thus not to commit a speech act). Behaviors to be performed with the coordination of language, for example, include Rule (6) (both borrowing and returning involve the use of language unless you are a dumb), and Rule (7) (valuing something often needs speaking it out and so involves the coordination of language. But you may also value it in your mind, in which case you need not use language). Besides, there are also some nonverbal behaviors, for example, opening/closing, screwing/unscrewing, locking/unlocking, messing/ cleaning; they belong to the second of the aforementioned four broad categories and can be accomplished without the use of words. However, they can also be accomplished with the coordination of language.

For the sake of convenience, we may label those behaviors performed without language as *nonverbal behaviors*, and those performed with or in language as *verbal behaviors*.

Furthermore, we can spot a special kind of verbal behavior, that is, *formulaic verbal behavior* (for details, see 3.3). In performing them, the speaker follows a certain sort of formulaicity, or a set of conventional patterns and long-established customs in his utterances and actions. Three simple examples will suffice here. Take, for one example, the occasion of a formal meeting. On such an occasion, the chairperson often begins with some opening remarks, saying something like: "Ladies and gentlemen, quiet down please! Let's get started. Here is today's agenda... First...". During the course of the meeting, the chairperson usually adopts fixed expressions, such as "Now let's move on to the next item..." and "Finally...". When the meeting comes to an end, the chairperson announces, "I declare the meeting closed". For another example, in Wuhan, a city on the Yangtze River in Central China, family members tend to say to each other, 洗了睡 ([xǐle shuì] "Wash and sleep"), as they are turning off the TV every night. It is a typical match between formulaic utterances and

6 Introduction

behavior; each time they say 洗了睡, they routinely perform the action (of washing their feet after finishing watching TV programs).

As a third example, we look at a traditional Chinese wedding ceremony. Conventionally, the bride and groom (B & G for short) are supposed to kowtow in sequence to Heaven and Earth, to the groom's parents and to each other as the ceremony master shouts 一拜天地 ([Yī bài tiāndì] "First, kowtow to Heaven and Earth"), 二拜高堂 ([Èr bài gāotáng] "Second, kowtow to your parents"), and 夫妻对拜 ([Fūqī duìbài] "Kowtow to each other"). And finally, as the master says 送入洞房 ([Sòngrù dòngfáng] "Escort the bride and groom to the bridal bedroom"), B & G are escorted to their bedroom. Here prevails an obvious formulaic pattern. This four-move ritual has undergone no significant changes in the past fifty years since 1949; despite some impromptu gags and games in between, the old customs of B & G's bowing to the groom's parents and to each other and then being escorted to their bedroom have been largely preserved. Some minor changes can be observed, though. For instance, the first move has been changed into 一拜毛主席 ([Yī bài Máozhǔxí]) "First, kowtow to Chairman Mao") or 一拜毛老 ([Yī bài Máolǎo] "First, kowtow to His Excellency Mr Mao") in some rural areas, or 一拜国旗 ([Yī bàiguóqí] "First, kowtow to the national flag") or 一拜邓小平 ([Yī bài Dèng Xiǎopíng] "First, kowtow to Deng Xiaoping") or 一拜邓老 ([Yī bài Dènglǎo] "First, kowtow to His Excellency Mr Deng") in some rural areas. Besides, a new move is sometimes added, such as 向来宾致敬 ([Xiàng láibīn zhìjìng] "Pay your respect to the guests"). After some gags and games, the last move is always to escort the bride and groom to the bridal bedroom, which is often the tenth move because ten is a lucky number in Chinese culture, meaning "perfect and complete". Overall, the formulaic verbal behaviors in such a wedding ceremony remain basically unchanged.

Moreover, people or parties concerned are constrained by a set of institutionalized or noninstitutionalized conventions or procedures (such as oral agreements, game rules, and default practices) in many other language-related behaviors. These include, but are not confined to, speech events like court debates, court investigations, business talks, announcements (say, on diplomatic occasions), diplomatic protesting, negotiations (arms talks or international conferences), writing letters, introducing people, recommending, praising, ordering, reporting, asking for instructions, requesting, making statements, interviewing, lecturing, diagnosing, and bargaining, etc. In all these cases, a relatively stable match can be found between what is said and what is done.

It can thus be argued that in certain behaviors or activity types (for example, cattle markets, traditional Chinese medical (shortened as TCM) inquiries, and traditional Chinese weddings), some actions (nonlinguistic) co-occur with certain utterances, and the two of them constitute a stable match. The so-called stable match between actions and utterances means that as long as a certain verbal behavior or activity type remains unchanged, there will be: 1) A relatively fixed set of utterances; 2) a relatively fixed set of actions in relatively fixed move orders; and 3) a relatively fixed co-occurrence of the above two. *Any type of verbal behavior (or activity type) that presents the above three characteristics can be referred to as a formulaic verbal behavior.* However, it must be noted that such a set of utterances, though basically fixed, does not preclude possible diachronic variations and that it meets the minimal requirement of linguistic input for the behavior because further reduction of utterances will result in communication failures. The formulaicity of formulaic verbal behavior means not only that both the utterances and the actions are basically fixed, but also that the match between the two is basically fixed (for details, see 3.3.1.1).

Thus, formulaic verbal behaviors occur in speech events and a speech event that is characterized with formulaic verbal behaviors will be referred to as a *formulaic speech event.* The opposite of formulaic verbal behaviors are non-formulaic verbal behaviors (i.e., incidental, inadvertent, and unexpected verbal behaviors). *Formulaic verbal behaviors are certainly implemented in formulaic speech events,* but, since the point of departure of this book is the basic state of human existence, what concern us above all are human behaviors, and my arguments move along the following sequence: From behaviors through verbal behaviors to formulaic verbal behaviors. However, whenever we talk about a formulaic verbal behavior, it should always be kept in mind that such a verbal behavior must be performed in a formulaic speech event.

It should be remembered that, from stem to stern of a formulaic speech event, there is a set of institutionalized or noninstitutionalized conventions or procedures (such as oral agreements, game rules, and default practices). More importantly, it is worth noting that such a procedure, apart from the need for behavioral coordination, starts with some formulaic opening remarks (starters), unfolds with some formulaic utterances (accompaniers), and finally ends with some formulaic closing remarks (enders).

In the above example of a formal meeting, the starters are the chairperson's opening remarks ("Ladies and gentlemen, quiet down please! Let's get started. Here is today's agenda…"), followed by some accompaniers, such as "First…", "Next…", and "Finally…" and speeches given by various participants in the course of the meeting, and the ender is the chairperson's announcement ("I declare the meeting closed").

In the case of a traditional Chinese wedding ceremony, the starter is the ceremony master's chanting 一拜天地 ("First, kowtow to Heaven and Earth"), followed by such accompaniers as 二拜高堂 ("Second, kowtow to your parents"), and 夫妻对拜 ("Kowtow to each other"). The ender is 送入洞房 ("Escort the bride and groom to the bridal bedroom").

The above two examples roughly demonstrate the paradigm of formulaic verbal behaviors (though with some variations not mentioned for the time being). A more detailed elaboration of formulaic verbal behaviors is to be provided in 3.3.

Admittedly, some speech events may have no institutionalized rules or conventionalized procedures. They are *non-formulaic speech events.* Even

8 Introduction

though some speech events may become formulaic, some others may remain non-formulaic (*de facto*). We do not want to exaggerate the limits and scope of formulaic speech events, but would only like to uncover and analyze (both philosophically and pragmatically) the implications of this phenomenon for human existence and development. We are also concerned about the variability in certain formulaic speech events (to be discussed in detail in 3.3, and in passing in other parts of the book). Rather, the formulaicity and variability of speech events coexist, making human communication effective (and maximally beneficial) and conducive to the individualized development of human beings.

The present research aims not to study all human behaviors, but only verbal behaviors and formulaic speech events. Nor does it intend to make a general survey of verbal behaviors and formulaic speech events, but to investigate them both philosophically and pragmatically. The ultimate goal of the philosophical and pragmatic probe is to explain the dependence of human existence on language and the relationship between humans and language, as well as to give language a philosophical account (but definitely not to answer the millennium problem in Western philosophy, that is, what is Being) and a pragmatic observation. In this sense, this book is concerned with the basic state of human existence, or basic human behaviors – mankind's living in language, mankind's having to live in language, and mankind's living in formulaic verbal behavior. The three livings, as I see it, reveal one of the basic facets of human existence. This is of great theoretical significance in explaining: 1) Humans' life activities; 2) the fact that language is the final fingerprint and heritage of an ethnic group; 3) the existence of a nation and the falling or lasting of a civilization; 4) linguistic determinism and its mechanism; and 5) when and why language will betray mankind.

Verbal behaviors and formulaic speech events can be studied not only from philosophical and pragmatic perspectives adopted in the present research, but also from perspectives of sociolinguistics, praxeology, and communication research. Therefore, a study of behaviors, verbal behaviors, and formulaic verbal behaviors, I hope, will draw the attention of scholars from all these diverse disciplines.

Now it is time to answer the question: In what sense can it be said that, given that formulaic verbal behavior is the core of verbal behavior, a probe into formulaic verbal behavior is basically a study of verbal behavior? As mentioned above, some verbal behaviors are non-formulaic (hence corresponding non-formulaic speech events). Even though some speech events may become formulaic, some others may remain non-formulaic (*de facto*). And, as also argued above, the formulaicity and variability of speech events coexist, making human communication effective (and maximally beneficial) and conducive to individualized development of human beings. Also, we shall not forget that human verbal behaviors are dominated by two types of events. One is of major speech events, including wedding ceremonies, court debates, court investigations, business talks, announcements (as on diplomatic

Introduction 9

occasions), negotiations (arms talks and international conferences), diplomatic protests, and so on. The other covers basic speech events that are not major, but are indispensable for human existence, including writing letters, introducing people, recommending, defending oneself, interviewing, negotiating, lecturing, bargaining on markets, diagnosing and TCM inquiries, etc. Neither of these two types of speech events can be separated from a set of institutionalized or noninstitutionalized conventions or procedures (such as oral agreements, game rules, and default practices). Moreover, *the more significant a speech event is, the more likely it is to be a basic speech event indispensable for human existence, and the more likely it is formulaic*, characterized by: 1) A relatively fixed set of utterances; 2) a relatively fixed set of actions in relatively fixed move orders; and 3) relatively fixed co-occurrence of the above two. Why is it that? Because in a major speech event or a basic speech event indispensable for human existence, it is all the more necessary to enhance efficiency, collaboration, expectation, cultural stability, relevance, economy, and benefit maximization, so that positive effects can be achieved and negative effects avoided. Therefore, it is safe to say that formulaic verbal behaviors are at the core of verbal behaviors, although numerous non-formulaic speech events do occur in human life. In this sense, a probe into formulaic verbal behaviors is basically the investigation of verbal behaviors in general.

1.3 The three livings and the basic state of human existence

In what sense can it be argued that the three livings – mankind lives in language, mankind has to live in language, and mankind lives in formulaic verbal behavior – constitute one of the basic facets of human existence?

Among the basic human-specific attributes, physiological ones, sociocultural ones, and rational thinking are the most prominent. The physiological attributes indicate that men are living entities, but they are not what defines human beings, as animals and plants are also living entities. The sociocultural attributes of humans suggest that, in order to survive and develop, human individuals have to participate in activities with others, as a result of which various social relations are established in cooperation or in hostility. However, sociality is not unique to humans, because animals are social, too. Nonetheless, it is a great leap for humans to grow from mere social beings to cultural beings and distinguish themselves from animals, for only human beings are able to carry out cultural activities – spiritual activities, aesthetic activities, symbolic activities, and superstructure activities – and have created a glorious civilization that is peculiar to mankind. Therefore, comparatively speaking, human cultural attributes are more important than their social attributes, and the ability to think is at the highest level of human-specific attributes.

It must be observed that, without the coordination and help of language, the three basic groups of human-specific attributes could not be activated. Interestingly, *they are closely correlated to language*. First, human physiological attributes are explicitly evident in their verbal behaviors – for when

10   *Introduction*

a person speaks, voicing, aspirating, and breathing are involved and they are all life activities. A detailed discussion about this can be found in "Congruity of Two Dynamic Balanced Structures: The Case of Life Consciousness in Speech", a section in *Aesthetic Linguistics* (G. Qian, 1993, pp. 62–73). This is also true of human sociocultural attributes. It is a truism that high-level effective communication is impossible without language, even though low-level social communication may be achieved. It also goes without saying that high-level effective cultural creations cannot be divorced from language, and that even low-level cultural activities cannot be independent of language. Finally, the human thinking attribute, a human-specific ability, depends heavily on language. Some might argue that animals also think because they can obtain food with their brains. But it is definitely not thinking. Genuine thinking should be logical, linguistic, and categorized. *If and only if something is successfully expressed with words can it be a thought, which generally takes on a logical, conceptualized, and even categorized form.*

In other words, mankind's basic human-specific attributes can only be activated to the fullest through language. Moreover, mankind's thinking ability, the third attribute, develops with language. That is why we insist that the three livings – mankind lives in language, mankind has to live in language, and mankind lives in formulaic verbal behavior – constitute one of the basic facets of human existence.

In addition, to examine the three livings is to study mankind's form of life. As Wittgenstein (1953, p. 8) puts it, "To imagine a language means to imagine a form of life". In explaining what a language game is, he (*ibid*. p. 11) remarks, "the term '*language-game*' is meant to bring into prominence the fact that the *speaking* of language is part of an activity, or of a form of life" (emphasis original). Malinowski (1923, p. 312) is in complete agreement with this point:

> ... [L]anguage in its primitive forms ought to be regarded and studied against the background of human activities and as a mode of human behavior in practical matters. ... Language is used by people engaged in practical work, in which utterances are embedded in action.

In another place, he (1935/1978, p. 7) puts it more explicitly and straightforwardly: "[T]he main function of language is not to express thought, not to duplicate mental processes, but rather to play an active pragmatic part in human behavior". Obviously, what Malinowski stresses here is that the use of language itself is a sort of pragmatic and effective behavior.

1.4 The reincarnation of pragmatics in China: Two signs

It is true that pragmatics originated from the Western philosophy of language. The motive of philosophers' study of meaning is to see the world, reality, and entities through language. However, in pursuit of sentential meanings, they gradually focused their attention on the speaker's intentions (Austin, 1962),

Introduction 11

which gave rise to speaker meaning, and then a contrast between natural meaning and non-natural meaning (Grice, 1957/1989). As an eventual result, an orthodox view arose, that is, the meaning of a sentence can be generated only in the context, which lays the primary foundation of pragmatics. Then, a distinction emerged between Anglo-American pragmatics, which places particular emphasis on specific units of analysis (Levinson, 1983), and European Continental pragmatics, which centers around a general pragmatic perspective. According to the latter view (Verschueren, 1999), there should be no specific units of analysis in pragmatics, because pragmatics is not a branch of the linguistics of language resources (such as phonemes, words, and sentences), but a branch of the linguistics of language use (for every level of language can be explored from a pragmatic perspective).

In the past two decades, Chinese scholars have fully absorbed the nutrition from Western pragmatics, and gradually developed their own pragmatic theories. It was against this background that *Pragmatics in Chinese Culture* (G. Qian, 1997/2002) was published. In this book, the "three-to-one theory" is put forward on the basis of Chinese culture, which defines pragmatics as a theory of linguistic functions. Specifically, Chinese pragmatics studies how language users interpret the nonliteral meaning of utterances (the *one* implied meaning beyond words) using the interlocutors' symbolic clues (such as physical entities they have when they speak as well as their facial expressions, gestures, voices and pitches, etc.), contextual knowledge, and intellectual reasoning (the *three* extralinguistic factors). Just as Shi and Cui (2002) observe, "*Pragmatics in Chinese Culture*, having got rid of the fetters of the Western pragmatic paradigm, tries to work out a new one suitable for the reality of Chinese language, that is, the 'three-to-one theory'". They (*ibid.*) further add, "This is an innovative pragmatic paradigm, and our book *A New Approach of Chinese Pragmatics* tries to take a new approach which is different from Qian's pragmatics".

The reincarnation of pragmatics in China may be marked by two signs. The first sign is the effort made by Chinese scholars to develop innovative theoretical frameworks. The "three-to-one theory" proposed in *Pragmatics in Chinese Culture* is a case in point, and another is the view of language as mankind's homestead developed in the present book, which is both philosophical and pragmatic in nature.

Philosophically speaking, the view of language as mankind's last homestead can be summarized as follows. Humans' heavy dependence on language is one of the basic facets of human existence, which is embodied by the three livings: Mankind lives in language, mankind has to live in language, and mankind lives in formulaic verbal behavior. It is in such a basic state of Being that we live as we do and we are as we are. Especially when we, by speaking, make a thing (actual or virtual) in the world present, we also make ourselves present in the world. The presence of human beings in the world is of greater significance than that of things, for it is human presence that makes possible the presence of things (for details, see 3.4.2).

12   *Introduction*

From the perspective of pragmatics, the view of language as humans' homestead goes roughly as follows. Language use is related to other human social behaviors, and different pragmatic analysis frameworks are established in accordance with different activity types. Ordinary language can be analyzed by the three types of pragmatics. Mankind uses language through the three livings, and plays language games (in the Wittgensteinian sense).

A second sign of the reincarnation of pragmatics in China is the use of data purely rooted in Chinese language and culture. This is already evident in my *Pragmatics in Chinese Culture*. In this present book, the data were collected from: 1) Traditional Chinese wedding ceremonies; 2) mischiefs in bridal bedrooms; 3) cattle markets; 4) vegetable markets; 5) street fortune-tellers; 6) family dinners on Chinese New Year's Eve; 7) folk dispute settlements; and 8) TCM inquiries. Language use in the context of Chinese culture – one of the oldest civilizations in the world – will certainly feature some peculiar communication rules, discourse patterns, and pragmatic strategies (G. Qian, 1997/ 2002). I am not saying that Western data are useless to Chinese scholars. The only thing I want to do is to supplement the general principles of pragmatics with Chinese data. This will not go awry, I suppose.

2 Philosophical and pragmatic perspectives

It is always advisable to view an object for research from more than one perspective. The study on the basic state of human existence can, accordingly, be conducted in the dimensions both of philosophy and of pragmatics.

2.1 A philosophical perspective

Here we look into the basic state of human existence from two perspectives: That of Western philosophy, especially the Western philosophy of language, and that of Chinese philosophy. As it stands, a much larger space is to be dedicated to the former than the latter. Why is that so? An explanation is to be given in Sections 2.1.3 and 3.4.3.

"Language is the house of Being" is a philosophical proposition, an affirmation of the significance of language for existence: Being dwells in language. "Language is the last homestead of human beings" is an integrated proposition of philosophy and pragmatics, unveiling the dependence of human existence on language and the relationship between human beings and their language, thus finding for language a niche in philosophy (but of course this is not intended to answer the age-old question in Western philosophy: What is there?). In this view, "human beings live in language". The two propositions are obviously different, but there ought to be a transition from the one to the other. Let us begin from the philosophical proposition that "language is the house of Being" and proceed on to why the existence of human beings should be so dependent on language (i.e., language is the last homestead of human beings).

Since we shall refer to "Being" frequently hereinafter, it is necessary, at the start, to clarify the difference between "beings" (*das Seinde* in German and το ον in Greek, equivalent to "the being" in English, and όντα in Greek to "beings" in English) and "Being" (*Sein/sein* in German) (Wang & Wang, 2002, p. 17).[1]

The traditional schools of metaphysics, fettered by the "subject-object" dichotomy, adhered to there being things out there. However, that the

14   *Philosophical and pragmatic perspectives*

things are there differs from that they are present, or appear; that is, what there *is* may not necessarily be present, or appear in experiences.

(S. Zhang, 1998)

In other words, "beings" can be understood as things or individuals with their presence or appearance out there, but they differ from "Being" and its presence. It is very important to accept that the Being may not be present. Otherwise, one cannot apprehend the second level of the universe. Is there such a Being? The answer is positive. Objective laws *are*, but with no presence. Information *is*, but with no presence, either. Coexisting with real things out there are virtual entities (the objective Being of real things). Q. Zhang (1998) points out that there are two categories of virtual entities: Social and physical. Virtual social entities include the material-based signs of social information (signs of shape/sound, thought, culture, and language, etc.). Virtual physical entities include material-based signs of various waves, like electromagnetic waves, acoustic waves, biological waves, gravitational waves, etc. A virtual social entity generally resides in a physical thing or takes a real thing as its carrier. What is called a "virtual entity" here is the objective Being of real things. All real things (whether as huge as celestial bodies or as tiny as particles) exist as visible (material) beings, while all virtual entities exist as the invisible Being, void of materiality. The realm of real things is only the surface of the universe (the first level), while that of virtual entities is the second level. For instance, "God" as a virtual entity of idea exists only in the mind of disciples. No one has ever seen the real form "God", since "God" is not substantive in the true sense of the word. As phenomena, objective laws exist and cannot be modified by any means, but they are invisible and intangible. The phenomenon of human spirit is a conceptual virtual entity. If one anatomizes a human brain, one sees just the "material" and is never able to locate the "spirit". However, the intangible Being is no less, and can be, a state of existence. If we do not admit its existence (can we deny the existence of spiritual or information phenomena?), how can we set out to study it? Virtual entities do exist in a formless way.

Heidegger (1996) found earlier that in the history of metaphysics, beings were mistaken for Being, while the true meaning of Being was forgotten, and these ontological differences had led metaphysics astray. About this topic, Umberto Eco (1932–2016), the Italian literary critic and semiotician well known in Europe and America, proposed that "Being" has been expressed in various ways, of which the most accurate definition is what is coded in language in various senses (Eco, 1984). This means that Being is not some concrete thing that can be caught hold of (i.e., tangible objects that exist), but a language expression (what is expressed may be intangible, but it is and can be). This gives us the initial inspiration that "language is the house of Being".

2.1.1 *"Language is the house of Being"*

We shall demonstrate from three aspects why "language is the house of Being": First of all, the original idea of Heidegger, who puts forward the

Philosophical and pragmatic perspectives 15

proposition; second, the meaning of the proposition in the light of the word *das Sein*; and third, analytic philosophers' taking language (analysis) as the key to resolving the problem of existence.

2.1.1.1 Heidegger's original idea of the proposition

After proposing that "Language is the house of Being" in his *Letter on Humanism*, Heidegger (1982) expounds it many times, among which the following eight statements are direct and clear.

The first statement appears as follows.

> The being of anything that is resides in the word. Therefore, this statement holds true: Language is the house of Being.
>
> (Heidegger, 1982, p. 63)

This statement – direct, clear, straightforward, and unequivocal – comes closest to being the declaration of the Western philosophy of language. It is true that Heidegger's essays are rarely included in the collections edited by Anglo-American analytic philosophers under the titles similar to *Modern Philosophy of Language*, but I do not think this rejection of Heidegger disavows his status in the philosophy of language. If one asks, "what does 'language is the house of Being' mean in the sense of the Western philosophy of language?", The most succinct answer is: "The Being of all beings resides in language".

The second statement goes as follows.

> Language has been called "the house of Being". It is the keeper of being present, in that its coming to light remains entrusted to the appropriating show of Saying. Language is the house of Being because language, as Saying, is the mode of appropriation.
>
> (Heidegger, 1982, p. 135)

The key point of this passage is that language is the keeper of being present because its coming to light is entrusted to Saying. So far, this point has been clearly made: It is language that gives Being its presence, making it appear, so that Being is disclosed and sheltered in language. It is language that enables the Being of all beings to reside in words. How is this idea reinforced by Heidegger himself time and again?

What follows is the third statement, in which Heidegger says that language is the house of Being.

> With that expression ["house of Being" – translator's note], I do not mean the Being of beings represented metaphysically, but the presence of Being, more precisely the presence of the two-fold,[2] Being and beings – but this two-fold understood in respect of its importance for thinking them.
>
> (Heidegger, 1982, pp. 26–27)

16 *Philosophical and pragmatic perspectives*

What is particularly worth highlighting here is that Heidegger's phrase "the presence of Being" means more precisely "the presence of the two-fold, Being and beings", because this is of very great philosophical significance. His elaboration of the presence of the two-fold (Being and beings) should be regarded as a solution to the entangled problem of "What is existence?" in Western philosophy. For, once Being and beings are distinguished, then:

- Virtual entities related to actual entities (things) acquire their status;
- an entity can *be* without being present; intangible Being *is* and can *be*;
- the major defect of "the beings were taken for the Being and the Being is lost in oblivion" is rectified.

The fourth statement goes as follows.

> ... something *is* only where the appropriate and therefore competent word names a thing as being, and so establishes the given being as a being. Does this mean, also, that there is being only where the appropriate word is speaking?
>
> (Heidegger, 1982, p. 63; emphasis original)

The fifth statement, "No thing is where the word breaks off",[3] lays bare the relationship between "word" and "thing"; the word itself is the relation because the word gives being to the thing and keeps the thing as the being. Heidegger (1982, p. 73) holds, "If the word did not have this bearing, the whole of things, the 'world', would sink into obscurity". It is "word" that endows a thing with being and keeps the thing as the being, thus casting light on the world.

The sixth statement goes as follows.

> Accordingly, if the word is to endow the thing with being, it too must be before anything is – thus it must inescapably be itself a thing. We would then be faced with the situation that one thing, the word, conveys being to another thing.
>
> (Heidegger, 1982, p. 86)

Please notice that Heidegger raises a new question here: Apart from being able to endow the being, the word itself is a thing, a real entity out there, too. Why is it so? His answer is: "Everybody, after all, sees and hears words in writing and in sound. They are; they can be like things, palpable to the senses" (1982, p. 87).

The seventh statement is: "The word itself is the giver. What does it give? ... the word gives Being" (*ibid.*, p. 88).

The eighth statement goes like this: "To say means to show, to make appear, the lighting-concealing-releasing offer of world" (*ibid.*, p. 107).

Philosophical and pragmatic perspectives 17

Besides the above eight direct elaborations of the proposition, Heidegger enunciated his original idea many times in other places, too. Because language is elevated to a status on a par with that of ontology, he stands firmly against regarding language as a mere instrument for idea exchanges, which he thinks is a debasement of the significance of language as logos. Similar to Heidegger in terms of the attitude to language, Gadamer holds that language is not just something human beings own in the world; rather, it is by language that human beings own the world (Y. Xu et al., 1996, pp. 235–237). Inherent in his thought, Heidegger insisted that to regard language merely as an instrument for idea exchanges among human beings belittles its value and that *the more profound value of language is that it makes Being present*.

In brief, the above eight quotations suffice to show Heidegger's original meaning of "language is the house of Being", which can be summarized in one statement: *The Being of beings resides in words*.

2.1.1.2 Discussions on the proposition

DISCUSSION I: THE THREE SITUATIONS WHERE THE BEING OF BEINGS RESIDES IN WORDS

The three different situations discussed below are not Heidegger's original ideas, but my thoughts over the question, "how does the Being of beings reside in words?" or "how can language be the homestead in which human beings exist?"

In the first situation, concrete things are tied up with language and a language expression is backed by a real thing. For instance, words like "water" and "computer" give presence to some visible, tangible, or otherwise perceivable substance or entity, i.e., water and computer. Every real person alive is sheltered in his or her name. For some names – "Socrates" (470–399 BC), "Plato" (429–347 BC), "Shakespeare", "Dan Li",[4] and so on – one cannot find real entities at present that correspond to them, but there is no reason to deny that these four names are linked with the persons that once lived.

In a second situation, language invents some individuals or things as beings, though those beings cannot be seen, touched, or otherwise sensed. Yet the Being of a fictitious being cannot be brushed off, because its Being is significant. For Being and beings are not the same. For example, words of "Hamlet", "Daiyu Lin", "gold mountain", "Flaming Mountain",[5] and "Pegasus", etc., have fabricated a series of individuals or things that are not real, but you cannot dismiss them as meaningless beings. They are real in your mind, existing in your spirit.

Closely related to this situation are the cases that demonstrate more vividly how saying makes Being appear and be kept in language and how the Being of beings resides in words. One case in point is a certain tall mountain rock or cliff that comes to be, under the force of erosions, in various shapes. People feel that it is very beautiful and looks just like something for which they do not have a word for the time being. After many trials of naming, one person

18   *Philosophical and pragmatic perspectives*

finally points at a rock in some shape and says, "Look! a turtle sticks out its head!" Another person points at another spot and says, "A monkey fishes in the sea!" And still another one points at a rock and says, "That's Ashima!" Accordingly, people decide to officially name these scenic spots "Turtle Sticking Out Head", "Monkey Fishing in the Sea", and "Ashima", respectively. Later visitors to these places for sightseeing would say that it really is a turtle sticking out the head, or a monkey fishing in the sea, or Ashima. What should be asked here is: Are the visitors appreciating the shapes of the rocks, or the labels tacked on to them in language? There is no turtle that is sticking out its head (the rock on the hummock is not at all a turtle, nor can it stick out a head); there is no monkey that is fishing in the sea (the rock on the hill is not a monkey and cannot fish in the sea); and Ashima simply does not exist (not only that the rock on the hill is not Ashima, but also that Ashima herself is a figure in a fairy tale and not a real person that ever lived). Why is it the case that all these things come to be what they are, once language labels are tacked onto them? What is the being that really is? The being that visitors appreciate is not the real entity (a rock in a certain shape), nor anything out there, nor purely a language expression (if you said "Look! A turtle sticks out its head!" in the absence of the particular hill or rock, or "Look! A monkey fishes in the sea!" pointing to a table, people would simply believe you are out of your mind!). But when you hear your companions say "Look! A monkey fishes in the sea" while seeing the hill and the rock in a particular shape, you may conjure up instantly in your mind the figure or image of a monkey fishing in the sea. But a corresponding mental image would not be conjured up, if either the entity in sight or the language expression heard is dispensed with. Of course, such an entity for appreciation is empty as a being (null-being, non-existent), but it is meanwhile a meaningful being! This is a being fabricated by the sustenance object in collaboration with the language label. It lives neither in the sustenance object, nor entirely in the language expression, but is reliant on both the sustenance object and the language expression. One thing we cannot deny is that it is the sayings ("Turtle Sticking Out Head", "Monkey Fishing in the Sea", and "Ashima"[6]) that enable those virtual entities (the figures and images conjured up in the mind of the appreciator) to show up, to appear and be kept in language. Such a being – a mental object which exists in experience (the turtle, the monkey, or Ashima, etc.) – does reside in word!

In the third situation, pure perception, reflection, thought, and idea come into being by right of their successful categorization and conceptualization in words. Examples abound: "Language game", "the Theory of Games", "logical thinking", "market economy", "the bio-holographic law", to list just several. A good case in point is this book, unfolded in front of the readers. All that is written, when the manuscript is finalized, is distilled into one proposition that "language is the last homestead of human beings". This generalized proposition, as a thought resulting from categorization and conceptualization, has now an existence on its own. In so saying, I am certainly not referring to the Chinese book *per se*, entitled *Language: The Last Homestead of*

Philosophical and pragmatic perspectives 19

Human Beings, as a real entity composed of visible and readable paper sheets. What I intend to illustrate is that the invisible and intangible experience made to appear and substantiated in language has no less a form of existence. It is language that makes this possible. The more such distilled pure ideas (in fact, language expressions) a civilization has in its possession, the more mature and highly advanced that civilization will be.

DISCUSSION II: WORD GIVES BEING TO BEINGS – TWO DISTINCT TERMS OF EXISTENCE

The fifth to the eighth of Heidegger's quotations listed above assert repeatedly that a thing has its Being only when a word names it. This is a controversial issue, nevertheless. The controversy reflects not only the difference in the philosophical standpoints between the East and the West as well as in the debates between realism and nominalism, but also in the historical disputes between materialism and idealism. With some self-confidence, a high-school student may well question an idealist: Do things, such as a rocket, atom bomb, atomic reactor, etc., come into being only after they are named? Don't they exist before the naming? (This also touches upon the "inverting" and "concealing" function of language, which we shall talk about in Discussion III that follows.) Heidegger (1982) seemed to have anticipated such a question, for he already asked and answered it himself.

> Yet how can a mere word accomplish this? The true situation is obviously the reverse. Take the sputnik. This thing, if such it is, *is* obviously independent of that name which was later tacked on to it.[7] ...[8] modern technology which would be the last to admit the thought that what gives things their being is the word. ... if the word framing that order and challenge had not spoken: then there would be no sputnik. No thing is where the word is lacking. Thus the puzzle remains: the word of language and its relation to the thing, to every thing that is – that it is and the way it is.
>
> (p. 62)

The point Heidegger made in answering the question is: A thing must be spoken before it is given its presence. *A thing cannot be talked about if it is not named and a thing that cannot be talked about cannot be brought to presence or is not made to appear.* He did not evade the question whether real entities (satellite, rocket, atom bomb, atomic reactor) exist or not. A philosopher is not so naive as to think that an unnamed thing does not exist out there (didn't he himself state clearly: "Take the sputnik. This thing, if such it is, *is* obviously independent of that name which was later tacked on to it"?). Obviously, Being and beings that Western philosophers talk about are not the same story. Therefore, Heidegger emphasizes the issue of the two-fold of Being and beings. "Word itself is a relation, because it gives a thing the presence and shelters it there" (Y. Xu et al., 1996, p. 153). How is a thing sheltered in speaking? Words name things and a true naming is an invitation; it calls out a

20 *Philosophical and pragmatic perspectives*

thing so that the thing as the thing is concerned by humans (*ibid.*). It is such a naming that gives presence to a thing its being, and the thing comes to be what it is and not be what it is not (*ibid.*, p. 154). To name a thing ("bowl", "knowledge economy", etc.) is to make the thing appear as the thing (a bowl, knowledge economy, etc.). Does the thing exist before it is named? It is not said here, but at least the thing is not brought into the spotlight. In what follows, we shall discuss this situation (the existence of beings before naming). The Being of beings is present only by the time they are named and, starting from that time, the beings are what they are and not what they are not; for instance, a bowl is a bowl and is not a knowledge economy. Here, Heidegger already had the idea that existence appears in word. To put it briefly, "word" has the function of naming what is, the presence of Being is called out by word, "No thing is where word breaks off", and the Being of all beings resides in words.

In line with Heidegger's statements, I now want to make a distinction between the existence of things before naming (in a broader sense, being expressed in language) and the existence of things after naming, for this issue is quite puzzling. Let's imagine an instance. Sealed in a bottle is oxygen (what exists, i.e., beings), but before people labeled it with "oxygen", the expression should be: "Oxygen exists but is not present". When people decide to attach the label of "oxygen" to the oxygen sealed in the bottle, then the expression has to be: "Oxygen exists and is present". In the same way, the artificial satellite mentioned above would have this difference before and after naming; "The artificial satellite exists but is not present" applies to the existence of the satellite before it is named, while "The artificial satellite exists and is present" applies to its existence after it is named.

To generalize, the expression "A thing exists but is not present (the existence of a thing without its presence)" applies to the former state (the existence of a thing before a name is given to it), while "A thing exists and is present (the existence of a thing with its presence)" applies to the latter state (the existence of a thing after it is named).

There is an advantage to this distinction: It acknowledges the Being of what indeed exists out there, and meanwhile caters to Heidegger's proposition of "the phrase 'the house of Being' ... [means] the presence of the two-fold, Being and beings" (Heidegger, 1982, pp. 26–27). One issue concerning word making "existence" present is the argument between realists and nominalists. Nominalists hold that there exist only concrete individuals in the world, such as San Zhang, Si Li, this man, that woman, this child, that old man, and that a general term like "man" is a virtual name, not existing in the same sense as San Zhang and Si Li really do. Who can see an abstract man, a universal man, or man as mankind? This school of thought is referred to as nominalism. Realists, on the other hand, insist that a universal man and thing is real and more real than a specific individual man or thing, because it is *a priori*, more complete, and eternal. Individuals are the derivation from or the particular instantiation of such a real entity. Nominalists do not accept the existence of any universal man claim.

Philosophical and pragmatic perspectives 21

Such entities are all empty names (discourse) and not real. There is no wholeness without individuals, and without referring to the whole, individuals exist. Therefore, individuals are real and the wholeness is non-physical but just a name or a phrase.

(Jin, 1998)

We should note his phrase of "the wholeness is non-physical but just a name or a phrase". 人类 ([rénlèi] "mankind") that we Chinese say, or "mankind" that Anglo-Americans speak of, do not exist actually, but mankind are what they are only after we use this word or phrase (人类 in Chinese or "mankind" in English) to label them. In the eyes of nominalists, the existence that we talk about is what is made to appear or called out by word.

DISCUSSION III: THE "INVERTING" AND "CONCEALING" FUNCTIONS OF LANGUAGE

This issue was mentioned in the foregoing discussion, when we came to the question, raised by ordinary people, of whether a thing *per se* exists on its own or it cannot exist until it is named. At that point we did an analysis of the two-fold of Being and beings to make the distinction between the thing as a being and its Being. But since this is an issue of great importance, we now elaborate on it again under a separate subtitle.

Two dogs can communicate with each other in the face of a bone, a thing that exists whose being is present and has appeared, but they are unable to discuss with each other what is above and beyond the bone – what is a bone, where does the bone come from, what is the function of the bone, what other uses can be made of the bone other than being eaten, or what is the molecular structure of the bone, etc.? Human beings can talk about an electric lamp in its presence, but, more marvelously, they are able to, by means of language, talk about various things behind the electric lamp that are not present and have not appeared, such as the direction, the polarity, and the current of electricity, the magnetic field caused by electricity, and so on. Aristotle said that man is a creature of logos, and the primary meaning of logos is language. It is logos that enables human beings to transcend present things and brings them to an existence that is not yet present and is yet to appear. No animals other than humans, however, are capable of this transcendence. Animals rely on the things that are immediately present to communicate with each other, but human beings, equipped with language, can speak of what is non-present and hidden, thereby realizing a shared life through mutual communication and understanding. S. Zhang (1998) points out,

The fundamental property of language is its capability of expressing things that are non-present and hidden. … Thinking can only be carried on in language. It is through learning language and speech that we grow up, form concepts, and know about the world. … Language and speech play a fully significant role where something is hidden. … In fact, without

22   *Philosophical and pragmatic perspectives*

language, thinking cannot be carried on, because concepts cannot be formed otherwise. Concept construction is constrained by language.

It is the very function of language to express the existence that is non-present and hidden that makes mankind as mankind that differs from all the other animals. For this reason, it is right to claim that "the issue of existence will draw us most intimately to the issue of language" (existence is "what is expressed in language in various ways"), and it is more correct to say that only language can enable us to draw out what is most inherently non-present. In a word, language not only makes what is on the spot appear, but also gives presence to what is non-present and hidden. It is in this sense that we say that thinking proceeds on the path of speech. In the general run of things, to say that thinking proceeds on the path of speech might well be taken to mean that where thought goes, speech shows. But in fact, *it is speech that draws out the non-present existence (thought)*.

What has been said above is the core idea that human beings cannot transcend time and space, but language helps them realize such a transcendence. For things and ideas not immediately present, language comes to presence in their place when people talk about them. About this point, there has long been a certain mistaken idea. This error in comprehension is reflected in people's use of terms like "inverting" or "concealing" to refer to the capability of language to help human beings transcend time and space and the ability to abstract and to categorize in language. Huang and Wang (1998) observed,

> As to the concealing of language, Shaomang Deng has given an elaboration, in the first chapters of his book, *Stress of Thinking*, published in 1994, on the "inverting" process of language beginning from Plato. The inverting function of language appears to be most clearly in Aristotle's philosophy. Originally, the physical matter was *a priori*, and the ancient Greeks were accustomed to the enumerative way of knowing about the classification of things; e.g., the concept of "man" was represented by the set of living individuals like San Zhang, Si Li, and so on. Aristotle, profoundly influenced by biological taxonomy, tended to name first the classification of things with an abstract concept of class, as a result of which it came to be accepted that there had to be an abstract concept or idea, before there could be concrete individual things and that concrete things were just the finite realization of the infinite idea in the world and were therefore relative. With this shift, the world of language and concept became what was *a priori* to the actual world. This is the "inverting" function of language. In Hegel's *Phänomenologie des Geistes*, when "This is a tree" is spoken, the reality is in fact obscured, for a really living tree is thrown under an abstract concept of class. So where there is language, there may be concealment. Laozi might have had his perception of the inverting property of language and signs, which was probably behind

Philosophical and pragmatic perspectives 23

his saying: "Truly great argument does not say anything, truly great voice does not have a sound, and truly great form does not have a shape".

In everyday life, people only see a poplar, a willow, an oak, and so on, but cannot see a tree. "Tree" is a concept word. We simply cannot see a concept. When someone points at a willow and says "This is a tree", it is indeed a concealment of the concrete thing (poplar, willow, or oak, etc.), a substitution of the thing with the pronouncement of an abstract concept word.

In fact, a human being usually starts to understand things from knowing the concrete instances, and thereby an abstract concept is formed at the end; e.g., coffee + cocoa + tea + soda water + ... = beverage. The advantage of abstract and categorized concept formation is that it is conducive to scientific research and helpful for language learners in learning and thinking. It is only in such cases that the process goes from the abstract to the concrete; e.g., beverage = coffee + cocoa + tea + soda water + ... Language only helps human beings to pin down what is abstracted and categorized in their mind. *After the abstract and categorized concepts are formed, they come to stand between human beings and the real world, and in this sense we can say the world of language and concept became what was* a priori *to the actual world.* This saying applies to mankind as a whole. For individual human beings, however, the way to knowledge is generally that the acquisition of "the world of language and concept (such as 'beverage' ...)" is accomplished after they are acquainted with real concrete objects (coffee, cocoa, tea, soda water ...) and not before this acquaintance.

However, problems occur in two situations where inverting happens. One is that the concept of a set or a class has already been implanted forcibly in the mind before an individual gets in touch with concrete things (quite common in practice and normal in education). Consequently, the individual has to begin from the concept of a class or a set and then goes back to learn words for concrete instances in order to know the things in specifics. There is another situation of inverting. When an adult points at a willow and says to a young child who is acquiring language: "This is a tree", this constitutes undoubtedly a confusion and concealment for the child. The child would have to straighten out the order that has been inverted in the following-up process of learning: "Oh, it turns out that what I see is not a tree, but a poplar or a willow or an oak ... Well, of course I can group these specific poplars, willows, or oaks ... into the set of 'tree'". The child is able to make the rectification of what has previously been inverted only when he/she is able to make such an utterance.

In using words to talk about those things, people make things appear, by way of abstraction and categorization – including those that do not appear of themselves (such as the knowledge economy) – bring to be here (this space) the things that are not here, and show the presence of things that are not present. For instance, a talk in a living room about a blade of grass on the Kunlun Mountain Range is a move beyond the limitation of space. When

24 *Philosophical and pragmatic perspectives*

people take as the topic what does not exist or is not happening at the time of their talk, such as discussing an event of 500 years ago, they move beyond the limitation of time. Human beings cannot transcend time and space, but language enables them to do so, because it is language that comes to be present in place of things. In a word, it is language that gives presence to beings.

It is a form of inverting to say that an abstract and ideal language (things *a priori* to the real world) has already existed before an individual is born. If this is so, is it true to say that "where there is language, there may be concealment"? Well, concealment can only be said to have occurred if, in face of a concrete thing, the pronouncement is made not with the name for the concrete thing, but in a concept word only (such as saying "This is a tree" instead of "This is a willow" in the face of a willow). What is at issue here is that concept words help human beings to classify and categorize the world, which should be regarded as the abstract words' function for cognition and not their concealment of the world. It is true that we cannot see abstract concepts, but we do abstract thinking and we do it in concepts. Besides, in terms of the law of cognition, we cannot conduct mature thinking without using words of abstract concepts. For this reason, *to think in words of abstract concepts is not to conceal; rather, it is the readiness to successfully bring the being to its presence.*

It has long been recognized that language is not omnipotent. What and how something is (including the eternal *Dao* in Laozi's philosophy) can be said clearly, but not always so. Therefore, Laozi said: "The *Dao* can be said, but what is said is not the eternal *Dao*". If you take language abstraction and categorization for concealment, an imperfect description, and interpret "not the external *Dao*" as the *Dao* being concealed, then such concealment obviously does have its *raison d'être*. For the "inverting" and "concealing" functions of language, please also refer to Section 4.2 of this book.

2.1.1.3 *The word* das Sein

Another meaning originates in the word *das Sein*.

"*Sein* itself is the Being that determines beings as beings". Both affirmative and negative judgments abound in speeches, and so the word "to be" is of very high frequency in language use.

What does the word *das Sein* mean in Heidegger's proposition "Die Sprache ist das Haus des Seins"? In the German language, *das Sein* means in Chinese 是 ([shì] "to be"), 在 ([zài] "to exist; to be at a location") and 存在 ([cúnzài] "there be; Being; existence"). Its English equivalent is "Being". The meaning of this proposition in the eyes of us Chinese is more or less at variance with that in the eyes of the people who speak Western languages. The key issue involved here is that the word *sein* in German expresses two meanings: Predication and existence. This is also the case with the counterpart of *sein* in English, "to be", which plays the role of predication and means "to exist". These two are in one while the one is of two, a relationship of two and one, one and two. But in the

Philosophical and pragmatic perspectives 25

Chinese language, there is no such a relationship, because the characters of Chinese 是 ("to be") and 存在 ("to exist; existence") express respectively two different concepts. Jin (1997, p. 197) points out:

> The word 存在 [cúnzaì] is a loanword in Chinese and a very bothersome one. It is all quite simple in the European and Indian languages. They have one word to express both "to be" and "to exist". … In the Chinese language, however, 是 ([shì] "to be") and 有 ([yoǔ] "to exist; to have") are not expressed by one word, since 有 [yoǔ] is ambiguous, meaning "to have" in the sense of possession apart from its meaning of "to exist". So the character string of 存在 ("existence") is adopted in Chinese translation, in which the character 存 [cún] denotes the temporal extension while 在 [zaì], the spatial location.

Let's put aside for the time being the temporal and spatial significance of the character string 存在 ([cúnzaì] "existence") and pay attention to just one point that interests us here: In the Indo-European languages, there is a single word that means both "to be" and "existence", while in Chinese two separate words must be used to express these two concepts.

Now, think about the character 是 [shì] in the Chinese discourse system. It is first a copula that links up two things, showing that the two things are the same or that the latter thing is the class the former is in or the property the former has. For example, 《红楼梦》的前八十回作者是曹雪芹 ([Hónglóumèng de qiánbāshíhuí zuòzhě shì Cáoxuěqín] "The author of the first 80 chapters of *A Dream of Red Mansions* is Cao Xueqin") or 某某是人 ([Mǒumǒu shì rén] "So-and-so is a human being"). A second usage of the character is to classify, as in 木棉是红的 ([Mùmián shì hóng de] "Kapoks are red"). A third usage of 是 is a connection of two things, indicating that the object asserted is in the condition described after the link verb, as in 外面是闹哄哄一片，里面是世外桃园 ([Wàimiàn shì nàohōnghōng yīpiàn, lǐmiàn shì shìwài táoyuán] "The outside is all hustle and bustle, while the inside is a tranquil retreat"). A fourth meaning of 是 expresses what is there, where the subject is usually a phrase of location and the thing that is in the location comes after the link verb, as in 教学大楼前是两棵高大的红棉 ([Jiàoxué dàlóu qián shì liǎng kē gāodà de hóngmián] "In front of the teaching building are two tall Mayreus"). There are other usages, but it does not appear necessary to list them all here.

Now let us turn to 存在 ([cúnzaì] "to exist; existence") in the Chinese discourse system. First, it means that a thing continues to be in time and space; it is there and has not yet disappeared. Second, it means philosophically the objective world that does not rely on the subjective consciousness of human beings and is independent of their will; i.e., the physical things (in the eyes of some Western philosophers, especially Heidegger, Being may be used to refer to a nonphysical entity).

With that being said, the comparison underlines the distinction between 是 ([shì] "to be") and 存在 ([cúnzaì] "to exist; existence") in the mind of the

26 *Philosophical and pragmatic perspectives*

people whose mother language is Chinese. As a result, when reading the Chinese translation of "language is the house of Being", the Chinese tend to understand "Being" to mean the objective world only, unaware of the sense of "to be". However, in the minds of the Germans, who read the original statement of "Die Sprache ist das Haus des Seins", the word *Seins* (roughly equivalent to 存在 ([cúnzài] "to exist; existence") in Chinese) at the end of the sentence and the copula *ist* are derived from the same thing and are the same thing! This is illustrated by the following figure.

Die Sprache ist das Haus des Seins.
⇓ ⇓
sein *Sein*

That is exactly what Heidegger refers to by *das Sein*. Now, let's look at Jiaying Chen's remarks.

> Heidegger's lifelong thinking was on *das Sein*, "to be", Being and existence. ... This all-purpose *Sein* connects the individual and the universal, entity and essence, concept and concept. ... *Sein* is a copula through which things and things, concepts and concepts, and things and concepts are all "linked" together. ... The role the copula *Sein* plays here is miraculous indeed. However, what Heidegger is most concerned with is not the connection between "beings" and "beings", but is "Being" itself, the Being that determines beings as beings.
>
> (Xu et al., 1996, pp. 145–146)

Here, the phrase "'Being' itself, the Being that determines beings as beings" is of key importance. We realize immediately that Heidegger's saying "language is the house of Being" can be in truth more appropriately rephrased as "language is the house of 'to be'". Language is the house of "to be" in that language is filled with "to be" or "to be not" judgments; i.e., what speakers say every day are full of affirmative or negative judgments made by using "to be" or "to be not". In doing something, a person (the subject) would make a judgment of the target of action (the object) before taking an action. The frequency with which we talk about "to be" vocally is already high enough, but the frequency with which they do it non-vocally is even much higher. In doing anything, one has to judge what is and what is not, before attempting and accomplishing it. When I want to enter my study to write a book on the computer, I must first judge whether the room I am approaching is the study or not, and if it is not, I have to look for the study at once. Next, I must judge whether the object I approach is my computer or not, as I can turn it on only if it is; if it is not a computer, I have to turn around to where the computer is. After I turn on my computer, I must find the file that I have been processing among so many files and, if the file is not the right one, I have to search again for the one I have been working on. This may go on and on. Only

Philosophical and pragmatic perspectives 27

Heaven knows how many times I say "to be" or "to be not" silently every day! Therefore, Jiaying Chen goes on to say:

> As soon as we deal with the beings, we already hear the sound of Being. What is heard first is not "A well is ..." but "... is a well". When I go across the courtyard to fetch water from a well, I have already been saying this is a courtyard and that is a well, though without any word uttered. The courtyard as the courtyard, the well as the well, and the beings as the beings, in all of these, the *Sein* is saying and language is there. ... Humans are saying *Sein* and *seins* in various ways all the time and everywhere, but the most often said "it is" (*Es ist*) is said non-vocally. It is "a well" and it is "a courtyard", and further, "The well is outside the courtyard".
>
> (Xu et al., 1996, p. 146)

Indeed, in our daily life, "the most often said 'it is' (*Es ist*) is said non-vocally".

In order to show the ubiquitous use of "to be" in language, I did a survey of its use in several languages.

Let's first take a look at the Russian language. In his paper entitled "Event Case and the Meaning of Sentences", Xiyin Li (1998) quotes three paragraphs in Russian to illustrate the idea of three worlds (inanimate world, animal world, and human world). The first paragraph contains nine expressions to which the third-person form of the present tense of the verb (есть) can be added. Есть is used five times in the second paragraph. And in the third paragraph the verbs are of a wide variety. This shows that in the Russian language the verb есть appears considerably frequently.[9]

Then, how about the English language? Look at the following passage, for example. It should be mentioned here that this passage is not selected purposefully but randomly; it was chosen simply because I happened to open the journal *PRAGMATICS* (June 1998) and it is the first paragraph of the first paper in it, which goes as follows.

> Interviewing *is* a widespread social practice which many practitioners or institutional representatives carry out in their daily professional routines. In various institutional settings, clinical interviews *are* the most common devices institutional representatives use to establish a relationship with their clients and perform their roles. At a practical and descriptive level, clinical interviews can be defined as verbal interactions which aim at making a diagnosis, a therapy, or at eliciting information from a subject in a research setting. One common characteristic of this type of interviews *is* that they do not rely on a fixed and predetermined set of questions, even though they might be based upon some routines. Another common characteristic *is* that they aim at eliciting the interviewee's discourse and most of the time involve his/her emotional commitment or at least a reference to his/her personal experience, to such an extent that sometimes the interviewee him or herself *is* the main topic of the

28 *Philosophical and pragmatic perspectives*

conversation. The construction of a relationship between institutional representatives and their clients, the way they make sense of the situation and construe the meaning of their discourse *are* thus essential features of clinical interviews.

(Emphasis added)

Altogether, there are 16 predicate verbs, of which six are linking verbs in the sense of "to be", without counting the "be" in the passive voices (because they do not mean "to be" or "to exist"). The linking verb "to be" accounts for one third of all the predicate verbs, with a wide variety of other verbs making up the remaining two-thirds. Incidentally, none of the link verbs ("to be") in this paragraph is of the existential usage as in "there be". Even so, it is truly amazing that this one verb "to be" should be in such a large proportion. It is thus no exaggeration to say that Western languages are the house of "to be".

The last paragraph of the last paper in the same issue of the journal goes as follows.

The ninth chapter treats so-called "nonnative varieties" of English around the world. The landmark against which these languages are commonly treated *is* not simply "standard" English, but rather, "Western" English(es). Varieties that *are* spoken in and by the Western world but that are clearly remote from standard English never seem to count as "nonnative" varieties, or they are simply given the status of additional standards – a privilege from which the non-Western varieties are excluded. The enterprise *is*, as such, fundamentally imperialist in nature: it always treats the "nonnative" varieties as aberrations of the landmark, rather than vice-versa. The last three chapters deal with issues of lexicography, the synthesis of politics and linguistics, and probability theory, respectively. The book closes off with a general list of references and an index of names and languages.

(Emphasis added)

There are altogether 13 predicate verbs, of which three are "to be", or one quarter of the total. Again, "to be" makes up a quite large proportion, even though none of the link verbs ("to be") in this paragraph is of the existential usage as in "there be", either.

Now, let's look at the Chinese language. Likewise, the following samples are not selected by this author purposefully but randomly from the Chinese journal *Xinhua News Digest*. They are the last paragraphs respectively of the last three articles of the August issue of 1998.

Sample I
《三重火焰》是对爱情的充分肯定，是对西方爱情观念的理论总结和剖析，同时也是对爱情的基础——人与自由的坚定捍卫。对爱情这种人类精神如此重要的感情，帕斯通过本书提出了独到的理论见解，做

Philosophical and pragmatic perspectives 29

出了诗意的贡献。这本书也可说是帕斯一生著述的总结，因为他所有著作的中心主题就是试图证明，人能够通过爱情和艺术创造性来克服他生存的孤独感。帕斯的书被翻译成中文的似乎不多，因而我们希望广大中国读者能通过这本书进一步认识和理解帕斯的思想和艺术。

[Sānchóng huǒyàn shì duì àiqíng de chōngfèn kěndìng, shì duì xīfāng àiqíng guānniàn de lǐlùn zǒngjié hé pōuxī, tóngshí yě shì duì àiqíng de jīchǔ——rén yǔ zìyóu de jiāndìng hànwèi. Duì àiqíng zhèzhǒng rénlèi jīngshén rúcǐ zhòngyào de gǎnqíng, pàsī tōngguò běnshū tíchūle dúdào de lǐlùn jiànjiě, zuò chūle shīyì de gòngxiàn. Zhèběn shū yě kě shuō shì pàsī yīshēng zhùshù de zǒngjié, yīnwèi tā suǒyǒu zhùzuò de zhōngxīn zhǔtí jiùshì shìtú zhèngmíng, rén nénggòu tōngguò àiqíng hé yìshù chuàngzàoxìng lái kèfú tā shēngcún de gūdúgǎn. Pàsī de shū bèi fānyì chéng zhōngwén de sìhū bùduō, yīn'ér wǒmen xīwàng guǎngdà zhōngguó dúzhě néng tōngguò zhèběn shū jìnyībù rènshí hé lǐjiě pàsī de sīxiǎng hé yìshù.]

The Triple Flame is entirely positive of love, *is* a theoretical summary and analysis of Western concept of love, and at the same time *is* a firm defense of the foundation of love – human being and freedom. On love as the affection so important to human spirit, Paz has raised his unique theoretical viewpoint in this book and made a poetic contribution to love. This book can be said to *be* the summary of his works in all his life, because in all his writings the central theme *is* to try to prove that a person can overcome his loneliness of existence by virtue of love and artistic creativity. Paz' writings have scarcely been translated into Chinese, and therefore we hope the readers in China can come to know and understand the idea and art of Paz by reading this book.

In this paragraph, the Chinese copula 是 ([shì] "to be") appears five times, while there are six other predicate verbs (including those in the sub-clauses). The copula 是 ([shì] "to be") makes up over two-thirds of all, which is quite amazing a proportion.

Sample II

因此，对出书速度要作具体分析。一般图书尤其是时效性强的图书尽可能争取快，而对有的工具书就不能单纯要求快。工具书的特点之一是具有稳定性，这就决定了它不可能在短时间内有轰动效应。但它随之而来的生命力相对较长，"失效期"也来得较迟。因此，不同的图书有不同的规律、不同的出版周期，出书速度不能超越图书自身的规律，超越了会受到惩罚的。

[Yīncǐ, duì chūshū sùdù yào zuò jùtǐ fēnxī. Yībān túshū yóuqíshì shíxiàoxìng qiáng de túshū jǐn kěnéng zhēngqǔ kuài, ér duì yǒude gōngjùshū jiù bùnéng dānchún yāoqiú kuài. Gōngjùshū de tèdiǎn zhīyī shì jùyǒu wěndìngxìng, zhè jiù juédìngle tā bù kěnéng zài duǎnshíjiān nèi yǒu hōngdòng xiàoyìng. Dàn tā suízhī ér lái de shēngmìnglì xiāngduì jiàozhǎng, "shīxiào qí" yě láidé jiàochí. Yīncǐ, bùtóng de túshū yǒu bùtóng

30 *Philosophical and pragmatic perspectives*

de guīlǜ, bùtóng de chūbǎn zhōuqí, chūshū sùdù bùnéng chāoyuè túshū zìshēn de guīlǜ, chāoyuèle huì shòudào chéngfá de.]

Therefore, one should do a concrete analysis of the speed of book publication. We should publish as quickly as possible ordinary books, especially those with immediacy, but do not press too hard for the publication of tool-books. One of the characteristics of the tool-book *is* its stability, which makes it impossible for the book to cause a sensation in a short time. But such a book has a relatively long life-expectancy and its "expiration" comes too slowly. In all, different books have different patterns and the speed of publication should not overstep cycles of publication; overstepping them spells penalty.

There are 12 predicate verbs in this paragraph, but only one is copula 是 ([shì] "to be"). This proportion is not impressive. After all, the copula 是 is used relatively less frequently in Chinese than this linking verb in Western languages.

Sample III
我所以列举上述例证，并不是说马克思的理论是一成不变的，"同时胜利"的论点仍然是正确的。相反，任何理论都是不断发展的，马克思主义也不例外，只是为了说明理论要符合实际。

[Wǒ suǒyǐ lièjǔ shàngshù lìzhèng, bìng bùshì shuō mǎkèsī de lǐlùn shì yīchéngbùbiàn de, "tóngshí shènglì" de lùndiǎn réngrán shì zhèngquè de. Xiāngfǎn, rènhé lǐlùn dōu shì bùduàn fāzhǎn de, mǎkèsī zhǔyì yě bù lìwài, zhǐshì wèile shuōmíng lǐlùn yào fúhé shíjì.]

By listing the above cases in point, I am not saying that Marx' theory *is* immutable and that his argument of "victory at the same time" *is* still correct. On the contrary, all theories *are* constantly developing and Marxism is no exception; I just want to show that theories must accord with reality.

In this short Chinese paragraph, there are altogether six predicate verbs (including verbs in sub-clauses), of which three are 是 ([shì] "to be"), half of the total.

The above-quoted cases serve the purpose of showing that in the three languages, быть (present tense есть), "to be" and 是 ([shì] "to be") appear in very high frequency. Heidegger said, "language is the house of Being", and we can say: Language is the house of "to be".

2.1.1.4 *Analysis of language: Solution to age-old philosophical problems*

What has directly motivated the trend of Anglo-American analytic philosophy is the attempt to resolve the age-old philosophical problem of ontology by means of language analysis. "The label 'analytical philosophy' usually refers to

Philosophical and pragmatic perspectives 31

a certain range of philosophical inquiries and doctrines which have developed from the last decade of the 19th century to present times" (Sbisà, 1995, p. 28). Most of them belong to the Anglo-American philosophical camp, but among the founders of the Anglo-American philosophy camp, Gottlob Frege was German and Wittgenstein was Austrian. However, the influence of these two philosophers was widely felt first in Anglo-American inquiries. Moreover, as Sbisà observes,

> ... the analytical-philosophical style has now spread into many different countries. Most of them share an effort towards a precise and detailed formulation of philosophical questions as well as towards a careful argumentative style in philosophical answers. Many of them are connected with the empiricist tradition and many of them are committed to the idea that the only propositions that we know with certainty as true are analytic ones. Many of them conceive of philosophy as an analytical activity and/or *envisage the study of language as necessary for tackling or perhaps solving philosophical problems.*
>
> (1995, p. 28; emphasis added)

The last two features (empiricist tradition, the idea that the only propositions that we know to be true with certainty are analytic ones, and envisaging the study of language as necessary for tackling or perhaps solving philosophical problems) are "perhaps most important for an understanding of the origins of the label 'analytical philosophy'" (Sbisà, 1995, p. 28).

As observed by Rorty (1967, p. 15), many philosophers, facing the enormous progresses of the sciences that resulted from cooperation between scientists who accept each other's conclusions when they are proved to be true, have started to search for criteria for rational agreements in philosophy. With such a goal in mind, they have focused their attention not on humans, things in the world, and so on, but on the language we use to talk about all this. Either an ideal language or an ideal understanding of our ordinary language could avoid misunderstandings among philosophers and promote rational agreements. The change of questions raised is the explicit sign of the change of the central issue of philosophical inquiries. Sbisà holds as follows.

> This move involves a *reconsideration of most traditional philosophical problems as problems of language.* For example, the fundamental ethical question "What is good?" becomes a question about the meaning of "good", or the way in which "good" can have meaning. The ontological question "What is there?" becomes a question about when and how we can refer to objects. ... According to Dummett, what distinguishes analytic philosophy from other schools is the belief, first, that a philosophical account of thought can be attained through a philosophical account of language, and, secondly, that a comprehensive account of thought can only be so attained.
>
> (Sbisà, 1995, p. 29; emphasis added)

32   *Philosophical and pragmatic perspectives*

The Anglo-American philosophy of language was founded by the German philosopher Gottlob Frege and has developed and become popular in English-speaking countries, such as Britain, the United States, Canada, Australia, and New Zealand. Nevertheless, the other countries on the European continent also made their contributions. Russell and Wittgenstein were the initiators of the turn, too. George Edward Moore was the forerunner of ordinary language analysis, with his patient and meticulous speculations on the subtle nuance between sentences. Around World War II, ordinary language analysis, represented by Gilbert Ryle, John Langshaw Austin, and Peter Frederick Strawson of Oxford, became the mainstream of philosophy of language, and later Wittgenstein's (1964) famous book *Philosophical Investigations* (*Philosophische Untersuchungen*) was a brilliant representative work of this line of thought. In the later development of the philosophy of language, Paul Grice and John Searle introduced speakers as an important aspect of meaning, which has been the central inquiry since the linguistic turn in philosophy (Xu et al., 1996, pp. 34–35).

In brief, Anglo-American analytic philosophy holds the following beliefs: 1) That the inquiry into human thinking and cognitive ability should yield to the inquiry into the meaning of language expressions, because only the latter is public, objective, and direct; 2) that most of the philosophical traditions are the product of metaphysical speculation and the most efficient way to reveal its errors is to point out its erroneous use of language; and 3) that even if there are different opinions on the status and function of language, at least one agreement can be reached: To avoid pointless arguments so as to tackle philosophical problems more effectively, it is a desirable approach to set aside the ontological issue of the object represented by language and make comparison of the language uses that everyone agrees on.

2.1.2 *"Being" drawing human beings into language*

The significance of the proposition "language is the house of Being" can be generalized briefly into the following three points. First, the original idea of the proponent is that Being comes to appear by virtue of language. Second, the word most frequently used by human beings is the copula *sein* (noun form *das Sein*, equivalent to "to be"), meaning "to be" and "to exist". Human beings are the sole species able to utter "to be"/*das Sein*/Being – the Being that determines beings as beings. Just as one can say land is the homestead of human beings because the land they have is remolded into their home for living, so can language be the homestead in which human beings exist. Third, analytic philosophers envisage language (analysis) as the fundamental solution to the problem of existence. Seen in this way, "language is the house of Being" is not only a proposition of Heidegger's, but also an aphorism of the entire Western philosophy.

Heidegger said on the one hand that language is the house of Being, and on the other hand that it is human beings that dwell in the house (Heidegger,

Philosophical and pragmatic perspectives 33

1993, p. 217). Thus, there is an overlapping relationship between Being–language–human beings. A deep comprehension of this overlapping relationship is rather helpful for appreciating the proposition "language is the last homestead of human beings".

A human being is a being, but one that speaks about all other beings. Such a being exists as a real individual out there, but innately this individual thinks about Being and this thinking is simply impossible without language. Therefore, it is the question of Being that draws human beings intrinsically into language from being out there. Heidegger (2000, p. 54) thus says, "... because the fate of language is grounded in the particular relation of a people to Being, the question of Being will be most intimately intertwined with the question about language for us".

To see if the question of Being is intimately intertwined with the question of language, one needs to see also whether such intertwining involves the basic state of human existence. It so happens that all the three livings of mankind (the kernel idea of this book, presented in Chapter 3) do involve language. For this reason, the three livings are the basic states of human existence. Thus, a study on the three livings constitutes a most profound perspective of philosophy, because *the three livings fully demonstrate how the question of Being is intimately intertwined with the question about language*. Consequently, it is just natural enough to regard language as the last homestead of human beings.

About the question of Being intimately intertwined with the question about language, Heidegger said further in his dialog with a Japanese, Tomio Tezuka, "Being itself – that is to say: the presence of present beings, the two-fold of the two in virtue of their simple oneness. This is what makes its claim on man, calling him to its essential being" (1982, p. 30). After Tomio Tezuka replied, "Man, then, realizes his nature as man by corresponding to the call of the two-fold, and bears witness to it in its message", Heidegger said further, "Accordingly, what prevails in and bears up the relation of human nature to the two-fold is language. Language defines the hermeneutic relation" (*ibid.*).

To understand the above passage more clearly, we now provide the following diagram of the relation between 1) human nature, 2) the presence and present being, and 3) language as "what prevails in and bears up the relation".

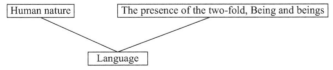

Heidegger's phrasing "the presence of the two-fold, Being and beings" (Heidegger, 1982, p. 26) is consistent with his speaking of the two-fold of "presence and present being" (*ibid.*, p. 30).

From the above diagram, we see that language is the supporting base and is clearly what prevails in and bears up the triangular relation. It is also very

34 *Philosophical and pragmatic perspectives*

clear that the question of human existence is intimately intertwined with the question of language.

Besides what is said above, one should be reminded that in the overlapping relationship between existence, language and human beings, language itself is the Being that determines beings as beings and makes them present.

Let us sort out the overlapping relationship between existence, language and human beings.

1) Human beings are the beings that speak about all the other beings.
2) Human beings exist as individuals out there.
3) Human beings think over existence and such thinking cannot be divorced from language.
4) "Language is the house of Being".
5) Language itself is the Being that determines beings as beings and makes them present.
6) The question of existence is intimately intertwined with the question about language.

Now, we can outline concisely the standpoint of this book: The study on the basic state of human existence (especially the three livings) can be philosophical (it can also be biological, sociological, historical, and so on), because, first, the question of existence is intimately intertwined with the question about language (the first viewpoint of philosophy), and, second, human beings make themselves present by speaking (the second viewpoint of philosophy, but this conclusion cannot be formally drawn until the end of Chapter 3. Please refer to 3.4.1). *This is the first aspect of the central theme of this book, as indicated in its subtitle.*

2.1.3 *How is the spirit of Chinese philosophy involved?*

As said at the beginning of this chapter, we examine the basic state of human existence from two perspectives, one being that of Western philosophy, especially the Western philosophy of language, and the other being that of Chinese philosophy. Thus far, a lot of space has been attributed to the elaboration of the former perspective. The discussion of the latter one, however, will take much less space, without citing any classic sayings in Chinese philosophy. Why is that so?

Here are three reasons.

First, the word "philosophy" describes what is grounded in Western institutions. The principal part of philosophy consists of questions about the world and about Being. In the Chinese language, however, there is no such a thing as "Being" (*das Sein*).

Second, closely related to the first reason is that pragmatics has a "blood tie" with Western philosophy, especially the Western philosophy of language.

Philosophical and pragmatic perspectives   35

Since we conduct both pragmatics study and philosophical study in this book, we have to keep a keen eye on the "birth mother" of pragmatics – Western philosophy.

Third, the basic state of existence of mankind, at least that of the Chinese people, might as well be inspected in the spirit of Chinese philosophy. Then, why is no such effort made in this book? That is a good question. What follows is an attempted answer. To begin with, it is beyond my capability, though I wish I were capable, to inspect human verbal behavior in the two weighty perspectives of both Chinese and Western philosophies. I choose to take only the Western philosophical perspective to see if it works to interpret the life of the people who speak the Chinese language, particularly with the viewpoints that the question of Being is intimately intertwined with the question about language and that human beings make themselves present by speaking. This work has not yet been done. In contrast, there is already an immense quantity of writings on the verbal behavior of the Chinese from the perspective of Chinese philosophy. I cannot make much new contribution to this mansion of work by adding merely one more brick or tile. Second, and more importantly, the spirit of Chinese philosophy is embedded in the verbal behavior of the Chinese in the mode of perfect integration, which makes it unnecessary to check up just a few items. That no separate space is given to Chinese philosophy does not indicate any underestimation of it on my part. On the contrary, it shows the full importance that I attach to it on the basis of my evaluation of its special value in this respect: The spirit of Chinese philosophy that we speak about, as the deposited essence of the soul and the thought of Chinese culture, is already incorporated in the verbal behavior of Chinese people, which is a seamless fusion of flesh and blood. Writing a book of this nature means merely producing one more book on Chinese culture itself.

What, then, is the spirit of Chinese philosophy? I endorse generally the following view held by Youlan Feng (1998, p. 2).

> Chinese philosophy focuses on society rather than the universe, on the ethics of secular pursuit rather than Heaven and Hell, and on the present life of man rather than the world to come for man. Chinese philosophy does seek after the highest state, but seems reluctant to set aside the ethics of daily pursuit. Such a state is at once in this world and away from this world. A solution provided to this problem is a contribution made by Chinese philosophy.

For this reason, it is appropriate for our purpose that we regard the entirety of Chapter 3 as an annotation of this spirit.

That is also, approximately, the spirit of Chinese culture, with an emphasis on society, on the ethics of secular pursuit and on the present life. What we speak of as the perspective of Chinese philosophy is thus the perspective of the spirit of Chinese culture.

2.2 A pragmatics perspective

2.2.1 *Language use and other forms of human social behavior*

The proposition that "language is the last homestead of human beings" and its concern with the gate-keeper of the house or the ordinary user of language relate the philosophical proposition itself to pragmatics. Individuals from all walks of life live by utilizing language and thereby make speaking a special type of human behavior. Indeed, *language comes into being as a result of mankind's existence and human beings, thanks to the language they use, can become what they are and achieve whatever they want.* They achieve their existence in the world created by language and develop themselves in the activities realized in language. *Language is, on the one hand, the form of existence that makes other forms of existence possible and, on the other hand, the form of behavior that makes other forms of human behavior possible.* In other words, language is the most basic form of human behavior and the most essential form of human life. It is on this basis that one can claim language to be the last homestead of human beings.

Pragmatics is basically specified by the Belgian pragmatician Jef Verschueren as "a cognitive, social, and cultural perspective on language phenomena in relation to their usage in forms of behavior" (1999, p. 7). Clearly, pragmatics examines language phenomena and the process of language use along such dimensions as the cognitive factors involved in the process of language use and the social and cultural contexts wherein the verbal behavior occurs. More importantly, pragmatics studies the verbal behavior of human beings in relation to their other forms of behavior. From the perspective of pragmatics, this means that there exists a multi-dimensional, dynamic, and interactive relation between verbal behavior and other forms of human behavior. On the one hand, one should study the behavior of language in relation to other forms of behavior because verbal behavior as a form of human behavior is embedded in these forms of human behavior. On the other hand, one can start by examining the behavior of language and thereby achieve an understanding of these forms of human behavior. It is in this sense that a study of how language is the last homestead of human beings is by nature a pragmatic probe into the basic state of human existence. *This is the second aspect of the central theme of this book, as indicated in its subtitle.*

Compared with a study of other forms of behavior, the study of verbal behavior enjoys a multitude of advantages. *One is that the occurrence, enfolding, and end of verbal behavior is often accompanied by a formulaic phrasing* (see Section 3.3). Thus, by using expressions or forms of language as the point of departure one can capture the verbal behavior and thereby manage to achieve an understanding of other forms of human behavior. A natural consequence of this is that pragmatics gets involved in the study of the basic form of human behavior and the basic state of human existence.

Philosophical and pragmatic perspectives   37

Indeed, even before the very emergence of pragmatics, anthropologists started to accord their attention to this concomitant but subordinate relationship between language and other forms of human behavior. In the 1920s and 1930s, the anthropologist Bronislaw Malinowski, for example, did his anthropological field work on the Trobriand Islands in Papua New Guinea and found that the traditional grammatical analysis could not help to elucidate the meanings of words or sentences of the local language because the meanings of these expressions were found to depend to a great extent on the practical experience of the speakers and the immediate contexts in which these expressions were uttered. Based on observations of this kind, Malinowski concluded that "language in its primitive forms ought to be regarded and studied against the background of human activities and as a mode of human behavior in practical matters" (1923, p. 312), because "language is used by people engaged in practical work, in which utterances are embedded in action" (*ibid.*). On this basis, he pointed out further "that language in its primitive function and original form has an essentially pragmatic character; that it is a mode of behavior, an indispensable element of concerted human action" (*ibid.*, p. 316). Later Malinowski elaborated that "the main function of language is not to express thought, not to duplicate mental processes, but rather to play an active pragmatic part in human behavior" (1935/1978, p. 7). This is the function language performs when it is involved in the regulation of human collective behavior. Also it should be noted that Malinowski here does not attempt to deny that language can be used to perform other functions (e.g., the expression of thought) but merely asserts how language in its original form and primitive function is related to human behavior and experience. For the American linguistic anthropologist Alessandro Duranti (1997), Malinowski's anthropological analysis of language serves to reveal the various pragmatic dimensions involved in language use and thereby anticipate the interdisciplinarity of pragmatics. In fact, the concept "concerted human action" will be mentioned repeatedly in 3.3.2, which attempts to answer why there is a constant coordination between formulaic actions and formulaic utterances.

Malinowski's observations are reflected to various extents in later works of pragmatics. In his *Foundations of the Theory of Signs* (1938), a foundational work in pragmatics, Charles Morris clearly referred to it as the branch of semiotics that studies the relation of signs to their interpreters. Later Morris specified pragmatics as the study of "the origin, uses and effects of the sign within the total behavior of the interpreters of signs" (1946, p. 219). For Morris, the behavior of the interpreters of signs is reciprocal and thus social. He regarded the process during which signs are produced and received in human social behavior as communication and classified it as conflictive, competitive, and symbiotic according to the ways in which users or interpreters of signs attain their common goals. In this case, communication occurs in social behavior and thus becomes related to it in different ways. On the whole, these relations can be divided into two types. On the one hand, communication can help

38 *Philosophical and pragmatic perspectives*

an individual to integrate himself with society and become socialized, and thereby make social behavior cooperative. On the other hand, communication does not have to achieve consistency in the way individuals evaluate and behave, or attain cooperation in their social behavior but to incur and increase conflicts, competition, and control in their social behavior. A consequence of sharing a language with others is that one is endowed with a most mysterious and powerful tool to control them for one's own purposes. Morris believes, however, that communication does not mean or guarantee cooperation but it is a basic way of achieving, maintaining, and extending the integration of an individual with a society. This two-sided nature of communication reveals the diversity and complexity of human social behavior. The cooperativeness and conflictiveness of communication will be described objectively in 3.3.4.3.

Wittgenstein's concern with the relation between language and social behavior started in the 1920s. His thoughts about the relation between language and social behavior were focused on two concepts: "Language game" and "form of life" (Wittgenstein, 1958). For Wittgenstein, "language game" refers to "ways of using signs simpler than those in which we use the signs of our highly complicated everyday language" (*ibid.*, p. 17), "the forms of language with which a child begins to make use of words", or "complete systems of human communication" (*ibid.*, p. 81), and the study of language games is the study of "primitive forms of language or primitive languages" (*ibid.*, p. 17). Later he defined it as "the whole, consisting of language and the actions into which it is woven" (1953, §7). Clearly, what has been called "language game" by Wittgenstein could be understood as a social communicative activity intended to achieve a certain communicative intention, and for Wittgenstein this activity can be exemplified as "giving orders, and obeying them", "describing the appearance of an object, or giving its measurements", "reporting an event", and "asking, thanking, cursing, greeting, praying" (*ibid.*). Structurally, the activity of a game, simple or complicated, consists of two components: Language (or the speaking of language) and the social behavior accompanying (the speaking of) language. Later, the above-mentioned language games became "speech events" for pragmatics. Indeed, formulaic verbal behaviors to be discussed in Section 3.3 of this book have been *solidified* out of such speech events.

The concept of "language game" has opened a new path to the nature of language. First, speaking as an element of language game is regarded as an activity, or, rather, as an activity occurring between subjects. In this case, the communicative and social nature of language features in the concept of language game. Second, the theory of "language game" has motivated a description of the intersubjective function of language. In the dialogue between the builder and his assistant, "Block!", "Pillar!", "Slab!", and "Beam!" are not words in the real sense but units of language serving to perform some communicative functions (*ibid.*, §2). Or in terms of speech act theory, these words are used as utterances to perform speech acts (e.g., ordering, or requesting an assistant to supply building materials), a process completed during the

Philosophical and pragmatic perspectives   39

process of a language game. Or rather, such communicative functions of words have emanated from its matrix behavior or the human social behavior of the language game; words (or other elements) of language are embedded in such behavior and thereby obtain their communicative values. Also related is that the analysis of the meaning of language cannot limit itself merely to an analysis of its structure but has to take into consideration the process during which language is woven and embedded into the behavior accompanying and concomitant with it. More importantly, with language game as the point of departure, the study of language will necessarily direct its attention to language users who live and exist intersubjectively as realistic social beings. These beings, from the perspective of this book, are gate-keepers of the last homestead of human beings.

Indeed, the concept "form of life" occurred in *Philosophical Investigations* just a few times. It is, however, a key concept in the system of Wittgenstein's philosophy of language. "Form of life" is used usually when Wittgenstein thinks about and discusses problems of language, as in "to imagine a language means to imagine a form of life" (1953, §19) or "the *speaking* of language is part of an activity, or of a form of life" (*ibid.*, §23; emphasis original), although he gives no definition of it. Van Peurson maintains that a form of life is "the way people of a given age and culture behave" (1970, p.69). Baghramian defines it as "the social context in which a language game can be played (and interpreted)" (1999, p. 87) and illustrates this by using the language game of prayer, which "can be understood only within the context of a religious form of life" (*ibid.*). Clearly, no matter how it is defined, as a form of behavior or a social context, "form of life" is a historical, cultural, and social concept that is shared by the participants of language games and makes it possible for the games to be conducted and interpreted as well.

According to the way it occurs in *Philosophical Investigations*, Sheng (2000), relatively completely, summarizes the concept of "form of life" in four points, as follows. First, he believes that as far as its content is concerned, "form of life" finds its expression in the way people speak in their everyday life. Second, to stress the importance of "form of life" for language understanding itself means that an emphasis has to be placed on intersubjectivity.[10] Speaking is by nature an interactive activity, which occurs and unfolds between subjects. On this basis, it is safe to say that *"form of life" is the basic level for pragmatics.* Moreover, form of life is the basis on which language game occurs and is interpreted. Finally, form of life as the context in which ordinary activities of speaking and communicating occur is the basic situational condition on which participants of given language games achieve an agreement, rather than the lowest situational condition shared by different language games. Indeed, what Section 3.3 is to talk about is actually a result of the stabilization of the present "form of life".

In this case, *the three concepts of "language", "language game", and "form of life" constitute relations of mutual embedding and interpretation.* Of the three, what comes first is an element of what comes later, while what comes later is the

40   *Philosophical and pragmatic perspectives*

basis on which what comes first comes about and thus gets interpreted. Stated another way, one who studies language has to examine its bases: Language game and form of life; while one who attempts to understand a form of life or a language game has to understand the language involved. *The interdependence among the three brings about a wide perspective for pragmatics and a special approach to the way pragmatics becomes involved in the study of the basic human behavior and the basic states of human existence.*

Unlike Wittgenstein, Austin (1962) was engaged in his analysis of the complicated ordinary language with the care and rigor of an analytic philosopher. Like Malinowski (1923) and Wittgenstein (1953), Austin regards language as a form of human behavior, or, in his words, "saying is doing". Starting with an analysis of language, however, he specified the action of speaking or "doing" as the smallest unit, "act", and defined its linguistic realization as utterance. In this view, by speaking, the speaker utters an utterance and thereby performs three speech acts: Locutionary, illocutionary, and perlocutionary. Of the three acts, the locutionary act is a pure act of speaking whose function is merely to utter a sentence that is phonetically, semantically, and grammatically normative. As an act of speaking functioning to realize the speaker's intention, the illocutionary act achieves this by changing the situation involved and thereby bringing about changes in relations between the interlocutors. The perlocutionary act is often known as an intended response or effect achieved in the audience's cognition and behavior when the speaker is attempting to perform an illocutionary act. The core of the three is the illocutionary act, which serves to realize the performative intention of the action of speaking and the communicative relationships established thereby. Austin referred to this intention or force, which inheres and operates in the action of speaking, as an illocutionary force and thereby distinguished it from the meaning captured and dealt with in semantics.

Of the theories that established themselves by criticizing and developing the speech act theory of Austin (1962) and Searle (1965), Wunderlich's (1972) speech act theory undoubtedly was unique and effective. Unlike Austin and Searle, Wunderlich started by examining speech acts along the interactive or intersubjective dimension. In his approach, speech act is defined as an interactive move in a given context mutually constructed by the interlocutors (Wunderlich, 1972, p. 117). Therefore, one who attempts to understand such a move has to refer to its matrix context in which the interlocutors interact (Wunderlich, 1976). And such a context in which a speech act occurs and operates is defined as a social process always constructed and interpreted by the participants involved. This social process is structurally comprised of linguistic communication and social interaction. Linguistic communication is known as an activity where language is used as a means of achieving understanding, and social interaction is an activity that is extralinguistic and other-oriented in nature. Since speech acts are performed in a social process during which the interlocutors interact and the occurrence or ongoing of this process is not determined or constrained merely by the intention of

Philosophical and pragmatic perspectives 41

the speaker, the conditions on which a speech act is performed effectively cannot be the appropriacy or felicity as claimed by Austin and Searle. For this purpose, Wunderlich introduced the concept of *Erfolgreich-Sein* ("to be successful") (*ibid.*). In his view, a speech act is appropriately performed when its expected effect is achieved (mainly by the speaker); it is really "successfully" performed only when the interactive conditions activated by its performance are fully met in the further progression of the whole interaction (as cited in Yuan, 1989, p. 185). Moreover, a speech act is only "successful" when after its performance its effect can be found in the way the hearer behaves in the subsequent part of the interaction (*ibid.*).

Clearly, in his speech act theory, Wunderlich describes and interprets language as a form of behavior as well. The difference is that he describes speech act as a move in a social process whose function is to unite the linguistic communication and the extralinguistic interaction of the process. In this case, the performance of a speech act activates a series of interactive conditions and the speech act is effective only when these conditions are met or its social goal in the whole social process is finally achieved. Thus, by investigating speech acts at the intersubjective or discourse level, Wunderlich manages to resolve the persistent problems in Austin and Searle's "intention analysis" and advances the development of speech act theory. Meanwhile, examining human beings who perform speech acts (thus verbal behaviors in our sense) within the scope of social processes can help to reveal the nature of mankind as social beings. Indeed, human beings, as ordinary people, exist as they do, dwelling in the last homestead of language and living in verbal behaviors, and often formulaic verbal behaviors.

Also worth mentioning is Levinson's (1979) study of the relation between language and human behavior, which was derived from his concern with Wittgenstein's theory of "language game" and the speech act theory of Austin and Searle. For Levinson, all the theoretical models of speech acts are attempts to apply the concept of speech act to solve the problem of Wittgenstein, i.e., how language is embedded within human social activities and how the activities restrict and constrain the way language (discourse) is understood. According to Levinson (1979), Austin and Searle try to reduce the use of language to speech acts, Lakoff (1975), Lewis (1972), and Sadock (1974) attempt to reduce speech acts to the propositional core of language, and Stenius (1972) distinguishes speech acts from propositional content, and applies Wittgenstein's "language games" mode of analysis to speech acts. Yet none of these models can (nor is it possible for them to) adequately capture the concern Wittgenstein implied by the notion of "language game" about the relationship between language and human behavior. There exists between speech acts and speech activities (close to what we call verbal behaviors) a fundamental interconnection that only a thorough-going pragmatic theory is adequate to describe. From his point of view, such a theory of pragmatics can be constructed only on the basis of an activity type, in contrast to speech act theory, which is based upon an utterance or speech acts. Activity type refers to

42 *Philosophical and pragmatic perspectives*

"any culturally recognized activity, whether or not that activity is coextensive with a period of speech or indeed whether any talk takes place in it at all" – paradigm examples being teaching, a job interview, a jural interrogation, a football game, a task in a workshop, a dinner party, and so on (Levinson, 1979, p. 368). From a prototypical point of view, the members of an activity type for him do not have the same membership but differ to various extents from the prototypical members.

To capture the variation among the members of an activity type, Levinson (1979) introduces three parameters: Scriptedness, verbalness, and formality. An extreme example of scriptedness is an activity where all the speech has been scripted and the speaker speaks merely in accordance with the script; another extreme example of scriptedness is an encounter talk in which both the speakers work impromptu. Verbalness varies from such activities as telephone dialogues, lectures, and TV interviews, which are almost linguistically constituted to those like football games, where language is seldom used or even not used at all. Formality is associated with the genre or style of language use. The formality of a style varies in the choice of words and sentences as well as in the choice of forms of address.

Clearly, Levinson's activity type refers to a type of communicative activities which are embedded into a sociocultural situation and oriented to goals. In such an activity, the use of language and the extralinguistic part are often interwoven and entangled in different ways. It is here that Levinson's activity type and Wunderlich's social process are quite similar. Likewise, our arguments that mankind lives in language (see Section 3.1) and that mankind has to live in language (see Section 3.2) mean that mankind lives in language games and "forms of life" (situations of life). In particular, *formulaic verbal behaviors* (the central topic of Section 3.3) *are actually highly formulaic activity types.*

Language coexists and is thus entangled with other forms of human social behavior; as social animals, human beings live in their matrix of social behavior, which includes language and is constructed by means of language. A consequence of the complicated relationship between language and other forms of human social behavior is that sciences of human behavior will have their attention accorded to the use of language and meanwhile studies of language use will become interested in other forms of human social behavior. On this basis, this section has reviewed studies of language and other forms of human behavior in fields such as pragmatics, anthropology, and philosophy with a view to getting prepared for the development of a tentative theoretical framework for the involvement of pragmatics in the study of human basic behavior and way of existence.

2.2.2 *A pragmatic framework for the analysis of activity types*

Before coming to the major concern of this section, let's briefly go over the propositions that "language is the house of Being" and that language is the last homestead of human beings.

Philosophical and pragmatic perspectives 43

As the philosophical and pragmatic proposition pervading this whole book, that language is the last homestead of human beings concerns how the basic behavior and state of existence of human beings rely on language. By using language, people establish social relations of different types with others, and, on this basis, establish, develop, and derive all other types of human behavior, thereby forming social communities of different kinds. In this sense, the world in which man exists is constituted by the social activities they perform, and the limitations of these social activities are the limitations of the world of their existence. The activities which constitute the world are by and large established and thus parasitic upon the activity of speaking, and the limitations of language are the limitations of the world of activities. Stated another way, people who are social members will have to live unavoidably in a world of activities that are constructed by means of language and in which they achieve themselves. For every social being, this world is the most fundamental and inherent and is thus his or her last house. Living at the gate of the house are not only thinkers or poets, but also ordinary users of language. The study of ordinary people's activity of speaking has been the task of pragmatics. Therefore, it is a matter of course for pragmatics to become involved in the description of language users' behavior and state of existence.

Based on the review of 2.2.1 and that of the basic behavior and state of existence of the human beings, we can come to assume the way pragmatics is involved in the study of human basic behavior as follows. First, we accept Levinson's (1979) concept of activity type and based on its goals divide human basic behavior into different activity types. Like Levinson, we regard activity types as culturally embedded, socially constituted and bounded communicative events that, constrained by their own goals, have different characteristics of their own. Second, to describe language and the social activities entangled with it, we assume that each activity type has its own activity structure that is an intermediate level between the linguistic and the extralinguistic forms of social behavior. At the level of activity structure, *the linguistic and the extralinguistic forms of social behavior are isomorphic* in that many factors of the extralinguistic social behavior, including the structural episodes and formulas of the activity, can enter linguistic behavior through the operation of this level so that *the linguistic and the extralinguistic forms of social behavior become similar to each other in different ways and to different extents.* Meanwhile we believe as well that each type of activity has a series of constraints of its own. Apart from the structural constraints concerning the way the activity is organized, the constraints of an activity include the interpersonal-cultural (social) constraints, the cognitive-psychological constraints, and the situational-physical constraints. *The performance of each activity derives from the way its participants interact with one another according to the activity-specific structural formula within the constraints of the activity* (see 3.3).

For the time being we label our descriptive framework as *a pragmatic framework for the analysis of activity types.* Needless to say, it is a framework of pragmatic analysis; it is one for analyzing activity types because it serves

44 *Philosophical and pragmatic perspectives*

to deal with the various kinds of activity-oriented goals and types; variations and parameters; structures and formulae; and constraints and conditions. This descriptive framework comprises the following major parts.

ACTIVITY GOALS AND ACTIVITY TYPES

At this pragmatic organizational level, an activity can be regarded as a social process or communicative event intended to accomplish a social goal. In accordance with the goals they are intended to attain, activities are classified into different types such as clinical interviews in traditional Chinese medicine (shortened as TCM), countryside mediations, dinner talks, judicial trials, service encounters, teasing the newlyweds on their wedding night, bargaining, fortune-telling, and quarrel mediations. Some types of activities, like TCM clinical interviews, family or house argument mediations, and teasing the newlyweds on their wedding night, are culture-specific, while other types of activities, like service encounters, can be found in commercial societies but work in different ways across cultures. For example, people from different cultures invite others to dinner and are engaged in dinner talks, but in China, dinner hosts are found to ask their guests to serve themselves or even offer to serve the guests themselves, and at times to show their sincerity dinner hosts are inclined to downplay the quality and quantity of the food by expressing their regret over its poor quality and low quantity. Such Chinese dinner talks cannot be found in the West. A court trial of the same transnational business dispute can go easily and be lively if it occurs in an Australian court, but it may go tensely and solemnly if it takes place in a Chinese court (of course, the results are almost the same). Of clinical interviews, TCM clinical interviews are easier and more flexible and thus less institutional, while Western clinical interviews are, on the other hand, less flexible and thus more institutional (see Mey, 2001, for more discussion on the institutional characteristics of Western clinical interviews). It is worth noting that differences between TCM and Western clinical interviews have to do with Chinese and Western cultural differences as well as characteristics of the two types of activities.

TYPE VARIATION AND VARIATION PARAMETERS

Type variation refers to the extents to which participants of an activity type differ from one another along some dimensions or in some parameters. According to the extents to which members of activity types vary in the preparedness, use, and stylistic formality, Levinson (1979), for instance, distinguishes three parameters: Scriptedness, verbalness, and formality. Building on Levinson's system, Clark (1996) distinguishes two more parameters: Cooperativeness and governance. For Clark, neither of the two parameters is homogeneous but vague. Cooperativeness, for instance, ranges from cooperation to competition and governance, which concerns the roles and positions of the activity participants, ranges from equality of roles

Philosophical and pragmatic perspectives   45

assumed by all the participants (e.g., equal roles played by all teachers and students on the same bus before they arrive at a practice workshop) to governance, where a participant takes a governing role and controls the progression of an activity (e.g., the teachers become instructors while the students follow their instructions once they arrive at the workshop). Of course, roles are assigned according to some social conventions. In this book, we take it for granted that variation across members of activity types is open-ended rather than limited to the above-mentioned dimensions or parameters. More parameters will indeed be identified as more analysis is conducted.

ACTIVITY STRUCTURE AND STRUCTURAL FORMULA

As far as the structural elements of an activity are concerned, Levinson (1979) distinguishes the concepts of activity episode and activity sequence. Yet in fact the structure of an activity can be analyzed further to thus include such smaller units as turns, which can be further specified as utterances, which can be analyzed further into different types of speech acts that these utterances are employed to perform. Related to this is that an activity always progresses in accordance with some formula, and we, therefore, claim that mankind lives in formulaic verbal behavior (see 3.3). Ontologically speaking, the formulaicity of an activity is determined by the aim it serves to achieve (see 3.3.2.4.1 and 3.3.2.4.2). Studies of the history of languages indicate that in their early history human ancestors chose to behave collectively so as to adapt themselves to the pressures of survival and the environment they had to confront (Arndt & Richard, 1987). To accomplish these collective activities, participants of these activities had to cooperate in various ways, and a consequence of this cooperation is the *formulaicity* occurring at different structural levels of an activity and the *conventionality* found to exist at different structural levels of a language system (see 3.3.2.1). Indeed, *the formulaicity of an activity and the conventionality of a linguistic sign have proved to have greatly improved the efficiency of human collective activities and thereby strengthened the ability of the human species as a whole to survive* (see 3.3.2). And this occurs as well in the way an individual activity operates because in the development of such an activity both participants involved are always inclined to accomplish the goal of the activity in the most economical and efficient way (see 3.3.2.4.2), and they always choose to perform the activity and achieve its goal by following the *optimal formula* they know. In a normal and typical TCM clinical interview, for instance, the doctor always starts his diagnosis by asking the patient questions, and then, after the steps of observation, listening/smelling, and pulse-taking, he finally comes to the end of the interview by writing the prescription, because this formula can best help to achieve the aim of the activity.

Also worth clarifying is that the formulaicity of an activity is realized to different extents at each level of the activity. At the episodic level, for instance, the formula of an activity is realized as the way the episodes of the activity occur according to a linear and temporal order (see 1.2 and 3.3.1.1). Again,

46   *Philosophical and pragmatic perspectives*

take a TCM clinical interview, for example. Normally, a typical TCM clinical interview always starts with the episode of asking the patient questions, which is followed first by the doctor's identification of and inference about the symptoms, then the prescription is made according to the symptoms, and finally directions are given by the doctor to the patient as to how to simmer and take the decoction. At the level of adjacency pairs, the way turns are organized and taken is formulaic to some extent. First, the turns are organized according to some time order. In one turn, for instance, only one speaker can hold the floor. Second, in some types of activity, topics in different episodes change and rotate in light of some formula. In a TCM clinical interview, for instance, the first turn in the initial adjacency pair of the question episode is generally initiated by the doctor while the patient is generally required to answer. Even when some patients happen to start the interviews by asking questions, the doctors will attempt to regain the floor to maintain the formula of the episode. In the treatment-negotiating (i.e., the last) episode, however, patients can have more floor. They can, for example, ask the doctors questions about how to simmer and take the decoction prescribed. At this time, the turn-taking formula will become flexible to various extents.

Formulaicity varies not only within an activity type or across the different episodes of an activity type but also across different activity types. Small talk and formal business talk, for instance, differ greatly in formulaicity. Although both consist of the general beginning-body-end formula (see 1.2 and 3.3.1.1), business talk has a much more complicated and rigorous formula than small talk does. Clearly, formulaicity is a prototypical concept. For an elaboration of the formulaicity of activities, see 3.3.

ACTIVITY CONSTRAINTS AND CONSTRAINT CONDITIONS

That an activity has to progress within the constraints of a multitude of factors affects its formulaicity. In fact, the rules for Wittgenstein's language games, the felicitous conditions for the speech acts of Austin and Searle, the interactive conditions governing the fruitfulness of Wunderlich's speech acts, and the structural constraints of Levinson's activity types are all attempts to explore this topic on different levels and dimensions. By their very nature, the rules for Wittgenstein's language games concern the way such games operate effectively at the intersubjective level, and the social and psychological dimensions along which these games unfold and develop. The felicitous conditions for the speech acts of Austin and Searle concern the validity with which speech acts are performed at the subject or utterance level, and these conditions relate as well to the formulaicity in which the speech acts are performed and the social and psychological constraints involved therein. Like Wittgenstein, Wunderlich and Levinson both examine at the intersubjective level the constraints within which speech acts or activities are performed. The only difference is that while Wunderlich is concerned with how the interactive factors work in a social process to condition the effect which a speech act is

Philosophical and pragmatic perspectives 47

performed to achieve, Levinson studies the constraints that are requirements made by an intention-motivated activity for the way its elements are organized. For more details about this, see 3.3.4.

Based on the above-mentioned studies of activity goals and activity types, type variations and variation parameters, activity structures and structural formulae, and activity constraints and constraint conditions, we believe that as speech events occur at the intersubjective level, activities must progress within the constraints operating at this level. Apart from Levinson's (1979) structural constraints, the progression of an activity is meanwhile constrained by factors that are by nature sociocultural (interpersonal), cognitive-psychological, and situational-physical. Activities of various types are always found to occur or anchor themselves in certain language communities or communicative contexts. A result of this is that the special sociocultural factors of the communities or contexts will surely enter the activities and thus influence to different extents the way these activities are performed and interpreted. In the history of pragmatics, social factors constraining the use of language have been regarded as persistent topics of which the most influential one is the study of politeness phenomena that emerged at the end of the 1970s (Brown & Levinson, 1978/1987; Leech, 1983). Besides, I have analyzed (G. Qian (1997/2002) many phenomena of language use occurring against the backdrop of Chinese culture and concluded that pragmatics is speechology in humanistic networks. And from an ethical perspective, R. Chen (2001) analyzes the sociocultural constraints within which Chinese is used. Thus, it is safe to say that at least against the background of Chinese culture, the use of language is always related to the way one conducts oneself and the social responsibilities one has to shoulder: *Saying is doing and how one does things is how one conducts oneself.* Such old sayings are good examples of this kind, such as "An utterance can make a state prosperous", "An utterance can destroy a state" (*Zilu, The Analects*), and "When a gentleman writes or speaks, he does not mean to practice using his tongue or lips, but to work for the state, its community, its people and its administration" (Part II, *Feiming, Mozi*). All of this constitutes the starting point for us to understand the social constraints for activity types occurring in Chinese cultural contexts (see 3.3.4).

Cognitive-psychological constraints influence the performance of an activity in two ways. First, at the cognitive level, the progression and unfolding of an activity are always constrained by the cognitive ability of its participants. Specifically, the way the participants perceive, represent, or conceptualize an activity from a macro or micro perspective, the way they plan the process of an activity, and the way their working memory influences the progression of an activity all constitute factors determining the occurrence and interpretation of the activity. Second, at the psychological level, the extent to which an emotive investment is made by the two participants of an activity definitely determines how the activity starts, progresses, and comes to its end, as can be found especially in the institutionalized types of activities. Compared with the other types of activities, institutionalized activities involve participants who

48 *Philosophical and pragmatic perspectives*

have a clear asymmetrical power, and therefore the more institutionalized the activities are, the more asymmetrical the power becomes. A result of this is that this power asymmetry will surely exert negative influence on the progression of the activities. As has been found in sociolinguistic studies, the more powerful party in an asymmetrical discourse is inclined to adopt active strategies (e.g., tag questions) to regulate the emotion of the less powerful party so that the activity itself can develop smoothly (Cameron, McAlinden, & O'Leary, 1988).

Situational and physical factors refer to the situational and physical context in which an activity is anchored. No activity can occur in a vacuum; on the contrary, every activity takes place and unfolds along temporal and spatial dimensions. Therefore, in different ways and to different extents the time and space in which the activity is embedded will surely influence the way it progresses. A greeting activity, for instance, will work differently depending on whether it occurs in a hurry or at ease. In the same vein, a greeting activity will operate differently depending on whether it occurs between two participants who are close at hand, or between two participants who are far away from each other. An activity of greeting will vary more significantly across different times of the day, e.g., in the morning or in the afternoon, at a meal time, at an unexpected meeting in a restroom, or at a meeting in other public places.

Indeed, the pattern of a discourse progression as the linguistic realization of an activity results from an interaction between the structural formula and the various constraints of the activity. *It is human beings who conduct interactions and undertake activities.* Furthermore, *the process during which human beings create an activity is a process during which the human participants themselves are created by the activity.* In this sense, any human being who is a social being has to live in activities of different types in which he or she becomes himself or herself, and behaves in his or her own way. Stated another way, people live in activities and they have to live in activities. A natural consequence of this is the following conclusion: Mankind lives in language, mankind has to live in language, and mankind lives in formulaic verbal behaviors. That is because language or verbal behavior is the social habitat in which one dwells for living and the last homestead that he owns as a social being.

2.2.3 A case of civil mediation from a countryside judicial center

In this section we are going to employ the model of pragmatics presented and described above to analyze a countryside judicial mediating activity. Strictly, such an activity cannot be a judicial mediating activity in the real sense but it belongs to a medial type of activity between a formal judicial mediating activity and an informal civil one. In such an activity, the mediator does not always attempt to resolve the conflicts involved on the basis of related rules of the law but often manages to regulate and balance the conflicts according to the role the parties involved have played and the responsibility they thus have to shoulder therein so that an acceptable result is finally achieved. Of

Philosophical and pragmatic perspectives 49

course, such mediation is not purely civil in nature since it still follows a set of procedures and regulations similar to that of a judicial court activity. Yet such a mediating activity is not institutionalized enough, and therefore in such an activity both the mediator and the conflictive parties involved have a much larger space and more freedom for interaction. However, the mediator plays a more important role in the final result of the mediation.

Mediation is a popular type of language activity in the rural areas of China. All over the country, people living in the countryside regard villages and towns as their residential communities and the area surrounding the villages and towns as their crop fields. A result of this is that, although villages and towns are no longer units of production in the residents' "commune" system since the implementation of the household-responsibility system in China in the late 1970s, they are still the sites of people's residence, production, and other types of behavior. This limited space of behavior and production has, on the one hand, made it possible for people to establish social relationships of different kinds and, on the other, resulted in disputes and conflicts of different kinds. Consequently, conflicts concerning support of parents, division of property, sites where houses may be built, and other ordinary issues have become common between members of a family, families, villagers of a village, or villagers of different villages.

These conflicts and disputes need to be resolved before they become more serious, because for the villagers who meet each other frequently every day, "a good neighbor close at hand is better than a brother far off", as an old Chinese saying goes. As it often happens, a family elder will work as the mediator if a family dispute occurs, a village head will work as the mediator if a dispute occurs between two families, and a leader from a higher rank or leaders from the villages involved will come to mediate if a dispute arises between villagers from two different villages. If the mediation does not work, the court of the town will come and resolve the dispute through arbitration following certain legal procedures and rules. Yet in this case, the town court will work under more and unnecessary pressure, because many disputes are civil and not judicial in nature. And what's more, even if a dispute is resolved through judicial procedures, the parties involved may not be satisfied. In the recent years, therefore, a new section – the social conflict mediation center – has been established in the township judicial office.

The social conflict mediation center has become appreciated soon after its emergence for two reasons. First, from a synchronic perspective, mediation of this kind agrees with the idea that average Chinese citizens, especially those from rural areas, have developed an understanding of the importance of law – an "order of law" that has been established on the basis of 情 ([qíng] "compassion") and 理 ([lǐ] "reason") (an "order of law" established on "compassion" thus often becomes aggravated). When disputes arise, they have to be resolved with justice and reason in a harmonious way. This justice, however, is not justice in the strict legal sense, and this reason is not reason in legal terms but mainly justice in terms of feeling, a type of justice that is more important

50 *Philosophical and pragmatic perspectives*

than justice in the legal sense. According to Y. Chen (2002, p. 69), 情 [qíng] can refer to some type of plot, circumstance, and the mood or emotion of the people involved, as well as the face (情面 [qíngmiàn], 面子 [miànzi]) of those involved in some situations. 理 ([lǐ] "reason") generally refers to principles, methods, or the Confucian天理 ([tiānlǐ] "heavenly justice"). Compassion and reason simultaneously oppose and complement each other, thus constituting 情理 ([qínglǐ] "emotive reason"), the Chinese intellect or conscience. Meanwhile, 理 ([lí] "reason") has a sense coinciding with礼 ([lí] "rite"). Thus compassion, reason, and law constitute the basis of the traditional judicial system in China. It is in this sense that one can claim that civil mediation has reflected the traditional Chinese idea of law and satisfied the needs of the rural citizens all over the country.

Second, from a diachronic perspective, the traditional Chinese society was a ritualistic society established on the feudal hierarchy. In such a society, all social relations and norms of social order were defined in terms of rites, and the legal definitions of the norms of people's behavior were based on norms of rites. The practice of regarding rule by rites as the basis of rule by law has been a popular idea in China for thousands of years. This idea has been not only the basis of the legal systems of different dynasties in China but also the deep-rooted idea of law held by the Chinese people as well. This situation lasted in China without being challenged for thousands of years until the beginning of the twentieth century, when Jiaben Shen was appointed viceminister of justice of the Qing Empire and took the responsibility of initiating a reform in the legal system of the empire. Over the past 100 plus years, indeed, the modernization of law in China has been a history of argumentation and even opposition between the school of law and the school of rites. So far, however, a consensus has been reached as to a combination of modern Western law and local traditional Chinese law, thereby promoting the modernization of the country and society through the modernization of rule by law. Yet the gradual formation and improvement of a new legal system does not mean that the idea of modern law has completely replaced the traditional idea of rule by rites. In fact, this is merely the very beginning of the modernization of Chinese law, just as Y. Chen observes.

> The modernization of Chinese law initiated by Jiaben Shen is by nature a struggle for the dominion power of Chinese society between a new system, a new idea of law and a new order on the one hand and an old order based on the rule by rites of thousands of years on the other. Its essential aim has been to construct in China a new structure of social relationships and the basic principle for a new social order. The final realization of the legal modernization in China will be marked by a complete replacement of the rule by rites with the rule by law, a long historical process which will likely last for at least a thousand years.
>
> (Y. Chen, 2002, p. 69)

Philosophical and pragmatic perspectives 51

If we do not look at the historical significance of legal construction and/or the differences between the traditional view of law and the modern view of law, then we can come to believe that the above-mentioned rural judicial mediation is by nature just a combination of the modern view of law and the traditional idea of law, or rather a realization of the traditional idea of law in the modern life of law. More importantly, from philosophical, pragmatic, and even anthropological perspectives, such an activity type epitomizes a form of behavior or a form of life popular among the rural people all over the country. Therefore, its study will be of essential significance to the research of the present project.

In what follows, we are going to illustrate, by analyzing a rural mediating activity, how pragmatics is involved in the study of the essential behavior of human beings. The case for analysis[11] here in this section was collected from the Social Conflict Mediation Center of Midong Township Judicial Office, Mile City, Yunnan Province. The mediation in this case was about an injury resulting from a traffic accident. Each mediating activity comprises three steps. In the first step, one of the parties involved applies to the center for mediation, and the center, responsible for organizing the mediation, informs and tells the other party to come to the mediation. Step two is the mediation itself. In the third step, the center will prepare a traditional written agreement concerning the result of the mediation, called 甘结 ([gānjié]), in which both parties sign and promise to fulfill their responsibilities or obligations and the punishments for not fulfilling the responsibilities or obligations are also stated. The center will work to help ensure that the parties involved fulfill their responsibilities or obligations as stated therein. The following is a transcription of a recorded mediating activity, where Q indicates a question by the mediator and A means an answer from the questioned party involved. In this transcription all the names of the parties involved are pseudonyms. Besides, expressions and syntactic structures from the local Chinese dialect were transcribed as they were although they may sound awkward in Mandarin Chinese.

(The mediator reads out the application for mediation to the two parties, and declares the procedures and rules for the mediating activity.)

1. Q: 郑家强，除了你申请书上所说的，格还有哪样要补充的？
   [Zhèngjiāqiáng, chúle nǐ shēnqǐngshū shàng suǒshuō de, gé háiyǒu nǎyàng yào bǔchōng de?]
   Jiaqiang Zheng, apart from what you've stated in the application, do you have anything else to add?

   A: 我的脚经过医院检查，有碎骨头在里面，还要动手术，这些费用要商量一下。其他不有得了。
   [Wǒ de jiǎo jīngguò yīyuàn jiǎnchá, yǒu suìgǔtou zài lǐmiàn, háiyào dòngshǒushù, zhèxiē fèiyòng yào shāngliáng yīxià. Qítā bù yǒu dé le.]
   A medical examination shows that my foot still suffers from some pieces of broken bones in it. Another operation is needed, and so the cost has to be negotiated. That's all.

52 *Philosophical and pragmatic perspectives*

2. Q: 高维云，郑家强申请书中所提出的内容，你有哪样要说的？

[Gāowéiyún, zhèngjiāqiáng shēnqǐngshū zhōng suǒ tíchū de nèiróng, nǐ yǒu nǎyàng yàoshuō de?]

Gao Weiyun, do you have anything to say about Zheng's application?

A: 是郑家强催我（为他办）出院（手续）的。当时他只是回家养伤。至于说骨头咋个伤，那我想的不合我承担。

[Shì zhèngjiāqiáng cuī wǒ (wèi tā bàn) chūyuàn (shǒuxù) de. Dāngshí tā zhǐshì huíjiā yǎngshāng. Zhìyú shuō gǔtou zǎgè shāng, nà wǒ xiǎng de bùhé wǒ chéngdān.]

It was Zheng who urged me to have him released from the hospital. After that, he stayed at home for recovery. As far as his bone injuries are concerned, I don't think that I'm responsible to them.

3. Q: 请你将事情发生的经过复述一下。

[Qǐng nǐ jiāng shìqíng fāshēng de jīngguò fùshù yīxià.]

Please describe the whole incident.

A: 2月8日早上，我要到阿乌（弥东乡一村子）去拿针水，在面粉厂见着他们。他们请我将他们拉去雨补水库那边。在秧田村后的半坡上，我的刹车拉杆断掉，有四个人跳车。我把车开到半坡的一个石脚地基上挡住。由于地势不平，加上郑家强坐这边重，就翻了，伤着他们。

[2 yuè 8 rì zǎoshang, wǒ yào dào āwū (mí dōngxiāng yī cūnzi) qù ná zhēnshuǐ, zài miànfěnchǎng jiànzhe tāmen. Tāmen qǐng wǒ jiāng tāmen lā qù yǔbǔshuǐkù nàbiān. Zài yāngtiáncūn hòu de bànpō shàng, wǒ de shāchē lāgǎn duàndiào, yǒu sì gè rén tiàochē. Wǒ bǎ chē kāidào bànpō de yīgè shíjiǎo dìjī shàng dǎngzhù. Yóuyú dìshì bùpíng, jiāshàng zhèngjiāqiáng zuò zhèbiān zhòng, jiù fānle, shāngzhe tāmen.]

On the morning of February 8, I was going to the Awu Village for some injection but came across them at the Flour Mill. They asked me to take them to the Yubu Reservoir. On the slope behind the Yangtian Village, the brake handle of my vehicle broke and four of them jumped down. My vehicle was stopped by the stone base of a house. Because of the rough terrain and the weight of Mr Zheng, my vehicle turned over and they got injured.

4. Q: 你认为这起事故的主要责任应由哪个承担？

[Nǐ rènwéi zhèqǐ shìgù de zhǔyào zérèn yīngyóu nǎge chéngdān?]

Who do you think should be responsible for this accident?

A: 当然是我承担。

[Dāngrán shì wǒ chéngdān.]

Of course I should.

5. Q: 郑家强申请中提出要你赔偿各种费用8683.05元。你认为如何？

[Zhèngjiāqiáng shēnqǐng zhōng tíchū yào nǐ péicháng gèzhǒng fèiyòng 8683.05 Yuán. Nǐ rènwéi rúhé?]

Philosophical and pragmatic perspectives 53

Jiaqiang Zheng has asked you to pay him 8683.05 yuan to cover all his medical bills and other involved costs. What do you think?

A: 我现在无能力，但按以前他家说过的500元，可以。
[Wǒ xiànzài wú nénglì, dàn àn yǐqián tājiā shuōguò de 500 yuán, kěyǐ.]
I don't have the ability, but if the compensation is 500 yuan as he asked for previously, I'll agree.

6. Q: 郑家强，你所提出的赔偿数目格还可以协商？
[Zhèngjiāqiáng, nǐ suǒ tíchū de péicháng shùmù gé hái kěyǐ xiéshāng?]
Jiaqiang Zheng, is the amount of the money you are asking negotiable?

A: 可以。
[Kěyǐ.]
Yes.

7. Q: 高维云，你所提出赔偿500元这个数目格还可以协商？
[Gāowéiyún, nǐ suǒ tíchū péicháng 500 yuán zhège shùmù gé hái kěyǐ xiéshāng?]
Weiyun Gao, can the compensation of 500 yuan you have offered be negotiated?

A: 可以。
[Kěyǐ.]
Yes.

8. Q: 郑家强，你现在说说，要求高维云承担多少？
[Zhèngjiāqiáng, nǐ xiànzài shuōshuō, yāoqiú gāowéiyún chéngdān duōshǎo?]
Now, Jiaqiang Zheng, tell us how much you would like Weiyun Gao to pay to cover your expenses.

A: 6000元。
[6000 yuán.]
6000 yuan.

9. Q: 高维云，你说说。
[Gāowéiyún, nǐ shuōshuō.]
Weiyun Gao, tell us what you think.

A: 再承担300元，总共800元。
[Zài chéngdān 300 yuán, zǒnggòng 800 yuán.]
Another 300 yuan, altogether 800 yuan.

10. Q: 郑家强，格还能下点儿？
[Zhèngjiāqiáng, gé hái néng xià diǎn er?]
Jiaqiang Zheng, could you slightly bring down the compensation?

54 *Philosophical and pragmatic perspectives*

A: 下1000元，按5000元算。
[Xià 1000 yuán, àn 5000 yuán suàn.]
Yes, but only 1000 yuan, so altogether 5000 yuan.

11. Q: 高维云，你上多少？
[Gāowéiyún, nǐ shàng duōshǎo?]
Weiyun Gao, how much will you add to your offer?

A: 可以承担1500元。
[Kěyǐ chéngdān 1500 yuán.]
At most 1500 yuan.

12. Q: 高维云，你能承担多少，一句话说说。
[Gāowéiyún, nǐ néng chéngdān duōshǎo, yī jùhuà shuō shuō.]
Weiyun Gao, in a word, how much are you able to to compensate him?

A: 2500元。只有这个能力。
[2500 Yuán. Zhǐyǒu zhège nénglì.]
At most 2500 yuan. That's all I can offer.

13. Q: 那你们如何支付？
[Nà nǐmen rúhé zhīfù?]
How would you like to pay?

A: 春节前付500元，其他的待6月份之前付清。
[Chūnjié qián fù 500 yuán, qítā de dài 6 yuèfèn zhīqián fùqīng.]
500 yuan before the Spring Festival, the rest before the end of April.

14. Q: 郑家强，高维云只愿意承担2500元。你格同意？
[Zhèngjiāqiáng, gāowéiyún zhǐ yuànyì chéngdān 2500 yuán. Nǐ gé tóngyì?]
Jiaqiang Zheng, Weiyun Gao would like to compensate you 2500 yuan. Do you accept it?

A: 可以呢。我同意，但要一次性支付现金。
[Kěyǐ ne. Wǒ tóngyì, dàn yào yīcìxìng zhīfù xiànjīn.]
I agree, but he needs to pay me cash, in one payment.

15. Q: 如果一次性支付不了，咋个整？
[Rúguǒ yīcìxìng zhīfù bùliǎo, zǎgèzhěng?]
What if he can't?

A: 要求他先付1000元，余款4月底以前付清。
[Yāoqiú tā xiān fù 1000 yuán, yúkuǎn 4 yuèdǐ yǐqián fùqīng.]
1000 yuan first, the rest before the end of April.

Philosophical and pragmatic perspectives 55

Let's have a look at the general structural formula of the mediating activity itself. Like other transcribed mediating activities of this type, the structural formula of such an activity often starts with an episode during which the mediator reads off the application form from the plaintiff to both of them and meanwhile announces the procedures and rules of mediation (rules of the game). Then comes the formal mediating activity itself. In this part of the activity, the mediator starts by consulting the two parties involved about the details of what the plaintiff was asking for and then moves onto the negotiation stage, where the two parties negotiate to resolve their differences between what the plaintiff was asking and what the other party was willing to pay. In the final part of the activity, he comes up with a written statement of agreement, which is signed, sealed, or fingerprinted by the two parties involved in the mediation. If there exist too significant differences between the two parties, they will be separated and each of them will work with a separate mediator. When the differences are negotiated and an agreement has been reached, they will be brought together for the mediation itself. Reasonably, this is the best formula to be followed by a mediating activity in order to accomplish its aims and purposes (3.3.1.1).

We now look at the constraints within which this type of activities progresses and operates.

We begin with structural constraints. As far as the way the turns are organized is concerned, it could be found that almost all the adjacency pairs are initiated by the mediator with directive speech acts realized generally as imperatives and yes/no questions, while the parties merely have to answer the questions or make statements as required by the procedures and rules of mediation. Consequently, each adjacency pair is constituted by the question of the mediator and the answer of the party addressed by the mediator through naming. Further, as far as the discourse roles are concerned, the role assumed by the mediator, as determined by the nature and the goal of this activity type, is always impartial in that he cannot speak for one of the parties or appear to be more favorable to one of the parties. Besides, as stipulated by the rules of mediation, neither of the two parties can interact with the other, i.e., they can only interact with the mediator. As shown in the case analyzed in this section, the two parties both stay in the same room, but they mention each other on the third-person basis. Clearly, in this activity, the topics and content of both the mediator and the parties have been stipulated and assigned by the activity type itself.

As far as the sociocultural (interpersonal) constraints are concerned, a mediating activity has its own features. The mediator, for instance, has to make all his efforts to maintain an impartial role during the whole process of mediation. He cannot appeal to his institutional power even when he comes across obstacles but has to resolve the differences between the two parties by virtue of compassion, reason, and law (mainly emotion and reason) so as to achieve an optimal balance between them. In this situation, the choice of an appropriate pragmatic strategy is the best way out. A frequently chosen

56 *Philosophical and pragmatic perspectives*

strategy is the narration of an event. In this case, when he hears, for example, that the party responsible for this accident is trying to shun the responsibility he should take (as shown at the end of the first turn), the mediator does not resort to laws but asks the responsible party to describe the accident (the circumstance or the plot) and then asks him who should take the responsibility of the accident (the reason). In this case, the responsible party finally has to take the responsibility (turns 3 and 4). Suppose that in this activity the mediator who hears that the responsible party is not willing to take the responsibility for the accident directly asserts that he should be responsible for this accident, the latter's face will be damaged so that the mediating activity cannot go smoothly. Understanding who should be responsible for the accident can therefore help to lay a foundation for the core of the mediating activity, negotiating the amount of the compensation.

As far as the cognitive-psychological constraints are concerned, we will focus on analyzing the emotive manipulation involved in the process of mediation. The emotive investment psychologically guarantees the way an activity occurs, unfolds, and progresses, as is realized most clearly in asymmetrical activity types. A characteristic of an asymmetrical activity is that power is not distributed evenly between the interactants. A result of this is that the floor is not shared equally in a dialogue between the two sides, which therefore influences the extent to which dialogic cooperation takes place. In this case, to make it possible for the dialogue to go smoothly, the more powerful side will attempt to reduce his own floor and meanwhile increase the floor of the less powerful side. As indicated in studies of sociolinguistics (Cameron, McAlinden, & O'Leary, 1988), a strategy often adopted by the more powerful side is mitigation, and the linguistic device that serves to realize it is the use of tag questions. In our case, we have found that the mediator has adopted a more direct device, which is linguistically realized as a question or an imperative, such as "do you still have anything more to say?" (Q1), "do you have anything to say about…?" (Q2), "What do you think?" (Q5), "Now … tell us how much…?" (Q8), and "tell us what you think" (Q9).

Also in this case, the use of emotive manipulation strategies has to help facilitate the negotiation of the amount of compensation in question. Since an activity of this type involves more compassion than law and the compassion involved tends to be driven by interest, the applicant is inclined to apply for a compensation which, like the selling price of a market, will be much greater than the real price or cost, and the compensation offered by the responsible party will be much lower than the amount offered by the buyer. In such a situation, what the mediator should do is to make all efforts to reduce the differences between the two sides so as to strike an optimal balance. As is shown in this case, the initial compensation asked for by the applicant was 8683.05 yuan, but the compensation offered by the responsible party was only 500 yuan. In this situation, the mediator was trying on one hand to maintain an impartial role and making efforts on the other to reduce and shorten the distance between the two parties. To achieve this goal, he employed two

Philosophical and pragmatic perspectives   57

linguistic devices: Yes/no questions and diminutive expressions. Examples of the former were "is the amount of the money you are asking negotiable?" (Q6), "can the compensation of 500 yuan you have offered be negotiated?" (Q7), or "could you slightly bring down the compensation?" (Q10). Here it could be found that the use of such pragmatic strategies makes it possible for the mediator to avoid hurting the emotion of the hearer while meanwhile managing to reduce in a comparatively implicit way the size of imposition resulting from the speech acts so as to effectively reduce the conflicts between the two parties and obtain the goal of the mediation at an optimal and satisfactory point, i.e., the compensation of 2500 yuan accepted by both parties. Of course, this result does not have to conform to a certain article of law, but it is reasonable and therefore acceptable to both sides.

The situational-physical constraints do not operate significantly in this very case, but looking at other activities of this type, one will find that constraints of this kind still play an important part in this activity type. For example, the mediator and the related parties stay in the same room, and a result of this is that what the mediator can or cannot say to either of the parties is constrained by the presence of the other side. In this case, when there are too great differences between the two, two mediators will come to separate the two sides and interact with them separately. Without the presence of the other party, therefore, the mediator and the party involved can enjoy much more freedom, although this freedom may not be accepted later by the absent third side. Further, as required by the mediation procedures, the two parties in this case cannot interact directly with each other. Consequently, when one of the sides mentions or refers to the other side, he does not use the second-person pronoun, or make any direct eye contact with him. This is a typical example showing how physical constraints operate to limit the use of language.

Now an essential question has to be answered. As can be seen clearly, our analysis of the above case can be an analysis of sociology, or an analysis of anthropological linguistics, or an analysis of judicial procedures, or more likely an analysis done by a community worker characterizing a new development in Chinese society. Then, on what accounts can we claim that our above analysis is a pragmatic one?

For one thing, the theoretical framework with which we processed the data is predicated on Wittgenstein's theory of "language games", Levinson's theory of "activity types", Wunderlich's concept of "social process", and Austin's speech act theory. These theories are by nature those of pragmatics. And our *activity-type-based pragmatic analytical framework*, which includes such basic concepts as activity goals and activity types, type variations and variation parameters, activity structures and structural formulae, and activity constraints and constraint conditions, is therefore by its very nature pragmatic as well. For another, any study that involves an analysis of language use can be generally included in pragmatics.

The major points of this section can be summarized as follows. First, verbal and nonverbal social behavior are entangled with each other, and thereby

58 *Philosophical and pragmatic perspectives*

constitute the basic behavior or the basic existential state of human beings. Second, in terms of goals of language use, the basic behavior of human beings can be divided into different activity types. Third, as a level of behavioral organization, an activity type constitutes a basic unit of pragmatic analysis and is thus a unity and development of Wittgenstein's "language games", Wunderlich's "social process", and Austin's "speech act theory" at the crosspoint of pragmatics and human behavior. Finally, and also most importantly, with activity type as our basic unit of analysis, we can gradually come to clarify the nature of human basic behavior and human ways of existence, and thereby gain further knowledge about language as the last homestead of human beings. It is in this sense that we can claim that the involvement of pragmatics is not only possible but also necessary and fruitful.

2.2.4 *Three types of pragmatic analyses of ordinary language*

As mentioned earlier in Section 1.4, the three different types of pragmatics refer to: 1) Pragmatics as a discipline with specific linguistic units of analysis (Levinson, 1983); 2) pragmatics as a perspective with no specific linguistic units of analysis (Verschueren, 1999); and 3) pragmatics in the narrow sense against the background of Chinese culture (G. Qian, 1997/2002).

When talking about how different types of pragmatics are involved in the analysis of human linguistic behavior and human ways of existence, we have to say that the data we have collected are everyday language data, including five cases from vegetable markets in Guangzhou and eight cases from vegetable markets in Chongqing. Given the limit of space, in what follows we will just analyze one of the cases from vegetable markets in Chongqing.

> The vendor: A middle-aged man (hereinafter "Vendor" for short)
> The buyer: Young lady 1 (hereinafter "Lady 1" for short) and young lady 2 (hereinafter "Lady 2" for short)
> Time: About 9 o'clock, on the morning of July 24, 2002
> Place: The Tiansheng Vegetable Market, Beibei, Chongqing
> Notes: Vendor keeps a fixed stand

> LADY 1: 姜朗个卖嘛？
> [Jiāng lǎnggè mài ma?]
> How do you sell the ginger?
> Vendor (reading a newspaper, and looking up lazily): 块五！
> [Kuàiwǔ!]
> 1.5 yuan (per 500g).
> LADY 1: 哎？
> [Āi?]
> Pardon?
> VENDOR: 块五的，块二就称。
> [Kuàiwǔ de, kuàièr jiù chēng.]

Philosophical and pragmatic perspectives 59

1.5 yuan, but 1.2 yuan is OK.

(Lady 1 looks down at the ginger)

VENDOR (standing up for his scale):　要啊？

[Yào a?]

Do you want some?

LADY 2:　你买这个做什么？

[Nǐ mǎi zhège zuò shénme?]

What do you want this for?

LADY 1:　泡噻！

[Pào sāi!]

Oh, for pickling!

VENDOR:　这个姜就是要泡起来吃才最舒服。好嫩嘛！你看哈儿！

[Zhège jiāng jiùshì yào pàoqǐlái chī cái zuìshūfú. Hǎonèn ma! Nǐ kànha er!]

This ginger tastes good when pickled. It's fresh and tender! Just take a look yourself!

LADY 1:　少点儿！

[Shǎo diǎn er!]

Lower the price!

VENDOR:　先看了东西了来。你们有些人一来就是不看东西好坏。

[Xiān kànle dōngxī le lái. Nǐmen yǒuxiērén yīlái jiùshì bùkàn dōngxī hǎohuài.]

Take a look at the goods first. Some of you simply bargain without considering the quality of the product.

LADY 1:　看了噻！

[Kànle sāi!]

I have already looked.

VENDOR:　你要泡姜就要买水嫩水嫩的这种。指拇儿一掐——哎！你莫掐重了哈——像梨儿一样的嫩，泡出来嚼起才巴实。

[Nǐ yào pàojiāng jiù yāomǎi shuǐnèn shuǐnèn de zhèzhǒng. Zhǐmǔ er yīqiā——āi! Nǐ mò qiāzhòngle hā——xiàng líer yīyàng de nèn, pàochūlái juéqǐ cái bāshí]

To make pickled ginger, you need to have ginger as fresh and tender as this. Just squeeze it with your thumb like this! Hey, don't squeeze it too strongly – ginger as fresh and tender as a pear tastes really good when pickled.

LADY 1:　好多哎？

[Hǎoduō āi?]

How much is the ginger?

VENDOR:　块二！

[Kuài èr!]

1.2 yuan.

LADY 1:　一块！

[Yīkuài!]

One yuan.

60 *Philosophical and pragmatic perspectives*

VENDOR: 嘿！你这个人！我给你说先把东西看了再说！

[Hēi! Nǐ zhège rén! Wǒ gěinǐshuō xiān bǎ dōngxī kànle zàishuō!]

Hey, you! I've told you to have a look at my ginger first!

LADY 1: 一块钱！少点儿零头下来。

[Yīkuài qián! Shǎo diǎn er língtóu xiàlái.]

One yuan. Take away the odds.

VENDOR: 说起来扯哟，你！我把这点儿零头给你少了，我们赚点儿啥子吃哎？不得行！

[Shuōqǐlái chě yāo, nǐ! Wǒ bǎ zhèdiǎn er língtóu gěinǐ shǎole, wǒmen zhuàndiǎn er sházi chī āi? Bùdé xíng!]

You're kidding! If I remove the odds for you, how can I make a living by making no money? No way!

(Lady 1 is hesitating and the vendor begins to put ginger into a plastic bag)

LADY 1: 哎！哎！我还没说要！

[Āi! Āi! Wǒ hái méishuō yào!]

Hey! Hey! I haven't decided to take your ginger!

VENDOR: 你先少买点儿回去泡。吃了再说！三天进嘴巴！你喜欢味道儿重点儿呢，就泡久点儿。你先吃了再说！你再也找不到更嫩的了！飘[12]！

[Nǐ xiān shǎo mǎidiǎn er huíqù pào. Chīle zàishuō! Sāntiān jìn zuǐbā! Nǐ xǐhuān wèidào er zhòngdiǎn er ne, jiù pào jiǔdiǎn er. Nǐ xiānchīle zàishuō! Nǐ zài yě zhǎobùdào gèngnèn dele! Piāo!]

Just have some, get it pickled, and have a try first! It's ready to eat in three days. If you have a strong taste, just pickle it for a longer period. Just have a try! You can find no ginger fresher or more tender than this, I bet!

LADY 1: 好好好……

[Hǎo hǎo hǎo…]

OK, OK, OK!…

Let's first analyze the dialogue using the type of pragmatics represented by Levinson, pragmatics with fixed units of analysis (such as deixis, speech act, implicature, and dialogue). We soon find that the case is first of all a bargaining dialogue with three participants and that from the speech act perspective, the opening turn is a question. In terms of implicature, when the vendor says "don't squeeze it too strongly – ginger as fresh and tender as a pear tastes really good when pickled", he is likely to imply that the ginger he is selling is of perfect quality and that one who wants to buy ginger has to buy his ginger and thus accept his price, etc.

For Verschueren (1999, p. 7), any "general cognitive, social, and cultural perspective on linguistic phenomena in relation to their usage in forms of behavior", a perspective with no fixed units of analysis, can be called pragmatics. From this perspective, it will be found that apart from general features of Chinese society and cognitive and psychological features shared by

Philosophical and pragmatic perspectives 61

Chinese sellers and buyers, bargaining at vegetable markets in Chongqing has its own specific cognitive, social, and cultural characteristics. What needs to be analyzed first is the formula of bargaining: Price-asking by the buyer; self-praising by the seller; price-cutting by the buyer; making or failing to make a deal. Also worth mentioning are formulaic expressions used in vegetable markets. For instance, in Chongqing, …朗个卖嘛? ([… lǎnggè mài ma?] "How do you sell …?") serves as a price-asking expression (while in Guangzhou, 丁(个)卖? ([Dīng (gè) mài?] "How to sell this?") is used[13]). Furthermore, in Chongqing, one yuan and five jiao is expressed as 块五 ([Kuàiwǔ] literally, "yuan five"); likewise, one yuan and two jiao is expressed as 块二 ([Kuàièr] literally, "yuan two"). The vendor will say 赚点儿啥子吃哎? ([zhuàndiǎn er sházi chī āi?] "How can I make a living by making no money?") to reject a price offer that is too low for him to make a profit. Especially, the local people use 飘 ([piāo] literally, "flutter") instead of Mandarin 赌一把 ([dǔyībǎ], "make a bet") to mean "I bet". From this case, we can have a glance at the psychological, social, and cultural characteristics of both the sellers and the buyers at vegetable markets in Chongqing. Unlike vegetable markets in Chongqing, in the final episode of a vegetable market bargain in Guangzhou, if the buyer is determined to leave the stand, the seller will generally make a compromise and the final price will be the one offered by the buyer.

The type of pragmatics that I put forward is also known as the "three-to-one theory" of pragmatics. According to this theory, an utterance carries an implicature that is beyond what the utterance says due to the operation, separately or together, of the cluster of signs concomitant with the speaker, the context, and the intelligence of both the speakers and hearers, on pragmatic inference. In this case, if we start with the three factors and analyze dialogues between sellers and customers, we will come up with a new landscape of findings, i.e., various types of implicature beyond what is actually said.

We can also analyze this case with pragmatics as a linguistic regulation theory (LRT for short) proposed by Y. Huo (2006).[14] As a theory of pragmatics, LRT is based on the following assumptions: 1) As a form of human social behavior, the use of language is embedded in other forms of human social behavior to regulate and manage the performance of these forms of behavior so as to achieve different forms of harmony; 2) language performs its regulating function within the category of an activity type with speech acts as its basic units; 3) language and its use have three features, variability, negotiability, and adaptability, which make it possible for language to perform its function of regulation; 4) the metapragmatic awareness of language users can constitute the cognitive presupposition for linguistic regulation to occur.

The first assumption can be the aim of this theory, i.e., to achieve all forms of harmony. The fact that the bargaining at the vegetable market in Chongqing was finished in a friendly way indicates that the aim of harmony was achieved finally in it. According to the second assumption, within an activity type, and with speech acts as its units, the activity of this case is bargaining by nature. The third assumption relates to the possibility of linguistic regulation; this

62 *Philosophical and pragmatic perspectives*

case is in fact a full realization of variability (bargaining at a vegetable market in Chongqing might be different from bargaining in other places in China), negotiability (both the seller and the buyer approach each other through bargaining), and adaptability (the seller is trying to adapt himself to the quality and price offered by the buyer and the buyer is trying to adapt herself to the self-praising advertisement and price-offering of the seller).

Due to their familiarity to Chinese readers of pragmatics, we will not go into details of the analyses by the three types of pragmatics but just mention them briefly. The reason for this is as follows. First, we aim merely to show that the three different paradigms of pragmatics can be involved but not to go into details of the whole process during which the involvement itself occurs, which will in turn engage an enormous amount of data (of course readers will not like to see this). Second, we have analyzed a case at the vegetable market just to demonstrate our great focus on ordinary language use because the whole process of pragmatic analysis has taken root in data of ordinary language use. In the philosophical trend after the linguistic turn (starting at the end of the nineteenth century and lasting until the 1970s), also known as analytic philosophy, Frege, Russell, and early Wittgenstein became dissatisfied with the coarseness, vagueness, and inexactitude of ordinary language, and the misunderstanding and nonsense of philosophical propositions arising therefrom, and the zest arose out of this for the so-called ideal language. Later, however, philosophers came to realize that ordinary language can really help resolve philosophical problems. Later Wittgenstein, for example, abandoned his early complaints about ordinary language and advised people to come back to the rough ground when he said,

> We have got on to slippery ice where there is no friction, and so, in a certain sense, the conditions are ideal; but also, just because of that, we are unable to walk. We want to walk: so we need *friction*. Back to the rough ground!
>
> (1953, §107; emphasis original)

Later, he continued, "What we do is to bring words back from their metaphysical to their everyday use" (*ibid.*, §116). Thus, Western analytic philosophy came back to regard ordinary language as its object of research (marked by "the Oxford school" or "the Ordinary Language [Analytic] school" and opposed to "the Ideal Language school" or "the Logical Language school"). Pragmatics originated from analytic philosophy and thus it needs to be close to the "rough ground".

2.3 Summary: "Philosophical" and "pragmatic"

A study in pragmatics should be very ordinary and full of life. All the data of this book were collected from the use of language in our daily life. Here a simple logic can be identified: Since human basic behavior and human basic

Philosophical and pragmatic perspectives 63

states of existence have been regarded as the object of research, what philosophy and pragmatics engage in has to be what happens daily, and full of life, but this does not have to mean that this engagement is not very philosophical. Philosophy is in fact not something based upon nothing, but something that moves through the real use of language, then turns a somersault[15] and thereby develops at a higher level thoughts about thoughts and thinking about thinking.

It is quite clear that this topic is a pragmatic one by nature. For if we attempt to analyze the data by using the present pragmatic frameworks with success, our analysis will be a pragmatic one by nature. Yet on what accounts could we claim that the present research is by nature philosophical as well? Our answer to this question is to be given at the very beginning of Chapter 3.

Notes

1 Wang & Wang (2002, p. 17) observe,

> "In Greek an article can be added before the participle to form *to on*, equivalent to *the being* in English, and *ta onta*, equivalent to *beings*, which can be translated into Chinese as 是的东西 [shì de dōngxī], meaning 'what is'. Now, it is generally translated as 存在事物 [cúnzài shìwù] meaning 'that which exists'…"

2 Some Chinese scholars (e.g., Sun, 1999), translate the two-fold as 二重性 [èrchóngxìng], which is puzzling, because the Chinese term means literally the manifestation of two properties of the same thing. But here, it is clear that "two-fold" denotes unmistakably the two things of *Being* and *beings*. So in my Chinese version of this book, I choose to name it 二重体 [èrchóngtǐ] ("dual entity").

3 This was first written by the poet Stefan George, whose poem *The Word* finished with this line: "Where word breaks off no thing may be." Heidegger rephrased this verse with an affirmative: "Kein Ding ist, wo das Wort gebricht" ("No thing is where the word breaks off") (Heidegger, 1982, p. 60).

4 Dan Li was the name of Laozi. In his *Outline of Chinese Philosophy*, Shi Hu thought Laozi lived during the late Spring and Autumn Period (770–476 BC) and placed him prior to Confucius.

5 Daiyu Lin is the heroine in *A Dream of Red Mansions*; Flaming Mountain is a well-known place in *Journey to the West*. Both works are Chinese classics. (The translator's note.)

6 Ashima is the heroine, beautiful and brave, in a well-known legend of Yi nationality in Yunnan Province, China.

7 Materialists think this way, which is typical of their position.

8 Things like rockets, atom bombs, atomic reactors are mentioned here by Heidegger.

9 Readers interested in the original Russian paragraphs are referred to Li (1998) for the details. It is simply for technical reasons that the passages are not reproduced here. By the way, Li's article is not concerned about how frequently the verb есть appears in Russian.

10 What is intersubjectivity? According to Stegmuller, a contemporary German philosopher, if one is just thinking about his knowledge of something, then his

64 *Philosophical and pragmatic perspectives*

knowledge cannot be scientific. For science occurs only when this thought becomes something communicable, i.e., something understandable, something that can be discussed and argued about. In other words, intersubjectivity, i.e., communicability or understandability between subjects, has replaced the human knowing ability and its origin and limitation and become the central topic of philosophy.

11 In the study of this project, we have recorded twenty rural mediating activities. For lack of space, we just analyze one of these cases here in detail.

12 飘 [Piāo], an expression in the Chongqing dialect meaning "I bet".

13 An interesting phenomenon often observed at a vegetable market in Guangzhou is that in an interaction between two people from Guangzhou, Cantonese is used as the medium, while in an interaction between one from Guangzhou and one from another place, the seller will offer to speak Mandarin Chinese. The reason for this is that since the implementation of the open policy, many people from other places started to move into Guangzhou and the vegetable sellers have adapted themselves to this market change. Sellers are especially inclined to greet the customers in Mandarin Chinese when they find that the latter are intellectuals. The first episode of such an interaction generally starts when the customer, pointing at the vegetable, asks: 这个怎么卖？ ([Zhège zěnme mài?] "How much is this?") (or 多大价？ ([Duōdà jià?] "What is the price?"). A Cantonese buyer asks about the price by saying 丁(个)卖? ([Dīng (gè) mài?] "How to sell this?").

14 Y. Huo finished his PhD thesis under G. Qian's supervision in 2003, which was later published with the title *Mitigation and Pragmatics as a Linguistic Regulation Theory: The Case of TCM Clinical Interviews*, in 2006. (The translator's note.)

15 The philosophical relevance of "turning a somersault" can be found in *Einfuhrung in die Metaphysik* (Heidegger 1953) in which the author states that the old types of metaphysics can but think of what exists as what exists. Over the past 2000-plus years, they have been searching the reason for what exists to be what exists, and yet the result is still a type of existence. Any true theory is a revolt against the thought out of which it has arisen, and philosophy can, by virtue of a unique leap out of its own way of existence, enter this whole world of different possible forms. To accomplish such a leap, three conditions have to be satisfied: To give what exists as a whole its space; to liberate one from the idol that everybody has and implicitly admires; to go back to the basic problems of metaphysics. See Cheng & Jiang (2003, p. 296).

3 Language
Mankind's last homestead

Introduction: There is no presence of mankind where the word is lacking

In what sense is this research philosophical?

In Section 2.1, the elaborated theme was that "Being" draws mankind into language. Now, we are to demonstrate that human beings make themselves present by speaking. Why on earth is it reasonable to say that an investigation of the basic state of human existence is philosophical? Mankind's basic state of existence is manifested in the three livings that this chapter is devoted to. The three livings all lead to the same conclusion, that human beings make themselves present by speaking. "There is being only where the appropriate word is speaking", says Heidegger (1982, p. 63). From the poem *The Word* by Stefan George, Heidegger repeatedly quotes the line "Where word breaks off no thing may be" (*ibid.*, p. 60) so that many people even believe that this is what Heidegger himself composed. Anyway, both two quotations above boil down to one point, i.e., *something may be only when the word speaks appropriately*. Nevertheless, the philosophical point of the present book is that *mankind makes himself present by speaking* – a proposition that is different from that of Heidegger.

This entire chapter is devoted to the proposition that mankind presents himself by speaking. It can be claimed that without this chapter, readers may have no reason to believe that the topic of this book is one of philosophy. Just as the poet Stefan George repeatedly states, "Where word breaks off no thing may be" (cited in Heidegger, 1982, p. 60), so repeated in this chapter is our claim: *There is no presence of mankind where the word is lacking.* Though the latter has been inspired by the former, they are two different propositions: "Where word breaks off no thing may be" concerns the relation between word uttered by mankind and the thing it refers to, while "there is no presence of mankind where the word is lacking" concerns the relation between word and mankind, the reaction of word to mankind, i.e., it makes mankind present in the world.

Here, a few words are necessary about the word "last" in "language is the last homestead of human beings". "Last" so used has nothing to do with the

66 *Language: Mankind's last homestead*

dimension of time, but rather of space. In fact, it indicates that language is the most basic way of human existence, and the most reliable "house" of human beings as well. Just as a snail carries a shell on its back, and the shell is its house, language is the shell mankind carries on his back and it is mankind's house. Moreover, wherever he stays, this home is with him. Zhongshu Qian (1997, p. 460) states, "Where mankind stays, there is a world – a world of human beings". His remarks can be perfectly continued with this: The world of human beings is actually a world of language in which human beings reside.

It is impossible for mankind to be completely alone in the world. Even though he has lost everything he owns in this world, he still has a most reliable property on which he can survive, the home that he can continue to maintain in the final resort – language. Language is a way in which mankind's life exists and the home in which mankind finds himself dwelling. Language is a warm home most suitable for human dwelling. Thus this "last" has the sense of being the most reliable, and the most suitable for survival. Here "suitable for survival" is not of a figurative use but of a literal one. We can understand it this way: While thinking about language, we not only try to master it but also bring ourselves into its existence so that we ourselves begin to dwell in it. That is, we are dwelling in the way we speak, rather than in ourselves (S. Yang, 1996, p. 254). This takes us back to the famous statement "language speaks (for itself)" by Heidegger (1975, p. 190), who believes that things can work automatically in their own way while mankind is just involved and thus participates in their work.

Therefore, the truth of the proposition "language is the last house of mankind" depends to a large extent on whether mankind lives in language, whether mankind has to live in language, and whether mankind has to live in formulaic verbal behavior.

3.1 Living in language

Living in this world, we find that we ourselves are always confined to merely one part of the world. This, of course, does not mean that we do not like to occupy the whole world as it is, but that we are doomed to fail to do so. We can, however, make attempts to go beyond the part to which we are confined. To achieve this, we have to enter the world of language, in which we can travel back to ancient times (along the temporal dimension) or manage to talk about the verge of, or even beyond, Heaven (along the spatial dimension). Most of the real world is obscure for us, far away and even unreal (if, for instance, you have never been to Hawaii, it is obscure for you, far away and unreal), but the world presented and stated in language is all the more real. The life that unfolds in language is reliable and specific. When mankind pursues a meaningful life (animals do not know how to pursue a meaningful life), what he can turn to is the use of language, almost the only way to make his life meaningful. For it is words, and only words, that present to mankind a world that is closer to his own world than the objective world of nature (even during his whole

Language: Mankind's last homestead 67

life, what mankind can experience is only a very small part of this objective world of nature); it is also words that can truly link up with his happiness and misgivings (again, the happiness and misgivings one can experience during his whole lifetime are only a very small part of the happiness and misgivings of the world). As Wu observes,

> The maze of Chinese, a gift of dangerous beauty, is the last house in which we can dwell. ... The world of language is a world which is more real than the real world. ... Language is here no longer a picture of the world, and our existence in language can make it easier for us to experience the dependability and reality of life. ... Living in language is living in a world of deeper meaning and in a world of infinite and varied possibilities that can be presented by existence.
>
> (1999, p. 136)

Mankind starts to cry the moment he is born, and starts gesticulating with hands and feet while chirping to give a response. He is rushing to language, rushing to life, and rushing to a life of variety and magnificence.

Therefore, speech is really the most concrete and tangible form of life because most other forms of our behavior are parasitic on speech; speech is truly the most real life because mankind dwells in linguistic discourse.

3.1.1 Major forms of human behavior are parasitic on speaking

Almost all other forms of human behavior are parasitic on verbal behavior.

All the achievements of human civilizations have been preserved and passed down via language. Austin is correct in his claim that "the common stock of knowledge that has been passed down from generation to generation, through established linguistic usage, is reliable" (Baghramian, 1999, pp. 107–108). Austin also points out at the same time that this is an underused source of philosophical illumination. Without language, human beings, like animals, would not be able to pass down their experiences and wisdom from generation to generation. Without language, there would have been no externalization of their mental activities. There would have been no thinking about thinking, i.e., philosophy (certainly there would not have been Plato's speech on philosophy, Socrates' speculative dialogues, or Confucius' worldly teaching to his pupils), the establishment and development of sciences based on mathematics, different literary activities (including the oral production of poems, songs, and plays, and the writing of novels and articles), or different forms of religious life (certainly there would have been no Jesus Christ's preachings, Buddhist lectures, or Zen Buddhist dialogues). Without language, there would have been no advancement of human productive activities through new technology (including all types of technological inventions) and without language there would have been no social communication in a family or a nation, or communication between the countryside and cities; consequently, cultural activities

68 *Language: Mankind's last homestead*

of all kinds by the public would have been nonexistent. Human beings who nowadays have flown to the moon and to Mars are often so inclined to ignore the trap after they have caught the fish that they have forgotten all about the basic fact that we have been dwelling in and amid language. Therefore, with this most fundamental fact clearly explained and highlighted, the proposition that language is the last homestead of human beings will come to the fore as a matter of course.

Mankind lives mainly in four types of behavior. First, mankind lives in spontaneous physiological behaviors such as metabolism. Second, he does things, mainly to produce (products or goods). Third, he uses language to perform some behavior (speech acts). Finally, he lives in purely mental behavior (purely mental behaviors can be verbally realized, but can also be nonverbal or barely verbal). All other forms of behavior are derived from these four types of behavior. The exchange of goods, for example, has obviously arisen out of the production of goods. Military battles and wars, or taking others' products or resources (as large as land, population, or large-scale resources and as small as oil) by military force, have come from production as well. Temple fairs in old times were a mixture of productive activities (like the exchange of products) and spiritual activities (like burning incense to worship gods, praying for wishes, and respecting ancestors). The various academic conferences convened in modern times are obviously derived from human introspective and creative activities. The list can still go on.

What especially matters, of all the four major types of human behavior mentioned above, is that only a part of the spontaneous physiological behavior can exist without relying on language, while the other forms of human behavior, particularly *production, part of physiological behavior, introspection* (which has been misunderstood by some as not working in language; see below for an analysis), *and creative behavior, are all parasitic on verbal behavior*. Really, the existence of mankind relies on society or the presupposition of a society shared by all its members, i.e., a network of speech or language. Language thus viewed is an enormous network that is, on the one hand, a basis for social communication and, on the other, a system of all such human cultural symbols as literature, art, religion, science, and ideology – the aforementioned introspection and creative behavior of human beings.

While attempting to stress the intersubjectivity among linguistic relationships by virtue of language and to remove the subjectivity of human beings, Jacques Lacan (1902–1981, professor of College de France, a representative of post-structuralism) points out that human beings as language animals manage to have themselves accepted by language, and that "speech is always a contract, an agreement by which an individual manages to enter an contractual relationship and become a member therein" (cited in Zhao, 1994). The self of an individual cannot exist without this, nor can it stand alone out of this network of relationships. Speaking is not a monologue in that both the speaker and the hearer often switch their roles. In this sense, the subject is a

Language: Mankind's last homestead 69

temporary phenomenon, relatively speaking. According to the logic of intersubjectivity, both sides enter a contract by virtue of language, and thereby establish a mutually accepted intersubjective relationship.

Leaving aside Lacan's intention to dissolve the subjectivity of human beings, we now focus our attention on the proposition that most of mankind's behavior is parasitic on verbal behavior, and activities, such as production, introspection, and creation, cannot exist without language even just for one second. Collective production and large-scale production activities need language to regulate relations between producers involved and thus make possible the coordinated action required for such production. Otherwise, the whole activity of large-scale production would break down. Production by individuals also requires language to coordinate the relations between the individuals involved and their emotion therein so that the production of the individuals can go smoothly. Spiritual creative activities (e.g., reading, literary creation, artistic creation, and history-writing) all seem to be activities of individual thinking. Yet communication and evaluation, which must occur in and after the activities themselves, have to involve the use of language and cooperation between the agents and those involved. Even the activities of the most individualized introspection and thinking need the use of language in order for them to occur. The dependence of introspection on language may be summarized as follows: *Thought is held by virtue of words. When your thought is locked in words, you may stay silent but you must use words, though without pronouncing them aloud.* Now the self as an object of existence dwells comfortably in words. Indeed, the kind of thinking that does not rely on words as its medium is, by nature, primitive and fragmented with broken pieces of thought only, and can never constitute an unbroken line of thought. No one can complete a thought before he speaks it out or writes it down, but instead he writes or speaks as meaning gradually emerges, or speaks as thought gradually emerges. Here "gradually" indicates a process during which thought is revised while speaking or speech is unfolding. *Language therefore brings existence back home and thought to formation.*

Activities of production, introspection, and creation, whose completion all depends on language, are therefore all parasitic activities, activities that are parasitic on verbal behavior. Hence, as Kasher claims, it is "impossible to understand any of these basic elements of human existence without understanding language" (Kasher, 1995, p. 410).

Mankind can do things with words because he has retained the following formula.

> *Speaking* (the base) + *activities of production, introspection or creation* (parasitic behaviors) = *doing things with words*

In this formula "the base" refers to speaking (different from Austin's "speech act"); "parasitic behaviors" mean behaviors that are parasitic on verbal behaviors. Stated another way, *among human behaviors, purely "verbal*

70 *Language: Mankind's last homestead*

behaviors" without their accompanying activities do not exist! How could it be possible that one just speaks without performing any actions or bringing about any effects from his speaking? One who starts to speak intends to commit somebody to something (e.g., a promise, a threat, etc.), declare something, direct something (e.g., suggestions, requests, or orders), express something (like apology, complaint, thanks, or congratulation) or represent something (e.g., claim, proposal, or report) (see also Searle, 1965, pp. 221–239; Austin, 1970, pp. 233–252). Linguists from the West would rather phrase our proposition that "major forms of human behavior are parasitic on speaking" as the concept "speech act", and thus claim that "saying is doing something". For Wittgenstein (1953, §27), "we do the most various things with our sentences". Indeed, the performance of these various acts will bring about various events and subsequent effects. For instance, a war stops after a talk (and this occurred even in ancient times). After Mozi and Ban Gongshu practiced their attack and defense before the king of Chu, Ban Gongshu, who was defeated, initiated an argument with Mozi. When Gongshu said: "I know how to defeat you, but I won't say it out (loud)", Mozi responded: "I know how you are going to defeat me, but I won't say it out (loud)". Everybody knew what Gongshu Ban meant to say (i.e., he meant to kill Mozi), but the state of Chu finally gave up the idea of attacking the state of Song. *Can this be considered the earliest recorded example of winning a battle at the language level?* As another example, goods are sent after a discussion of some minutes on the phone; one party bursts into tears or laughter after a loud quarrel; somebody decides not to steal any longer after a Buddhist lecture; one manages to kill another person after somebody has whispered in his ear; one can speak English fluently after he has been trained by his teacher for years. In other words, activities of speaking like persuading one to pursue truth, teaching one to do good deeds, and teaching one to love beauty result in, i.e., are followed by, related actions or acts.

Of course, there are numerous examples about how to make use of language to teach one to cheat, urge one to do evil, or instigate one to pursue indecencies. So some people say that language is a double-edged knife because it can be used by one to kill his enemy and himself or his own friends as well. Or as held by some, since quarrels, misgivings, hatred, tempests, and misunderstanding all have resulted from the use of a tongue, what one should do is to cut the tongue off. Indeed, there have been tales or facts in history about how people gave up their own tongues (by biting them off by themselves) so as to stop their misgivings. In Greece, there are many philosophical stories about this. In China a Zen Buddhist story goes as follows. A boatman who was pushing his boat from ashore into the river had a lot of crabs, conches, and shrimps crushed and killed along the way. At this a lay-Buddhist, who pretended to be pious, asked a Zen master nearby, "Is this the fault of the passenger or the fault of the boatman?" "It is neither the fault of the passenger nor the fault of the boatman", answered the master. Feeling conceited, the lay-Buddhist asked, "Since neither of them has erred, who on earth then

Language: Mankind's last homestead 71

is to blame?" Angrily, the master pointed at the layman with both his index finger and middle finger, stared at him and shouted, "It's you yourself who is to blame!" The master's reasoning goes like this: The boatman pushed the boat just for a living, the passenger boarded the boat just for his business, and the crabs and the shrimps were crushed just for hiding themselves, and therefore none of the three is to blame. The reason for this is that "sin, which is by nature empty, has resulted from the mind, and it will disappear if no mind is placed on it". An error that has been made with no intention is not a real error, and even though an error has been made, that error was not an intentional one. At fault are those (including the conceited lay-Buddhist in the story) who are inclined to gloat, to make something out of nothing, to raise the devil, and to cause quarrels and human evils (Fang, 1996, p. 220). Disasters that are said to emanate from the mouth actually come from the people involved, i.e., their gloating, their making something out of nothing, and their devil-raising. The metaphor that "language is a double-edged knife" is a maltreatment of speaking in that speaking is merely the base upon which the parasitic activities (like production, introspection, and creation) are built, and the effects of these activities are not determined by the activity of speaking itself but by the agents of these activities.

In any case, there cannot be a pure verbal behavior that results in no subsequent actions or effects. In other words, *the major forms of human behavior depend on speaking as their house* and language is therefore the last homestead of human beings. However, *when we claim that "language is the last homestead of human beings", we mean that "the major forms of human behavior depend on speaking as their house or base".*

This mode of human life, speaking (the base)+production, introspection, or creation (the parasites), reminds us of Wittgenstein's theory of "language game" and gives us a better understanding of it. Stated another way, we, after a study of this mode of life, come back to Wittgenstein's theory of language game and can have a true understanding of it. In his definition, "language game" is characterized as "the whole, consisting of language and the activities into which it is woven" (1953, §7). Wittgenstein's concept of "the whole, consisting of language and the activities into which it is woven" is exactly what is characterized by our aforementioned mode of "speaking (the base)+production, introspection, or creation (the parasites)". This is the field of discourse. It is in this field that we human beings are found to bargain, chat, teach others a lesson, cooperate, make trouble, etc. In doing so, we follow some rules on the basis of which our games are what they actually are. In brief, *we are now entrusting our behaviors (activities) to speaking*. Hence, it is by no means strange to say "language is the last homestead of human beings".

The major forms of human behavior are parasitic on speaking for one more reason. Patterns of social behavior in a society are likely to correspond to sentence-types in the structural system of the language spoken therein. Sentence-types thus result from behavioral patterns of people in their social

72 *Language: Mankind's last homestead*

life. Commenting on the functional explanations of pragmatics, Levinson states,

> One might observe the fact that nearly all the world's languages have the three basic sentence-types: imperative, interrogative and declarative (Sadock & Zwicky, in press). On the grounds that these seem to be used paradigmatically for ordering, questioning and asserting, respectively, one might argue that it is pointless to search for internal linguistic motivations for these three sentence types: they recur in the languages of the world because humans are, perhaps, specifically concerned with three functions of language in particular – the organizing of other persons' actions, the eliciting of information, and the conveying of information. (Such an explanation is of course suspiciously *post hoc*[1]: we would need independent evidence that these three activities are indeed predominant in social life.)
>
> (1983, p. 40)

For Levinson, clearly, the interpretation that is to the point made here starts with the three specific functions of language. What we need to prove is that the three activities – organizing others' actions, eliciting (others') information, and conveying (our own) information – are the *three predominating activities* in the human societies of this world. And the reason for the three activities to be predominant is merely that humans who want to survive and live well have to "organize others' actions" (i.e., produce imperatives), to "elicit (others') information" (i.e., ask questions), and to "convey (their own) information" (i.e., make statements). In fact, it may go without saying that patterns of social behavior in a society are likely to correspond to sentence-types in the structural system of the language spoken therein. If a sentence-type does not reflect human behavior, how could humans have created this sentence-type to bother themselves with? Humans have made types of sentences to satisfy their own needs, just as they have built houses and made steam engines or diet pills for their own needs. On the other hand, major forms of human behavior are always parasitic on speaking. It is based on this that we can claim that language is the last homestead of human beings.

3.1.2 Mankind exists in discourse fields

Human beings create discourse fields, and at the same time they live in the discourse fields they have created. *Discourse fields are verbal communication networks and the resulting sediments of discourse that have a lasting impact on speakers (even when they are not speaking). Discourse sediments are sometimes a result of spontaneous production, but are usually well established, often with some situation-bound usages* (see Section 3.1.2.4).

Mankind speaks because he has to. The reason for this is that as soon as he is born, he is confronted with a given set of discourse patterns, or a discourse field. By its very nature, this discourse field can be regarded as the natural

Language: Mankind's last homestead 73

situation where a child acquires his mother tongue, or as *a set of discourse patterns that the child can do nothing but accept*. Whether we acknowledge this or not is of great importance.

As far as an individual is concerned, the discourse field begins when he starts to speak, but it does not disappear after his speaking stops. This resonates with the concept in pragmatics of the perlocutionary act (Austin, 1962). It is because of this that pragmatics is involved in this research.

The saying that "all written works in this world are results of copying" is quite right. By "written works", we mean, however, not really plagiarized ones, but honest writings themselves, even famous works. Any famous work has to be written by its author in collaboration with other authors; such works cannot be written by just one author. In living within a certain discourse field, the author is always making use of the resources available within it. Otherwise, he cannot communicate with others. Of course, he can create, but only in terms of new concepts and thoughts. In fact, one who has created new concepts and thoughts can claim to be a real creative author himself. In the same vein, speaking is also copying! Speaking presupposes the use of public rules and words. A number of philosophers have rejected that there exists in this world a language used merely by an individual person. As far as language and its rules are concerned, it could be claimed that linguistic communication is a type of rule-governed behavior. Since there is in this world no language spoken by just one person, all people speak the same language in their given community. Isn't this a type of mutual "copying"? Creativity in the use of language manifests itself in speaking in two ways only: 1) Individual new words (or concepts) whose reception has to undergo a process, "an aesthetic process of making choices" (G. Qian, 1993, pp. 212–219); and 2) new thoughts and opinions. *That both articles and speaking are results of copying indicates and proves the existence of discourse fields.* Both the speaker and the author live in the discourse fields in which they are found to speak or write. One does not have to write, but one has to speak. One has to live in a discourse field, and this is a truth beyond doubt.

There exists more than one discourse field. Often a larger discourse field consists of many smaller discourse fields. Smaller discourses can be classified according to the professions, the circles of life, and the conditions of knowledge involved therein, or according to the events they involve, such as court decrees, bargaining, war negotiations, trade talks, and the like.

3.1.2.1 Listening and speaking: A primary form of human life

As Austin argues, the common stock of knowledge that has been passed down from generation to generation, through established linguistic usage, is a reliable but underused source of philosophical illumination (Baghramian, 1999, pp. 107–108).

Listening and speaking constitute a primary form of human life; what is said is meaningful only in the flow of being said.

74 *Language: Mankind's last homestead*

Human beings live, mainly, in spontaneous physiological behaviors (e.g., metabolism), production activities (e.g., producing products and commodities), speech acts, and purely mental behaviors. All other behaviors are subsets of these four kinds of behaviors. It is worth noting that among the four primary kinds of behaviors, only a part of spontaneous physiological behaviors can be divorced from language. All the other human behaviors, including production activities, speech acts, purely mental behaviors, and part of spontaneous physiological behaviors, are parasitic on verbal behaviors. This point will be further elaborated in Sections 3.2 and 3.3.

When it comes to the difference between humans and animals, the first thing that comes to one's mind is nothing but the ability to speak, the most striking and prominent feature of human beings, though the other features of human beings also matter. Greeks, for example, define human beings as *zoon logon echon*, which means animals that can speak. Listening and speaking (as well as reading and writing after the rise of civilization) constitute not only a visible and sensible form of mankind's living in the world, but also a primary one.

Common sense tells us that human society is comprised of human beings. However, according to Zhuangzi, human sounds are comprised of the speech made by human beings (Feng, 1996, p. 97). Instead of saying that human society is comprised of human beings, Zhuangzi claims that the human sounds are comprised of speech, attaching more importance to speech than to human beings (which happens to coincide with Greek's definition of human beings). As Youlan Feng analyzes, in the book *On the Equality of Things* Zhuangzi first describes wind and the various distinct sounds made by wind and calls them "the sounds of Nature" (*ibid.*). In addition, there are some sounds that are called "human sounds", comprised of the speech made by human society. Human sounds are different from the sounds of Nature in that speeches produced by human beings represent their thoughts, namely the positive or negative opinions every individual develops from their unique limited viewpoints. Feng goes on to emphasize the limitations of every individual's opinions, which is right but will not be covered here. Then why did Zhuangzi claim that "human sounds are comprised of speech" and thus give priority to speech over human beings? Personally, I think it is because he believed that verbal behaviors constitute a primary form of mankind's living in the world. Then isn't it the same as the idea that mankind lives in discourse fields?

It is speech that helps create a wonderful material world and a realm of meaning for mankind. This is a reward for mankind's living in discourse fields. How many utterances will a person produce in his lifetime? Apart from spontaneous speeches, we have so many things, events, stories, and cases to share with others in our lifetime. We can retell the story of how eighteen farmers in the hometown of the founding emperor of the Ming Dynasty portioned out the community-owned land to households prior to official approvals at the end of the 1970s (November 24, 1978), or describe a 62-kilogram watermelon that grew in a so-and-so's farmland,[2] or gossip about the daughter of a

Language: Mankind's last homestead 75

county magistrate who, having eloped with a sole trader, was caught and sent back home by police officers sent by her father, or spread the news of finding a human-shaped plant,[3] and the list can go on. Speakers never think that the events (things, stories, and cases) they talk about will add anything to or make any difference to the material world and the realm of meaning for mankind world. They never realize that their accounts are indicative of supporting or rejecting a theory of economic politics (preferably political economy in China) (e.g., privately portioning the community-owned land to households), discovering some cases of biological gene mutations (e.g., the 62-kilogram watermelon or the human-shaped plant), and supporting or opposing a certain article of law, say, marriage law (e.g., the county magistrate who sent police officers to catch and bring home his daughter, who had eloped with a sole trader). However, in the eyes of an expert, narrators of events are making revisions to what actually happened based on their own experience. D. Wang argues as follows.

> The test of various theories should be carried out from generation to generation so as to judge by accumulated experience whether a theory is good or not, and this is "tradition". When I tell a story, the significance of my story is that it adds new experience to some intellectual tradition and, in combination with others' stories, either supports or rejects a certain theory. In this sense, my story can make a difference to the credibility of a theory in its tradition, namely its probability of being considered correct ... speaking is meaningful only in the tradition of speaking. Likewise, thinking can only be the thinking of das Sein in the tradition of thinking ... In other words, thinking and speaking are meaningful only in existing concrete traditions.
>
> (1997, pp. 138–141)

The events spoken by every individual change traditions, and hence play a role in constructing or dissolving a theory (in the meaning world). For instance, when you spread the news of a human-shaped plant, you are actually supporting the Universal Holographic Law – every holographic unit in the universe contains all the information of another holographic unit (Wang & Yan, 1995). When you say a certain phrase develops into a sentence, you are actually supporting the Linguistic Holographic Law – every structural unit on a certain level of language (phoneme, syllable, word, phrase, sentence, paragraph, and even discourse) contains all the information of another structural unit on the same level or an upper level (syllable is the superordinate level of phoneme) (G. Qian, 2002).

Suppose a person talks about a case of committing crimes with a computer; a second one shares a case of destroying computer hardware by spreading computer viruses, causing a worldwide stir; and a third one tells that a computer software, like a busy-boy, will underline in red an English sentence occupying five lines, indicating there is an error in it. If you inquire what is wrong, say, by

76 *Language: Mankind's last homestead*

clicking the "Spelling and Grammar" tab in the "Tool" menu, you will be told to rewrite the sentence because it is an "unduly long sentence". How annoying it would be! In formal English literature, a sentence occupying ten lines may not be taken as unduly long at all, let alone a sentence occupying five lines. A sentence with more than one hundred words can also be found sometimes! How irritating it is to find all English sentences occupying five lines underlined in red by the computer software! A fourth one speaks of a case of sexual harassment with computers and a fifth shares an event of posting big-character posters online; a sixth shares another distressing story caused by computers and a seventh talks about another painful computer-related story; an eighth reports that the fact that everyone is able to voice their superficial opinions online increases a sense of loss among intellectuals, causing them to feel that such online writings not only deprive them of their sense of pride resulting from publishing in established formal venues, and of their pride in receiving handsome remunerations to buy a high-class electrical appliance, but also rob them of the sense of achievement from the careers they have been building up in their lifetime... Aren't all these accounts preparing for the elimination of computers in the twenty-fifth century? Because the more such accounts there are, the less perceived value computers will have. However, there is also the possibility that a certain individual enumerates the advantages of computers and a second one talks about how amazing computers are, and a third, a fourth... an xth person... Aren't all these accounts helpful in designing a new plan for "super-computers" or "super-brain computers" in the twenty-sixth century? This is because the more such accounts appear, the more perceived value computers will have.

It is just in this sense that we say speech helps create a wonderful material world full of meanings that is habitable for mankind.

Listening is one important part of mankind's living in discourse fields. Listening is a form of living. There are two kinds of listening. One is listening with the aim of having a conversation with others, in which case one first yields the turn (as called by pragmatists) and then takes the floor. The other is listening only for information, with no intention to take the floor later. This includes, but is not limited to: 1) Listening to a lecture, a project report, a court trial, an announcement made by a government spokesperson, an inaugural speech, or a story; 2) listening to the radio; 3) listening to (and watching) television; and 4) going to a tea shop where most people go not for saying something, but simply for listening. In other words, this kind of listening involves obtaining and storing information in the brain without a conversation. By the purpose of listening, listening can be categorized into three types: Listening for information, listening for entertainment (of others' speech resources), and listening for both information and entertainment. For the third type, consider as a case in point the example of listening to Zhongshu Qian talk about art, as recalled by many people. When Qian commented on a historical figure, whether modern or ancient, he not only talked about their merits, but also their follies and anecdotes, revealing the true face of the person under discussion.

Now we can see that personal speeches can also be a type of resource. In our discourse fields, large or small, there are numerous resources for us to enjoy or employ. Therefore, listening is a form of life.

A special case of listening for entertainment is watching debates on television. Enjoying such debates is more a way of living in discourse fields than a solid evidence of mankind's living in discourse fields. Regardless of the intention of the television station involved, for the audience, the purpose of listening to such debates is two-fold. For one, the listener wishes to seek truth from the debate, trying to make head or tail of the issues under debate, but having no interest in who debates better (or who wins the debate). For another, the listener simply appreciates the wits of debaters and the beauty of their critical thoughts, ignoring the issues under debate or, if they are already well acquainted with the questions under debate, they only take the debate as an aesthetic object. As a result, the debate turns into a "competition" and finally an object of appreciation. As I see it, this symbolizes an increasingly mature degree of human civilization. Debates that took place in Greece thousands of years ago did not reach such maturity; modern debates in developed countries have usually, and I think rightly, taken practical aims as the first priority, telling the audience, for example, who should be elected the president, whether a certain heavy expenditure is reasonable, and whether a certain region should be governed under the jurisdiction of a given country. Such debates are not yet an aesthetic object. Unfortunately, for a rather long history in China, public debates are labelled a form of "false democracy" in the eyes of Chinese people, who are down-to-earth and look down upon slick talkers. The Chinese saying 身教重于言教 ([Shēnjiào zhòngyú yánjiào] "Example is always better than precept") presupposes that the precept is empty talk. Another Chinese proverb, "Judge people by their deeds, not just by their words", attaches more importance to "deeds" than "words", as words can turn out to be lies. Most often, "Stop bragging" serves as a warning that debases language. In such a tradition, Ah Q, the protagonist in one of Xun Lu's novels, can only say how good he is at "doing", rather than how good he is at "bragging" or "talking". However, the 1960s (specifically the period of the Cultural Revolution from 1966 to 1976) witnessed a sharp turn in the attitude towards debates in the sense that all the Chinese people became debaters; 700 million people became elocutionists and orators, walking on the streets and making impassioned speeches, speaking in a positive tone or in an attractive way. When such debates escalated, they rolled up their sleeves... and let guns "speak". Unfortunately, it is now clear that the debates that took place in the Cultural Revolution were indeed forms of "false democracy" as the debaters took delight in insulting each other's dignity and trampling on laws. To be fair, in some cases, words do not work. For example, we cannot produce food or construct information highways with words. Yet there are cases where words matter, like answering such questions as what should serve as the criterion of truth and how it can be more effective to crack down on corruption. Nowadays in China, debates have become an aesthetic object,

78　*Language: Mankind's last homestead*

which undoubtedly indicates that the concept of mankind "living in discourse fields" has stepped into an advanced phase.

3.1.2.2　*The preexistence of discourse fields*

In the beginning of Section 3.1.2, we roughly defined a discourse field as a verbal communication network and the resulting sediments of discourse that have a lasting impact on speakers (even when they are not speaking). Discourse sediments are sometimes a result of spontaneous production, but are usually well established, often with some situation-bound usages. *A super discourse field already exists even before one speaks*, and it is of greater importance than the specific discourse field in which one speaks. Discourse fields are more than linguistic in nature. Mankind always lives in discourse fields, for speech crystallizes ideas, including ideas that are part of our collective unconsciousness. Those ideas that are part of collective unconsciousness tend to be dominant thoughts. Very often, people justify what they are doing, what they want to do, or what they have done by turning to a saying, a creed, or a precept, saying "I remember there is... (a saying, creed, or precept)". This phenomenon is clear evidence of mankind living in discourse fields. Human beings do things by following some ideas, precepts, and experience, all of which happen to be crystallized in human minds by speech. Men with different views of life often take the following creeds and aphorisms as their guidelines for action: 1) "Heaven destroys those who do not think for themselves"; 2) "Know yourself and know the enemy; feel for others"; 3) "A thousand cups of wine are not too many when drinking with close friends; when the conversation gets disagreeable, to say one word more is a waste of breath"; and 4) "Respect your teacher as you do your father". Old sayings such as "Do as you would be done by others", "Do everything for others' benefit and nothing for your own", "Time is money", "Knowledge is power", and "Failure is the mother of success" serve as ruling thoughts that guide and discipline people. New ideas such as "Surf the Internet" and "Take the highway" are just like popular slogans that agitate, tempt, and manipulate people (for a more detailed discussion, see Section 3.1.2.3). All these thoughts and beliefs have come into being as a result of crystallization by speech. Put differently, they are the crystallization of the doctrinal ideology of the times, the sedimentation of economics, culture, politics, morality, and wisdom, and the crystallization of various social institutions.

As an indication of the fact that humans remain in a state of speaking even when they do not speak, there are many dialect chunks or phonetic chunks in discourse fields, such as the (native) dialect chunks speakers acquire at an early age, and the native standard language and, if any, the foreign language(s) they learn later. All these phonetic chunks, which usually stay with us all our lives, exist in our subconsciousness. When one becomes carried away, like being mad, overjoyed, or panicked, some intimate sounds "idle" deep in the mind may be activated. For example, when in a fit of anger, a person will speak his

Language: Mankind's last homestead 79

vernacular (or mother tongue) that he seldom speaks for years. This shows one's attachment to his or her home accent or mother tongue, on the one hand, and, on the other, indicates that *one never strays out of the discourse field of his.* With some stimulus, various phonetic chunks in the discourse field will be in full swing again.

Men are born into preexisting discourse fields. *Living in tradition is living in the preexisting discourse fields and living in the sediments of discourse.*

Every era has its own dictums and aphorisms, which function as a special preexisting discourse field, guiding people to think (or replacing people's thoughts in special periods), live, and act in a given way. A dictum may cause a series of actions, and, at certain times, individuals might even become slaves to these dictums and aphorisms. Some dictums and aphorisms are kept on record, such as Confucian ideas of loyalty and piety, benevolence and righteousness, benevolent governance, and the Dao of the king, as well as self-cultivation and self-restraint, and the Confucian creeds like "Don't do to others what you don't want others to do to you" and "Extend the respect of the elder in one's family to those of other families and extend the love of the young in one' own family to those of other families". Similar ideas also find expression in the neo-Confucianist works starting from the Song Dynasty (e.g., "Maintaining a true and sincere heart, developing one's own self, making one's family harmonious, and ruling the country and the world with good policies") in *A Collection of Traditional Chinese Wise Sayings* (增广贤文 [Zēngguǎngxiánwén] "Expanded collection of essays on virtues") that came out in the early years of the Republic of China, and in the various versions of *Quotations from Chairman Mao* (aka *The Little Red Book*). However, more ideas have been passed down from generation to generation not in writing, but by word of mouth. It would be naive to believe that quotations are mere words written in books. Words can leap and have leapt out of the bound of books. During the Cultural Revolution, Mao's quotations, worshipped by all, were supposed to "be carried and studied wherever you go". They were used by both the heads of revolutionary committees and some "gangsters". What effect can a single quotation produce? What would have happened if all the quotations had been put into practice? A quotation can lead to incessant actions. For example, following the quotation that "Once class struggle is solved, all problems will be solved", we have caught so many class enemies! A quotation can bring about novelty. For example, as a result of quotations like "Revolutionary committees are good", "People's communes are good", and "Barefoot doctors are good", a great number of revolutionary committees, people's communes, and barefoot doctors sprung up like mushrooms in China. During that period, we lived by those quotations, just as we had lived by those off-the-record aphorisms. Since the 1980s and the 1990s, the dictum "Falling behind leaves one vulnerable to attacks by others" has inspired many science and technology workers, ordinary people, and administrative officials to carry out their plans, actions, and projects! We are indeed living in discourse fields.

80 *Language: Mankind's last homestead*

As a matter of fact, the various discourse fields we live in are dynamic and ever-changing. Just as the thoughts of a paper or a book are crystallized as keywords, the value judgments, moral standards, and sentiments of our times are also crystallized as keywords in respective discourse fields. That is to say, we all live under the guidance of these keywords, just as the readers of a paper are guided, consciously or unconsciously, by its keywords. During the hottest months in 1998, Chinese people, especially people along the Yangtze River, were greatly influenced by such keywords as "combatting the flood", "doubling the guard and holding fast to the last", "liberation army", "protecting the embankments", "support", and "donation". Then, starting from September 10 of that year, Chinese people began living in such keywords as "anti-smuggling", "8 percent GDP growth", and "drawing a lesson from the bitter experience of the flood". Changes in the keywords used represent the changes of the Chinese people's lives, events, and thoughts. A change of discourse fields is just like switching channels.

The view that a huge discourse field already exists even before one speaks can also be evidenced by the prints of the past generations. Such prints can be referred to as "solidified discourse fields". Typical examples include *The Analects of Confucius, Daodejing,* and *Zhuangzi,* the three of which constitute the pillar of the Chinese civilization, together with various quotations, anthologies, and proverbs from the past. Other examples include *A Collection of Traditional Chinese Wise Sayings* and *Moral Stories* (善书 [Shànshū] "book on good"). The latter is a versed storybook about good deeds; good people in the book are always polite and respectful, often with touching words and deeds, while bad guys are malicious and cruel, whom readers or listeners condemn. When I was a child, I used to listen to my family read various versions of *Moral Stories* to me. Isn't it a way of living?

This kind of solidified discourse field exists for readers, so reading becomes a way of living for professionals and those who want to become professionals. A case in point is professional publications. Reading professional publications can be a productive activity of gaining information (to innovate, create, discover, or make theoretical breakthroughs) or achieving a maximal productivity level. For example, an innovation will help to reap maximum economic benefits, and a theoretical breakthrough will bring great reputation, which further leads to professional titles, ranks, and rewards. In this case, discourse fields function as symbolic capitals, helping people to accomplish their goals. This kind of reading is utilitarian reading, which, nevertheless, brings about remarkable social progress. Another case of a solidified discourse field is literary magazines, pop-culture magazines, and entertainment magazines (never assume that literary magazines and pop-culture magazines cannot be entertaining). This kind of reading is non-utilitarian as people often read simply to seek spiritual pleasure or receive a spiritual baptism. They are free from the social discourse systems that keep them within bounds and can even escape from a lifelong professional discourse system so as to have a break, have fun, or enjoy themselves as onlookers. They are living in reading and are never tired of reading all their lives. Such readers are not reading for the purpose of making inventions or seeking fame and fortune, let alone for earning a living. They, as chosen readers, are comfortable with the affinity of publications, and they read perhaps to find a new world and life style or a new type of people – anything that is different from what they already know. Or perhaps they read to confirm their knowledge and taste, to appreciate a certain writing style, or to savor some thoughts. Furthermore, reading masterpieces that touch our hearts is a way of experiencing humanity if one has never experienced a sense of dignity in his own life. In a nutshell, reading itself is a way of living. Mankind lives in solidified discourse fields. Yet for people without a reading habit or ability, there is no such thing as reading, not to mention reading as a way of living. Therefore, reading is only a possible way of living. And as the degree of civilization develops, possibility will turn into necessity.

For individuals or groups without any reading ability or habit, discourse fields exist by word of mouth, a way that is of more essential significance. We will come back to this point later.

Discourse fields also serve as a rectification mechanism for society. In society, some people are kind, and some are evil. In China's thousands of years of history, average people cannot afford to read classics and are in want of a religious spirit (compared with Westerners, who devote themselves to religion), then how do they avoid wrong acts? For one thing, they can rely on family education, more specifically, the teaching by parents and other senior family members; for another, they can count on discourse fields, which is the most basic way. They follow and spread such teachings as "Good and evil will have their karmic rewards and retributions respectively when their time comes", "A good conscience is a soft pillow", "He who is unjust is doomed to destruction", and "Polluting the environment is destroying the future of our descendants". By following such teachings, the Chinese try to modify their cost and benefit analysis (the most basic one is that good brings about good and evil brings about evil) and nip the vicious desires in the bud. These circulated sayings, which warn people of consequences and guide people to do good deeds, are a deterrent more powerful than family education and the admonishments of the elder. Another solidified discourse field serving as a preventative correction mechanism is Spring Festival couplets. A typical case in point is the first line of a couplet that says, "Virtue and happiness are mother and daughter". Apparently, this couplet is persuading people to do good deeds, and it simultaneously implies a warning that may go like "Evil and misfortune are father and son".

A discourse field can also function as a checking mechanism. Mankind does not passively live in dictums, aphorisms, sayings, quotations, and keywords. In other words, all such things do not always entail the absence of individual thinking because discourse fields also function as a checking mechanism. Dictums and aphorisms are in a dialogical relationship with the checking mechanism, and dialogues can see to it that sayings and quotations will not

82 *Language: Mankind's last homestead*

go to extremes and become utter falsehood. Nan (1998) is right in making the following remarks.

> Every conclusion must be drawn after necessary check and correction. It will help to prevent any conclusion from running along a slippery slope. With dialogic constraints, even if a specific opinion may go to an extreme, the convergence of numerous speeches will basically ensure that the society is in line with the rational expectations of the majority.

If each era has its own ruling thoughts, then it also has its own dominant discourse system. *The dominant discourse system is often a symbol of consensus and we live in consensus.* Dominance is not necessary interpreted in a political sense, because there are also ideological dominance, economic dominance, and cultural dominance. Let us examine whether the so-called dominant discourse system represents the ruling thoughts discourse (Does this sound weird? An explanation is to be made below). The following quoted discourses (or discourse segments), listed roughly in the chronological order, are graded into three levels, Level 1 (L1), Level 2 (L2), and Level 3 (L3), by a single standard, that is, the degree of popularity and acceptance of the discourse. L1 is the most dominant. No value judgements will be made here about any of the discourses, be they positive or negative, good or bad, beneficial or harmful. Some of the discourses are cited from M. Wang (1997, p. 117). Some of them are taken from various prints, but most of them have been passed down merely by word of mouth.

> 忠孝、仁义、仁政、王道。[Zhōngxiào, rényì, rénzhèng, wángdào.] (L1)
> Loyalty and piety, benevolence and righteousness, benevolent governance, the Dao of the king.

> 三省、绝四、慎独、爱人。[Sānshěng, juésì, shèndú, àirén.] (L3)
> Repeated examination of one's conscience, complete eradication of four problems, self-restraint; love for others.

> 己所不欲，勿施于人。[Jǐsuǒbùyù, wùshīyúrén.] (L1)
> Don't do to others what you don't want others to do to you.

> 老吾老以及人之老，幼吾幼以及人之幼。[Lǎo wúlǎo yǐjí rénzhīlǎo, yòu wúyòu yǐjí rénzhīyòu.] (L3)
> Extend the respect of the elder in one's family to those of other families and extend the love of the young in one' own family to those of other families.

> 知之为知之，不知为不知，是知也。[Zhīzhī wéi zhīzhī, bùzhī wéi bùzhī, shì zhīyě.] (L1)
> Say you know when you know, and say you do not when you do not; that is true knowledge.

> (All the above are doctrines of Confucius and Mencius.)

Language: Mankind's last homestead 83

祸兮福所依，福兮祸所伏。[Huò xī fúsuǒyī, fú xī huòsuǒfú.] (L1)
Misfortune might be a blessing in disguise and vice versa.

道可道，非常道。[Dào kě dào, fēi chángdào.] (L3)
The Tao (way) that can be told is not the eternal Tao (way).
   (The above two were put forward by Laozi.)

正心、诚意、修身、齐家、治国、平天下。[Zhèngxīn, chéngyì, xiūshēn, qíjiā, zhìguó, píngtiānxià.] (L2)
Maintaining a true and sincere heart, developing one's own self, making one's family harmonious, ruling the country and the world with good policies.
   (Doctrine of neo-Confucianism in the Song Dynasty.)

天下为公。[Tiānxiàwèigōng.] (L1)
The world is for all.
   (Sun Yat-sen's motto.)

人不为己，天诛地灭。[Rénbùwéijǐ, tiānzhūdìmiè.] (L1)
Heaven destroys those who do not think for themselves.

砍头不要紧，只要主义真。[Kǎntóu bùyàojǐn, zhǐyào zhǔyìzhēn.] (L2)
We are willing to die for truth.

敌人不投降就叫他灭亡。[Dírén bù tóuxiáng jiù jiàotā mièwáng.] (L3)
Destroy the enemy who will not surrender.

为革命而……（种田，学习等）[Wèi gémìng ér……(zhòngtián, xuéxí děng).] (L1)
Let's… (e.g., farm, study, etc.) for the revolution.

为了世界上三分之二的没有解放的人民。[Wèile shìjiè shàng sānfēnzhīèr de méiyǒu jiěfàng de rénmín.] (L3)
Fight for the two-thirds of the world population who are not enmancipated.

人有多大胆，地有多大产。[Rén yǒu duōdàdǎn, dì yǒu duōdàchǎn.] (L2)
The bolder people are, the more productive the fields will be.

兴无灭资。[Xìngwúmièzī.] (L1)
Foster what is proletarian and eliminate what is bourgeois.

毫不利己，专门利人。[Háobùlìjǐ, zhuānménlìrén.] (L1)
Do everything for others' benefit and nothing for your own.
   (By Zedong Mao.)

个人主义是万恶之源。[Gèrénzhǔyì shì wàn'è zhī yuán.] (L2)
Self-centeredness is the root of all evils.

一不怕苦，二不怕死。[Yī bùpàkǔ, èr bùpàsǐ.] (L1)
Fear neither hardship nor death.

84　Language: Mankind's last homestead

一人当兵，全家光荣。[Yīrén dāngbīng, quánjiā guāngróng.] (L1)
When a member of a family becomes a soldier, the whole family are bestowed with pride and glory.

敢想敢说敢干敢闯。[Gǎnxiǎng gǎnshuō gǎngàn gǎnchuǎng.] (L2)
Dare to think, to say, to do, and to forge ahead.

鼓足干劲，力争上游，多快好省地建设社会主义。[Gǔzú gànjìn, lìzhēng shàngyóu, duōkuàihǎoshěng dì jiànshè shèhuìzhǔyì.] (L1)
Go all-out to aim high and build socialism with greater, faster, better, and more economical results.

活到老，学到老。[Huódàolǎo, xuédàolǎo.] (L1)
Learn for one's whole life.

见荣誉就让，见困难就上，见先进就学，见后进就帮。[Jiànróngyù jiùràng, jiànkùnnàn jiùshàng, jiànxiānjìn jiùxué, jiànhòujìn jiùbāng.] (L2)
Claim no credit, tackle the problems head-on, learn from the best, and help those in need.

脱裤子割尾巴。[Tuō kùzi gē wěibā.] (L2)
Take off the dogmatic trousers and cut the capitalist tail.

共产党的哲学是斗争哲学。[Gòngchǎndǎng de zhéxué shì dòuzhēngzhéxué.] (L1)
The philosophy of the Communist Party is the philosophy of struggle.

三年超英，五年赶美。[Sānnián chāoyīng, wǔnián gǎnměi.] (L2)
Overtake England in three years and catch up with America in five years.

宁要社会主义的草，不要资本主义的苗。[Níngyào shèhuìzhǔyì de cǎo, bùyào zīběnzhǔyì de miáo.] (L2)
Prefer socialist weeds to capitalist seedlings.

革命不是请客吃饭。[Gémìng bùshì qǐngkèchīfàn.] (L2)
Revolution is not a dinner party.
　(By Zedong Mao.)

造反有理。[Zàofǎn yǒulǐ.] (L2)
Rebelling is justified.

理解的要执行，不理解的也要执行。[Lǐjiěde yāozhíxíng, bùlǐjiěde yě yàozhíxíng.] (L1)
Carry it out when it is understood and carry it out even when it is not understood.

活学活用……[Huóxuéhuóyòng……] (L1)
Creatively learn and apply…

念念不忘……[Niànniànbùwàng……] (L1)
Bear in mind constantly…
　(The above three were advocated by Biao Lin.)

Language: Mankind's last homestead 85

振兴中华。[Zhènxīng zhōnghuá.] (L1)
Revitalize China.

四项基本原则是立国之本。[Sìxiàng jīběnyuánzé shì lìguózhīběn.] (L1)
The Four Cardinal Principles are the very foundation on which we build our country.

实践是检验真理的唯一标准。[Shíjiàn shì jiǎnyàn zhēnlǐ de wéiyī biāozhǔn.] (L1)
Being tested in practice is the sole criterion for testing truth.

解放思想，实事求是。[Jiěfàngsīxiǎng, shíshìqiúshì.] (L2)
Emancipate our mind and seek truth from facts.

不唯上，不唯书，只唯实。[Bùwéishàng, bùwéishū, zhǐwéishí.] (L3)
Never comply blindly with authority or books, but be practical and realistic.
 (Advocated by Yun Chen.)

空谈误国，实干兴邦。[Kōngtán wùguó, shígàn xīngbāng.] (L3)
Actions speak louder than words in revitalizing our nation.

不管白猫黑猫，抓住老鼠就是好猫。[Bùguǎn báimāo hēimāo, zhuāzhù lǎoshǔ jiùshì hǎomāo.] (L1)
It doesn't matter whether a cat is black or white; it is a good cat as long as it catches mice.

摸着石头过河。[Mōzhe shítou guòhé.] (L1)
Crossing the river by feeling the stones in it.

不搞无谓的争论。[Bùgǎo wúwèide zhēnglùn.] (L3)
Don't engage in meaningless arguments.

胆子再大一点，步子再快一点。[Dǎnzi zài dàyīdiǎn, bùzi zài kuàiyīdiǎn.] (L2)
Be bolder and move faster.
 (The above four were advocated by Xiaoping Deng.)

一人结扎，全家光荣。[Yīrén jiézā, quánjiā guāngróng.] (L2)
A wife's ligation is a matter of honor for your family. (This sounds ridiculous, for how can the father-in-law and the young children in the family feel honored about it?)

观念更新。[Guānniàn gēngxīn.] (L1)
Renew ideas.

走向世界。[Zǒuxiàng shìjiè.] (L1)
Lead China to the world.

打假。[Dǎjiǎ.] (L1)
Crack down on counterfeits.

86 *Language: Mankind's last homestead*

反腐倡廉。[Fǎnfǔ chànglián.] (L1)
Combat corruption and build a clean government.

转换机制。[Zhuǎnhuàn jīzhì.] (L3)
Transforming mechanisms.

时间就是金钱。[Shíjiān jiùshì jīnqián.] (L1)
Time is money.

质量就是生命。[Zhìliàng jiùshì shēngmìng.] (L3)
Quality is life.

搞活经济，搞活企业。[Gǎohuó jīngjì, gǎohuó qǐyè.] (L3)
Invigorate the economy and enterprises.

精英意识。[Jīngyīng yìshí.] (L3)
Elite consciousness.

使命感。[Shǐmìnggǎn.] (L3)
Sense of mission.

超前意识。[Chāoqián yìshí.] (L3)
Foresight awareness.

宽容。[Kuānróng.] (L3)
Tolerance.

知识经济。[Zhīshìjīngjì.] (L1)
Knowledge economy.
　WTO (L1)
　World Trade Organization.

奥运。[Àoyùn.] (L1)
The Olympic Games.

小康。[Xiǎokāng.] (L1)
Moderately prosperous.

三个代表。[Sāngèdàibiǎo.] (L1)
Three represents.

学术泡沫。[Xuéshù pàomò.] (L2)
Academic bubble.

海龟派。[Hǎiguīpài.] (L3)
Sea turtles (a homophone for海归 [Hǎiguī], overseas Chinese who returned to China).

非典。[Fēidiǎn.] (L1)
SARS.

Language: Mankind's last homestead 87

Can you separate the predominant thoughts of the times from the above discourses? Obviously, ruling thoughts are crystallized in popular discourse, which, in turn, is the mode of presentation of ruling thoughts. That is why I integrated the two into one single concept, the "ruling thoughts discourse", as a makeshift solution to the intertwining relationship between them. However, the integrated concept makes it clear that the predominant thoughts of a certain era can hardly be separated from the then dominant discourse. It is in this sense that we say *the rule of predominant thoughts is the rule of dominant discourses. We live in the field of dominant discourses.*

A certain discourse, though not qualified as part of the ruling thoughts, may represent popular sentiments and values. Typical examples include political jokes and tongue-twisters. They are also a kind of discourse field in which mankind lives. In special times, people really have to live by such jokes. As a case in point, in 1997, the seventh issue of *Star* published a "philosophical joke" once popular in the USSR entitled "Dictatorship Philosophy as a Joke" (Lin, 1998, p. 45). The Russians, an extremely humorous and satirical people, tend to "laugh" in the face of immense hardships, and spoke out their innermost agony and indignation by means of satirical jokes, which are often a combination of tears and joy. The political jokes once popular in the USSR have been widely appreciated all over the world.

Why does mankind live in such jokes? Mankind lives to create (in pursuit of happiness and pleasure), to enjoy (material and spiritual wealth), or to experience sufferings. Some live to enjoy, others live to create, but none live to bear hardships, which, however, is a destiny for all, and still others live simply to live. Generally speaking, one need not be wise to enjoy material wealth (this is why ordinary people, let alone those simple-minded and evil-minded people, tend to be headed on the wrong track of life or even plunge into the abyss of crimes). By contrast, both creation and endurance of sufferings require great wisdom (this is why creative people and pioneers not afraid of troubles tend to be noble and wise). Most importantly, profound wisdom makes it easier to experience and overcome hardships. Happiness and suffering often go hand-in-hand in our lives. This suggests that we may spend half of our lives in experiencing and overcoming hardships. Basically, getting rid of hardships consists in removing the source of hardships (for instance, in curing a certain illness with a medical treatment or medicine). But in order to remove the source of hardships, one often needs to pay a more painful price (for example, when medieval Europe tried to abolish dictatorship in the Dark Ages). In case one cannot eradicate the source of hardships for the time being, it may be an effective and even a primary way to live through agonies and speak out the innermost indignation by means of humorous discourse. That is exactly what the prisoners of war during World War II did to alleviate their physiological and mental suffering. In such special circumstances, people are more directly required to live in discourse fields.

88 *Language: Mankind's last homestead*

3.1.2.3 *One or two sayings may control our entire life*

One or two sayings may control most of your life, even your whole life. You listen to and follow a saying most of your life, even all your life. Even if you change your mind, you have to be under the thumb of another saying.

Some individuals believe "A horse can't grow fat without extra feed", and have been working on securing "extra feed" all their lives. Some other individuals are convinced that "Ruthlessness is the mark of a truly great man", and have been following this saying until disgrace and ruin are brought upon themselves. Without doubt, many more people listen to the following sayings: "Peace is the greatest happiness", "Dedication is a pleasure", "Ignorance is a rare bliss", "To take a penny that is not yours will invite punishment", "Save yourself all by yourself", "Follow your own course, and let people talk", "Do not wait for Heaven to open a door for you, but just do your own business", and so on. Once we believe that "It is unlimited fun to fight against Heaven, to fight against the Earth and to fight against other people", needless to say, we will have a lifetime of fight. Once upon a time, China was an experimental field of such "unlimited fun". It was later realized that we must live in harmony with, rather than plunder from, Heaven and Earth. There is no need to struggle against others, either. By the time we realized this, the country's economy was on the verge of collapse, and the culture was also ruined. Therefore, we turned to the other two sayings: "Development is the fundamental principle" and "To protect the environment is to protect ourselves".

You may say that this is not to listen to a saying, but just to adhere to a belief. You may be right, but how do you keep the belief? We have no idea. How can you adhere to a vague, fragmentary thought? If I ask you "What is the belief you have been keeping all your life?" and force you to answer the question, what you do have to do is to give me a sentence. Thus, you search around, repeat trial and error, and finally you speak it out and tell it to me. This situation is what Heidegger describes, and can be quoted as follows.

> Only where the word for the thing has been found is the thing a thing. Only thus *is* it. Accordingly, we must stress as follows: no thing *is* where the word, that is, the name is lacking. The word alone gives being to the thing.
>
> (1959/1982, p. 62; emphasis original)

Heidegger thus concluded, "Language is the house of Being". Only when you tell me your idea in words clearly do I know clearly what belief you are adhering to. *If you are unable to speak it out, you have not yet clearly formed the belief that you claim.* As Dummett (cited in Baghramian, 1999, p. 310) holds, "our capacity for thought is not separable from our ability to use language; that is, fully fledged thought cannot be acquired before the acquisition of language". Therefore, what you keep are not some naked beliefs, values, life styles, psychological states, or spiritual pursuits, but some utterances. You can change the beliefs you do not want to hold, but you cannot change the utterances you have already produced. Listening to sayings means listening to the values, life styles, mental states, or spiritual pursuits we successfully express through language. At last, we certainly have to admit that we do listen to a saying and are controlled by it, which is not bad for us to know. This sort of mysterious process, which the author of this book experienced once, can serve as an example. My father died in 1975 and he left the world without any illness and pain. I once tried my best to generalize this kind of death, and called it "the wise death" (G. Qian, 1995). However, I had never been able to find an appropriate expression (or statement) that could best summarize the spirit. Twenty-eight years later, on the early morning of September 2, 2003, when I looked over a column of *English Salon* (an English magazine published in China), "We Learn and We Laugh Together", I read the words of an American, Dr Robert S. Herman: "We are not always able to choose how we are going to die. But we can decide how we are going to live". Immediately, I refuted his view, saying in my heart, "My father is able to choose how he is going to die, and wisely". This again forced me to sum up my father's death into the following statement: "To choose a simple life without extravagance is to choose an easy and painless death". This statement may as well influence my own life. The point is that a vague belief, which had been in my mind for twenty-eight years, turned into a sentence only when I forced myself to put it in words. If I had not forced myself to say it out loud, it would have remained a vague and fragmentary belief.

A statement that expresses a belief, a life style, a value, or a spiritual pursuit can control the whole life of a person. Among the five idols, which constitute the most famous part of Bacon's philosophy, is the idol of the marketplace, which Bacon used to mean that language controls our hearts, and our minds cannot easily escape the influence of words (Russell, 1972, p. 544).

M. Wang (1997, p. 117) distinguishes five kinds of Chinese sayings and aphorisms, as follows.

1) Some sayings and aphorisms constitute the mainstream values of Chinese traditional culture; they are at least the most popular part of traditional cultural values. Examples include the following.

> 学而时习之，不亦说乎，有朋自远方来不亦乐乎，人不知而不愠，不亦君子乎？ [Xué ér shíxízhī, bùyìyuèhū, yǒupéng zìyuǎnfānglái buyìlèhū, rénbùzhī ér bùyùn, bùyì jūnzǐhū?]
> Is it not a pleasure to learn with a constant perseverance and application? Is it not delightful to have friends coming from distant quarters? To tolerate being misunderstood, and to get along with those unwise ones, isn't this clement enough to be called a gentleman?

> 吾日三省吾身。[Wú rì sānxǐng wúshēn.]
> I examine myself three times a day.

Language: Mankind's last homestead

朝闻道夕死可也。[Zháowéndào xīsǐkěyě.]
Having heard the Way in the morning, one may die content in the evening.

吾十有五而志于学。[Wú shíyǒuwǔ ér zhìyúxué.]
At the age of fifteen, I had my mind bent on learning.

舍生而取义。[Shěshēng ér qǔyì.]
Give up one's life for a just cause.

人生自古谁无死，留取丹心照汗青。[Rénshēng zìgǔ shéiwúsǐ, liúqǔ dānxīn zhàohànqīng.]
Everyone must die; let me die and leave a loyal heart shining on the pages of history.

天降大任于斯人也，必先苦其心志劳其筋骨。[Tiānjiàng dàrèn yú sīrén yě, bìxiān kǔqíxīnzhì láoqíjīngǔ.]
When Heaven is about to place a great responsibility on a great man, it always first frustrates his spirit and will, exhausts his muscles and bones...

2) Many literary languages make up and beautify the expressions of emotion, the mode of expressions and mental state.

举头望明月，低头思故乡。[Jǔtóu wàngmíngyuè, dītóu sīgùxiāng.]
Looking up, I find the moon bright. Bowing, I am drowned in homesickness.

贫贱夫妻百事哀。[Pínjiànfūqī bǎishìāi.]
To a destitute couple, nothing goes well.

但愿人长久，千里共婵娟。[Dànyuàn rénchángjiǔ, qiānlǐ gòng chánjuān.]
May we all be blessed with longevity. Though far apart, we are still able to share the beauty of the moon together.

僵卧孤村不自哀，尚思为国戍轮台。[Jiāngwò gūcūn bùzìāi, shàngsī wèiguó shùlúntái.]
Lying alone in a lonely village without self-pity, I am still concerned about the Luntai Garrison.

3) Some folk words have a significant influence on the formation of a person's spiritual outlook.

一寸光阴一寸金。[Yīcùn guāngyīn yīcù jīn.]
As every thread of gold is valuable, so is every moment of time.

守身如执玉，积德胜遗金。[Shǒushēn rú zhíyù, jīdé shèng yíjīn.]
Keep your body as jade, and an accumulation of moral merits prevails over gold gifts.

Language: Mankind's last homestead 91

一言既出，驷马难追。[Yīyán jìchū, sìmǎ nánzhuī.]
A word spoken is an arrow let fly and cannot be retracted.

大丈夫四海为家。[Dàzhàngfū sìhǎiwéijiā.]
A true man makes his home wherever he is.

种瓜得瓜，种豆得豆。[Zhǒngguā déguā, zhǒngdòu dédòu.]
One reaps what he sows.

家贫出孝子，国难出忠臣。[Jiāpín chūxiàozǐ, guónàn chūzhōngchén.]
A poor family brings up dutiful sons; national calamities produce
loyal officials.

家有良田千顷，不如薄艺随身。[Jiāyǒu liángtián qiānqǐng, bùrú
báoyì suíshēn.]
It is better to master a few skills than to own a thousand hectares of
good field.

只要工夫深，铁杵磨成针。[Zhǐyào gōngfūshēn, tiěchǔ móchén
gzhēn.]
If you work at it hard enough, you can grind an iron rod into a needle
(or, Constant dripping wears away a stone).

4) The spreading of ruthless and evil words from the outlaw or the gangland
or trite remarks is also one of the life styles. Although they are neither
"useful suggestions" nor "epigrams", they are essential for the study of
the society. Examples are as follows.

量小非君子，无毒不丈夫。[Liàngxiǎo fēijūnzǐ, wúdú bùzhàngfū.]
He who is not generous or broad-minded is not a gentleman; he who
is not vicious to his enemies will not become a real man.

最毒妇人心。[Zuìdú fùrénxīn.]
The most vicious thing is a woman's heart.

马无夜草不肥，人无外财不富。[Mǎwúyècǎo bùféi, rénwúwàicái
bùfù.]
A horse can't grow fat without extra feed; a person can't become rich
without wealth obtained illegally.

好死不如赖活。[Hǎosǐ bùrú làihuó.]
A bad living is better than a good death.

官不打送礼的。[Guān bùdǎ sònglǐde.]
Officials will not make things difficult for the gift-givers.

礼多人不怪。[Lǐduō rénbùguài.]
Courtesy costs nothing.

少说话，多磕头。[Shǎoshuōhuà, duōkētóu.]
Talk less; bow more.

92 *Language: Mankind's last homestead*

5) Celebrated dictums, words of wisdom, or common sayings also present an exotic life style, which indicates that discourse breaks the ethnic boundaries. Examples are as follows.

知识就是力量。[Zhīshì jiùshì lìliàng.]
Knowledge is power.

天才即是勤奋。[Tiāncái jíshì qínfèn.]
Geniuses come from diligence.

失败是成功之母。[Shībài shì chénggōngzhīmǔ.]
Failure is the mother of success.

在某某的字典上没有"难"字。[Zài mǒumǒude zìdiǎnshàng méiyǒu "nán" zì.]
The word "difficult" cannot be found in his or her dictionary.

物竞天择，适者生存。[Wùjìng tiānzé, shìzhě shēngcún.]
Only the fittest can survive from natural selection.

好话是银，沉默是金。[Hǎohuà shìyín, chénmò shìjīn.]
A nice word is silver, but silence is gold.

不自由，毋宁死。[Bùzìyóu, wúnìngsǐ.]
Give me liberty or give me death.

生命诚可贵，爱情价更高，若为自由故，两者皆可抛。[Shēng mìng chéngkěguì, àiqíng jiàgènggāo, ruòwèizìyóugù, liǎngzhě jiēkěpāo.]
Life is valuable and love values more, but for freedom, we can give up both.

民有，民治，民享。[Mínyǒu, mínzhì, mínxiǎng.]
(A government) of the people, by the people, and for the people.

吾爱吾师，吾更爱真理。[Wú àiwúshī, wú gèngài zhēnlǐ.]
I love my teacher, but I love truth more.

天助自助者。[Tiānzhù zìzhùzhě.]
God helps those who help themselves.

The first, the third, the fourth, and the fifth points in M. Wang's classification are closely related to our view of following a saying.

In fact, we are constantly following the instructions and arrangements from one saying to another in our lives. We are living in these sentences.

3.1.2.4 *The inheritance of discourse field is the inheritance of history*

Each nation has only one history, but there are two ways to inherit it: By writing and by speech. Books are written in words, including the writings by Mencius

Language: Mankind's last homestead 93

and the writings by Zhuangzi. Opposite to writing, speech is the spoken word, which Zhuangzi referred to as 言 ([yán] "speech") and Mencius called 辞 ([cí] "words").

Transmission of history by writing. The book *The Records of the Grand Historian* (史记 [Shǐjì]) records a variety of historical figures, and the work *History as a Mirror* (资治通鉴 [Zīzhì tōngjiàn]) documents various experiences and lessons of governing a country. History, through the years of the past, reminds the later generations of what happened in the land a long time ago. However, history passed down in this way has two problems. One is an innate limitation called 书不尽言(shūbùjìnyán), meaning that the books cannot record all the words uttered, which the pre-Qin thinkers had been aware of. It is not just that not all words can be recorded, but that virtually only a small portion is recorded! The words that are not recorded are always a lot more than those recorded. Generations of experience and knowledge cannot be all covered by word of mouth; most are lost, and only a small part is kept. The other problem is an acquired limitation, or a man-made issue. History in words is always curtailed or exaggerated, hence inaccurate, unclear, or can even be distorted and tampered with, intentionally or unintentionally. When Xun Lu was still alive, there was a thing often rising into his mind, which was to "rewrite history". He once wrote,

> Most of Chinese knowledge needs to be straightened out. Take history for an example; it should be rewritten. Our forefathers told us how powerful the Tang Dynasty was and how excellent the Ming Dynasty was! Actually there is much temperament of Hu's folk in the Tang Dynasty and there is no shortage of rogues in the Ming Dynasty. Such kinds of things ought to be stripped of their colorful garments, and shown with their truth so that young generations will never be muddle-headed or be at a loss.
>
> (Cited in Sanmu, 2003, p. 69)

It was advocated to rewrite history because history was found to be flawed with false information or disinformation. Because of this second limitation, history can sober us up on the one hand, and can confuse us on the other. What can confuse us is much more than what can sober us up. Nonetheless, the advantages of this mode of history inheritance through books weigh greater than its disadvantages. The creation of words pushes human beings to the Age of Civilization. The history, knowledge, and skills passed down from mouth to mouth in ancient times have begun to be recorded by various chapters, sections, and books (nowadays by books, compact disks, video disks, photographic films, among others). As a result, those treasures can be kept for a long time and can be spread far throughout the world. Just as Liu observes, as follows,

> Chinese characters were surely not produced in the Warring States period, but the process that words and writings took the place of songs,

94 *Language: Mankind's last homestead*

legends, and myths and became a main method of inheriting knowledge and history was, without doubt, completed in the Warring States period. The collapse of the traditional official (of professionals teaching people by word of mouth and deeds) system led to the end of the tradition of passing knowledge on by word of mouth.

(2003, p. 7)

Transmission of history by speech. The history before the Warring States period, needless to say, was transmitted by word of mouth. During the Warring States, characters and writings began to replace songs, legends, and myths, and became a main method of inheritance until now. Therefore, we should say, history is mainly passed down by word of mouth, though there are plenty of problems in this process. One of the problems is that meaning is beyond words, as realized by the pre-Qin thinkers. Meaning beyond words means what one has said does not convey all in one's mind, or, as Zhongshu Qian put it: Language is not everything. This problem has been much discussed in modern linguistics, so there is no point in repeating it. The second problem is that spoken words can neither be kept nor spread across time and space, which is the most intractable problem. An experience or lesson can only be passed down from father to son, from one neighbor to another. If you shout to a person who is two hills away, it is impossible for your shouting to reach the person, and the information will not be received. This is the limitation in space. The limitation in time is much bigger. It is a prolonged process, enough for a grandfather's words to be passed down to his grandchildren; it is an even longer process for his words to be transmitted to others' grandchildren. *It is precisely because of this innate limitation (i.e., words neither can be kept in nor be spread across time and space) that the history of human civilization passed down by word of mouth is not always recognized, and may even not be noticed. A history inherited by spoken words might thus sound like a fantasy.* Even if we have tried to give a place to the oral inheritance of history, it is of no help. The most direct reason is that what has been passed down by word of mouth has not yet appeared as "history". Guo and his colleagues' work provides some circumstantial evidence (Guo, 2003). They worked on a project titled "The Oral Data Collection of Chinese Rural Life in the Second Half of the Twentieth Century and Research Plan" and took Ji County, in the north of Shannxi Province, China, as one of their survey sites. During their interviews with the rural people, they asked them some questions about political mobilization, land transfer, family property valuation, and so on. The female villagers could, on appearance, hardly give as clear and accurate a description as the rural male ones. What they could give were just the feelings and memories hiding behind the mist of history that cannot be expressed clearly. In real life, as for rural women, what collectivization brought to them was that they began to walk outside of their homes and bring their families into the outside village society; they began to labor in the field instead of being confined to the kitchen. Their survey indicated that the place was a non-event realm; a mass of details of life was mixed up in a disordered way, there was no clear time boundary or logic relation, and it seemed to have no relation with the important historical points. Nonetheless, just in the description of the details of their lives, the process of collectivization that those rural women experienced and the history that belonged to them would emerge. The women's memories about this period of time would emerge only when the events had a personal relation to them. Specifically speaking, this phase of history was brought to reappear through their memories of physical pains, raising children, and the issue of food.

From Guo's (*ibid.*) work, I see two things. First, there are no authentic history textbooks, historical volumes, or historical archives to record women's memories of physical pain, the raising of children, and the issue of food. However, those things verify the agricultural cooperative movement that took place in that era. It is a revolutionary shift, for all farmers, to change from individual farming to collective farming. It was a transfer of property ownership and a transfer of the mode of labor and income distribution (Guo, 2003). History passed down by books might record texts as above; however, the memories about physical pains, the raising of children, and food, which were passed down by spoken words, have disappeared in distant time and space. There is an amount of such helplessness in history. Second, what if oral messages were recorded by someone? Recording itself is a kind of processing. In addition, the more responsibly you do it, the more it would be processed. We can never capture history as inherited by the original word of mouth. Nevertheless, we must recognize that, although each nation has only one history, there are two ways of inheritance: One is by writing, and the other is by speech. If we recognize the way of inheritance by word of mouth, we recognize that spoken discourse has kept *a history in a special form, which we cannot touch or observe*. The third problem of history inheritance by word of mouth is that the confidentiality of government affairs, the secrecy of family affairs, and especially the puzzle of superb skills that only God can know discount the inheritance of history by word of mouth. Passing down history by word of mouth lowers the process of incubation of civilization. Despite so many problems, *transmission by speech is still an essential method to inherit history, which is merely difficult to be discovered, believed, and confirmed*. During the period before the Warring States, history was only passed down in this way. Even nowadays, people take the spread of information as an "explosion", and I believe this information explosion cannot cover all the words, nor can it monopolize the inheritance of all words. For instance, the number of words said, but not recorded, must be more than the number recorded (i.e., those made into books, CDs, video disks, photographic films, and so on). The words recorded but not passed down must be more than those passed down. Chao (2003, p. 21) explains *oral history* as follows.

The aesthetic principles summarized in the reading rules are not always suitable for the works created for "listening". This is by no means simply

96   *Language: Mankind's last homestead*

a change of receiving organs, but also a change of rules. We sometimes realize that there are some differences between written and spoken languages, but we do not dig into their causes. *The immediacy, interactivity, and highly context-dependent nature of oral transmission determines that its aesthetic attributes are intrinsically linked to certain "auditory" effects.* Let us take formulaic expressions such as conventional phraseologies as an example. They are repulsive for reading, but for listening they cause no problem, and often create some particular aesthetic effect.

(Emphasis added)

History inheritance by writing and by speech are complementary to each other. However, just as Chao holds,

Elite cultural products in books have long been paid too much attention, while oral folk cultural traditions are despised. This kind of bias may result in an irretrievable loss to human beings. The United Nations Educational, Scientific and Cultural Organization accepted these views and compiled some documents, such as *Proposal on Protection of Traditional and Folk Culture.*

(2003, p. 18)

To continue to despise oral history is to maintain the ignorance of the unrevealed history. This book attaches a special importance to spoken discourse that retains history, which is a retort to that ignorance.

Discourse fields retain history, and the transmission of discourse fields is the inheritance of history. The continuity of history is also in the inheritance of discourse fields. There are only three things that can directly reveal history: Archeological findings, fossils, and language (its phonetic system at the first level and its writing system at the second level). The fossils of animals, plants, and human bones are ironclad evidence, or rather "stone" evidence, of life extension. Thus, the inheritance of life finds its way into "stone" evidence. Then, what can prove that the language we are using is the inheritance of the language of a distant time away (albeit a change)? If there were no evidence, would it be nonsense to say that "things that can display history include language"? The possible evidence is the writing system of language – the oracle bone inscriptions, bronze scripts, characters on bronze tripods, the change of Chinese characters, and so on. Written records, in writing forms, are just one aspect of the evidence; they are not sound (phonetic) records. What can prove that speech sounds we now use are the ones changed from those in the distant past? The answer is that diachronic studies on real dialects (not writings) can provide phonetic evidence, for a real and living dialect can certainly be used as original evidence. This is another type of evidence.

Can we imagine that the original discourse could be transmitted to the next generations? Or we can ask in another way: What can prove the inheritance of discourse? Inheritance of history is the inheritance of human behavior in

Language: Mankind's last homestead 97

a certain location, which flows in time. While the passing of time has been confirmed by physical experiment, how can we prove the inheritance of human behavior, especially the inheritance of discourse?

Whether or not we actually discovered the original discourse field, it can be concluded that as long as the history of a nation has been long passed down, the discourse field of that nation must have been passed down accordingly. If a nation obviously has a long history, *it is illogical to think that its discourse field has not been passed down*. In other words, history is inherited by discourse; or history is the inheritance of discourse field. Discourse fields are composed of various language uses in certain contexts. When Baghramian comments on the analytic philosopher Austin's work, she points out,

> It is Austin's view that the common stock of knowledge that has been handed down from generation to generation, through established linguistic usage, is a reliable but underused source of philosophical illumination.
>
> (1999, pp. 107–108)

Austin's view entails two propositions: 1) The common stock of knowledge is handed down from generation to generation; 2) this handing down is completed through established linguistic usages. The first proposition is precisely about the inheritance of history, and the second proposition is correctly concerned with the mode of inheritance, that is, through established linguistic usages.

Classics can be evidence of the inheritance of a discourse field. It is correct that most parts of the classics are records of discourse. Take *The Analects* as an example. This classic recorded the dialogues between Confucius and his disciples, which were the speeches in the discourse of their time. Such dialogues have been handed down by written words, which must have been modified and polished. However, the speech situations at that time can be seen on the whole, though they are not the original discourse. (This tells us that *we should make records of spoken discourses by tapes, compact disks, and other equipment for descendants thousands of years from now so that the linguists of their time can have access to them*). Besides, a considerable part, or even a major part, of the classics are not records of speeches but records of thoughts and thinking. Records of thoughts (thinking, cogitation, or speculation) are not the same as those of speeches.

Hegel in his *Aesthetics* asserts that there is no national epic in China. This view was still held by a book of introduction to Chinese literature published several years ago. This is so ridiculous! We do not have to say that some ethnic groups in China have been found to possess their own epics, an important aspect of the original discourse of a nation. Even if such epics had not been discovered yet, we could deduce and find that kind of original discourse, according to the logic, "If a nation obviously has a long history, it is illogical to think that its discourse field has not been passed down".

98 *Language: Mankind's last homestead*

The strongest proof of the inheritance of discourse lies in the *original ancient songs* of histories and stories, heroic and mythical *epics, myths, folk legends*, etc. that nations have *passed down by word of mouth* from generation to generation. For instance, the Miao people had no writings in the past, but they had good knowledge of their ancestors' history. How did this happen? The Miaos passed it down by mouth-to-mouth transmission of their ancient songs, myths, and legends. In order for people to easily inherit these things orally without being ruined, they were made in rhyme, and in prose. The ancient songs, myths, and legends have been passed down from generation to generation for thousands of years and still live among the folk people, which is the evidence of the inheritance of discourse accumulations.

The first evidence for the Miaos is provided by more than twenty-eight books titled *Selective Series of Guizhou Folk Literature* and *Research Series of Guizhou Folk Culture*, which were recently published. They provide us with original records of folklore discourse. According to Duan (1998), one of the books, *Ancient Songs of the Miao People*, with the length of 5000 lines, includes thirteen long songs, such as *Song of the Creation of Heaven and Earth*, *Song of the Origin of Mankind*, *Song of the Deluge*, and *Song of Travelling over Rivers and Lands*, and so on. In addition, this song book includes such songs as *Pangu* (*Pangu* was the creator of the universe in Chinese mythology), *Yangya Shooting the Sun and Moon, the Migration of Chiyou and Miao*, and *Ancient Epoch: The Beginning of the World*. Another book, *Guizhou Long Folk Poems*, is a collection of the mythical epics of the Yi, Shui, and Dong people. Another such book, *Mojing Literature of the Buyi People*, is a collection of ancient mythological songs including mythological epics, historical songs, and story songs.

A second piece of evidence comes from a case in my hometown (Shahu Town, Xiantao City, Hubei Province). In my childhood, I sang folk ballads that had been sung by generations. From whom did the past generations learn those ballads? From grandfathers, grandfathers' grandfathers, great grandfathers' grandfathers... In this way, the very origin can be traced too. I, as a witness, can say for sure that the following ballads or folk songs are not taken from any books but are handed down by spoken words in the local dialect. They *are spoken discourses that directly align with a distant history*. The cruder these ballads are and the more mistakes, errors, and ambiguity are found in pronunciation or spelling, the more credible they are as original discourses. Their roughness, pronunciation errors, and semantic ambiguities indicate that they are unlikely to be works by literati. Before we look at the ballads, some background information is necessary to help avoid confusions and/or misunderstandings. 1) The ballads are kept in their original forms as much as possible, with possible mistakes and ambiguity left unchanged. My own interpretations are put in brackets. 2) The Chinese characters and corresponding pinyin do not accurately represent the dialectal accent of my hometown, which is different from that of Mandarin. Rhymes that go in the local dialect disappear once read aloud in Mandarin. 3) The sign ★ in front of the ballad means that it is sung not only by children but also sung or muttered by adults. 4) The English version for each ballad is only an interpretation of it to the best of our ability.

★天皇皇，地皇皇，我家有个小儿郎，过路君子念一遍，一觉睡到大天光。

[Tiān huánghuáng, di huánghuáng, wǒjiā yǒugè xiǎoérláng, guòlù jūnzǐ niànyībiàn, yījiào shuìdào dàtiānguāng.]

Heaven is vast, and the Earth is vast; the little baby in my family will be asleep till broad daylight (or dawn), if passers-by read the words on the paper.

(As long as a child keeps crying at sleeping time, his parents will write the above words on a yellow paper (burned as money for ghosts to use) and paste it on the street walls. It is believed by the local people that passers-by may read it when they see it, and that the more people read it, the better the child will sleep.)

4月亮哥，跟我走，走到南山买巴篓。巴篓巴，换糍巴。糍巴软，换竹片。竹片尖，杵上天。天又高，好打刀。刀又快，好切菜。菜又甜，好过年 …

[Yuèliànggē, gēnwǒzǒu, zǒudào nánshān mǎibālǒu. Bālǒubā, huàncíbā. Cíbāruǎn, huànzhúpiàn. Zhúpiànjiān, chǔshàngtiān. Tiānyòugāo, hǎodǎdāo. Dāoyòukuài, hǎoqiēcài. Càiyòutián, hǎoguònián…]

Brother Moon, walk with me, to South Mount to buy Balou. Balou Ba, barter for Ciba. Soft Ciba, barter for bamboo strips. Sharp bamboo strips pestle the sky. The sky is high, thus making it easy to fabricate knives. Knives are sharp and cut vegetables easily. Delicious vegetables bring a happy new year…

(巴篓 is a kind of shallow basket weaved with fine peeled wicker, which is rarely seen now. The second 巴 in 巴篓巴, I guess, should be 背 ([bēi] "carry"), and thus, 巴篓巴means that the basket is easy to carry. 糍巴 is cooked pastry made of glutinous rice, square or round in shape. It gets soft when heated, and it can be fried or roasted.)

★背砣砣，换酒喝。酒冷了，换茶喝。茶冷了，把尿你喝。

[Bèituótuó, huànjiǔhē. Jiǔlěngle, huàncháhē. Chálěngle, bǎniàonǐhē.]

Carry Tuotuo to exchange for some liquor to drink. When the liquor gets cold, exchange it for a cup of tea. When the tea gets cold, I give you some urine to drink.

(It is not clear whether Tuotuo refers to a grind mound or a weight of a steelyard.)

牵杆杆，卖枣枣，卖到河那边狗子咬。狗子狗子你不咬，买个粑粑你过早。

[Qiāngāngān, màizǎozǎo, màidào hénàbiān gǒuziyǎo. Gǒuzi gǒuzi nǐbùyǎo, mǎigèbābā nǐguòzǎo.]

100   *Language: Mankind's last homestead*

Holding a stick, I'm selling dates. When I arrive at the other side of the river, a dog barks at me. Dog, dog don't bite me; I'll buy you some cooked pastry for your breakfast.

三岁的娃，会推磨，推的粉子磨不过，做的粑粑甜不过。婆婆吃了两三个，半夜起来摸茶喝，炊子撞了前脑壳，门闩撞了后脑壳。嚷的嚷，喊的喊，婆婆到了田中间。

[Sānsuìdewá, huìtuīmó, tuīdefěnzi mòbuguò, zuòdebābā tiánbùguò. Pópo chīle liǎngsāngè, bànyèqǐlái mōcháhē, chuīzi zhuàngle qiánnǎoké, ménshuān zhuàngle hòunǎoké. Rǎngderǎng, hǎndehǎn, pópo dàole tiánzhōngjiān.]

A three-year-old boy can push the grinder, the rice powder is too coarse, but the cooked pastry made of it is very sweet. Grandma ate two or three pieces. In the midnight, she got up in the darkness, looking for some tea to drink. Her forehead bumped against a kitchen pot and the back of her head bumped against the bolt of the door. People yelling and crying, Grandma was in the middle of the field.

(In the local dialect, 个 is pronounced as guò, 喝 as huō, so that they rhyme with 磨 and过. Likewise, 间 is pronounced as gān so that it rhymes with 喊. The last sentence in the song implies grandma died and got buried in the field.)

★地米菜，蒸蒸菜，好吃婆娘来碗来。

[Dìmǐcài, zhēngzhēngcài, hàochī póniáng láiwǎnlái.]

Shepherd's purse makes a dish when steamed; an edacious woman eats a bowl of it.

(地米菜is the local term for wild shepherd's purse. In old days, it was used for food in China in the early spring, which may witness food shortage between two harvests.)

摇摆手，家家的走。搭洋船，下汉口，搭不到洋船步路走。

[Yáobǎishǒu, jiājiādezǒu. Dāyángchuán, xiàhànkǒu, dābùdào yángchuán bùlùzǒu.]

Waving hands, go to Grandma's home. Take a steamboat to Hankou. Just walk all the way to it if you fail to catch a steamboat.

(In the local dialect, 家家is pronounced as gāga, referring to the maternal grandmother. Steamboats were named 洋船 (literally, "foreign boats") because they were made by foreign/imported techniques.)

★沙湖沔阳州，十年九不收。要是收一年，狗子不吃糯米粥。

[Shāhú miǎnyángzhōu, shínián jiǔbùshōu. Yàoshi shōuyīnián, gǒuzi bùchī nuòmǐzhōu.]

Shahu, Mianyang County, does not harvest nine years out of ten. If there is one year of harvest, the dogs do not eat glutinous rice porridge.

From the above songs, we can see some contextual or background information for the rural discourse in Shahu Town, Xiantao City, Hubei Province

Language: Mankind's last homestead 101

before 1949. First, there was language worship (as shown by the first song). Words were used to expel evils and ghosts and give children peace and safety. Placards with such words gave the whole town a somewhat mysterious and horrifying atmosphere. The wordings of the time, the most typical of which are 糍粑 [cíbā] and 过年 [guònián], are not much different from those of today (at the time this book is being written, pressed, and marketed). The grandmother on the father's side is still called 婆婆 [pópo] and the maternal grandmother is still called 家家 [gaga]; a kind of cooking pot is still called 炊子 [chuīzi] instead of 炊壶 [chuīhú] in Mandarin Chinese. Likewise, shepherd's purse is still called 地米菜 ([dìmǐcài] literally, "field rice vege-table"). However, things have changed with a few expressions. For example, since Shahu residents do not use 巴篓 [bālǒu] baskets any more, the word for such baskets is no longer heard. Mandarin 过春节 ([guòchūnjié] "to cele-brate the Spring Festival") is used more often than 过年 [guònián] when they talk about celebrating the Lunar New Year. Now no one would use ballads, such as the first one, to treat the illness of their children, which is a kind of progress. Besides, a steamboat is no longer called 洋船 ([yángchuán] "for-eign boat"). (Unfortunately, boats can no longer run along the Tongshun River, because several dams have been built on it.) Furthermore, no one calls Shahu Town Mianyang County any more. Third, children's songs can best reflect the traditional moral values of a nation. If adults believe that a cer-tain virtue must be inherited, they will hand it down in children's songs. For example, a three-year-old boy was said to push a grinder to grind rice into powder and make cooked pastry for his grandmother to show filial piety. Fourth, in folk songs, we can see local social and economic changes and developments. The last ballad was one of the most widely circulated ballads through "Three Bar Drums", a kind of folk opera. It was still sung occasion-ally by some elderly people inside and outside the province before the local water conservancy facilities removed the floods in the 1970s and 1980s. The ballad indicates that there were once frequent floods in these areas, but the soil was fertile and rich in production. At that time, the productive force of Jianghan Plain in Hubei Province (which is precisely the geographical infor-mation revealed by the original ballad: 搭洋船，下汉口, to take a steamboat to Hankou) was nothing more than going to Nanshan to buy baskets and cooked rice pastry, to trade for bamboo strips, to smith knives, and to have delicious vegetables for a happy New Year, which all displayed a picture of agricultural life. The most enjoyable treat of modern civilization was nothing but boarding a little steamboat to Hankou, but failure to catch a little steam-boat led to distress and inconvenience (just walk all the way to it if you fail to catch a steamboat). However, the production activities of Shahu Town people are much more than those things. The historical value of ballads becomes apparent over the comparison between the two time periods. As for commercial transportation, now there are numerous people going to Hankou to do business every day. Unfortunately, the Tongshun River where ships could travel to Wuhan is no longer navigable for boats or ships. What is

102 *Language: Mankind's last homestead*

even more serious is that if no efficient measures are taken, the Tongshun River itself will disappear. If that happens, we will ruin our descendants' jobs and destroy their happiness. How can we continue to inherit and sing such enchanting, heart-warming songs as 摇摆手，家家的走 ("Waving hands, go to Grandma's home")? Fifth, genuine folk songs passed down by word of mouth are always full of a sense of humor, which is the best ingredient of a nation's culture. Humor can be seen in such ballads as "When the tea gets cold, I give you some urine to drink", "Dog, Dog, don't bite me; I'll buy you some cooked pastry for your breakfast", "Shepherd's purse makes a dish when steamed; an edacious woman eats a bowl of it". In fact, the shepherd's purse dish is so delicious that, I am afraid, everyone who sees it would like to be an "edacious woman". Sixth, the most gratifying thing is that the phonetic system that kept the history is still being handed down and down. The children in my hometown are still singing such sweet songs as "Brother Moon, walk with me". The fact that *a discourse filed of the remote past has been successfully passed down is of great importance because it is a sign that history is still being passed down.* If the songs were no longer handed down by word of mouth, it would be a very serious matter. The reason why I repeatedly emphasize the importance of inheritance by word of mouth is that written records of things often fail to stay faithful to their original states. You have to know that those children's songs and ballads that have been modified (and should be regarded as "destroyed") by the literati will not be accepted by grandmothers, mothers, and elder sisters (women). The reason is that the modification by the literati often erased the original and lively flavor. That is to say, the essence of history is modified away. The ballads and children's songs that children can sing in Shahu Town, as long as you check, have been taught orally by grandmothers, mothers, and older sisters (women). Here is an important fact: Ballads are taught by women. Of course, the final determinant of the value of these ballads and songs is that children love to sing. The key to children's love is that these songs must be fun and the rhymes must be catchy. Therefore, the following argument that appears to be irrelevant on the surface is in line with the law: *To enliven children's songs is to let women sing them.* The same is true of ballads: *To enliven ballads is to let women sing them.* The ballads that seem to be sung together by both men and women are actually taught by women. This fact is not complicated. The effects of the impeccable, steady, and modest kind of things written in the books, if they are not taught by word of mouth, will be more or less discounted. Moreover, I dare say that it is absolutely useless for the literati to write new children's songs and new ballads with their own wishful thinking. Children's songs and ballads of any kind, such as ancient songs (historical songs and story songs), epic poems (heroic epic and mythical epic), myths, folklore, and so on, *must appear naturally among people, accumulated and inherited by word of mouth from generation to generation.* Any songs written under the guidance of "the main theme" advocated by the government will be futile, no matter how good

Language: Mankind's last homestead 103

the subjective wishes are. The national epics in the world and some ethnic epics in China are all preserved by word of mouth. Written records are all the work of later literati. The Indian *Veda* is a timeless classic inherited by word of mouth (Jin, 1995). The undistorted records are certainly meritorious and positive. However, the records that have been modified selectively are more likely to have the most real things in the history "modified" away.

A third piece of evidence comes from this fact: In some places (such as the remote mountain areas inhabited by ethnic minorities) and communities, speech texts (the texts that record speech) are still bound to the context of cultural transmission by spoken words, or, in other words, cannot be interpreted in isolation from their ritual backgrounds.

Every ethnic group has some form of speech texts, such as myths, epochs, and stories, in fixed procedural pattern, that are passed down from one generation to the next in the form of performances like talk-and-sing arts, chants, or panegyrics. For this very reason, these activities are history *per se*. During my childhood in Shahu Town of Xiantao City, Hubei Province, I listened to the "virtue-story-telling", quite popular in the Jianghan Plain. This performance art sang out the story texts in melodies very pleasant to the ear, persuading people to do good deeds and accumulate virtues. Some story-tellers practiced the virtue stories so much that they could sing them out with the script put aside, achieving a better artistic effect, moving the audience to tears. Again, when a ritual was enacted to save the soul of a dead person from purgatory, the merits and virtues in the whole life of the dead were presented in the form of telling and singing all along the spectacular Buddhist service or Daoist rite. In modern days, a funeral ceremony is held instead. The ritual remains but has varied; the chanting is less often a part. Someone would now read a drafted text that gives an official comment on the life of the dead, but the emotional expressions that should have been most significant are reduced. The only non-official funeral ceremony I have ever attended was that for my eldest brother. No one of any official rank was there to read a memorial speech, yet the official procedure was transplanted with one of his former friends reading a pre-drafted memorial speech on the spot. That was a true friend's speech, an accurate and passionate presentation of the detailed life-story, filled with true and touching feelings, everyone present being so moved that they sobbed, face in hands, or cried loudly, bathed in tears. Similar contents of this kind of speech have been repeated year after year and generation after generation since the primordial time. For today's people, these oral texts are hard to interpret, primarily because the situations that backed them up – rituals such as pleading for rain, praying to Buddha or Heaven, conducting Daoist rites, a man marrying a woman into his family or a woman being married off, worshipping the ancestry, a mourning ceremony for the soul of the dead – no longer reoccur and so the procedural activities attached to these situations have become rare or lost. However, these procedural activities were once true historical occurrences. Some of them

104 *Language: Mankind's last homestead*

remain intact still. In the out-of-the-way mountain areas or isolated regions inhabited by ethnic minority groups, performances of this kind (tell-and-sing arts, chants, or panegyrics) are as popular as they were before. They form an "oral history" with unique characteristics. How many of these primitive art forms of tell-and-sing arts, chants, or panegyrics will survive and go down to posterity, with the change of time and the accelerating urbanization of rural areas? This question is hard to answer. The reason why I sigh my worries about the fate of these arts in the future is that they have been vivid records of how people once really lived.

The birth and growth of discourse fields are natural, cumulative from generation to generation, and, as a norm, orally imparted. Seen from the above-described activities and events, we can say that it is the discourse field that keeps history. The inheritance of a discourse field is the inheritance of history.

Being the crystallization of discourse fields, words keep history. *Investigation into words is thus investigation into history. This is what we call the fossil function of words.* The supporting facts to be discussed below are taken from G. Qian (1986).

Frequently one witnesses the renewed use of obsolete words in newspapers, broadcasts, and television in Guangzhou. They look like new coinage, but are not. Hence, the fossil metaphor I am using; these resurgent words function much like fossils. As I pointed out earlier in this section, mankind relies on three things for a direct dialog with his own past: Archeological findings, fossils, and language (both speech and writing). Fossils offer definitive explanatory evidence for the ancient histories of material civilization and nature, even though the excavation of valuable fossils may have sometimes occurred by chance. There is a surprising similarity between fossils and language in their role as historical testimonies.

The need to address the reemerging things that once were in the past brings about the resurgence of some words that have already become obsolete. Around 1990, in cities of Guangzhou, Shanghai, Hong Kong, Macao, and Shenzhen, people began to notice the reuse of obsolete words, such as 经纪人 ([jīngjìrén] "broker"), 股民 ([gǔmín] "stockholder"), and 顶上 ([dǐngshàng] "best") (these words are often heard and are well known nowadays). Of the three, the first two are familiar to all; what we need to address is the third word, dǐngshàng, heard in Guangzhou. This word is formed on the analogy of 顶好 ([dǐnghǎo] literally "top-good", "best"), which was no longer in use after the 1950s in mainland China. The word had appeared in the phrase 顶上的补喉糖片 ([dǐngshàngde bǔhóutángpiàn] "Best sugar-coated tablets for nurturing throats") by Yutang Lin (who migrated to the United States in 1936 and finally settled down in Taiwan in 1966) in his essay, *On My Quitting Smoking*. Currently, this word is used in Guangdong, as in 顶上泰国香米 ([dǐngshàng tàiguó xiāngmǐ] "Best Thai fragrant rice"; printed on the rice package).

These words that have come back to life are living fossils. Take 经纪人 ("broker"), for example.

Before 1949: 经纪人 in use
///

(No 经纪人 in use)

///
After 1990: 经纪人 in use

Between 1949 and 1990 there was a gap of around forty years when the word was not seen in use. What is the reason for this long absence? Let's suppose three hundred years from now someone finds that this word was absent from speech for forty years, but was widely used before 1949, only to be reused on a large scale after 1990. It is highly likely that the people then would immediately associate this gap with the social history of the forty years. With this association, many interesting questions would crop up. The forty-year gap occurred exactly during the period of a planned economy. There was no place for professionals, such as brokers or drummers (salesmen to the door) in a planned economy, but such professionals were just indispensable in the market economy that has been in place since the 1990s. A glimpse at the economy from the angle of words is a glimpse at the historical and the social vicissitudes. The same is also the case with the word "stockholder". Such revived words play the role of fossils because they once "died". Having "died" and then become resurrected again, these words are endowed with high value for research.

Some new expressions (e.g., 群死群伤 ([qúnsǐqúnshāng] "large group casualty") are coined and may disappear in the future. They can then be regarded as fossils too. For instance, we can assume there is a gap in time before such new expressions come to the scene. And after they begin to be used, they may be used repeatedly for a short or long time. Whatever the case, they live through, or are a constant throughout, a certain period of time. But after this time period, there will be another gap. Between the two temporal gaps is the time when they are in active use, which makes it meaningful to inquire into them. These new words may fade out along with the disappearance of the things they represent. It is exactly for this possibility of disappearance that words acquire their fossil function. If they are gone for good, never to return, people would look into the reason why this is the case; and if some words are absent for some time and resurface in use again, people would also ask why this is the case. Both these situations constitute the fossil function of words.

Now let's look at the example of 群死群伤 ("large group casualty").

(No 群死群伤 in use)
///

Shortly before the Spring Festival of 1994 to X: 群死群伤 in use

///
(No 群死群伤 in use)

106 *Language: Mankind's last homestead*

In the above figure, the X means the unknown year that will witness the absence of the expression.

Some years later when people look back, they may find that 群死群伤 ("large group casualty") is prevalently used between 1994 to a certain year (Year X), and that it was not used before 1994 and after Year X. This is a case opposite to that of 经纪人 ("broker"). Why this is the case would certainly be the question raised. Various experts may find something interesting to their respective disciplines. An economist could reason that with the deepening of the reform and opening up of China, there was a further development of the economy, resulting in acceleration of urbanization and the need for rural labor on the market. For this reason, peasant workers from the hinterland provinces swarmed to Guangdong for job opportunities. At the time of the Spring Festival, all these workers had to hurry back home for their family reunions, which caused a crowded traffic and an insufficient public transportation capacity, leading to fatal road accidents. A transportation expert, on the other hand, may conclude that the traffic during this period was a bottleneck, handicapping passenger transportation, and that because of a serious lack of adequate transportation capacity, some avaricious bus-owners, for the sake of profit, must have grossly overloaded their buses and/or been driving dangerously long hours without needed rest, resulting in accidents with a large number of casualties. Likewise, a legal expert may be convinced that the urbanization process could not be stopped at the time and employment laws were lacking or inadequate, while at the same time Western China was underdeveloped and hence lacked employment opportunities (and indeed there was no relevant state policy in favor of Western China). When no law was decreed to regulate the distribution of the labor force, the population had no alternative but to flood its way to the coastal cities. The economist may further realize that the then rural policies were not working so the difficulties of the countryside, the peasant, and agriculture remained largely unimproved too. With no implementation of appropriate and effective economic policies to protect them, the peasants were forced to abandon farming for employment in manufacturing and other businesses in large cities. Sociologists may come up with interesting findings that the Chinese people paid too high a cost for their Spring Festival reunions, since they, after a whole year of hardworking, needed to rush in haste back home for the reunion dinner on the eve of Chinese Lunar New Year, in spite of the dangers awaiting to happen around the Spring Festival thanks to a crowded and inadequate traffic system. In other words, the overwhelmed transport capacity was the reason behind the large group casualties. Those who study culture, however, may concentrate on the great attractive power of the Spring Festival reunion in China and the magnetic force of the family as a cell of the society. Does this diversity of multi-dimensional research findings show that the new coinage does function powerfully as a living fossil?

The living-fossil function of words can be compared to fossils in nature, which provide us with a chance to know the conditions of climate, terrain,

Language: Mankind's last homestead 107

and fauna and flora of many years ago. In the same way we can, by examining words in use, obtain an understanding of the conditions of the productive capacity, the relationships involved in production, culture, and the technologies of the human society in the past.

If a word is always active, being used all the time, and therefore has a stable meaning, then it is impossible for it to have any culture-loaded usage that ever sank into oblivion. In the language of every nation, there are in use such stable words, which we cannot expect to have fossil functions.[5]

To examine the words of a discourse field is to inquire into history.

3.1.2.5 A summary

We have elaborated that mankind lives in discourse fields in four perspectives: 1) That listening and saying constitute a primary form of mankind's living in the world; that *what is said* is meaningful only in the dynamic context in which it is being said; 2) that a super discourse field exists, even before one speaks, and it is of greater importance than the specific discourse field in which one speaks, for it postulates a matrix discourse field; and 3) that the aphorisms that a nation has are in fact its people's mode (paradigm) of living. Besides, it is the discourse field that keeps record of history, which is made possible by and in language with its sound system (primary) and writing system (secondary). The inheritance of a discourse field is the inheritance of history as the words in the former are the record of the latter.

What we have shown in the discussion of the most basic form of human existence is that we live in language and in discourse fields. Language is the last homestead of human beings, as is shown by history and by our present being.

About mankind's being living in discourse fields, one more word needs to be said. Zen Buddhism has been reiterating this warning: "In sayings, one dies; beyond sayings, one lives" or "One may demise under a saying". *"To demise under a saying" is a hazard hidden in the discourse field, a danger of living in the discourse field.* For this reason, we have in particular talked about the rectification and checking mechanisms of the discourse field. We do so because, first, no discourse field of any historical age can avoid being infiltrated by certain speeches that temporarily hide, deviate from, or even distort the truth, and second, even the discourses that are correct or that represent objective truth can go nowhere if one adheres solely to their literal meanings. About this, Zhongshu Qian made the following comment.

> Those formulaic clichés (such as 门户开放 ([ménhùkāifàng] "open-door"), 走向世界 ([zǒuxiàng shìjiè] "heading onto the world arena") and so on) are quite conducive to memory, for, as headlines or slogans, they stay within easy reach and make smooth reading. However, the progress of history does not seem to take care of the convenience of historians by pushing ahead in a straightforward and programmatic fashion. In our daily life, both the doors and windows can be wide-open sometimes, or

108 *Language: Mankind's last homestead*

the windows are wide-open or half-open but the doors are closed, or both the doors and windows are closed with just a crack or a key-hole to let in a bit of air. When both are wide-open, the old and the weak cannot expect to be immune from getting a cold; but if both are closed tight, the house turns out over-stifling with too many inhabitants in it; however, if both are half-open, the effect might well be a mere strike of pose, just like a male and a female going dating for the first time.

(Z. Qian, 1997, p. 461)

I quote Zhongshu Qian here just to stress that it is not a must to insist rigidly on the literal meaning of the so-called aphorisms, or to "carry it out even when it is not understood". Things go astray when compliance is blind.

3.2 Having to live in language

3.2.1 Language as a kind of life activity

When we say that language is itself a kind of life activity, the word "language" denotes "verbal behavior". In the eyes of a biologist, human beings exist as flesh-and-blood entities. In the eyes of a philosopher, practice (behavior) is the mode of human existence, which results in both material and spiritual products. Both kinds of products can exist independently of human beings, but the human potential can be reflected from their existence.

Nevertheless, existence is expressed through language in multifarious ways (X. Zhang, 1996). That is to say, existence is not something concrete that can be held in grip but is expressed through language. Language exists concurrently with the visible flesh-and-blood beings, and for this reason it can be regarded as the immediate way of human existence. Human beings are inseparable from language; rather, they dwell in it. It is because language (after it was created) exists prior to any human individuals that language acquisition is rendered possible. Children can learn to speak without teachers there to teach them because an ocean of language has already been there. To be born into the world is to be born into the ocean of language.

The only reason for claiming that language is the immediate way of human existence is that language itself is a kind of human life activity. To observe verbal behaviors is to observe human life activities. For this point, much evidence can be seen in *Esthetic Linguistics* (G. Qian, 1993, pp. 62–72). The study of language is thus the study of human beings themselves. What follows is a brief summary of the evidence I provided in *Esthetic Linguistics* so that the readers may quickly gain a gist of the main ideas.

Verbal behavior itself is a kind of human life activity. This can be witnessed in mankind's hearing and seeing. What is audible (or the audible expression) is the voicing pattern (including the speech sound, the breath power, and the tone of utterance) that keeps a concerted pace with the speaker's physiological rhythm and changes of emotion. This is a state of life. What

Language: Mankind's last homestead 109

are visible (or the visible expression) are the speaker's facial expressions and postures that stay in harmony with the act of speaking. Facial expressions and postures are thus the speaker's state of life that co-occurs with his/her speaking.

The voicing pattern has the following features. First, it is individual-unique, varying from person to person. Second, if a sentence is coupled with opposite voicing patterns, there will be opposite interpretations of its meaning. Likewise, a sentence produced with different voicing patterns conveys different meanings. Besides, an utterance is inseparable from its audible expressions and visible expressions. When the speaker dies, their speaking ceases and their voicing pattern is gone as well.

Facial expressions and postures are visible aspects of an utterance. Facial expressions and postures can be independent of language, for they are present even while one is not speaking; but speaking cannot go without facial expressions and postures, i.e., one can never speak without facial expressions and postures.

Physiological disharmony in one's body leads to the weakening of his voicing pattern, while physiological harmony leads to the strengthening of it. Consequently, the accordance of the phonetic sounds, intonation, and breath power with the articulated utterance reflects in turn physiological harmony. In the final analysis, the esthetic effect of language should be a part of the effect of harmonious human life, for the esthetic choice-making at every level of language goes in accordance with the harmony of life.

That concludes our brief review. What follows is my latest finding.

Zhongshu Qian makes some comments on the voicing pattern. According to him,

> Breathing (of air) is the rhythm flowing within the human body, such as the so-called "implicit charm of *qi* (air, vitality) movement". Air pressure is a technical term in physics, while (air) breathing is a parable of life, the former being extrovert and the latter introvert.
>
> (Z. Qian, 1997, p. 403)

Z. Qian does not say what he calls breathing is the voicing pattern contained in an utterance. But what he calls breathing is exactly what I call the voicing pattern in *Esthetic Linguistics* (G. Qian, 1993). In *Esthetic Linguistics*, it is elaborated that the voicing pattern is a state of human life inherent in speech (living people's speaking acts), while Z. Qian says that breathing is the rhythm flowing within the human body, an implicit charm of *qi* movement, a parable of life and an introvert being. These two sayings are surely parallel. When arguing that a writer's writing style tells who the writer is, Z. Qian points out,

> R. de Gourmont thinks that a piece of writing is a physiological product (*un produit physiologique*), which comes under the influence of health, diet, housing, and other life functions. A piece of writing reflects the

110 *Language: Mankind's last homestead*

writer's state of life. Gourmont only attempts to explain the writing style in terms of the writer's physiology, which he deems to be beyond or behind the style, but our literary critique claims outright that the style has in itself various functions and structures of life, such as breathing, bone, spirit and pulse.

(Z. Qian, 1997, p. 394)

Of course, "writing style" and speech are not the same thing, but the two are obviously commensurable. A piece of writing reflects the writer's state of life; speaking reflects the speaker's state of life even more thoroughly. Speaking involves the internal movement of *qi*, the skeletal framing and the spiritual pulsing. Take Yusheng Luo,[6] for instance. At the age of 83 (when she gave a performance on China Central TV in 1998), she still spoke in a resonantly booming voice and drawled with a delicate lingering sound. Isn't this a phenomenon of life to the core? That "a piece of writing reflects the writer's state of life" and that "breathing is the rhythm flowing within the human body, the implicit charm of *qi* movement and the parable of life" work together, supporting the claim that language is a form of human existence. What follows are two more cases supporting this claim, which were not mentioned in *Esthetic Linguistics* (G. Qian, 1993).

Zhongshu Qian says,

The eye is the window to the mind. We see what is outside and let others see what is inside us meanwhile. The eye follows often the way the mind turns, which is why Mencius has commented that "There is no better way to tell a person than reading his eyes". The lovers in M. Maeterlinck's drama are not allowed to close the eyes when they kiss, in order that one can see how much of the kiss wells up to the lips from deep in the other's heart. This is also the reason why when we talk with a man wearing sunglasses, we feel it hard to catch his intention, as if he were behind a mask.

(Z. Qian, 1997, p. 16)

The speaker veils up, by wearing sunglasses, the most animated part of his facial expressions and postures, and, with it, his way of existence is obscured and his flow of life hidden from view. As the result, no one can catch his intention.

The other case is a story told by Yingtai Long (1996, p. 53). One night in Austria, Long read aloud her own writing in German. At the end, the audience came up to shake hands with her one after another. A middle-aged German woman looked fixedly at her and said: "I've been looking at your eyes. When you were speaking, I felt so familiar with your eye expression, which was like that of us Europeans. Have you been living in Europe for long?" About this experience, Yingtai Long writes,

Language: Mankind's last homestead 111

I can clearly perceive from their eye movement whether what radiates is a ridicule or an appreciation, humor or sarcasm ... contempt or fondness, suspicion or affirmation. I can understand the most delicate jokes they tell and detect their weariness that they attempt to gloss over. If the eye expression is a language, and yes it is, then clearly I have been, without my knowing it, using the European eye expression to communicate with them. ... And there is the body language, or how we pose and behave ourselves. As a Chinese who has lived in the West for nearly two decades, I am already very different from the one who has not been affected by any experiences in the West in our manners of walking, sitting, gestures for expressing agreement or disagreement, physical distance habitually kept in conversation, on-the-spot decision to shake hands or to embrace at farewell bidding ... The German woman with her keen observation felt a "familiarity" in me, because I communicated with her that night in the eye expression and body language of Europeans.

(1996, p. 53)

This is a good story indeed. It may help many outsiders in an alien land (a foreign country, or even a dialectal region totally different from one's own) understand why on earth they do not have any speech power. Without a relevant life state of verbal behavior, one would have virtually lost language, in spite of the ability to use blunt words and sentences in dialogs. *For a human being, the loss of language means the loss of oneself, the loss of what one is.* To have lost language is to be ousted, for the invisible is usually neglected.

Therefore, we declare that the life state of speech *per se* is the immediate reality, the direct way, of existence of mankind, based on which we further claim that *to study language is to study human beings themselves.* One may as well come up to say "People live just for pleasures all their life"; or, conversely, "People live to suffer all their life". In fact, however, one, throughout his life, does much more speaking than having pleasures or sufferings. Leshan Dong says in his memory of Ningkun Wu,

So I appreciate especially what he (Ningkun Wu) says in the following well-known saying by Caesar the Great[7]: "I came, I suffered, I survived." This is a proclamation full of pride, applicable in general to the Chinese intellectuals of this generation who have gone through too many sufferings but survived by virtue of this spirit.

(Dong, 1994, p. 103)

Nevertheless, before "I came", there should be "I say" – "I say: I came, I suffered, I survived". That is to say, verbal behavior is one of the most important human behaviors. When human beings themselves become the object for study, the act of speaking is of course one of the most important research projects.

112   *Language: Mankind's last homestead*

What you say and what you write are the material forms of personal quality or the state of life. Speeches reflect who the speaker is, and writings reflect who the writer is. Likewise, we can judge an individual by what he says or writes. Both tell the relationship between language and the state of human life. Language is the most true-to-life record of an individual's form of living and the most typical stamp of his/her life. Of course, in the process of the materialization, there may be certain false facial expressions. Speakers or writers may plot to conceal themselves, ending up in the phenomena of "not speaking one's mind" or "writing the contrary of what one means". Such cases can be found everywhere, but they are not worth listing here. For the sake of certain interest or purpose, the oral or written speech one offers to the society and the same one living in it may not be in coherence. To disguise oneself by verbal behavior is also one of the functions of language.

During the Cultural Revolution in China, a Japanese newspaper published a piece of news that all the 120 workers in a factory in China were slaughtered, which was appalling indeed. Checking the original Chinese report, however, one found that it was the workers who rose up in rebellion, which the reporter described by using the then prevalent phrase of 杀出来了 ([shā chūláile] "killing the way out"). The incompetent Japanese translator failed to realize that the word 杀 ([shā] "kill") can be used in the Chinese language to mean making or forcing one's way out. A Japanese once said, "If Japanese people don't regard China as a society with a different culture, the Chinese language may impede their understanding of China" (cited in Dai, 1996, p. 108). This probably explains why the writer who has quoted the above story asks: How do the Chinese talk? The "killing the way out" mentioned above is not the only phrase of this nature. The Chinese speak with a choking smell of gunpower, as if they were all over-charged with it. Even a very common thing or a trivially significant event can be talked about in the terms of war. Problems must be "combated"; there are "the front and rear areas, the battlefront and the protracted warfare" in working against a flood; a university president has the "bearing of an army general"; to realize the four modernizations is a "new Long March"; someone's revealing a seamy side can have done a "blood-shedding piercing"; "struggle" hard for one hundred days to complete the construction of a road; "fight" a good "battle" in doing a job (such as studying for a college entrance examination); one should cast away the burden of worries in order to "go to the battlefront with a light pack"; the exhaustion of something (like a box of instant noodles being used up) can be called "running out of ammunition and food supplies"; putting everything one has into overcoming adversity is to "fight with one's back to the river"; someone shying away from something (such as from drinking liquor) is an "army deserter" or is said to "desert his ranks in the battlefront"; being too timid to show up before a big crowd is to be "battle-shy"; a reckless and desperate action is to "go into battle stripped to the waist"; to do something bravely or brazenly (such as cutting the line when picking up a meal in the cafeteria) can be mocked as "charging into the enemy lines"; to confront

Language: Mankind's last homestead 113

someone throughout is to "fight a bloody battle to the end"... and so on and so forth; it is very hard to put in a nutshell.

Such a way of speaking among the Chinese has probably to do with a rather long history of turbulences they have experienced (from the wars and massacres in the days of old to the large-scale armed violence during the so-called Cultural Revolution in contemporary times: Uprisings and rebellions, resistances against foreign aggressions, and internal feuds). This underlies the fact that *the study on how the Chinese talk is none other than the study on their state of survival and their way of existence*. Isn't it true that the very real state of survival, the way of existence, of the Chinese people has its embodied presence in such lavish use of terms, smacking of war, as "killing the way out"?

3.2.2 Language as the last fingerprint and heritage of an ethnic group

3.2.2.1 Religion and language in ethnic identity

Religion or language: Which should be given precedence as the marker of ethnic identity? For the Jews, it seems that religion takes precedence; for the Chinese, vice versa.

L. Hou (2001, p. 95) points out that the Jews have been "rootless" through thousands of years, except hundreds of years of transitory settlement since their arrival at Canaan from Exodus. When the Roman legions burned down the Second Temple in 70 AD, most Jewish people were deprived of their homeland and dispersed as diaspora. Only in their memory survived such landscape icons like the Holy Temple and the Mount of Zion, which embody their home for the soul. From 70 AD onwards, Jewish people have been dispersed around the world (e.g., in Henan, China) until the founding of Israel in 1948. Though their homeland is far away, their mother tongue lost, even their complexion adapted, they stand firm as the vulnerable amid the ordeals of survival and retain their ethnic character against the corrosion of mainstream culture. They survive today on an irreplaceable strength – Judaism, their religion. The Jewish people celebrate abundant religious holidays: New Moon, Passover, Unleavened Bread, Sacrifice of First-fruits, Pentecost, Trumpets, Atonement, Tabernacles, Dedication, Purim, Sabbath, Jubilee, etc. In the absence of a mother tongue, on what ground do they identify themselves as Jews and then return to Jerusalem for reclaiming sovereignty? And on what ground are they identified as Jews? In the absence of a mother tongue, the only testimony is their religious faith: "These are our festivals". Complexion is not a credible marker for ethnic identification, as never before. In the case of the Jews, while their mother tongue died out, their religion stood out. Similarly, the Hui people in China, although they lost track of their ancestors' mother tongue – Arabian or Persian – they adhere to the Muslim faith, Islam (an imam who is illiterate of Chinese characters is literate of Arabian and Persian). In this sense, we identify them as the Hui.

114   *Language: Mankind's last homestead*

An opposite case is found in China (in specific, among the Han people). It is true to a large extent that pre-1949 China adopted Buddhism as its national religion. But town folks historically neither held regular Buddhist events widely, nor followed any Buddhist holidays. In my large family around 1939, for instance, my grandmother was the only committed Buddhist follower. She burned ritual incense and went fasting on the first and fifteenth day of every lunar month. But she did it in hopes of longevity (i.e., out of a utilitarian motive, yet ignorant of what makes Buddhism as it is). In the countryside of Shahu Town in Xiantao City of Hubei province, Buddhist events were relatively popular, as evidenced by monastery or temple visits to burn incense and offer prayers. Nonetheless, there were no widely recognized Buddhist holidays. Chinese people implore the Goddess of Mercy (Guanyin) only in foul weather (like childlessness, peril, illness, or poverty); in fair weather, they turn away (or probably return with votive offerings if their prayers for progeny and power have been fulfilled). Being so pragmatic and utilitarian, even to the point of losing one's integrity (so ungrateful for the favors bestowed), such religious acts, in the strict sense, display no piety at all. He who holds faith as it is, not for favor, and who holds it even when gods help not, is pious indeed. For Chinese, the days of fasting are not meant to be the celebration of religious holidays. None of their favorite holidays such as Chinese Spring Festival, Lantern Festival, Tomb-sweeping Day, Dragon Boat Festival, Mid-autumn Festival, Senior's Day, etc. is religious. Although religious freedom has been proclaimed in the Chinese constitution since 1949, god-worshipping has not been popularized among people nationwide (despite sporadic reverences since the reform and opening up), and no religious holidays have ever been observed. However, nobody is blind to the existence and growth of the Han people. Their national identity is solely marked by the Chinese language, spoken and written, instead of by their complexion, which helps little in identifying the Han people from Japanese due to their close resemblance in complexion and build. In the case of the Chinese, it is the mother tongue that outshines religion as being a more important characteristic.

One single contrast between the Jews and the Chinese cannot adequately respond to the question, that is: Which should be the primary marker of ethnic identity, religion or language? This question remains to be answered in the future after *observing how language adapts itself during the tug-of-war between the so-called globalization and the preservation of local distinctions.* The process of ethnic identification involves an issue far more intricate than language and religion, namely the volition and decision of the target community to be identified.

Generally speaking, *given the means of communication and transportation we have now and will have in the near future, the most vital norms for ethnic identification are likely linguistic and paralinguistic features.*

At present, the features of an ethnic group (not a nation, but an ethnic group in a nation) become rather indistinguishable and unnoticeable. All the features once having been deemed unique may lose their uniqueness and

Language: Mankind's last homestead 115

distinction. Advances in technology bring the world and ethnic communities closer. Today, it is beyond the reach of any single nation, let alone any single ethnic group, to build the information highway or to tackle problems such as drug trafficking, environmental pollution (nuclear pollution, water pollution, air pollution), natural disasters (El Niño, anti-El Niño, etc.), and international corporation. Modern civilization has been sweeping across the world – jeans everywhere, Coca-Cola everywhere, farmers in Western dresses (probably without matching leather shoes), and even the remotest village has accessibility to six TV channels and direct calling. When this happens, what is the highly unique look and life style by which your ethnic group can be identified by outsiders? In other words, the rise of technology, i.e., the invention of the train, ship, automobile, plane, telephone, telegraph, camera, movie, television, fax, and information highway, comes to blur ethnic boundaries and boost ethnic assimilation. This proposition reveals a backward inference that, like arguing in opposite terms, for the aboriginals and ethnic groups on every continent, their uniqueness emanates right from the "blocks". What has "blocked" them from each other? The gap in information and transportation tops the list of blocks. Other blocks, be they gaps left by remote land or high mountains or vast oceans, stand insignificant compared with the gaps left by the poor conditions of information and transportation. Once information and transportation improve to pave the way for ethnic assimilation, the assimilation will elbow forward and be unstoppable.

The idea that ethnic assimilation follows readily from the improvement of information and transportation has been attested by our fieldwork (conducted by my student Yongshou Huo and me). Parts of our fieldwork notes are included below.

On August 17, 2001, we were invited to a real Mosuo family of the "Kingdom of Women", in a village (Walabie) on the shores of the exotic and beautiful Lugu Lake, Yongning Town in Ninglang Autonomous county, Yunnan province. By "real Mosuo", we mean that these villagers are dwelling in the same homestead where their ancestors have lived, thrived, and rested, not in a tourist fabrication. They still practice the same traditions of 走婚 ([zǒuhūn] "walking marriage"). They build and style their houses as their ancestors have done. Their ethnic dress codes remain unchanged, and so does the tradition of seeking medical treatment from a senior villager who can converse with gods (probably such healers bear certain titles, but we forgot to ask. The saving grace is that, during our visit to the Mosuo family, Yongshou Huo happened to film the episode of a patient showing up for a medical interview with the matriarch, with whom I ceased talking).

We were received by a woman in her thirties, Aqi Duzhima Lixin Yang (now she is addressed as Lixin Yang, the name given by herself in the Han naming style during the Cultural Revolution. This add-on Han name suggests the beginning of ethnic absorption into the Han culture). Yang's *axia* (i.e., male companion, like *husband* in English) used to visit her home only at night, but now they stay together away from her home (not for the sake of starting

116 *Language: Mankind's last homestead*

an independent family, but for vending their handwoven items – a shift of life style from farming to commerce of Han Chinese culture). Yang speaks Mandarin very well. She also did well in school and went to the township's middle school, using textbooks in Chinese (which changed Yang and her peers fundamentally). She brought us to her home, a family of fifteen folks led by her mother, including her and her sisters' nine children. Our dialogue about the future of the Mosuo and their language is recorded below.

QIAN: *Do you think Mosuo customs and language will collapse in the end under the impact of Chinese culture and language?*

YANG: *Not really. The Mosuo language is our family language. Though I speak Chinese, I don't speak it to my children. They (learn to) speak the Mosuo language with the granny. For us, Chinese policies like "Five Disciplines and Four Graces" or "Learn from Lei Feng" are neither a push nor a pull, because in our family, to love each other, to respect the old and to care for the young, are sacred duties with no need for other disciplines. At the sight of an elder, kids move away and give a seat to them.*

QIAN: *Well. Will things remain unchanged as time goes by? Like two hundred years from now?*

YANG: *One hundred or two hundred years from now, the Mosuo language will be gone. The impact of Chinese culture may chip away the Mosuo language bit by bit every generation. By then, it might be gone. Not now.*

Regarding whether the Mosuo ethnic distinction and language will live on, Aqi Duzhima Lixin Yang shows concerns – well-grounded concerns, I reckon, based on the following reasons why the Mosuo embarked on an ethnic assimilation with Han Chinese. In the first place, transportation matters. Back in the Cultural Revolution era, when Yang was in middle school, transportation was not as developed as it is today there. So far, the county (Ninglang) has been connected with the town (Yongning) by a real road, but the road does not reach Lugu Lake yet. Traffic has to make through an unpaved course or even wade across it in flood season. Anyway, this does not put Lugu Lake in isolation. Indeed, there are motor tricycles serving transportation from Yongning to Walabie, the village where Yang lives. We took one, and traveled on a road, not deemed as modern, but fairly good for tractors, vans, motor tricycles, and the like to dart around the village. What matters more than transportation is that Yang had direct dialing in her own house. Such transportation and communication facilities welcome Han Chinese people and government-run middle schools to the doorstep. *Meanwhile, they pave the way for the arrival of Chinese teachers and Chinese textbooks, which are the leading resources for a fluent acquisition of Chinese in the case of Aqi Duzhima Lixin Yang.* It is from there that root changes take place. Given better transportation, along with greater supply of Chinese teachers and Chinese textbooks, Yang's coming generations are to be educated with better Chinese as well as stronger Chinese culture. Her belief, "from the granny, children (learn to) speak the Mosuo language", is untenable. What if the granny passes away? What if Yang herself grows to be a granny? She is, well, a granny that can speak Chinese. Hence, the development of transportation invites Chinese teachers and Chinese textbooks, and will then change everything there, including the Mosuo language. Since the day of interview with Yang, her remarks about how "every generation drops a bit" of the Mosuo language have been lingering to my ears as an insightful woe. "Every generation drops a bit" can be construed as "every generation takes on a bit" of Chinese influences heralded by language. The advent of Chinese vocabulary opens the door for the underlying Chinese ideals, thoughts, outlooks, production modes, and manners, which then transform local customs and habits slowly and silently. The hot spring (a natural bathing place) in Yang's village, which used to be a mixed-gender venue, was later partitioned into men-versus-women space during the Cultural Revolution, and now there are no bathers at all. Our nostalgia oozed at the sight of the abandoned pool. Many locals take on Chinese names. Each year, many researchers from Taiwan, Europe, Britain, America, and other provinces come to join the locals in the form of "three togethers" (eat together, live together, and work together). Modern music and dancing tunes from TV, radio, or recorder merrily tap the ears of men and women in Mosuo costume. However, modern drum beats are not as solemn and soul-touching as the traditional ones. Will current traditions of 走婚 ("walking marriage") and matriarchal family survive another fifty years, leaving this real "Kingdom of Women" intact? It is hard to tell.

Despite all the changes, we can still tell that the dwellers in this village are Mosuo people. Why? First, they interact in the Mosuo language. Second, women rule the family, as always, and walking marriage is still a living practice.

This case study reveals that *ethnic language is considered one of the most reliable markers for identifying an ethnic group*. Given the means of communication and transportation of today and tomorrow, it is the language differences that make an ethnic group who they are. The signature distinction rests on linguistic and paralinguistic features. Saying so, we by no means belittle other identification markers such as religion, mode of production, or cultural pattern. The fact is that *language serves as the cultural and psychological foundation on which ethnic unity rests. Where the foundation stands, nothing else runs aloof from it; where the foundation stands, everything else stays close to it (be it religion, cultural pattern, mode of thinking, customs and conventions, mode of production, life style, etc.)*. Current communication and transportation capacities provide even the remotest countryside with six to seven TV channels and direct dialing phone service at their fingertips, as well as ready access by traffic. Under such conditions, can any mode of production or life style be kept unknown, unshared, or unlearnable? In contrast, linguistic and paralinguistic features (G. Qian, 1997/2002) can be rather unique, the latter including symbolic clusters attached to man, say, facial expressions, postures, and pitch, volume, and prosody. Yinque Chen claims,

118　*Language: Mankind's last homestead*

The distinction between the Han and the Hu[8] lies more in culture than in bloodline. Whoever adapts himself to the Han culture looks like a Han person; whoever adapts himself to the Hu culture looks like a Hu person. His bloodline is not taken into account.

(Cited in Xie, 1997)

In Yinque Chen's era, bloodline was no longer the criterion for identifying ethnicity. Instead, what an individual actually became – a Han or a Hu individual – rose to be the yardstick of identification. What counts as being a Han individual? What counts as being a Hu individual? I believe there used to be a set of criteria for the distinction, among which language should be the leading one, since it is not possible for an individual who claims or is believed to have become Sinicized not to be able to speak Chinese.

Taking the position as the point of departure that ethnic language is considered to be one of the most reliable markers to identify an ethnic group, can we find out if there exists a real Manchu ethnic group in China? Definitely, the big family of China consists of fifty-six ethnic groups including Han, Man, Mongol, Hui, Zang, etc. Owning to Chinese culture's strong assimilating power, "it took only 300 years for Manchu to be reduced into a demographic entity today, with a rare number of people speaking and reading the Manchu language (when the Manchus took hold of Beijing and started ruling China 300 years ago, they came with their own language and writing). Now only one Manchu word stays widely known – *sachima*[9]" (N. Zhao, 1994, p. 350). What is the ground for the claim that Manchu has been reduced into a demographic entity? I suppose, the claim largely rests on the linguistic facts, namely the rarity of literates in the Manchu language.

A decade ago, when some regions (counties) appealed for the status of regional ethnic autonomy, the government was challenged by a critical question, "What qualifies you as an ethnic minority group?" This question, so far as I know, has confronted the government of Enshi in Hubei province during its process of appealing for the founding of a Tujia autonomous prefecture. Out of an interest as a language teacher, I raised a question, "Are there any indisputable credentials for this region (at that time covering eight counties of 2 million inhabitants) to claim its being of Tujia ethnicity?" My query may escape absurdity, thanks to my twenty-six to twenty-seven years of working as a local teacher there from 1962 to 1988, when I set foot far and deep into mountains and forests of Laifeng county, Badong county, Hefeng county, Xuan'en county, Enshi county, Jianshi county, and Xianfeng county. And therein, I witnessed the life of local folks in poverty and remoteness. Therefore, I am in the position to argue whether the locals are Tujia people, or, to say the least, whether there are Tujia people. What qualifies this region for a Tujia autonomous prefecture? Their ethnic clothing? Few locals dress in ethnic clothing except for performing on stage or receiving inspections from an authority. Most of the local people dress just like the Han people, with the exception of local male villagers donning impressively long head

Language: Mankind's last homestead 119

wraps. Does their Baishou dance[10] qualify them? Undeniably, the Baishou dance in Xuan'en and Laifeng is really "local" (it is not for stage performance in downtown), with their own dance halls. Does their Nuo opera qualify them? The Nuo opera may be a fascinating fossil of art, performed at the front entry or in the sitting room of one's home. But some minorities in other provinces also perform Nuo opera and also worship the Nuo god – the disease-dispelling god. These three questions/credentials that I raised – ethnic clothing, Baishou dance, and Nuo opera – fall short of qualitative significance altogether, even if I hope for the best in light of the locals. In the end, I realized the only credential that could pass identification was a fieldwork document of the Tujia language, which I have read. It records Tujia words and phrases (transcribed in Chinese scripts) spoken only by a few elderly people, but indecipherable by the young or the non-locals. Belittle not this reference (this record of Tujia words and phrases). *It is the last and best heritage of an ethnic group.*

Advances in societal modernization complicate the issue of ethnic identification. Increasing similarities in life style and increasing cultural exchanges will fail any attempt to identify ethnicity by means of life styles or cultural customs. Hence, language may come into play. For instance, the majority of the Zhuang people, spreading south of the Wuling[11] over the border regions between Hunan province and Guangxi province, between Guangdong province and Jiangxi province, can be identified by their own languages. The following examples are all taken from S. Lu (1998, p. 6). The Zhuang people refer to 田 ([tián] "field") as 那 [nà], 近山 ([jìnshān] "mountain nearby") as 挠[náo], 远山 ([yuǎnshān] "mountain in distance") as 陇 [lòng], 太阳([tàiyáng] "sun") as 腾云[téngwén] (in Cantonese pronunciation), 星 ([xīng] "star") as 老离 [láolí], 河([hé] "river") as 打[dǎ], 水 ([shuǐ] "water") as 饮 [yàng] (in Cantonese pronunciation). They refer to 父亲 ([fùqīn] "father") as 薄 [bò] or 傲 [ào], 母亲 ([mǔqīn] "mother") as 骨 [gu] or 咪 [mi], 哥哥 ([gēgē] "elder brother") as 撸 [lu], 嫂嫂 ([sǎosǎo] "wife of one's elder brother") as 流 [liù], 弟弟 ([dìdì] "younger brother") as 农 [nong], 伯父 ([bófù] "father's elder brother") as 龙 [lòng], etc. In their grammar, the modifier of a noun is postnominal, which is different from Mandarin, such as in 花红 ([huāhóng] literally, "flower red"), 衣新 ([yīxīn] literally, "clothes new"), 姐大 ([jiědà] literally, "sister the eldest"). The Zhuang language belongs to the Zhuang-Dai branch of the Zhuang-Dong group in the Sino-Tibetan family. Language differences nail down ethnic differences, as fingerprints tell individual differences.

Language holds an ethnic group's identity. Then, would a nation like Switzerland disappear due to the absence of a Swiss language? Quite to the contrary, Switzerland, dubbed "the world garden", stays there carefree. Interestingly, Switzerland, without a Swiss language, has German, French, Italian, and Rhaeto-Romance as its official languages. Its official documents are written and released in German, French, and Italian. Caution that there is no Swiss ethnic group in Switzerland; this country consists of multiple ethnic groups, German, French, Italian, and so on, 72 percent being Germans. This

120   *Language: Mankind's last homestead*

case testifies the other way round how *language and ethnicity guard each other*. In Switzerland, since there is no Swiss ethnic group, there is no Swiss language.

3.2.2.2 *The fingerprint value of language community*

Therefore, it is tenable to categorize the world by language into language communities, a concept neither geographical nor political. The world, in fact, is composed of communities speaking Chinese, English, Arabian, French, Spanish, etc. A language community can spread across the boundary of countries. For example, the Chinese-speaking community in Singapore is living in the language world of Chinese, like any other Chinese-speaking community beyond the borders of China. It is even so in the case of Hong Kong and Taiwan residents. The tenability of categorizing the world by language can be attributed to the distinctive traits of language, which Kachru (1985), Professor of English Typology at the University of Illinois in the United States, agrees with in his description of the spread of English in terms of three concentric circles. These circles represent three types of English spread based on historical, social, and cultural features. The Inner Circle, including the United Kingdom, the United States, Canada, Australia, and New Zealand, provides norms of English. The Outer Circle, formed by Malaysia, India, Singapore, Nigeria, Ghana, the Philippines, and other countries where English is used as an official or semi-official language, deviates and develops its norms. The Expanding Circle, like Japan, Russia, and China, learning and using English as a foreign language, depends on English norms. Both the Inner and the Outer Circles formulate language communities beyond territory boundary.

What is the significance of categorizing language communities? Does a language community embody any distinctive traits? Where do they present themselves?

On top of it, culture embodies distinctive traits, which is widely acknowledged. Because language and culture are holographic, it follows that language also embodies distinctive traits. This serves as the rationale for dividing the world into language communities. Many concepts, like "cultural organization", "cultural community", "cultural group", and so on, attest to the distinctive qualities of culture. Xiaotong Fei (1998) argues for the existence of "cultural communities" and "cultural groups". This is indeed true.

The account for the holographic relation between language and culture is presented in *The Theory of Language Holography* (G. Qian, 2002), which makes the following two claims. First, within the matrix of cosmos, its two sub-systems –language and culture – are mutually inclusive. There is no such thing as language stripped or devoid of culture. For if language and culture were disconnected and mutually exclusive, man would have developed schizophrenia. As far as we know, normal people do not suffer such a mental disorder. Second, as two parts of the whole, language and culture are isomorphic with their matrix – the cosmos. Language is isomorphic with the cosmos in sound, rhythm, and beauty. Their isomorphism is also found in

Language: Mankind's last homestead   121

features such as recursive structure, sets and discreteness, the uncertainty principle of boundary, periodic principle (shift and rhythm), synchronicity and diachronicity, manipulation and linearity of holography, structural hierarchy, etc. Culture also displays isomorphism with its matrix – the cosmos, in that the cosmos creates mankind, so man's modes of cultural behaviors repeat, replicate, while responding to the cosmos. As stated above, the cosmos, acting as a body of universal ties, holds everything fully open to everything else by means of mutual interaction, connection, and restriction. Therein lies everything or every node fully informed of mutual interaction, connection, and restriction with any other node. For that matter, every node becomes an information epitome of the whole cosmos. Because language and culture are the nodes of this cosmos, each of them becomes the information epitome of the cosmos. In other words, language and culture are holographic.

Therefore, one culture sustains one language. Every language community rests on a specific cultural cornerstone. We find that what works in Chinese-speaking communities fails in communities speaking Western languages, and vice versa. This is the cultural validity of a language community, which enlightens its distinctive traits. Thus, _blame not language for untranslatability; blame culture._ While translation between languages can always be done one way or another, fences between cultures can hardly be mended, and an irredeemable loss in translation is always a cultural loss. Language forms are often identifiable so that the argument, _language differences bear fingerprint distinctions_, is well-attested. This argument complements another argument, namely that language is the last heritage of its people and its creators (see 3.2.2.3).

I will now put aside the relationship between language and culture, since a wealth of existing literature can be referred to.

The second value of categorizing language community is to underscore the distinctive mode of thinking nurtured by every language community. _Speakers of different languages manifest different modes of thinking, proof of which will also prove the fingerprint value of language community as an index to the uniqueness of a mode of thinking._

To prove it, I can conduct a hypothetical experiment. Among a large number of factors affecting foreign-language learning, the top seven factors, in my opinion, include syntactic fluency, vocabulary size, cross-cultural sensitivity, knowledge model alignment, alignment of the sense of sound, interference of thinking mode, and psychological being. Grammarians often prioritize syntactic maturity and vocabulary size, while culture-minded teachers of foreign languages prioritize sensitivity to cross-cultural variations. In recent years, schema researchers underscore the alignment-of-knowledge model. All these well-informed views, if tailored to the specific needs of individual learners, will help those disadvantaged learners.

The alignment issue of the sense of sound, studied by few researchers, will receive only a brief discussion here since the current book is not ready to propose any conclusion due to the incompletion of an intended

122 *Language: Mankind's last homestead*

experiment. Let me just outline some ideas for examining this issue. Suppose a learner of a foreign language keeps in mind a mispronounced word or an intonation-misplaced sentence type (e.g., rising tone lost, sense group miscut, stress missed, main clause and subordinate clause unfairly timed, etc.). When he is exposed to the correct pronunciation of that word, or the properly managed intonation of that sentence type, *a dysfunction occurs as the result of the misaligned sense of sound, that is, the wrong sense of sound kept in mind repels the correct pronunciation.* However, having not gleaned sufficient data, I cannot estimate the impact of such misaligned sense of sound on a learner's listening performance. Readers interested in the issue may refer to my paper "The Calling of the Sense of Sound" (G. Qian, 1990), in which I presented an elementary rationale for the misaligned sense of sound.

Another issue, more essential than the above-mentioned one, is that the mode of thinking inherent in one's native language interferes with one's performance in listening to a foreign language. What underlies the issue is that *one language nurtures one mode of thinking.* Although no studies have been in sight, I intend to pursue this topic, not for the sake of improving listening competence (it is believed to help in this regard), but for *justifying the categorization of language community* and further attesting to the proposition that language is the last heritage of its people, the last homestead of mankind.

The hypothetical experiment is pictured as follows. A recorder is playing an English passage clearly read. For the moment, let us put aside six factors: Syntactic fluency, vocabulary size, cross-cultural sensitivity, knowledge alignment, alignment of the sense of sound, as well as psychological well-being. In other words, the visualized listener, a Chinese, has no problem whatsoever with the six factors. He has a strong command of syntactic constructions, a large lexicon, a strong cross-cultural sensitivity, a properly aligned knowledge model, a properly aligned sense of sound, and a normal psychological well-being. According to my hypothesis, the most natural listening takes place in this fashion: The listener thinks along the flow of the spoken or narrated English, rather than thinking back. This fashion suggests the convergence of the listener's flow of thoughts and the recording's flow of language. If the two flows diverge, the former flow always harasses the latter. When a Chinese listens to an English passage as follows, what will happen in his mind?

> In a quite ordinary sense, it is obvious that there can be private languages. There can be, because there are. A language may be said to be private when it is devised to enable a limited number of persons to communicate with one another in a way that is not intelligible to anyone outside the group. By this criterion, thieves' slang and family jargons are private languages. Such languages are not strictly private, in the sense that only one person uses and understands them, but there may very well be

Language: Mankind's last homestead 123

languages that are. Men have been known to keep diaries in codes which no one else is meant to understand.

(Ayer & Rhees, 1954, p. 63)

Sentence one: *In a quite ordinary sense, it is obvious that there can be private languages*. This English sentence, identical in structure with its Chinese counterpart (a construction also starts with an adverb 显然 ([xiǎnrán] "obviously"), may be easily comprehended by the Chinese listener. In this case, his train of thoughts matches the current of language being spoken (being delivered in progression), hence the convergence of the thoughts and language. However, if the listener is driven by a "correct" grammar (i.e., a resultant mode of thinking trained by his Chinese teacher of English), he will pick up the real subject and drop it where the grammatical subject stands. Only by mentally relocating *that there can be private languages* back to the lodge of *it* can he stop fidgeting and listen on with a peaceful mind. Fiddling in mind the linear order of this English sentence causes his train of thoughts to diverge for the first time from the audible flow of language, which may lead to distraction and affect his subsequent listening.

Sentence two: *There can be, because there are*. This sentence greets his ears with ease, because it unfolds in the same sequence of thoughts as its Chinese equivalent. In fact, the listener's train of thoughts synchronizes with the audible flow of language.

Sentence three: *A language may be said to be private when it is devised to enable a limited number of persons to communicate with one another in a way that is not intelligible to anyone outside the group*. Upon listening while obsessed with the Chinese mode of thinking, he will first figure out the Chinese meaning of *when it is devised to… the group* (or even worse, he will be tempted to translate it into Chinese). He will then revisit the foregoing part, *A language may be said to be private*. Such replay blocks for the second time the linear flow of the original sentence, and brings about one of the consequences, that is, when his mind flips the sentence back and forth he loses track of the ongoing flow of the recording (or the flow of the speaking). He may thus be upset and affected in the subsequent listening.

Sentence four: *By this criterion, thieves' slang and family jargons are private languages*. The listener understands the sentence effortlessly, thanks to the sequential consistency with its Chinese counterpart. This train of Chinese thought, in the same order with the English sentence, synchronizes with the audible flow of language.

Sentence five: *Such languages are not strictly private, in the sense that only one person uses and understands them, but there may very well be languages that are*. If the listener insists on decoding the meaning of *in the sense…* ahead of *Such languages are…*, he is justifiably applying the cause-effect order preferred by a Chinese thinking mode. But this backward glance of thoughts once again fails to synchronize with the flow of recording, so that the listener risks losing track of *but there may very well be languages that are*.

124   *Language: Mankind's last homestead*

Sentence six: *Men have been known to keep diaries in codes which no one else is meant to understand.* If the listener's flow of thoughts converges with that of the recording, he will render the sentence into an acceptable interpretation 我们知道有人用别人不理解的密码记日记 [wǒmēn zhīdào yǒurén yòng biérén bùlǐjiě de mìmǎ jìrìjì], even though such mental work of translation is not warranted by the rule of listening comprehension – according to the rule, listening comprehension should not co-occur with translation into one's mother tongue. Yet, the real problem lies in the conflicting sequence between the train of thoughts and the audible flow of language, which occurs when the sentence reaches the end. The listener conditioned by the Chinese thinking mode, namely preceding a noun with its attributive clause, cannot help but rewind in his mind the sentence into 我们知道有人用别人不理解的密码记日记.

Within this brief episode of listening, the listener's train of thoughts diverges from the flow of recording on two or three occasions. As a listener of a foreign language, sometimes *his mode of thinking is at odds with the linearity of the language spoken.* Two incompatible systems of encoding cannot operate on the same platform, let alone simultaneously. When the train of thought disrupts the linear flow of listening, can a foreign listener achieve accuracy of listening? (Since this section does not target at listening diagnosis, there is no point in discussing listening practice.)

The impotence proves that a gap between thinking modes is a matter of language gap. One people, one language, and one thinking mode – one nurtures the other. To categorize the world by language not only foregrounds its distinctive traits but also implies that *language frames and houses the thinking pattern of a people*; in other words, a language is the last homestead of the language community (it happens during the cultural assimilation that some minority groups may convert from speaking their own languages to speaking the dominant language in their country, voluntarily or involuntarily. See 3.2.2.3 for a detailed discussion).

A language community always emerges with a set of behaviors; different language communities entail different forms of behaviors, and each of them acquires individuality. The topic concerning linguistic determinism is to be discussed in 3.2.4.

3.2.2.3 The last heritage of a people

1) "Language is the heritage from our forefathers, the first heritage, also the last".

This remark made by Qiuyu Yu in an interview with China Central TV in 1998 accords with Shaogong Han's (1994) statement, "Only language holds the key to the past. Only language can walk from the depths of history to today as the last fingerprint and heritage of a people".

Language preserves history by two of its sub-systems: Its phonological and orthographic systems, as two keys to the past. Speech can be transmitted

Language: Mankind's last homestead 125

only from one generation to its immediate next, while writing can be passed down across gaps in generation. No wonder language is the only legacy of a people that cannot be taken away or taken down. (Here again involves the cases of some minority groups assimilated into a dominant language at the cost of their mother tongues, by or against their volition. See the below section on Emperor Xiaowen of the Northern Wei Dynasty giving up the ethnic language.)

As previously demonstrated, language is the most solid credential qualifying Enshi in Hubei province for a Tujia autonomous prefecture. Its language – the vocabulary spoken only by the elderly and understood by none of the young, walks from the depths of history as the last fingerprint and heritage of this ethnic group.

The key to the past and distant history is held in the hands of three messengers: Objects buried by ancestors, fossils, and language. But fossils (of plants and animals) are neither attached to, nor produced or possessed by, humans. Human skulls are not mental products of human beings; they are parts of human bodies. Unlike fossils, *language is bred by human minds, and in return language holds all the developmental records of human minds. While language passes on through generations, it carries the entire load of cultural and mental legacies of its speakers. The Analects*, those dialogues between Confucius and his disciples (which can be cited as data of discourse; see G. Qian, 1997/ 2002), reveal the history of the Spring and Autumn Period (an important period in Chinese history) via orthographic records, not phonological records like tapes. The dialogues in文心雕龙 ([wénxīn diāolóng] *The Literary Mind and the Carving of Dragons*, the first systemic Chinese literary criticism; also see G. Qian, *ibid.*) unfold the history of the Qi and Liang Dynasties, though also via orthographic, but not phonetic, records. Predictably, one thousand years from now, Chinese people might be channeled back to the ethos of their early-twenty-first-century fellow men through some oral Chinese dialogues (more important than written ones) recorded then. Such entry to the history through written language and more ideally through spoken language is of fingerprint quality. Every fingerprint is unique; none is identical with any other. With a fingerprint uniqueness, language serves as one of the most eligible markers of ethnic identity.

2) Every ethnic group guards their language as their last heritage.

One great example is the *Compendium of the Languages of the Turks*, its legendary birth and loss, its loss and rebirth, and its spread at length (Y. P. Lu, 2002). Actually, the collection is not a dictionary proper, but an encyclopedia of Turkic peoples about their languages, stories, poetry, history, geography, natural resources, and customs. The legend related to this dictionary started with Mahmud Kashgari, who was born in 1008 AD to a Khan father and a Khan grandfather of the Karakhanid Dynasty. Later Kashgari fled from a court coup, his clan slain, but his grand goal was set for the ensuing vagrant

126 *Language: Mankind's last homestead*

life. For fifteen years, this knowledgeable mind wandered far and wide among the Turkic tribes along the Ili River, the Chu River, the Syr River, and the Am River, gleaning and studying their dialects, determined to preserve those dying languages for eternity. Together with silk merchants, he headed to and settled down in Baghdad, dedicating twenty solitary years to composing *Compendium of the Languages of the Turks* in Arabic. This comprehensive dictionary with Turkic dialects, stories, and poetry is deemed the encyclopedia about Turkic peoples, valuable not only for the study of languages, literature, and art of Xinjiang and Central Asia, but also for the study of history, geography, natural resources, and social customs of Turkic peoples. In February 1074, Kashgari offered his manuscript to Abdullah, the king of the Abbasid Dynasty, and then made a long march back to his hometown as a village teacher. However, the war sweeping the Arab world burned down the palace; the dictionary once housed there was gone. After the war ended, the futile search for this book lasted over one hundred years until one day in the late twelfth century, when a disheveled woman beggar showed up with a bundle in a Baghdad street, approached the palace gate, and went straight into the palace. She was King Abdullah's descendent, whose family sheltered the dictionary under their wings for over one hundred years of exoduses. They lost a dynasty, but saved the dictionary, whereby they paid homage to the heart's desire of a scholar. When the beggar handed over the book, the overjoyed king issued a quick order, having dozens of copies made of this book. But a few years later, as the second expedition of the Crusades trampled on the Arabian lands, the dictionary was gone again and remained out of sight for the following six hundred years. In World War I, a bomb, as if knowing its way, blasted open the library of a book collector in the famous Turkish aristocrat Diverbeck family, and there the ancient book was found, the only copy of *Compendium of the Languages of the Turks* in the world. A teacher spent three years in Istanbul having it printed in three awe-inspiring volumes for scholars worldwide. The whole story is not a fiction; it is a fact of history. What is on the mind of these dictionary guardians, so vigilant and rational, so caring and daring in their 700-year relay race of protection? What can best account for it? *Only driven by the faith that language is the last heritage of a nation and an ethnic group can its peoples be united and unified as a whole.* They know that a language heritage preserved is an encyclopedia saved for its people. Such a strong sense of guarding a book and its success should only be seen in peoples mature with a long history of education. To our dismay, this legend was achieved by these nomadic peoples in wars either on their lands or beyond. This legendary story should cause us Chinese to think: With a long history of farming and cultural glory, what did we do to our cultural legacy? We were once quite cocky in our "valor" for stifling Confucianism, in our "gallantry" for trashing traditional thoughts, cultures, customs, and norms. We, government officials, scholars, and average individuals, should now become aware of the importance of saving or protecting Chinese classics. Given our national power and what we have today, it will not be a difficult

Language: Mankind's last homestead 127

job to do. However, are we ready to act as fulfilling guardians as devotedly as those Turkic peoples did?

No people will forsake their mother tongue without struggle. Stories of dying for their mother tongue recur in the past and present of China and elsewhere. Language conflicts also take place, even leading to warfare in defense of one's mother tongue. In Haley's 1976 novel *Roots: The Saga of an American Family*, the black slave Kunta Kinte would rather die hanged than give up his African name for an English one. Trivial as this plot for linguistics is, it is a supplement. Its counterpart can be found in the following historical event in China. Emperor Xiaowen of the Northern Wei Dynasty carried out a top-down Sinicization. He had the capital relocated to Luoyang, the language converted to Han Chinese (of the Central Plains), his family name changed from Tuoba to Yuan. The reform was destined to be a battle. His eldest son, Xun Yuan (aged fifteen), stood against him in defense of his mother tongue and his family name, in the end beheaded by his father, the emperor.

Emperor Xiaowen was as determined to kill as his son was determined to die, but in stark contrast – one for dropping the mother tongue, the other for keeping it. Why did that happen?

Hong Tuoba (476–499 CE), Emperor Xiaowen of the Northern Wei Dynasty, changed his surname to Yuan three years before his death in order to promote Sinicization. During his twenty-three-year tenure, to move the capital and to Sinicize his country were the most significant yet the most controversial measures. When the dice were cast for the relocation of both the capital and his people to Luoyang in the Central Plains, Emperor Xiaowen launched a stronger campaign for Sinicization, every move of which was confronted by the opposition. On December 2 in the eighteenth year of Taihe, Emperor Xiaowen forbade wearing "Hu clothes" (the clothes of northern ethnic groups such as Xianbei). On May 26, he proclaimed another decree,

The Xianbei language is banned. Han Chinese is the only authorized right pronunciation. Civil servants aged thirty or younger are forbidden to speak the Xianbei language. Any violation will result in a demotion or dismissal. Tolerance of adaptation is given to those civil servants over thirty years old.

On June 2, Emperor Xiaowen issued an edict forbidding the use of the Xianbei language in the court, and claiming to discharge all violators. In the process of Sinicization, the deadly blow to the opposition was to revoke the old family surname Tuoba and impose the new one Yuan. The reform proceeded against all odds, beheading the fifteen-year-old eldest son Xun Yuan who led the defiance, and executing a group of top-ranking ministers who attempted riots. Such radical policies of Sinicization were never reversed during Xiaowen's rule. Emperor Xiaowen's reform achieved far-reaching success, as the most intensive Sinicization in China ever fulfilled through the strongest initiative by a non-Han Chinese ruler in power (Ge, 1996).

Two insights are obtained from what Emperor Xiaowen did (including his giving up of his mother tongue). The first insight is, to defeat an ethnic group, just lead its language – its last legacy – to its downfall (make it die or let it die in

128 *Language: Mankind's last homestead*

the process of assimilation or dissolution). In the case of Emperor Xiaowen, Xianbei people chose to be assimilated with Han people. Japanese invaders in China schemed up language oppression by spreading Japanese classes; so did the Germans during their occupation of France, by banning French courses and erasing French from primary schools. Both the German and Japanese aggressors ill intended to "drain the pond to get at the fish". To account for Emperor Xiaowen's success in Sinicization, Ge (1996) attributes its thoroughness to the decree of renaming the Tuoba family Yuan. But I think otherwise. I think credit should be given to the decree that banned the Xianbei language and authorized the use of Chinese (spoken by the Han people of the Central Plains) as the only language. Enculturation does not follow from the renaming. Overseas Chinese, without dropping their Chinese names, can acquire those local languages because they grow up there as natives. In the local language environment, they are laden with local culture that leads to enculturation. The giant leap that led the Xianbei people to thorough Sinicization was leaving for the new capital Luoyang and speaking only Han Chinese; this was also a leap of uprooting themselves from their homes and taking new roots in the Central Plains (as Emperor Xiaowen desired). Only by leaving behind their language were they able to tear themselves away from the old home and build the new home (in the Central Plains) they wanted. What to give and what to take – this is a dialectical relationship. I will come back to this topic in Section 3.2.3.

The second insight concerns why some ethnic groups let go of their mother tongue – their last heritage. Ge (1996) attributes Emperor Xiaowen's reform resolution to his belief in the cultural superiority of Han Chinese and his vision of the Xianbei people's long-term benefits. This analysis seems unconvincing.

It is rather shocking that the Xianbei people, the Xianbei language, the Xianbei culture, pure as they had been for nearly one thousand years, quickly disappeared along with the Tuoba family. Other minorities would have rather stayed away from the material civilization and the vast territory of the Central Plains in order to maintain their purity against any attempts of Sinicization. Emperor Xiaowen, in contrast, hailed Sinicization with open arms and an iron fist. Was he a Xianbei traitor? This is well beyond my judgment; I leave it open for others to debate. I will reframe the discussion by standing in the shoes of Emperor Xiaowen. Without much difficulty, I can figure out the following reasons why he embraced Han culture: 1) If he did not set out for voluntary Sinicization, what would happen to the future of his people, or could they maintain their purity? Whenever those nomads inhabiting northern China or abroad stepped into the farmed regions of the Han Chinese, they were assimilated culturally, without exception. Examples were many since the Han Dynasty: Hun, Huan, Xianbei, Jie, Dingling, Tiele, Turk, Huihe, Shatuo, Qidan, and Jurchen (not to mention those non-Han groups in the pre-Qin Dynasty). Emperor Xiaowen must have known what happened to those past ethnic minorities before (being assimilated by the Han culture), though he could not see what would happen to the future minorities. Ge (1996) raises a question, "During the past two thousand years, none of the

Language: Mankind's last homestead 129

ethnic minorities has achieved better results than Xianbei people who had undergone Emperor Xiaowen's reform. Is it a sheer coincidence?" Emperor Xiaowen not only saw the necessity, but also seized it as a means to decide their fate. 2) He sought to strengthen his power by learning advanced modes of production and life styles. 3) In fact, if ethnic minority rulers did not open their front door to Sinicization, their people would sneak out the back door to join the Han Chinese, tempted by their developed modes of production and life styles. In the late Jin Dynasty, just as the Jurchens migrated to the Yellow River region, they learnt to speak Han Chinese, wear Han clothes, and bear Chinese surnames, against emperors' bans. Even some princes or dukes "were accustomed only to the Han customs from an early age", "illiterate of Jurchen written or spoken language", for which Emperor Shizong of the Jin Dynasty admonished them helplessly as "forgetting their roots" (Ge, 1996). To sum up, the root cause for why so many minorities in China voluntarily gave up their mother tongues – their last legacies – was their yearning for advanced production power and their needs to survive and develop. Other than that, it is unthinkable. However, history has witnessed quite a few cases where people died in vain, or not, to keep their mother tongues.

Laplanders inhabiting Yukasjervi, Sweden, can be cited as the latest example of voluntary assimilation, being ready to give up their mother tongue. According to a French encyclopedia, Laplanders, living in a village as a nomadic people more than 100 kilometers deep in the high-latitude Arctic Circle, may be on the verge of disappearance. They spread across Norway, Sweden, Russia, and Finland, with a population of only 20,000, half of them in Sweden. The village of Yukasjervi has become not only Laplanders' stop for rest and supply, but also the springboard to and school of urban civilization for those Laplanders tired of nomadic life. Whether this account is credible or not is open to discussion. Laplanders have their own spoken language, written language, cultural values, and traditions. If they wanted to assimilate into other peoples, they would disperse and readily trade their mother tongue for an urban life. If this were indeed the case, Laplanders would be another minority group willing to assimilate and give up their mother tongue. If this is not the case, saying that they are "on the verge of disappearance from the planet" is but fact-distorting.

3) Enlarge the share of one's language in the world for information transmission.

Language heritage has been endangered by existing language hegemony.

Political disputes triggered by language hegemony are legion. In *The Politics of Friendship*, Derrida (2005), best known for deconstructionism since the late 1960s, argues that "all the seemingly natural categories, together with those derivative concepts such as society, culture, nationality, and border, are entailed by language, hence conventional". Here language refers to discourse in general, not the counterpart of written language. In reviewing *Specters of*

130 *Language: Mankind's last homestead*

Marx: The State of the Debt, the Work of Mourning and the New International (Derrida, 1994), Yang Lu (1998) states,

> Derrida lashes out at "the New International" – the centralization of global capitalism and media, believing it as an unprecedented means of warfare to seek world hegemony. And according to Derrida's logic, hegemony and tyranny are not rooted in strong military power or wicked political system, but in language, and ultimately in philosophy. Back to the inscrutable subject of deconstructionism, in Derrida's terms, he aims at "neutralizing" language without a tilt left or right. If language is neutralized, politics will be neutralized in the end, or its overbearing air will be moderate.

If my understanding is not wrong, this posits the logic of world politics – political hegemony is driven by language hegemony. This logic is more evident in the statement – if language is neutralized, then politics will be neutralized. To understand the problem, it may be helpful to bring up a relevant topic, the ethnicity of language. In recent years, grumbles have been made against the Nobel Prize for having failed even the best Chinese writers. People blame either the poor English translation, or the curse of language ethnicity. But I believe this is the problem of language discrimination, namely language hegemony. Latin American writers have similar tales of woe. According to Du (1998),

> Latin American writers and critics are perplexed by the issue of wavering language, apart from their undetermined issue of complexion. They tend to write in English, as the result of the bilingual education advocated by American politics. Their acts of writing in English even about the life of ethnic minorities pose themselves as the mainstream elite and create a paradox in their discourse.

The ethnicity of Latin Americans is underrepresented in their works written in neither Spanish nor Portuguese. Using English can hardly render the life of Latin Americans, just as using English can hardly render that of Chinese, for there is a partition in between. *This partition makes impossible the preservation of one's ethnic fingerprint in others' language, or the transmission of one's cultural heritage.* Heidegger has a profound observation on this point in his dialogue on language between him (as Inquirer in the dialogue) and the Japanese scholar Tezuka Tomio (as Japanese in the dialogue) (Heidegger, 1982, p. 5).

JAPANESE: Now I am beginning to understand better where you smell the danger. The language of the dialogue constantly destroyed the possibility of saying what the dialogue was about.

Language: Mankind's last homestead   131

INQUIRER: Some time ago I called language, clumsily enough, the house of Being. If man by virtue of his language dwells within the claim and call of Being, then we Europeans presumably dwell in an entirely different house than Eastasian man.

JAPANESE: Assuming that the languages of the two are not merely different but are other in nature, and radically so.

INQUIRER: And so, a dialogue from house to house remains nearly impossible.

When they talked about the Japanese art in the European language, they knew the language was destroying what the talk was about, because "Man by virtue of his language dwells within the claim and call of Being". Different languages present Being in different ways. The language of a foreign house does not work for one's own house. "Europeans presumably dwell in an entirely different house than Eastasian man"; this is the very root cause for the assertion that others' language cannot preserve one's ethnic fingerprint, nor transmit one's cultural heritage. The conclusion "A dialogue from house to house remains nearly impossible" reminds us of those Latin American authors writing in English about the life of Latin Americans. They (due to some reluctant factors) take up English as the mainstream language for writing, and pose themselves as elites. This is not only a joke of political equality, but also a great detriment to the personas under their description (the life of Latin Americans).

In this era (the so-called post-modern age), the movement against "discourse hegemony" intensifies day by day, instead of slowing down. One example is the *World Guide* published in 1997 by Uruguay Third World Center, which carries highlights around the world, updated weekly and re-edited bi-annually. Its cover bears an impressive mission statement: *The World Seen from the South*, different from the one seen through the eyes of superpowers. In one issue, the editor's note said,

> *The World Guide*, since its publication in 1997, has been viewing the world with an unconventional eye. Today, while the world seems to be heading towards the same direction, our articles hail the uniqueness of more than 200 countries and regions. Every day, praises of "globalization" are over the loudspeaker, as though the "globalization" spaceship were flying a small bunch of billionaires and tycoons to the new millennium. In contrast, agonies of woe from millions of ordinary people are heard every day on our *Guide*. These people want no more than the basic medical supply, or a meal. Unlike any other reference books in defense of their being "objective", we openly admit our bias: we sympathize with women seeking justice, with indigenous people sticking to ethnicity, with farmers guarding their seeds, with workers fighting for the rights hard-earned through generations.

> (Quoted in Suo, 1999a)

132 *Language: Mankind's last homestead*

The World Guide was rivaling those superpowers for the right of discourse. Another event protesting discourse hegemony took place in 1992 in Brazil. While the United Nations held a conference on "Environment and Development", the World Indian Organization launched its convention in the same city and at the same time to protest manipulation by the developed countries and disrespect for the Indians incurred by the conference. It issued to the press *The Earth Charter*, voices from the bottom of the society. Such eye-for-eye rivalry also targets the right of discourse. Recently, along the worldwide trend of media networking, many non-governmental education radio stations across Latin America have been networking to form the Latin American Radio Stations Association of Education. Thus, they empowered themselves for the struggle of discourse right.

Discourse hegemony bred by technology monopoly has posed hard-to-swallow threats to the linguistic heritage of a people. One example comes in very handy. Because the technology of computers and networks is monopolized by some multinational corporations in the United States such as Intel, Microsoft, IBM, and Compaq, when one purchases the monopolized technology, he has to buy English as the medium of interaction (to think in English and "talk" in English with computer and network designed in English). There is no way for users to escape from this "coercion", unless they stay away from computers and the Internet. But staying away from computers requires the payment of high prices of information depravity that will inflict damage on industry, business, and more damage on national defense. For common folks in a non-English-speaking country, the choice is theirs, to enter the English world or not. There is no choice left for a country, for its government, for its departments of intelligence, defense, or technology. It fears not English; it fears risks of intelligence leakage; it fears being known inside-out. Such unspeakable pains gnaw it and torture especially those intellectual elites whose sense of national pride is more peculiar, deeper, and more fragile than that of the common people. French elites, for example, proud of their brilliant art and beautiful language, have been glancing at English just sideways. Russian elites, proud of their incomparably deep literary tradition, have sneered at American literature, but have had to swallow in recent years the painful loss of their national defense advantage. Chinese intellectual elites, proud of their long history, rich culture, and deep literary tradition, have to pocket their mother tongue when talking with a computer, even though they are still sulky with the history of humiliation (they fear not learning English. They are much quicker in learning English than some awkward British or American learners of Chinese). Having to be guided by English and ushered into English makes them feel lowly (ancient and graceful Chinese, French, and Russian are all in danger of exclusion), their self-esteem hurt indescribably. To pursue language equality has always been an earnest enterprise. Software experts in China, France, and Russia should take their time to design software in Chinese, French, and Russian so that they can compete with sweeping English on the Internet for the right of discourse. Shouldn't they? This competition is not

Language: Mankind's last homestead 133

driven by willfulness, but by the urge to guard the last heritage of a people. We cannot afford to have Chinese erased by formatting, or to let all the non-English languages die in the tide of the computer and the Internet. *Human civilization, in any sense, is not propelled by discourse hegemony. To struggle for language equality is not a matter of willfulness, because every language presents a unique form of life* (see 3.2.1).

How should one protect language equality, by appeals or by multilateral conventions? Who cares! In the coming era of information and data, superpowers will use information technology and data to stake out their territory in the virtual space as much as they want, leaving no room for latecomers. When the engine of information technology drives economic development, 80 percent of the information in the world is laden in language and over 80 percent of the information is transmitted by English. With the lion's share in the hand of English, many non-English-speaking countries have been reduced into language debtors. Who does not adapt her language to the Internet will be knocked out and excluded. Therefore, every government with a vision should take effective measures to expand its share of language in the world for information transmission. *This is not only a question of opposing language hegemony, but also of resisting the fate of being eliminated and excluded.*

On the issue of expanding one's language share in information transmission, here is a special case for reference: The Chinese-language education in Taiwan has gone astray. After Kuomingtang crossed the strait to Taiwan in 1949, Taiwan became, in just over ten years, the first region in China with Mandarin Chinese popularized. However, in the 1980s, the political climate dismissed Mandarin Chinese in favor of local dialects; Chinese pinyin was replaced with a new phonetic system, and teaching in dialect was promoted in the name of "teaching in the native language" or "teaching in the indigenous language". "To present the Taiwanese language in Chinese characters" (台语汉字化 [táiyǔ hànzìhuà]) or 汉字台语化 [hànzì táiyǔhuà]) was encouraged, resulting in expressions such as 俗俗卖 ([súsúmài] "cheap sale"), 强强滚 ([qiángqiánggǔn] "lively"), 白帅帅([báishuàishuài] "very handsome"), and 俗搁大碗 ([súgēdàwǎn] "cheap sale but good quality"), which are incomprehensible to most Chinese. The phonetic system of the early twentieth century was adhered to, and simplified Chinese advocated by mainland China was accused of sabotaging traditional Chinese culture (simplified Chinese characters may be displayed as unintelligible codes on a computer in Taiwan). Such language policies implemented by the Taiwan authorities were actually serving its politics, in the name of featuring the Chinese language with Taiwanese characteristics. However, these language policies will end up isolating Taiwan from the rest of the world (Zhou, 2004). This case suggests that Taiwan, as an island of China since the ancient times, attempted to erect itself as a state by removing and remolding its language inherently tied with the motherland. Everyone seems to know the crucial truth that *a state stands on the pedestal of language.* It proves once again that language is the last fingerprint and heritage of an ethnic group or a nation. Language plays an

134 *Language: Mankind's last homestead*

extremely important role in ethnic identification: It bears the fingerprint value to mark out language community and holds the last heritage of a people.

Where there is discourse hegemony, there are ongoing protests against it. From the 1880s to the 1960s, 30,000 Australian Aboriginal children were assimilated by force, known as the "Stolen Generations". According to the report disclosed in 1997 by the Australian Human Rights Committee (cited in Sun, 1999), children born to mixed white and Aboriginal parents were forcefully removed to missionary schools or white foster families by the Australian government under the racial assimilation policy. The purpose, the report assumes, was to take away the descendants' Aboriginal identity and put on them the identity of a white society. For the Aboriginal, this is genocide. Some of them have already filed a lawsuit in the Federal Court of Darwin, demanding compensation from the Australian government on the grounds that the racial policy of former governments split them from their parents and deprived them of their native language, causing lifelong trauma to their bodies and souls. The intergenerational lawsuit has been a fight for racial survival and language autonomy; it is not a language issue *per se*. In the world, *language issues – to defend the rights of one's mother tongue – are always correlated with human rights, racial rights, and motherland rights.* Imagine, for example, behind the sixteen official languages in India, what a vast tangle it is between races, areas, and regions that must be dealt with and attended to, a tangle of interwoven interests, friendship and enmity, clashes and conflicts. In Canada, French-speaking regions had minor or major clashes with English-speaking regions from time to time, which is not news at all. Weiming Du, an academician of the American Academy of Humanities and Sciences, a Harvard Professor of Philosophy and History, observes, "In Belgium the conflicts between two languages led to the division of the prestigious Rwandan University in Europe into two schools who cold-shoulder each other" (1998, p. 89). These is strong proof for the tight correlation between holding a language and keeping a civilization. The mother-tongue right is guarded as the last heritage of a nation. What will happen if the last heritage is gone?

The attitudes to discourse hegemony cannot be neatly couched in terms of *anti-this* or *anti-that*. Complexity exhibits in the relationship between the native languages of the Philippines (Tagalog, Pisa, etc.) and the languages of the colonial suzerains, first Spanish, then English. Before the Spanish arrived, more than one hundred languages lived in the Philippines (on more than 7,000 islands). The Spanish suppressed the Islamic influence centered on the southern Mindans and imposed Catholicism on the Filipinos, shaping the Philippines as the only Christian country in Asia. However, it did not become a Spanish-speaking country. Why is that so? Is that because of the merciful Spanish, or the fearless Filipinos and their successful protest? According Suo (1999b), it is because the Spanish colonial government had not seriously implemented Spanish education nationwide. It took it for granted that since missionaries had learnt to preach in local languages, there was no need to popularize Spanish. (This seemingly heedless decision was indeed calculated by the authorities.) Some conservative religious personages worried that the colonial language, if learnt by the indigenous people of different languages, would be exploited for rebellion in unison (please note that this colonial logic is quite different from that of Japan, which imposed Japanese in China, and Germany, which banned French classes in France during World War II). Their worries were not groundless. The Philippines' national hero, Jose Rizal, wrote anti-Spanish-colonialism masterpieces in Spanish, *Touch Me Not*, *The Reign of the Greed*, and other articles. It was not until 1862 that the Spanish royal family issued a decree making Spanish a compulsory course in colonial primary education, but it was opposed by the University of San Marcos in the Philippines (part of the Spanish colonial authorities, not the indigenous Philippines). Its reasoning went as follows.

> So far, the confrontation between different languages and ethnic groups has given us advantage, the Kagoyans against the Tagalogs, the Panpangos against the Ilocanos. The government defeated all of these uprisings. However, the unification of language will nurture harmony among them, in its wake come some of them to address the masses with inflammatory speeches in the same language.
>
> (Cited in Suo, 1999b)

History has witnessed that the Spanish authorities' worries did come true. Jose Rizal, along with many key members of the independence movement, launched the united revolt by arming themselves with the weapon – Spanish. Rizal felt very ambivalent about Spanish. On the one hand, he wrote all his works in Spanish. On the other, Spanish rankled with him because he was born to Gallup, his native language, but had grown up under Spanish rebukes. Rizal questioned,

> Why do we have to learn Spanish? We already have a wealth of Tagalog, Pisa, Ilocano... Is it just for learning those beautiful stories and theories about freedom, progress, and justice, then craving for them in agony? Is it just for learning their laws and our rights, then subjecting us to very different verdicts? What is the point of learning Spanish since one can reach God in any language? ... Is it just for understanding the insults and curses of the National Guard? If that is all, there is no need to learn Spanish: We can understand the language of whip and feel with our slightly sensitive body. What is the use of Spanish for us, without even the right to speak?
>
> (Cited in Suo, 1999b)

This reveals, on the one hand, that the colonized people were opposing the language hegemony of the suzerain and, on the other, that their struggle against colonialism utilized the language of the suzerain. Rizal's shower of whipping questions can be construed as expressions of sensations and emotions because

136 *Language: Mankind's last homestead*

what he resisted was in fact the political power of the suzerain, not the language – the carrier of culture. Spanish was chosen to write the most important documents in the Philippine Independence Movement and most works by the national martyrs. At any rate, the days of resistance are gone. Colonization of three hundred years has infused the Filipino soil with the suzerain culture: Catholicism accepted by the masses, the guitar popularized, Spanish loan words into the local language, especially those for architecture, religion, law, music, and eating. Aside from that, Spanish surnames and names have been carried on for generations in Filipino families; Spanish names for communities and roads are still used today... However, English did not go through so many bends and winds when it arrived in the Philippines later. Americans are by no means as pedantic as the old Spanish colonists. In December 1898, the US military was deployed in the Philippines under the Paris Peace Treaty. They have been encountering waves of anti-American struggles since then. However, English gains a free pass in Manila today. Americans have planned from the outset the spread of English and made striding progress in a short period of time. In 1901, the United States dispatched six hundred professional English teachers from home to the Philippines. Today learning English is obligatory there. Suo (1999b) points out,

> People's language selection was rigidly governed by pragmatism. They disliked English, but English was designated as a compulsory course; they were attached to Spanish, but not many of them would afford time just in memory of the past [Spanish is the language of the early suzerain, not the native language! Note by the author of this book]. ... Language reflects the vicissitudes of history; language holds the lifeblood of national culture. Chinese people blessed with profound and rich Chinese language should fulfill the mission of cherishing this wealth. Otherwise, the vicious circle of cultural anomaly and language degeneration would incur deep grief.

In the Philippine history between the two suzerains' languages and the native languages, its complex relationship suggests the following points. First, the so-called language issues in the world exist either between two or more ethnic groups or tribes within a nation, or between suzerains and their colonies, like the typical case of the Philippines. Second, the relationship between a suzerain's (colonizer's) language and the native language cannot be summarized in terms of *anti-this* or *anti-that*. Acceptance or rejection of the colonial language depends on three major factors: National sentiments, pragmatism of language, and national interest in the long run. The case of the Philippines, which accepted Spanish slowly and accepted English swiftly, illustrates the second and third factor. Emperor Xiaowen of the Northern Wei Dynasty of China was another example, who campaigned for thorough Sinicization – the capital relocated to Luoyang, the language shifted to the right pronunciation (Han Chinese of the Central Plains). Third, language issues, no matter whether they are between peoples in a nation or between nations, all bear patriotic sentiments – to guard the homestead of language for an ethnic group, for a tribe, or for a nation. Language holds the lifeblood of an ethnic culture. The compassion for the house of language is indeed the compassion for the lifeblood of an ethnic culture.

Not all language issues in the world are associated with the protection of mother-tongue rights, human rights, racial rights, or motherland rights. There is another type of trouble. In China, where language stability always prevails, with no dialects contending for the throne of official language and no harassment of discourse hegemony, language has been seized as a pilot breakthrough for the social progress movement, namely the New Culture movement that overthrew classical Chinese and established vernacular Chinese. From a historical point of view, the New Culture movement is a social development in line with the Reform Movement of 1898 and the Revolution of 1911. Its motive for language change is to eradicate poverty and backwardness, and to gain a sound footing in the world. *In China, language issues are closely intertwined with social changes, and the reform in language issues has usually taken place without unnecessary sacrifices on the part of language users, which is a true blessing.*

During the Meiji Restoration, despite some thinkers' desperate spur of "leaving Asia to enter Europe", Japan retained its language, surnames, and race. Its failure in Westernization may have been due to its preserved language, I think. Preventing its language from being Westernized seems to have been a lucky move for Japan.

Language issues, language hegemony, or language anti-hegemony within or between nations usually emerge on the surface, while political and cultural conquests are often hidden deep. Cultural conquests are bound to encounter resistance. This is the internal cause of language issues.

4) Language houses the true feelings of human beings.

Western philosophers are discontent with the instrumental understanding of language, mainly because it weakens and even denies the philosophical function of language as the house of Being. In arguing that language is the last homestead of human beings, here we focus on the emotional value of language to house the true feelings of human beings, rather than serving only as a tool or symbols, which is grounded on the evidence of the following five facts.

First, one acquires one's mother tongue, in the form of a specific dialect, typically in one's mother's arms. For grown-up Chinese who can speak the standard language, official language, or Putonghua, their mother-tongue dialect oozes out of the mouth and subconsciousness when expressing their deepest love and endearment, for example, to their parents or hometown folks.

Second, when driven by spontaneous emotions such as fury or fondness, people habitually pop out words and intonations of their mother-tongue dialect to curse or to adore someone or something.

138 *Language: Mankind's last homestead*

Third, although the majority of Hui people in China have lost their ancestors' mother tongue – Arabian or Persian (their Muslim faith well kept) – imams illiterate of Chinese characters still use Arabian or Persian. It is predicted that someday Muslims in other parts of the world may use the local language in their religious practice, but the Hui people in China will not because it is by their ancient mother tongue that they communicate with their long history (Suo, 2000, pp. 24–29).

Fourth, Suo (*ibid.*) tells an anecdote in which he chatted with a veteran translator of Spanish and several Argentine friends. The Argentines brought up a light question for the translator, "You teach your son Spanish at home, don't you?" The answer was, "No. He will study English in the future". "Why?" "Because Spanish is useless". This gave the Argentines an odd face, and after a pause, one said, "We should have the entire world to go for Spanish in the future". The translator just let out a simple fact about Spanish being useful or not, but this unintended hurtful comment added awkwardness to the listeners. Why is that so? That is because the nest for their national sentiment was accidentally ripped, and the flagstaff of their national sentiment was snapped. A close analogy may be that when we speak Chinese in a foreign country, we are often bothered with a repeated question, "Are you Japanese?" If a foreigner snaps to our face that Chinese is useless, our cheerful heart will be chilled.

Fifth, the spirits of national martyrs and sages can be best recollected if duplicated in their own language. Directors of some well-received TV series in China such as *Romance of the Three Kingdoms* and *Daming Palace* gave a thumb-up to classical dialogues after rounds of discussion. I reckon at the bottom of the human mind, language (ancient language) is regarded as the nest for men's true feelings. Whenever modern Chinese recall Yat-sen Sun, Father of the Republic, they can always recite his will, "余致力国民革命凡四十年 ([yú zhìlì guómíngémìng fán sìshínían] "Over forty years I have devoted to National Revolution")..." We quote the will as his own words, and no one ever renders it in a modern version, "我投身于革命活动共四十年 ([wǒ tóushēnyú gémìnghuódòng gòng sìshínían] "I have been engaged in revolutionary activities for forty years..."). Whenever we recall Liang Zhuge, we recite his *Northern Expedition Memorial*. Whenever we recall Dongpo Su, we quote his *Ode to the Red Cliff*. Why is that? Why do we usually recall them first in their works of words, other than the innumerable feats that Liang Zhuge is remembered by, other than the talents and anecdotes that Dongpo Su's wit or romance is known by word of mouth? It proves that language snugly nestles people's affections for ancestors and sages. Moreover, it proves that language can evoke their voices, looks and facial expressions – their forms of life, reveal their mentality – also their forms of life showcase their talents and feats, and record their thoughts and moods. *Because language keeps a true record of one's form of life and bears a brand of one's life* (see 3.2.1), no wonder the recollection of someone naturally tunes in to his speech (with his voice more prominent than looks and facial expressions).

3.2.2.4 Accent identity: Psychological homestead

"Psychological homestead" is an analogy of "geographical homestead". It is sought after by people who identify with their hometown accent when they are away from hometown (in another place at home or abroad). It is no less important than the hometown on the map, only much stronger and more enduring. This can be exemplified by the cases about the Chinese-language complex of three generations of Chinese in Singapore, as recorded by Qiuyu Yu (1998), which are summarized in the following.

For immigrants from Fujian, Guangdong, and other places to Singapore, their sense of self-defense and cohesion built up facing the mass of Malays, Indians, and Europeans. They first formed a large Chinese circle, and then smaller circles by provinces, counties, clans, and surnames, every circle marked out by accents. They set up region-based guildhalls one after another through disasters and duels – no one knows how many. However, the most enduring "guildhalls" are in nowhere but on one's tongue. The first words uttered can tell one's origin. In fact, the guildhalls set up in the cities across China by people from different parts of the country also serve the same function: To seek their psychological homestead.

Yu wrote about a Chinese Singaporean hairstylist, famous for styling Chinese hair and well sought-after by young Chinese ladies. They always visited his salon in company with their mothers – their interpreters, for the eccentric stylist spoke only Chinese to Chinese clients. On this, Qiuyu Yu comments that the senior hairdresser is trying to preserve ethnic harmony by creating a milieu where the hair color vibes with the language. This is, in my view, the hairdresser's gesture to seek psychological homestead via the accent, for he could not return to his hometown on the map.

Once, a Singaporean woman with fine tastes invited Qiuyu Yu to dinner in the "Li Bai Hall" of a luxury restaurant. The moment Yu rushed in, she (knowing that Yu is from Shanghai and speaks the Shanghai dialect) caught him in a downpour of Shanghai dialect, fluent and pure. Her early connection with Shanghai was quite clear as she started speaking. On that, Yu (1998) makes the following comment.

> Language is sometimes like a peculiar spell, whispered to lift up a lost world and to unlock a door of life. I know, this madam living in the English world has been left with few chances to speak Shanghai or Hunan dialects. But those symbols, those rhythms, dormant like secret codes in her veins, have never disappeared.

The Chinese Singaporean woman said that she dreamt fragments of dreams and in each she spoke different dialects (Hunan or Shanghai dialect). Her daughter, a fruitful and famous English writer, spoke to her mother in Chinese for conveying affections, although both were proficient in English. On this, Yu (1998) comments,

140 *Language: Mankind's last homestead*

If Chinese language was viewed as a "caring mother", she pulled an extremely long sewing thread to clothe her children overseas, body and soul. This thread has evolved into the cable for racial posterity, and into the fiber woven with historical changes.

In saying that the accent of one's birth place can "lift up a lost world", Yu, by "a lost world", means the physical hometown one cannot return to. In saying that the accent of one's birth place can "unlock a door of life", Yu refers to the search for one's psychological homestead.

Yu (1998) also recorded that one day, many elderly Chinese Singaporeans crowded into a theater to watch a comic dialogue from Taiwan. The director and Yu were very worried about if the whimsical lines in the Taiwan cross-talk could prompt laughter. The cross-talk turned out to fire the audience, every subtle line igniting a hall of laughter, which displayed a collective conformity among people unknown to each other. Yu holds that people can identify with each other by language or by laughter. The comedian of this dialogue, Liqun Li, poked and tickled Yu with words understandable only by Chinese, and the performance altogether was ecstatic of miscellaneous topics: Zen Buddhism, anomalies, whether Tianxiang Wen (a patriotic poet and politician in the last years of the Southern Song Dynasty) can do Qigong or not, the acme of the Heaven-and-man unity. To deliberately showcase the thick content of Chinese language on an exotic land, the messier, the merrier. Just as Yu's descriptions show, accent identification was "displayed in a collective conformity among people unknown to each other" and psychological homestead was found in "words understandable only by Chinese, and ... the ecstatic performance".

3.2.3 Language and the falling or lasting of a civilization

One of the frequently quoted sayings by Confucius goes as follows.

If terminology is not corrected, then what is said cannot be followed. If what is said cannot be followed, then work cannot be accomplished. If work cannot be accomplished, then ritual and music cannot be developed. If ritual and music cannot be developed, then criminal punishments are not appropriate. If criminal punishments are not appropriate, then people will be at a loss.

(Zilu, The Analects)

This quote is widely held as the "theory of naming". Shi Hu (1997, p. 68) emphasizes, "Look at the harms of wrong names: Ritual and music cannot be developed, criminal punishments are not appropriate, and people will be at a loss. What a severe problem it is!" This is indeed "a severe problem", but instead of focusing on its consequences, we focus on the destiny of human beings to live in language (not helplessly). We focus on whether if names are wrong nothing can be done. If nothing can be done, then we would be bogged

Language: Mankind's last homestead 141

deep in the most primitive production activities as isolated individuals. If survival is a problem, there is no room for this or that civilization, no hope of civilization at all.

Language shapes and solidifies a civilization. In this process, people use language to set up and develop a civilized social system, economic norms, moral system (norms of conduct), and ideology. Of course, there are other processes involved in the development of a civilization, including the processes to grope for development (developing economy), to defend the basic rights for survival and development (starting or resisting invasion), to distribute interests (staging civil wars or clashes), and to gratify spiritual needs (developing literature, arts, etc.). But *language serves as the cohesion for all the constituents of a civilization.* Gong Qi (1997, p. 90) holds,

> People use language to express and communicate ideas and thoughts; people use written language to spread language and record experiences, keeping them, accumulating them, and magnifying them. Language should be credited as one of the factors for the progress of human civilization and culture.

3.2.3.1 The most effective conquest and assimilation

An existing civilization may fall, like Mayan culture and ancient Chinese Loulan culture, which fell apart and died as natural conditions worsened.

Can a civilization be annihilated by a bloody conquest of alien people? If a civilization is conquered and finally annihilated by alien people, which may be more effective: A bloody conquest or a language-and-culture assimilation? In this section, a case will be examined to shed some light on this question. But a clarification should be made that the author of the book bears no presupposition in favor of conquests by bloody force or by language and culture. The author abhors any conquest in any form, and supports voluntary, peaceful, and win-win integration between peoples. By offering bygone historical facts, the case under discussion can highlight the role that language plays in the keeping or falling of a civilization.

A civilization under conquest by alien people for a short or long period of time will not necessarily evaporate. The conqueror and the conquered may form different types of relationships. One is that in the long process of conquest, the conquered have to give up their political rights and their language in order to survive, develop, and progress. The second one is that the conqueror overpowers the conquered by bloody force, and then infiltrates into the latter by means of language and cultural assimilation, and slowly subdues them. The third one, though very unusual, is the assimilation of the conqueror by the conquered, whose cultural genes are far too penetrating. Such a thing happened in the history of China. Emperor Xiaowen of the Northern Wei Dynasty, after ruling the Han Chinese, launched a thorough Sinicization – moving the capital to Luoyang, authorizing the right pronunciation (Han

142 *Language: Mankind's last homestead*

Chinese of the Central Plains), and changing the family name (Tuoba) to Yuan. The fourth one, the powerful conquest, did not go through in the end.

The fate of the American Indians revealed a process of being conquered by violence and then becoming assimilated through language and culture.

After Columbus' discovery of the American continent in 1492, Europeans broke in and seized it. Before that, American Indians had developed a mature and complex social system with a rich cultural tradition, as the result of thousands of years of evolution. In Central America, the Mexican plain witnessed the rise and fall of a succession of Indian civilizations: The Olmec civilization (1200–400 BC; with huge stone carvings and grand religious cere-monies, they learnt to cultivate corn and created probably the earliest writing in America), the Teotihuacan civilization (around the time of the Wei and Jin Dynasties in China; they built pyramids as colossal as Egyptian ones, with meticulous city planning and a population of nearly 200,000), the Mayan civilization (which coexisted with the Teotihuacan one and in which they developed intricate social hierarchies, smart urban networks, and a com-plete political system; they practiced intensive farming, created a logosyllabic script and a most sophisticated calendar; their power declined around 900 AD), the Toltec civilization and the Aztec civilization (its capital was present-day Mexico City, with a population of 250,000, when Paris at that time as the largest city in Europe had only about 100,000). During the two-century con-quest, the Europeans led by Spain slaughtered these civilized nations without a wink of mercy; they herded the Indians together and with swords stabbed them to death, men and women, old and young; they tied them to posts and roasted them to death over fire; they even dried the milk of nursing mothers and starved their babies to death. In commenting on this history, Huang (1999) writes,

> It is indisputable that after the conquest the Indian population plunged from tens of millions to millions. With such a sharp loss, the cultural tradition of the Indians came to a halt; a brilliant civilization was ruth-lessly annihilated.

Huang's remark, "a brilliant civilization was ruthlessly annihilated", brings my attention to two things: 1) The fact of depopulation, a drop in the number of language users; and 2) millions of survivors who spoke native Indian languages. The latter, especially, may be more meaningful for a civilization because it holds out a hope that *one day the civilization will be revived as long as Indian languages are in use*. This hope is not a fantasy. Think about the restoration of the Jews. When the Roman legions burned down the Second Temple in 70 AD, most Jewish people were deprived of their homeland and dispersed as diaspora. From 70 BC to 1948, over a thousand years, Jewish people have been dispersed around the world, with their homeland far away, their mother tongue lost, even their complexion adapted. Amid the ordeals of survival, they managed to restore their country. The complicated reasons

Language: Mankind's last homestead 143

for their success cannot be captured in this book. I want to say that, like the Jewish that scattered all over the world, lost the mother tongue, but have miraculously rebuilt their nation, there are chances that millions of remaining Indian speakers in South America *might rebuild a new Indian civilization, different from the old, yet still of their own. This is just a conjecture.*

So far, the discussion on American Indians (then Central and South America) is just half done. The fate of North American Indians is another story.

The most dramatic event is that the European conquest of the New World took root, thrived, and developed a superpower in North America: The United States. Europeans regard the United States as a satellite country of European civilization (Huang, 1999). Before the founding of the United States, the conquered North American Indians had already been slaughtered, encroached upon, discriminated against, and deprived of their homeland. How did the United States – the satellite country of European civilization – treat the natives (North American Indians) after its establishment?

The United States exercised administrative power to carry out language strategy, that is, to assimilate and conquer native Indians by means of language. North American native languages, also known as North American Indian languages, is the general term for hundreds of native languages in America. Half of them had disappeared within five hundred years since the arrival of Europeans (by 1992, Columbus had discovered the continent for five hundred years), and the rest will die out in the near future. According to Dr Michelle Klaus, president of the Native American Language Institute and director of the Alaska Native Language Center, Native American languages fall into four types: A-type languages are spoken by all generations, including children; B-type languages spoken only by parents; C-type languages only by grandparents; and D-type languages only by the elderly, with no more than ten speakers for each language (cited in Cai, 2002). The death of a language is marked mainly by the total loss of its users. Dr Klaus predicts that D-type languages will die out in 2010, unless saved by special measures or kissed by miracles, C-type languages in 2040, and B-type languages in 2060. By 2060, the around one hundred fifty existing Indian languages in the United States will be reduced to twenty, a critical point of decline. Dr Klaus holds that the language policy of the United States has played an unforgivable role in the process of their decay, and should be blamed for the demise of Indian languages (cited in Cai, 2002). Cai (2002) points out that for a long time, the US government has adopted an assimilation policy to exclude, suppress, and eliminate Indian languages, and that Indian languages have been wiped out by unceasing blows and corrosions from the American government, which intended the thorough assimilation of Indian people. He continues to say that *"unilingualism" and "language superiority", two core concepts that originated in Europe from Christian languages and cultures, became the theoretical and philosophical basis for the language policy of the West and later of America.* After its founding, the United States also pursued "linguistic unity" to establish English as the dominant language in North America,

144 *Language: Mankind's last homestead*

while also marginalizing, dismantling, and weakening the other languages. First and foremost, hundreds of Indian languages were victimized by the US policy towards the Indian languages, which was part of its policy towards the Indians. The relationship between the United States of America, which was built on Indian soil, and the Indians, has always been the relationship of conquest and assimilation. In Cai's (2002) view, *history proves that the most effective conquest and assimilation is achieved through the assimilation of language and culture*. Thus, it can be seen that the American Indian language policy is not only driven by the American concepts of language and culture, but also by their determination to subdue and assimilate the Indians. To dispel Indian languages is an important part of its assimilation policy. In fact, President Grant's "Peace Plan" issued after the Civil War aimed at such tenet and motive.

> Many misunderstandings between the American government and the Indians are caused by language. One third of our current troubles have stemmed from language differences. Language unity can foster unity of emotions, and then the assimilation of thoughts, habits, and traditions will take place. The troubles caused by language differences will vanish. Therefore, we should set up schools to host Indian children, educating them in English, eliminating and replacing their barbaric languages with English. From then on, differences will disappear and civilization will follow.
>
> (Cited in Cai, 2002)

In 1887, during President Grant's administration, Atkins, the director of the Office of Indian Affairs, submitted his annual report to the United States Department of the Interior, saying that *"there is nothing like language that can so surely and fully get the national hallmarks burnt into a person"* (cited in Cai, 2002; emphasis added). Schools established in the Indian reservations of the United States prohibited students from speaking their mother tongues under any circumstances. On October 30, 1990, President Bush signed the Native American Language Act (Title I of Public Law 101–477.1), declaring that the United States had an obligation to work with Native Indians taking measures to protect Native American cultures and languages because they had a special status. However, this was nothing more than a pretense, for many American Indian languages had already died by then, posing no threat to anywhere or anybody, and it is of little use endowing them such a special status (Cai, 2002). President Grant's postwar "Peace Plan" is the most telling historical testimony to the secret of conquest and assimilation, and also the password to the secret. What are the troubles of conquest by force? The "Peace Plan" claimed that "one third of our current troubles have stemmed from language differences" (cited in Cai, 2002). What steps should be taken to assimilate these native Indians? The "Peace Plan" proposed, "We should set up schools to host Indian children, educating them in English, eliminating and replacing

Language: Mankind's last homestead 145

their barbaric languages with English" (cited in Cai, 2002). Why is unity desirable between Native American languages and English? According to the "Peace Plan", it is because "language unity can foster unity of emotions, and then the assimilation of thoughts, habits, and traditions will take place" and "the troubles caused by language differences will vanish" (*ibid.*). The goal of the "Peace Plan" is that "from then on, differences will disappear and civilization will follow" (*ibid.*). As for the civilization finally established, whose civilization is it, the civilization of the conqueror or the conquered? The answer is clear now. *It must be an undeniable truth that when a language is destroyed, its civilization will fall apart (e.g., due to invasion).* From what happened to the Native American languages and civilizations, the most important lesson we should learn is, in Atkins's words, "There is nothing like language that can so surely and fully get the national hallmarks burnt into a person" (cited in Cai, 2002). As mentioned earlier, Japan imposed Japanese language education during its invasion of China, and Germany banned French courses during its conquest of France. Of course, their efforts did not succeed. The historical experience ("historical lessons" is also a correct wording) obtained here is that a conquest by means of "force" will never attain the end of "conquest". In contrast, Liang Zhuge's ideas and deeds in this regard during the Three Kingdoms period of China were sagacious.

To sum up, while Europeans conquered Central and South America mainly by force, the United States, dubbed "the satellite country of Europeans", mainly resorted to language-and-culture assimilation of Native American Indians. This case suggests that on the negative side, a civilization falls apart (e.g., due to invasion) when its language is destroyed; on the positive side, *to guard the mother tongue means a matter of life or death for a civilization.*

3.2.3.2 Mother tongue/mother culture: The warmest cradle of a civilization

Japan has spent a period in history attempting to Westernize itself from head to toe, but in vain. Why did it fail, though all the Japanese craved for it? On the contrary, in China, only a few wild cries for Westernization would rake people's nerves (actually, they are overreacting). Is it possible for China to be totally Westernized? Is there a danger of collapse if a civilization has learnt or imported ideology and life style from other cultures on a large scale?

In order to answer these questions, we have to find out what "Westernization" means. By this term, many people refer to how China or any nation in the East follows the West in ideology or life style, in particular, worshiping capitalism and liberalism. This understanding leaves something out and will lead to nowhere. Communism was also born in the West. The opening statement of the *Communist Manifesto*, published one hundred fifty years ago, is "A specter is haunting Europe – the specter of communism". Communism developed in Europe, traveled to the Soviet Union and then to China, a trajectory so vital but ignored by our concept of "Westernization". To worship or to decry an imported culture is simply insane and illusory. Equally bad, dumping one's

146   *Language: Mankind's last homestead*

mother culture and kneeling before a foreign culture will incur many foul consequences. "Westernization" so narrowly interpreted as capitalism and liberalism is but a submission to "West-centered dominance". A chewy "forgetting" should be mentioned here. In the 1950s to 1960s, China propagandized "leaning over to the Soviet Union", a downright Westernization slogan and policy. This failure has been kept as an unspoken secret and an unlearnt lesson. In contrast, another kind of Westernization, i.e., the pursuit of downright capitalism and liberalism, has swarmed people with oversensitivity and fear of being engulfed in a "wave" of *-ism*.

Even if Westernization is interpreted so narrowly (as the pursuit of downright capitalism and liberalism), I believe that *China cannot be Westernized unless Chinese is completely replaced by Western languages*. History has witnessed repeatedly that Chinese succeeded in assimilating other languages; it is impossible for Western languages to take the place of Chinese. It is impossible for any civilization to be Westernized (disintegrated) unless its mother tongue is completely replaced by a foreign language. Territory seized by foreign forces does not entail such Westernization.

When we contend that China cannot be totally Westernized and that Japan has not succeeded in Westernization, we are weighing the value of language for a nation, the value of the mother tongue and mother culture, not the ideological, military, or economic strength of a nation powerful enough or not to eject Westernization.

Therefore, our answer to the first question is that Japan, in the hopes of Westernization, has done this or that in vain because of its maintained mother tongue and mother culture. Japan has adopted a Western political system, yet it does not amount to being Westernized. The answer to the second question is that it is impossible for China to be totally Westernized. The answer to the third question is: Blind acceptance of the ideology and life style of different cultures is undesirable (so, in this sense, it is absolutely necessary for our government and scholars to promote Chinese culture and guide the younger generation to become informed of China's present-day situations).

In Japan, the process of modernization began with a vigorous advocacy of leaving Asia and joining Europe, the so-called "leaving Asia" frenzy (G. Sun, 1995). Japan "knelt" before almost everything Western, such as the Western cultural and economic hegemony, even the Western discourse of modernity, except the Western political hegemony that it defied. Japanese-look architecture blends with Western-style floor-to-ceiling doors and windows, and Tatami rooms adjoin spacious Nordic-style halls. Tables and chairs in the dining room are designed in Italy and made in Germany. Potted flowers on the windowsills that you pass by are probably European imports. Nowadays, the Katakana of loanwords quickly gobbles down once dominant Chinese characters in Japanese. You would attempt to argue that the biggest crisis facing Japan after the Meiji Restoration is its hot head to follow Western developed countries and Western values. That is true. However, you cannot deny that Japan in the end chose to counteract Westernization and maintain its identity, which

Language: Mankind's last homestead 147

reflected a more sophisticated and profound cultural orientation. According to the Japanese expert on the history of thoughts Hashikawa Miyako, the aforementioned "leaving Asia" frenzy pioneered by Fukuzawa Yukichi is one of the two orientations. Another orientation is "Asia is One" represented by Okakura Kakuzo. The former dismisses Confucian civilization, and the latter advocates "love" and "religion" to unite the Oriental as one. This is true not only for the past of Japan, but also for the present of East Asian countries. They have accepted the entire set of Western discourse of modernity together with the world framed by such rhetoric. Why did Japan in the past and those East Asian countries at present sleep on the West-dominant ideology? Very likely, they subject themselves to the discourse of modernity, presuming the process of modernization identical and homogeneous between the West and the East. On the surface, discourse dominance is so omnipotent that it precedes politics and economy, but the truth is that Western and Eastern cultures are incomparable and heterogeneous. The modernization of East Asian countries does not necessarily amount to Westernization. Therefore, the historical background and psychological context for accepting the dominant discourse of the West do not exist at all. This point will be discussed later.

In fact, *Japan achieved neither Westernization nor Sinicization.* It has tried painstakingly to learn from China, but has not learnt Chinese culture proper. To some extent, Japanese society has modelled itself on Chinese forms of life, but the life of the common Japanese has not been Sinicized. Japan has a cultural structure completely different from that of China, both in social organization and family structure. Its failure in the two attempts of Westernization can be attributed to its maintained mother tongue and mother culture.

The cultural norms of Japan are woven in Japanese, and those of China are woven in Chinese, just as *the cultural norms of every nation – or, more precisely, the norms of humanistic network – are woven in its mother tongue. As long as its mother tongue exists, the norms of a nation will not fall apart or die out.*

As for the reasons why Japan failed in its attempts at Westernization and why China does not have to worry about thorough Westernization, it is because the mother tongue carries the cultural norms, because the mother tongue keeps alive the norms of its nation, and because different cultures are meant to be complementary instead of being life-or-death mutually exclusive. Being incommensurable or heterogeneous, different civilizations or cultures are expected to complement each other, to foreground and interpret each other so as to set up collectively the common truth in the world, each of them being an indispensable component, none superior or inferior to the other. This is why incommensurable or heterogeneous civilizations can be complementary. According to Fu Yan, one of the axioms for mankind is as follows.

> If the ancient thoughts are true and ancient words credible, they cannot be blocked by gaps of time or space. They may be absent here, but present there. *They emerge in different places, but they share many similarities. Truth-seekers can borrow what they learn elsewhere to prove what we have*

148 *Language: Mankind's last homestead*

inherited from our ancestors. Doing so, truth-seekers will be enlightened and awakened.

(Cited in R. Zhang, 1998; emphasis added)

Put differently, our traditional culture will not die because of the introduction of Western civilization. Instead, Eastern and Western civilizations are mutually complementary and interpretive.

It is via the mother tongue that the mother culture solidifies in a person or a nation. *As the mother culture accumulates in a person or a nation, it becomes the root cause for why an Eastern nation cannot be Westernized outright. Hence, mother tongue and mother culture make the firmest and warmest cradle of a civilization.*

In this sense, some people cannot understand why Shi Hu, as a thinker of the Enlightenment movement, strongly advocated total Westernization (he later advocated "complete globalization and total Westernization"; R. Zhang, 1998). Some people regard Hu's advocacy as a strategy to urge conservative Chinese striving for thorough Westernization and hopefully achieving some progresses despite their conservativeness (L. Qi, 1998). I can understand Hu's strategy. He realized that the accumulation of a nation's mother culture is the deepest reason for why a nation cannot be Westernized outright. Hu had a deep understanding of the cultural bedrock of our nation. Knowing that China cannot be totally Westernized, Hu still advocated thorough Westernization in hope that his proposal might bring about some progress in China, even just some slight progress. Hu himself was not Westernized during a long period of overseas life; he did not practice any Western customs for his marriage, which matters quite a lot to any Chinese. Likewise, another famous scholar of Hu's time, Yinque Chen, having lived overseas for a long time, still wore a long gown after he returned to China to teach at a university and study Chinese history and literature. The same is true with Youlan Feng, who wore long black hair, beard, long gown, and Chinese jacket, while having a *Taiji* logo printed on his blue cloth book wrappers. Why Shi Hu proposed such a strategy is also understandable in view of the fact that he had profound insights into Chinese philosophy, being an initiator and vigorous practitioner of China's New Culture movement, and a great scholar on language and culture. Chiang Kai-shek once made an ungrounded boast, "My face is the only marker of my Oriental identity" (cited in Xiaoxiao, 2002). Chiang's mother tongue already entailed the mother culture upon him, as the most penetrating and innermost part, while his face was only an outside part. When in power, he often issued official documents in traditional Chinese (which were drafted by his secretary, Bulei Chen, though). Judging by this, his intrinsic ties with the Oriental identity were more than his face. Take Ziwen Song for another example (cited in Xiaoxiao, 2002). When Song headed the Ministry of Finance, the Ministry of Foreign Affairs, and the Executive Department of the Guomindang Government, he could only read the English translation of the Chinese official documents. It seemed that he had been completely "Westernized", but this was not the case

Language: Mankind's last homestead 149

(Xiaoxiao, 2002). Long before that, Song's mother tongue and mother culture had been accumulating since his early childhood with his parents. This was evidenced by his addressing his sisters as 阿姐 ([ājiě] "sister") when he was with them. Any Chinese with a full accumulation of his/her mother tongue and mother culture will bear some typical Chinese characteristics even to the very end of his life. Admittedly, Ziwen Song had an excellent command of English under the influence of Western culture. It is, however, rather dubious to assert his utter Westernization. Addressing terms like 阿姐 ([ājiě] "sister") or 阿弟([ādì] "brother"), though trivial, are an aroma emanating from the Chinese culture. These important personages mentioned above, who should have been Westernized as completely as possible, were not transformed that way at all, let alone the whole of China under Chiang Kai-shek's administration. It was nothing but a fantasy for China to be thoroughly Westernized.

Further evidence is provided by three culturally torn countries, Russia, Turkey, and Mexico. In *The Clash of Civilizations* (section 1, chapter VI of part III, "Torn Countries: The Failure of Civilization Shifting"), Huntington points out that "torn" refers to "cultural schizophrenia" and being "torn between two civilizations" (cited in Q. He, 1999). A country suddenly becomes sick and ashamed of its unique civilization, and attempts to shake it off while embracing another idolized civilization. Such a shift of identity to date has failed, hence a "torn country". Huntington examines three "torn countries", Russia, Turkey, and Mexico. Since the reign of Peter the Great, various forms (or aspects) of Westernization have considerably modernized the science and technology of Russia, but have not transformed its culture. Under the impact of the Orthodox Church and "Slavism", Russian people, deep down, have been rejecting Western culture and have fallen into a "torn country". Even at the peak of its "democratization" or Westernization, Russia has been shut out of the West as an "alien", which then had to withdraw and rekindle its cultural identity. Emulating Russia, Turkey has thoroughly Westernized its political, educational, and social system, etc. since the 1920s and especially after World War II. Nevertheless, the Ottoman Empire and Islamic tradition could not be erased from the mentality of the Turks or from the historical memory of Europeans. After the Cold War, Turkey has been moving itself closer to the West by appealing for EU membership, but Turkey has been given no place within Europe. Mexico was "torn" by the hesitation between the Spanish tradition of Latin America and Protestant capitalism of North America. All these facts prove that to abandon one's mother tongue and mother culture is not only impossible but also imprudent – self-destructively imprudent. Running away from one's own mother, foolishly yearning to embrace others' mothers, will end up in nowhere for one's home or protection. The "torn country" tragedy results from historical complexities and results in perplexities. It highlights the responsibility that humanistic intellectuals should shoulder for their country. Though the government of such a country and its short-sighted policies (a wishful convert to the West) should be to blame, humanistic intellectuals should also be held

150 *Language: Mankind's last homestead*

accountable. Their philosophical thinking on language and culture is for the nation and will be of the nation. If they think more deeply, the government and its people will mature enough to develop its civilization with less cost. It is not wise for any government or nation to stress only natural sciences but overlook humanities.

Regarding the accumulation of mother tongue and mother culture, we arrive at the conclusion: There is no way for Eastern countries to be Westernized, or Western countries "Easternized"; the best solution is "home is best" – staying at one's snug home of language, fine with its door and windows staying ajar.

3.2.3.3 *Language incommensurability stabilizes a civilization*

The concept of incommensurability, recurring in the earlier section, refers to the gap between two civilizations or cultures that is hard to fill, primarily due to their differences, which are not necessarily in opposition. This section is devoted to the discussion of language incommensurability.

One nation, one civilization. How do civilizations differ from each other? They differ primarily in cultural modes and languages. As their languages differ, so will their cultural modes. In this vein, among various determinants of cultural stability, language is the priority because its changes are most conservative (not in a bad sense). A nation and a civilization will survive, so long as its language stays alive.

In the countries speaking Indo-European languages, their scientific studies often adopt an analytic approach, the same as their cognitive mode of the world. As remarkable examples, Newton and Einstein adopt it to search for the primitive power of the universe. Where does their cognitive pattern stem from? From language. In contrast, the cognitive pattern of Chinese people seems to be synthetic, according to many Chinese scholars (e.g., Youlan Feng, Xianlin Ji, etc.). This synthetic approach was displayed in the science, technology, and philosophy of ancient China. Where does their synthetic pattern stem from? From language, too. English and Chinese exhibit marked differences in structure. English words often have multisyllables and morphological variations (in cases or inflections). As an alphabetic language, it is spoken as it is written. Both its morphology and logical syntax can stand analytical examination; overall, its grammar is rule-governed. However, Chinese words are monosyllabic and morphologically invariable. As an ideographic language, its phonological representation is different from its orthographical one. More strikingly, Chinese grammar seems fairly flexible and tricky (e.g., allowing for a bunch of conjunctions omitted from compound-complex sentences), though misunderstandings would not arise because of the speaker's and listener's reasoning. In this sense, Chinese seems to be "man-governed". The contrast between English and Chinese suggests their major incommensurability, which leads to cultural divergences in thinking modes (see 3.2.4), approaches to scientific studies, and philosophical inquiries. These divergences have intrinsic connections with language differences.

Language: Mankind's last homestead 151

Presumably, language incommensurability is the fundamental reason for why translations are often done between the two languages even though they are largely untranslatable and why communication between the languages is still happening though they are incommunicable. In analogy, just like doing the square root of 2 or dividing a circumference by its diameter, though inexhaustible, the progression can infinitely yield greater accuracy. For two nations speaking different languages, the language incommensurability guards each of them against "otherness". Even if China has achieved a full-scale modernization, it will not be completely Westernized. Thorough Westernization is impossible, as long as the mother tongue is still prevalent in its community, saving all the troubles of armed forces (of course needed at times of fighting for one's homeland), diplomats, and national security agents (tracking down spies). Therefore, Huntington (cited in Ji, 1997) exclaims, "They have achieved modernization, but they have not become people like us".

The Chinese discourse field is so absorptive that even Christianity – born in the West, was "Sinicized" after it entered China. This justifies the assertion that as long as the mother tongue is still prevalent in its community, thorough Westernization is impossible. According to Tan (1997), the contact between Chinese and Christianity can be dated back to the introduction of Nestorianism in 635 AD, the ninth year of the Reign of Zhenguan in the Tang Dynasty. Emperor Taizong was pleased about the Chinese transcriptions of Nestorianism and it subsequently spread out. The Nestorian documents found in China include *Ode to the Nestorian Monument in the Central Empire, Book of the Holy One: The Meditator, Monotheism, Book of Proclaiming the Beginning and Seeking the Origin, Chih Hsuan An Lo Ching, Praise the Trinity for Redemption, Book of Glory.* They are early attempts to introduce Christian doctrines to Chinese, and they are an important part of the origin of Christian theology. At the end of the thirteenth century, the Catholic Franciscan missionary John of Montecorvino brought Christianity again into the capital of the Yuan Dynasty. It is said that he had translated the Old Testament "Psalms" and the New Testament into the Uyghur used commonly by the Mongol ruling class in China then. But it was not until the arrival of Matteo Ricci in China (1582) that Catholicism flew in and its classics were translated into Chinese, which set out a systematic "fusion" of Christian tenets into Chinese language and culture. During the reign of Emperor Qianlong, a non-stop debate among missionaries wrestled with how to translate those Christian doctrines into Chinese, an unnoticed issue in the past. Matteo Ricci used 天主 ([tiānzhǔ] "the Lord of Heaven") from Chinese history books to render the Latin word *Dues* (the Holy God in Christianity). Discontented missionaries protested that the true meaning of *Dues* would be covered up or distorted by Chinese terms such as 天 ([tiān] "Heaven"), 天主 ([tiānzhǔ] "the Lord of Heaven"), and 上帝 ([shàngdì] "the Emperor of Heaven"). These Chinese terms usually refer to the god in the Chinese faith, not God revealed through Jesus Christ, as designated by *Dues*. To avoid confusion, the transliteration 陡斯 [dǒusī] was proposed for *Dues*,

152 *Language: Mankind's last homestead*

the Holy God in Christianity. 天, 天主, and 上帝 have acquired established meanings in Chinese context and represented traditional Chinese faith, so the use of them for *Dues* of Christianity is prone to misunderstanding. Just as Tan (1997) points out,

> The controversy is not a matter of busy-for-nothing, but is a serious issue. The question is whether the Chinese language can "host" the Christian faith as it is and, if so, how to preserve it as it is.

The controversy lends us an insight that a language can host something alien from it and tolerate a moderate "fusion" with it, but it cannot preserve the alien intact. This fact shows that it is unthinkable for native speakers to be "dissolved" by other civilizations if their mother tongue is still alive. In the case of Christianity's Sinicization, I do not take it for granted that Chinese can "Sinicize" those Western things outright. Just as when our Zen Buddhism was translated to the West, into Western languages, it cannot be Westernized outright, despite some loss of original intentions. It is quite clear that the Chinese language constitutes the greatest unbridgeable chasm against the complete Westernization of China. The chasm of language incommensurability defeats any attempt at complete Westernization of any civilization.

Philosophers interpret language incommensurability from another angle, viewing language as the house of Being, the house of existence, or the house of beings. Different languages are different houses.

Let us look at the excerpt of dialogue on language between Heidegger (as H in the dialogue) and the Japanese scholar Tezuka Tomio (as T in the dialogue) (Heidegger, 1982, pp. 2–15).

T: ... since the encounter with European thinking, there has come to light a certain incapacity in our language. (Heidegger, 1982, p. 2)

H: ... a true encounter with European existence is still not taking place, in spite of all assimilations and intermixtures. (*Ibid.*, p. 3)

T: What danger are you thinking of?

H: That we will let ourselves be led astray by the wealth of concepts which the spirit of the European languages has in store, and will look down upon what claims our existence, as on something that is vague and amorphous. (*Ibid.*, p. 3)

H: ... The danger arose from the dialogues themselves, in that they were dialogues. (*Ibid.*, p. 4)

H: The danger of our dialogues was hidden in language itself, not in what we discussed, nor in the *way in which* we tried to do so (original emphasis). (*Ibid.*, p. 4)

T: Now I am beginning to understand better where you smell the danger. The language of the dialogue constantly destroyed the possibility of saying what the dialogue was about.

Language: Mankind's last homestead 153

H: Some time ago I called language, clumsily enough, the house of Being. If man by virtue of his language dwells within the claim and call of Being, then we Europeans presumably dwell in an entirely different house than Eastasian man.

J: Assuming that the languages of the two are not merely different but are other in nature, and radically so.

H: And so, a dialogue from house to house remains nearly impossible. (*Ibid.*, p. 5)

T: But a source that would then still remain concealed from both language worlds.

H: That is what I mean. (*Ibid.*, p. 8)

T: You have already mentioned what prevented you: the language of the dialogue was European; but what was to be experienced and to be thought was the Eastasian nature of Japanese art. (*Ibid.*, p. 13)

H: Whatever we spoke about was from the start forced over into the sphere of European ideas. (*Ibid.*, p. 14)

H: Because I now see *still* more clearly the danger that the language of our dialogue might constantly destroy the possibility of saying that of which we are speaking. (*Ibid.*, p. 15)

This dialogue captures our attention to Heidegger's ideas as follows. European thinking exposes a certain incapacity in East Asian languages, and vice versa. European languages make East Asian existence amorphous, and vice versa. If man by virtue of his language dwells within the call of Being, then Europeans presumably dwell in an entirely different house than East Asians. Assuming that the languages of the two are not merely different but are "other" in nature, so a dialogue from house to house remains nearly impossible. Saying what the dialogue is about in two languages is a danger. Whatever is spoken about is from the start forced over into the sphere of ideas held by the language spoken. A language constantly destroys the possibility of what another language can speak about.

In my view, the ideal way of saying should be using language A when only language A makes sense, using language B when only language B makes sense, and using language C when only language C makes sense. Take a simple example. The English word *uncle* (too general) cannot specify different uncles in the Chinese humanistic network, i.e., uncles on the paternal or maternal side, younger or older than one's own parents, in-laws or not. Likewise, the Chinese word 雪 ([xuě] "snow") (also too general) cannot specify a variety of snow in the Eskimo humanistic network. Why is that? *Every language has its own unique humanistic network* (here the concept of "humanistic network" is broader and more accurate than "culture"). *Because the uniqueness of humanistic networks creates separation between them, language incommensurability stabilizes every civilization.*

154 *Language: Mankind's last homestead*

3.2.3.4 The stability of a language and its writing system safeguard a civilization

Language, spoken or written, is the most conservative (not in a bad sense) and fundamental component of a culture. Its stability results from time, on the one hand – very long stretches of time of formation (spoken language before written language) and evolution – and, on the other, it results from language speakers, all the speakers of a speech community taking part in and identifying with the changes of a language (till conventions are reached). These two facts lead to the third one, *the stabilized humanistic network behind language emerging from speech community's conventions over a long time.*

The two factors, time and participants, require a very long span of time to make even small subjective changes to spoken or written language out of man's desires. Every change involves the acceptance of a large number of participating users, and every change evokes the enduring humanistic network behind the language. This explains why the bubble for annihilating Chinese (advocated by Xuantong Qian in his *The Future Problems with Chinese Characters*) and replacing it with Esperanto finally burst, why the proposal for romanizing the Chinese characters was stillborn, and why the zeal for "Esperanto as the common language of the world" (Bajin, 1989, p. 84) was dampened. For a country, a few decades or centuries will be enough to achieve industrialization, modernization, and prosperity. However, any change in language and its writing system is the most fundamental and difficult change in a civilization, *owing to the long years, the large number of language users, and the humanistic network woven by language as enduring as Mount Tai.* The frenzy of annihilating Chinese characters amounts to annihilating the humanistic network. If Chinese pinyin took the place of Chinese characters, there would be nothing behind it but a void (a blank slate). In contrast, behind the Chinese characters was five thousand years of civilization as firm as Mount Tai. Saying that "Esperanto will become a common language for all the people" means saying that "all the people share the same humanistic network", or that all the people share the same cultural background, which is no less than a dreamy dream.

The language of a nation, spoken and written, stabilizes its deepest culture. Therefore, when one lives away from his hometown (in other provinces or countries), in order to preserve his civilization, he must first and foremost preserve his language (see 3.2.3.4 for the discussion of the Chinese language complex as recorded by Qiuyu Yu). Conversely, in order to survive on an alien land, one has to forsake his mother civilization by taking the first and most difficult step – to forsake his native language. For survival, when expatriates assimilate themselves into the host countries (which is common throughout history), dropping their modes of thinking, modes of living and production, they must first drop the hardest to drop, namely their language. What follows is a case recorded by Qiuyu Yu (1998, p. 486).

In many overseas Chinese families with three generations, the first generation speaks the Fujian dialect, the second speaks standard Chinese, and the third speaks English only. Interaction between generations needs translation; every move of translation waters down the original meaning and emotion. Language alone becomes the hurdle, hard to cross over even for the blood-tied family members under the same roof. No choice is left for parents who are upset by the neck-and-neck competition outside the door. None of them is willing to afford decades of their children's time bending over a very challenging but not quite useful language. Although parents do know that Chinese is connected both to the soul of their forefathers and the civilization of five thousand years, they pick the subject of English for their children while plucking away any Chinese subject. They trade the principles of kinship, affection, and culture for the principles of openness, practicality, and economy. This sets the historical milieu of the use of English by the third generation of Chinese Singaporeans. Only by English does the third generation feel at ease. By English, with distinct Nanyang accent though, they may erase all the divergences from their homeland, erase all the vicissitudes of their families, all the bitterness of their history, and in the end shake off the Chinese language and shake off their surnames. Concerning this process, Qiuyu Yu (1998) poses some questions: How much psychological transformation does a community undergo from learning a foreign language to unlearning their mother tongue, and how long does it take? Furthermore, how much psychological transformation does a community undergo from dropping their mother tongue to dropping their family name, and how long does it take? Yu laments that a language shift gives birth to a bunch of rootless "abstract people". More significantly, Yu predicts that Singaporean politicians, eager to modernize this Chinese-dominant country onto the international stage, must force over a new mode of thinking and a new tempo. According to Yu, nothing can achieve this goal more thoroughly and effectively than creating a different language vibe: *Because language is part of the cultural-psychological pedestal, once the pedestal is replaced, other parts will be in their place.*

Note that only when language is replaced can one be uprooted. Sometimes a person, some people, or a small number of people choose to uproot themselves by "forsaking their native language which is the most thorough and effective means to this end". Language vibe serves as the pedestal for everything else, the way of thinking, the way of living, the customs and habits, which are all "movables" along with "the removal of language". In this sense, *the stability of language is at the root of civilization stability, and forsaking a language is uprooting a civilization.*

3.2.3.5 The "septum" between languages safeguards a civilization

There is communication between languages (to be discussed in 3.2.3.6), but there is the "septum" between languages. Y. Cheng (1994) points out that *"it is language that best embodies the septum of human thought"* (emphasis added). Sometimes we think we are using the same concept, but in fact we are just talking to ourselves. Take the English word "tolerance /toleration"

156 *Language: Mankind's last homestead*

and its Chinese counterpart 宽容 [kuānróng], for example. The meaning of "tolerance" has been extended from "put up with others" to "not to infringe upon others' freedom of thought and action". It is to restrain the imposition of one's own will upon others, which is based on equality of human beings in personality and rationality. Thus, human beings have to be tolerant, otherwise they would be wrong or even guilty (as was specified in the Act of Toleration, the Chinese translation of which is 宽容法 [kuānróngfǎ], issued during the seventeenth-century revolution in England). And "tolerance" is almost "forgiveness", just as the Chinese sayings go, "Gentlemen do not bear a grudge against a villain for his wrongdoings" and "The prime minister's mind should be broad enough to sail a boat". Thus, to be tolerant has become a matter of magnanimity and self-cultivation, all depending on individuals' willingness. It is a virtue for a person to be of tolerance, but it is still human not to be tolerant, for the object of "forgiveness" is inherently reprehensible or at least contemptible. It can be seen that "tolerance" is not based on the principle of equality, but comes from a sense of superiority of elders, virtuous people, wise people, and, more commonly, kings (Cheng, 1994). In Chinese, 人文主义 [rénwénzhǔyì] is often taken as equivalent to "humanism", but the problem is that "humanism" has several senses. Alan Bullock once said,

> I spent my whole life at Oxford, where study on humanities has a long tradition, going back at least to Erasmus, John Colette, Thomas Moore, and the "new learning" in the Renaissance. Probably, this is why the notion of humanism is taken for granted. Until I was about sixty when I became vice-chancellor of Oxford … I have just discovered that no one has succeeded in defining the terms such as humanism, humanist, humanistic, and humanity in a way that others are also satisfied with. These words vary in meanings and mean different things to different people, which leaves lexicographers and encyclopedia-compilers scratching their heads.
>
> (Cited in Dong, 1993)

Chinese understandings of the term "humanism" are diverse: Some understand it as 人文主义 [rénwénzhǔyì], some translate it as 人本主义 [rénběnzhǔyì] or 人道主义 [réndàozhǔyì], and some others interpret it as 人性论 [rénxìnglùn]. Some even translate it as 唯人论 ([wéirénlùn] "theory only on human beings") and 人学 ([rénxué] "science of mankind"). In different historical stages, different specific environments required different emphases in interpretation. The separation between people leads to the septum of languages, which in turn results in confusions in translations.

Nevertheless, the septum between languages guards a civilization.

To translate one language into another is, in fact, to translate one life into another, which is essentially impossible. The ideal of translation is to make one kind of thought, culture, or life understood by another kind of thought,

Language: Mankind's last homestead 157

culture, or life. To achieve this ideal, the culture, society, and history on which language depends would have to be taken into account. Wittgenstein (1953, p. 5) calls "the whole, consisting of language and the actions into which it is woven, the 'language-game'" and claims that "to imagine a language means to imagine a form of life" (1953, p. 8). As a result, many people around the world who can write in a foreign language have similar complaints: It is inappropriate to express the thoughts of non-English-speakers in English and non-Chinese-speakers in Chinese. Such a kind of misfit is not in the subject under discussion, nor in the way of discussion, but hidden in the language itself (terminology, words). If Eastern concepts, such as 气 ([qì] "pneuma"), 道 ([dào] "logos") and 禅 ([chán] "Dhyana") are talked about in Western languages, there is always a wall, impenetrable no matter how you try to convey the truth. Similarly, if we use Chinese terms or words, such as 电脑化空间 ([diànnǎohuà kōngjiān] "computerized space"), 计算机空间 ([jìsuànjī kōngjiān] "computer space"), 信息空间 ([xìnxī kōngjiān] "information space"), 多维信息空间 ([duōwéi xìnxī kōngjiān] "multi-dimensional information space"), 多次元空间 ([duōcìyuán kōngjiān] "multi-dimensional space"), or 赛博空间[sàibó kōngjiān] "cyberspace") to talk about "cyberspace", we may fail to cover exactly what "cyberspace" means to a native English speaker, no matter how hard we try. It is possible that when a translator cannot understand the author's intention in the source text, they might do word-to-word translation, which either twists the original meaning or is simply incomprehensible (I call that violent communication). Violent communication happens to almost every translator, but a good translator reduces it to the lowest level possible.

Those translators who are ambitious invest a lot of effort in the cultural untranslatability, but the results are not always ideal, to which I hold a sympathetic attitude. These arduous translators often have the assumption that others fail to translate because they do not have enough knowledge or wisdom.

In fact, the separation itself between people, resulting in the septum between languages, is what people or civilizations need. Some compartments do not have to be rammed open, or knocked through, *just as a fence or a wall between two houses would make their dwellers feel secure.* How can you deny that the existence of the wall between Zhang's house and Li's is reasonable since it can make both house-owners feel safe and relieved? The partition wall makes property rights clear, enables privacy, and legalizes individual freedom and safety. Accordingly, to admit the legitimacy of this wall is wisdom. In this way, it seems unwise for translators to try to get through everything. As for the issue of untranslatability, my position is that there is indeed such a thing and *its existence is reasonable. It is necessary to make efforts to do translation while acknowledging untranslatability.*

The cultural septum is the root of the language septum. What happens when we mistake cultural differences for the cultural common core?[12] To use the target language with the lexical patterns, word order, rhetorical devices, and cultural patterns of image borrowing in the source language will cause

158   *Language: Mankind's last homestead*

communication failures. For instance, if you translate the Chinese phrase 一贫如洗 ([yīpínrúxǐ] "as poor as a church mouse") literally into "as poor as washing (洗 [xǐ])", it will make no sense to native English-speakers. What shall we do? We have to abandon the cultural pattern of the source language, adopt the one in the target language, and translate it into "as poor as a church mouse". Then communication succeeds, or equivalent communicative effect is achieved. However, in terms of linguistic form, the two expressions are not equivalent. Moreover, the cultural image in the source language is completely lost and the metaphorical meaning is also gone. The Chinese 如洗 [rúxǐ] means "clean as being washed by water", while the English counterpart "as a church mouse" means "like a mouse in the church which has nothing to eat". Although the metaphor of the two is the same, the cultural images of the two are totally unrelated. Take another example: If you translate the Chinese我只会马走日，象飞田 ([wǒ zhīhuì mǎzǒurì, xiàngfēitián] "I just know that the horse moves first one point along the horizontal/vertical lines, and then one point diagonally, within a frame like the Chinese character 日 ([rì] 'sun'), and that the Elephant moves exactly two points in any diagonal direction within a frame like the Chinese character 田 ([tián] 'farmland')") into "I only know the most basic moves", the cultural bearing of the Chinese chess in 马走日，象飞田([mǎzǒurì，xiàngfēitián] "The horse moves within a frame like the Chinese character 日([rì] 'sun') and the Elephant moves within a frame like the Chinese character 田 ([tián] 'farmland')") is totally lost. In a word, cultural loss is inevitable in translation, especially in interpretation. No matter what the source language is, there is a problem of cultural loss in translating it into another language (G. Qian, 1994).

Translation between two languages basically involves triple losses. The first step of translation is to comprehend the source text. A text is just a meaningless symbol before it is comprehended (if there is any meaning, it is uncertain and open). Only in understanding can the text be given a meaning or definite meaning. Moreover, since understanding itself is a way of human existence, the results of understanding are different manifestations of the various ways of existence. As meaning depends on understanding, it is reasonable for different readers to hold that there is no such thing as the same text. The meaning that the reader finally grasps must have been changed by understanding, and this is the so-called deviation. The second step is to translate the source text into the target text. Even a successful or faithful translation is just one interpretation of the source text. The process of interpretation is accompanied by the subjective interference from the interpreter, which means a loss for the source text. Youlan Feng also believes so, when he says,

> A translation is nothing more than an interpretation. For example, when one translates a sentence in Laozi, he gives his own interpretation of this sentence. However, this translation can only convey one meaning, but in fact, the source text may contain many other meanings. The source

Language: Mankind's last homestead 159

text is richly suggestive, while its translation is not and cannot be. Thus, the translation has lost much of the richness inherent in the source text.

(Feng, 1996, p. 13)

The third step is the reader's reading of the target text, which is also an interpretation. This is the third deviation, that is, the reader will do to the target text what the translator does to the source text. To this, Ni (1996) exclaims, "Awful, it [translation] has been casted with the triple curses of hermeneutics!" Is there a super translator who can escape the triple deviations? I do not think so. A good translator only deviates a little less.

Sapir (1929; in Mandelbaum, 1958, p. 162) claims, "In a sense, the network of cultural patterns of a civilization is *indexed in the language* which expresses that civilization". Based on his claim, we can say that a civilization is guarded by its language.

When one is born, he is put into a life style, which means that he has entered a limitation. It is difficult for a person to communicate with others; it is more difficult for one nation to communicate with other nations. The fact that language is untranslatable reflects that people are untranslatable. It follows that the septum in language is caused by the separation of people. Objectively, the "septum" in language guards a civilization.

Language locks up the essence of the civilization of a nation, i.e., literature, but objectively it guards the civilization. Many types of art are borderless owing to the universality of the materials used. The colors created by the pigment, the lines by brushes, and the tones and melodies by strings can be appreciated by people all over the world without translation. Zhongshu Qian cited several convincing examples and said,

> The ill-informed Chinese may love listening to foreign music, while the countrified foreigners may collect Chinese paintings and statues. Maybe they are not good at authentication, but their pleasure is real. Only literature is the stubbornest, refusing to tell its secrets to everyone. The literature produced in a certain language is limited and blocked by that language. Similarly, poetics in a country is always difficult for a foreigner to understand unless he is proficient in the language of that country. Otherwise, the translation is just like a boiled waxberry, which loses its charm.
>
> (Z. Qian, 1997, pp. 529–530)

God might be reproved as the original troublemaker. Humans wanted to build a tower to Heaven, which is against God's will. Therefore, God cursed and managed to confuse the languages of the tower-builders so that they could not understand each other and had to give up building the tower. This is the so-called "curse of Babel". In art, only literary communication requires the help of translation, but the translation is not authentic enough. This septum in translation has exerted significant negative influences. The reason

160 *Language: Mankind's last homestead*

why the Chinese cannot get the Nobel Prize in Literature is not that they have no excellent literary works, but that the so-called sinologists in foreign countries are not so proficient in Chinese. If you cannot enter the palace of Chinese literature, how can you comment on the Chinese literary works? The independence of literature is an important part of the independence of a civilization, and the independence of literature must rely on the uniqueness of language as the media.

Each language creates a unique cultural tradition, cognitive style, and thinking habit, which is also a kind of separation. The United Kingdom and France are separated by the English Channel, while the United Kingdom and the United States are separated by the Atlantic Ocean, which is geographically much wider. However, the difference between the United Kingdom and France is much larger than that between the United Kingdom and the United States. The reason is that the United Kingdom and the United States speak the same language, while the United Kingdom and France have different official languages. It is generally believed that language barriers can be removed by translation. However, symbolic differences are only at the shallow level of language barriers, while deep differences are those in cognitive styles and thinking habits, that is, the differences at the discourse level, in Foucault's words. We know that different languages lead to different classifications of the objective world and different categories (see 3.2.4 for a detailed discussion). Whorf points out,

> We dissect nature along lines laid down by our native languages. The categories and types that we isolate from the world of phenomena we do not find there because they stare every observer in the face; on the contrary, the world is presented in a kaleidoscope flux of impressions which has to be organized by our minds – and this means largely by the linguistic systems of our minds.
>
> (Whorf, 1940/1956, p. 213)

People who speak Chinese say 热水 ([rèshuǐ] "hot water") and people who speak English say "hot water", but people who speak Japanese do not say "atsu-i mizi" in a similar way. In Japanese, "mizi" refers only to cold water, so "atsu-i mizi" becomes "hot" and "cold water", which are incompatible. In Japanese, "oyu" refers specifically to hot water. This is a categorical difference. Eskimos classify snow differently from people of other nations (there are plenty of words for snow of different shapes and colors and falling times, but no word for ordinary snow). Chinese people's classification of relatives (for example, relatives who are age peers of one's own parents are subdivided into 叔父/母 ([shūfù/mǔ] "father's younger brother"/"the wife of father's younger brother"), 伯父/母 ([bófù/mǔ] "father's elder brother"/ "the wife of father's elder brother"), 姑父/母 ([gūfù/mǔ] "husband of father's sister"/"father's sister") and 舅父/母 ([jiùfù/mǔ] "mother's brother"/"the wife of mother's brother"), but there is no such general term as uncle/aunt) is

Language: Mankind's last homestead 161

different from that of British and American people (for example, relatives who are age peers of one's own parents are called collectively without any subcategories). The American Indians who speak Hopi only have one word for both 飞机 ([fēijī] "airplane"), 飞龙 ([fēilóng] "flying dragon") and 飞行员 ([fēixíngyuán] "pilot"), but use different words for water in the open air and water in a bottle. The way the Chinese describe the moon is different from that of British and American people, and the Chinese almost categorize food therapy and medical therapy (Chinese herbal medicine) into the same class (a meal recipe can have a specific therapeutic purpose. As the saying goes, "food is superior to medicine"). However, Westerners make a strict distinction between medicine and food. Westerners are good at scientific theories, especially the major theories generated by hypothesis testing, in which Chinese people are deficient. This can be traced back to their different cognitive styles: The former is adept at logical analysis, while the latter is deft at synthetic thinking. Why did Westerners invent such disciplines as geometry and algebra, which use accurate step-by-step deduction? Why was the mysterious and unspeakable Zen created by the Chinese? *Is this the result of accidental division of labor or linguistic differences?* The different creations were not accidental events because *it was impossible for the two to exchange inventions. This is caused by the differences in the series of language-cognitive style-habit of thinking.* The doctoral or master students studying in the United Kingdom and the United States have such a strange feeling; their papers written in relatively smooth English are not so smooth after being translated into Chinese by themselves! Moreover, the writings concerning British and American culture seem to be no longer narratives of English and American culture after being translated into Chinese! When we try to rewrite our own monographs in Chinese into English, we feel strongly that the original feeling has changed. The awkwardness during the process is obvious, and we may not believe much of what we have written. The reason for this interesting change is that we will change to use the corresponding cognitive style and thinking habit of the language in which we narrate. When the Chinese say 田 ([tián] "field, farmland"), the glyph information – the crisscrossed division of the land – is revealed together. When the British and American people say "field", "farmland", and "cropland", the crisscrossed division of the land is completely invisible from the word form. That is to say, the speaking of the Chinese character 田 [tián] in which the sound and glyph information appear at the same time has made Chinese people cognitively adopt such a kind of crisscrossed land division. The expressions that are unique in Chinese, such as the two-part allegorical sayings, can be explained from cognitive styles and ways of thinking. For example, in 孔夫子搬家—尽是输 ([kǒngfūzǐ bānjiā – jìnshìshū] "Confucius moves – all is lost"), 输 ([shū] "lose") has the same sound with another Chinese word 书 ([shū] "book"). There is in fact a pun in it with another meaning: Confucius moves with nothing but books. Likewise, the poems hiding the head (i.e., the first words of a few lines of a poem are combined into one sentence) and poems hiding the tail (the last words of a

162   *Language: Mankind's last homestead*

few lines of a poem are combined into one sentence) can also be explained from cognitive styles and ways of thinking. The word sound and character arrangement of Chinese, which allow vertical reading in horizontal rows and horizontal reading in vertical rows, allow or train Chinese people to have such cognitive styles and ways of thinking.

The septum between languages coexists with the septum between the systems of culture, morality, religion, law, etc. We bring this up because it is not appropriate to understand the septum between languages as being generated by languages solely. All of these septa actually coexist with one another. For example, the difference between the East and the West shall not be seen as merely a difference between languages, though it is the principal one, as there are other differences, such as differences between moral systems. As N. Zhao (1994) points out, the golden moral rule in China is "Do not do to others what you would not have them do to you", and the golden moral rule in the West is "Do to others as you would have them do to you". "What you would not have them do to you" refers to something that causes unpleasant feelings, and different people or cultures may agree to a higher degree on what they are. Things with negative evaluations such as pain, fatigue, poverty, insult, and hunger are unwanted for anyone. However, the concept of things wanted is more flexible and varies for different people or cultures. Everyone has different emphases on the pursuit of money, fame, power, knowledge, and religious beliefs. Therefore, it does not matter if a person who does not like eating stinky tofu does not put stinky tofu on the table every time he treats. However, it would be unpleasant if a stinky tofu lover put a plate of stinky tofu on the table every time he treats. In the former case, the consistency between what one does not like and what others do not like is often high; in the latter case, the consistency between what one likes and what others like is often low, but the one forces others to love the same thing, regardless of a large number of changes. This reminds us that today, when we can see each other even if we are thousands of miles apart by videophones, it does not mean that contemporary people have more opportunities than ever to share the common meaning of their words. On the contrary, in this world, whether it is a dialogue between the South and the North, or a dialogue between the East and the West, it has become increasingly difficult for human beings to find a common language and the common linguistic meaning. Geographically and linguistically, Kuwait and Iraq are "relatives". However, on February 5, 2003, the tens of thousands of military vehicles (entering the attack position) prepared by the US army to attack Iraq passed through the border of Kuwait. Different regions and nations (even the same country) are faced with strong and profound discourse conflicts among different language groups. In addition, the desire of the people in Quebec, Canada to speak French is well-known to the world. This shows that the linguistic septum is accompanied by a fundamental septum – the distribution of interests among countries, nations, and regions.

Language: Mankind's last homestead 163

3.2.3.6 The communication between languages increases the vitality of a civilization

In addition to the tendency to eliminate mutual impact, different language communities also promote each other and supplement each other. In other words, the mutual impact between languages has not only negative consequences for a civilization, but also positive ones.

When commenting on the Caribbean poet Derek Walcott, who received the Nobel Prize in Literature in 1992, the Russian-American poet Brodsky says,

> Civilization is limited, and there will be a moment in the life of every civilization when the center cannot be maintained. *It is not army groups but the language that prevents a civilization from falling apart.* This is true of Rome, and of ancient Greece. At this moment, the task of maintenance falls on those from other provinces and from the outside.
>
> (Cited in Huang, 1996)

The above citation is very important, although "civilization" is not well defined in it. Judged from the reference to Rome and ancient Greece, the "civilization" refers to the comprehensive development of a nation's economy, politics, and culture (this is exactly what we mean by "civilization"). However, judged from Huang's (1996) whole article, titled "The Change of English Styles", the words "civilization" and "civilization center" here seem to refer to the discourse center of a language (such as the center of English, the center of Chinese, etc.). This issue can be left aside, for even if the words "civilization" and "civilization center" refer to the discourse center (of English or Chinese), Huang's (1996) analysis supports our argument that communication between languages increases the vitality of a civilization. All the writers cited in the first part of Huang's 1996 article are winners of the Nobel Prize in Literature. They are not writers from mainstream English-speaking countries, but from other countries; Soyinka is from Nigeria, Gordimer from South Africa, Heaney from Ireland, and Brodsky from Russia. But without exception, "they use their own special talents and non-English experiences to enrich English styles and impact the center from the edge" (Huang, 1996). The Russian-American poet Brodsky wrote proses in English with proficiency that even the best English writers admire. In order to make their works novel and lively, many writers often borrow words from the fields of science and technology, natural science, sociology, and even political economy. In fact, in addition to the original intention of pursuing novelty, this practice also injects new blood into literature and greatly enriches linguistic expressions. The task of maintaining the center (of the English discourse) falls mainly on non-native English writers (so-called peripheral or marginal writers). They embrace diversity and have a wide range of experience in and knowledge about other countries

164 *Language: Mankind's last homestead*

in addition to the center. They are more flexible and sophisticated and have a broad and unique vision.

When talking about the impact form the edge on the English center, Huang (1996) also mentions the impact from translation, holding that translation from non-English languages into English is also an edge for writing in the English language. The above-mentioned non-native English writers who write in English (and won the Nobel Prize) benefit from the geographical marginality as well as the linguistic marginality in their unique styles. In fact, what they have done is not to maintain the central literature, but to greatly enrich the central literature. We can also say that the vitality of contemporary Chinese language mainly comes from translation. Actually, the flourishing of translation is not driven by the thirst for Western knowledge, but by the thirst for linguistic vitality. The passion of contemporary Chinese young poets for language exploration is not only out of curiosity, but also out of necessity. The nutrients they draw on are precisely translated works. When talking about the impact of translation from one language on another language center, Huang (1996) makes two points clear. On the one hand, the influence itself is important, always there to influence the potential reader. On the other, the affected people need the influence, and they are waiting for the emergence of this poignant influence. Once this influence flashes, they will instinctively exclaim, "It's coming!" In other words, the translated works are intended for potential readers to learn something from the target texts, while the readers of the translated works read the target texts in hope of learning something from them.

3.2.4 Linguistic determinism and its mechanism

The proposition that language determines thoughts is related to the proposition that "language is the house of Being". Since language is the house of Being, human beings who speak different languages live in different houses. That is why Heidegger says that "we Europeans presumably inhabit in a quite different house from Eastasians" (1982, p. 5). The so-called different houses mean that each language has its own unique conceptual framework. Is there a unique conceptual framework? We know that different languages dissect nature differently and end with different conceptual categories. But conversely, different languages cultivate different philosophies. There are the so-called existentialism, epistemology, and linguistic turn in Western philosophy, but none of them can be found in Chinese philosophy rooted in the Chinese language. The root of such a view is that in Western languages, the word *sein/* "to be" came into use very early to indicate a quality or a state or an identity, while its Chinese equivalent 是 ([shì] "be") came into use much later, and it did not become widely used until even later.

The necessity for the discussion of linguistic determinism and its mechanism arises for three reasons. First of all, this has been a major theoretical issue for a long time, but has not become a formal topic for public

Language: Mankind's last homestead   165

debate in China. It is not normal to be ignorant of such major theories. Therefore, I attempt to draw the attention of the linguistic field in China to this topic through this section. Second, there is a close relationship between "The theory that language determines thoughts" and the argument that "language is the homestead of mankind". If it is true that language regulates thoughts, it is also true that human beings with thoughts are also regulated by language. It is then logical in this context to say that human beings dwell in languages (as their homes). Third, another sense of language's being mankind's last homestead is that we are also limited by language. A language network envelops human beings. In addition, language embodies human beings' worldviews and practice. Sapir made an extreme statement: "Human beings ... are very much *at the mercy of* the particular language which has become the medium of expression for their society" (Sapir, 1929, in Mandelbaum, 1958, p. 162; emphasis added). Logic is the key to effective expressions. In turn, language trains speakers by logic. We Chinese used to be particularly fond of "dichotomy" not long before (in fact, the world is tripartite, for there is a large gray or middle area), which has something to do with the prevalence of antithesis in Chinese structure. In *Aesthetic Linguistics* (G. Qian, 1993), I referred to this phenomenon as the influence of a nation's aesthetic ideas on the construction of a nation's language structures, which seemed to tell only half of the story. The other half is that once a language structure is formed, it trains the way of thinking of new generations.

This section is divided into three parts. The first part is a review of the Sapir-Whorf hypothesis, which is based on my article "Verification or Falsification: Linguistic Determinism" (in G. Qian & Xie, 1998). That article does not explain the ins and outs of the falsification issue, which is to be supplemented and elaborated in what follows. The second part deals with the mechanism of linguistic determinism. The third part argues that to accept linguistic determinism is to admit that language is the pre-existing structure of an individual's cognition of the world (the language system already exists before every individual is born; see 3.2.4.4 for detailed explanation). In turn, to admit or not to admit that language is a pre-existing structure is of great importance to the understanding of linguistic determinism.

3.2.4.1 The Sapir-Whorf hypothesis

The following quotes from Sapir (Sapir, 1929, in Mandelbaum, 1958, pp. 160–166) represent the core of the Sapir-Whorf hypothesis.

Language powerfully *conditions* all our thinking.

(p. 162; emphasis added)

Thought is, to a significant extent, *determined* by language.

(p. 160; emphasis added)

166   *Language: Mankind's last homestead*

> Human beings ... are very much *at the mercy of* the particular language.
>
> (p. 162; emphasis added)

This famous hypothesis has trampled on the "sensitive areas" of both linguistics and philosophy in China, and many scholars disagree with it. As far as I know, among scholars doing foreign-language studies or Chinese studies in China, when this hypothesis is mentioned, some may criticize it mindlessly, some may completely deny it, and more will incidentally make simple and irrelevant sarcasm. Still, some, without reading the original works on the hypothesis, may even say that the theory is reactionary and idealistic. They seem to be particularly annoyed by the idea that human beings are trapped in language cages. However, these people just talk privately, and only a few publications are found to discuss and comment on the hypothesis. To the best of my knowledge, even fewer articles (for example, T. Wu, 1990) have been found to seriously argue against the hypothesis. In China, this is an issue that should be, but has never been, debated. Is the silence due to disdain, or lack of time, or other causes? No one can tell for sure. Nonetheless, one thing is for sure: In private, there is no lack of debates or criticisms, and there are even irresponsible attacks from large numbers of scholars (e.g., during the Cultural Revolution), but there is just no scholarly debate in the strict sense. Is it that our culture does not nurture such a serious debate?

However, the debate about the Sapir-Whorf hypothesis is not closed, though it is not seriously treated in China. Outside of China, views that conform to or oppose this hypothesis have repeatedly appeared in publications. The preface of Thomas S. Kuhn to the Chinese version *Kuhn's Selected Works of Philosophy of Science*[13] has made a stunning voice of the hypothesis in China (cited in Ji, 1997). It seems that we cannot avoid this debate. There should be more publications in which cordial objective and rational debates are made, but fewer private radical criticisms or attacks by those scholars who simply deny the validity of the hypothesis after taking a quick glance at the conclusions or topic sentences of the works advocating it, and interpreting them without taking the context into full consideration.

In our discussion of the Sapir-Whorf hypothesis, to avoid distortion or misrepresentation, we quote directly Sapir and Whorf. Let us first look at what Sapir said in *The Status of Linguistics as a Science* (1929; in Mandelbaum, 1958, pp. 160–166; emphasis added).

> Language is becoming increasingly valuable as a guide to the scientific study of a given culture. In a sense, the network of cultural patterns of a civilization is indexed in the language which expresses that civilization. It is an illusion to think that we can understand the significant outlines of a culture through sheer observation and without the guide of the linguistic symbolism which makes these outlines significant and intelligible to society. One day the attempt to master a primitive culture without the

Language: Mankind's last homestead 167

help of the language of its society will seem as amateurish as the labors of a historian who cannot handle the original documents of the civilization which he is describing.

Language is a guide to "social reality". Though language is not ordinarily thought of as of essential interest to the students of social science, it powerfully *conditions* all our thinking about social problems and processes. Human beings do not live in the objective world alone, nor alone in the world of social activity as ordinarily understood, but are very much *at the mercy of* the particular language that has become the medium of expression for their society. It is quite an illusion to imagine that one could adjust to reality essentially without the use of language and that language is merely an incidental means of solving specific problems of communication or reflection. The fact of the matter is that the "real world" is to a large extent unconsciously *built up on the language habits of the group*. The concise expression of this proposition is that the "real world" is built up on the language habits. No two languages are ever sufficiently similar to be considered as representing the same social reality. The worlds in which different societies live are distinct worlds, not merely the same world with *different labels* attached.

The understanding of a simple poem, for instance, involves not merely an understanding of the single words in their common meanings, but a full comprehension of the whole life of the community as it is mirrored in the words, or as it is suggested by their overtones. Even comparatively simple acts of perception are very much more *at the mercy of the patterns called words* than we might suppose. If one draws some dozen lines, for instance, of different shapes, one might perceive them as divisible into such categories as "straight", "crooked", "curved", "zigzag" because of the classificatory suggestiveness of the linguistic terms themselves. We see and hear or experience very largely as we do because the language habits of our community *predispose certain choices of interpretation*.

The above-quoted paragraphs represent the essence of Sapir's "linguistic determinism", which can be summarized into the following statements.

1) Language powerfully conditions all our thinking about social problems and processes; human beings are very much at the mercy of the language they speak; and their perceptions are very much more at the mercy of the patterns called words than we might suppose.
2) The network of cultural patterns of a civilization is indexed in the language that expresses that civilization; the "real world" is to a large extent unconsciously built up on the language habits of the group; and the language habits predispose certain choices of interpretation.
3) The linguistic terms have classificatory suggestiveness.

168   *Language: Mankind's last homestead*

The first one is the core proposition, which means that language conditions thoughts, people are at the mercy of the language, and people's perceptions are at the mercy of words. The second one describes the relationship between the objective world – cultural patterns and the real world – and language, that is, cultural patterns are indexed in the language, and the real world is built up on language habits. The third one tells that language has the function of segmenting nature, which can be specifically demonstrated in Whorf's linguistic relativity as follows.

Now, let's look at Whorf's "principle of linguistic relativity" (1940; in Carroll, 1956, pp. 212–214; emphasis added).

> ... It was found that the background linguistic system (in other words, the grammar) of each language is not merely a reproducing instrument for voicing ideas but rather is itself the *shaper* of ideas, the program and guide for the individual's mental activity, for his analysis of impressions, for his synthesis of his mental stock in trade. Formulation of ideas is not an independent process, strictly rational in the old sense, but is part of a particular grammar, and differs, from slightly to greatly, between different grammars. We *dissect nature along lines laid down by our native languages.* The categories and types that we abstract from the phenomenal world we do not find there because they stare every observer in the face; on the contrary, the world is presented in a kaleidoscopic flux of *impressions* which has to be organized by our minds – and this means largely *by the linguistic systems in our minds.* We cut nature up, organize it into concepts, and ascribe significances as we do, largely because we are parties to an agreement to weave it in this way – an agreement that holds throughout our speech community and *is codified in the patterns of our language.* The agreement is, of course, an implicit and unstated one, but its terms are absolutely obligatory; we cannot talk at all except by subscribing to the organization and classification of language materials which the agreement decrees.

This fact is very significant for modern science, for it means that no individual is free to describe nature with absolute impartiality but *is constrained to* certain modes of interpretation even while he thinks himself most free. The person most nearly free in such respects would be a linguist familiar with very many widely different linguistic systems. As yet no linguist is in any such position. We are thus introduced to a new *principle of relativity*, which holds that *all observers are not led by the same physical evidence to the same picture of the universe, unless their linguistic backgrounds are similar, or can in some way be calibrated.*

> When Semitic, Chinese, Tibetan, or African languages are contrasted with our own, the divergence in analysis of the world becomes more apparent; and, when we bring in the native languages of the Americas,

Language: Mankind's last homestead 169

where speech communities for many millenniums have gone their ways independently of each other and of the Old World, the fact that *languages dissect nature in many different ways* becomes patent. The *relativity* of all conceptual systems, ours included, and their dependence upon language stand revealed.

What Whorf calls the principle of linguistic relativity can be summarized as follows.

1) The linguistic system is itself the shaper of ideas.
2) We dissect nature along lines laid down by our native languages; any individual is always constrained to certain modes of interpretation; and languages dissect nature in many different ways.
3) The relativity principle: All observers are not led by the same physical evidence to the same picture of the universe, unless their linguistic backgrounds are similar, or can in some way be calibrated with each other.

The combination of Sapir's linguistic determinism and Whorf's principle of linguistic relativity is the Sapir-Whorf hypothesis. First, the first point of Whorf's principle that language is the shaper of ideas accords with Sapir's view that "language conditions all our thinking". Second, the second point of Whorf's principle is that human beings dissect nature along lines laid down by our native languages, and logically, languages dissect nature in many different ways. This idea agrees with Sapir's view that "the linguistic terms have classificatory suggestiveness". The two constitute one important aspect of the Sapir-Whorf hypothesis. Third, Whorf holds, "all observers are not led by the same physical evidence to the same picture of the universe", while Sapir claims, "the 'real world' is to a large extent unconsciously built up on the language habits of the group; and the language habits predispose certain choices of interpretation". This forms another important aspect of the hypothesis. The core idea of the Sapir-Whorf hypothesis is that language conditions our thinking; the different structures of different languages will affect the way people think and the way the world is divided into categories – the principle of linguistic relativity. On the one hand, "Languages dissect nature in many different ways"; on the other hand, "All observers are not led by the same physical evidence to the same picture of the universe".

Sapir proposed linguistic determinism in the 1920s, and Whorf proposed the principle of linguistic relativity in the 1940s. At least in the West, their assumptions were not fatally challenged (although there were many different opinions about them). Moreover, three decades later, in 1988, Thomas S. Kuhn proposed a new supportive view in the preface he wrote for a planned Chinese symposium entitled *Kuhn's Selected Works of Philosophy of Science*. This is an intriguing fact. Here presented are some of the relevant ideas in Kuhn's preface and Ji's interpretation of it (Ji, 1997, pp. 87–97). In the preface, Kuhn writes,

170 *Language: Mankind's last homestead*

They are just speech communities or dialogue communities, a group of individuals connected by shared words. These words make professional communication possible, but also confine communication to the professionals.

The above-mentioned concept "speech community" involves a series of more specific developments of my views. *The Structure of Scientific Revolutions* talks about many changes in word meaning that accompany the scientific revolution, as well as the changes in visual gestalt and in the way of seeing. Among them, the change of meaning is more fundamental. ... Neither the traditional theory of word meaning nor the new theory of attributing meaning to reference (from connotation to denotation) is adequate to illustrate this concept. ... I have been trying to figure out how words can be meaningful and *how meaningful words fit into the world they describe*. In other words, I have been looking for the basis of incommensurability.

... Since many generalizations made with old category names cannot be expressed easily, incommensurability has also become a form of untranslatability. ... The success in learning a second language does not mean that it can be translated into the translator's original language. Language learning can only lead to the use of two languages, but cannot enrich the original language. ... Although each individual *must select the word reference arranged by the community in a certain way*, different individuals can be distinguished in different ways. ... The scientific beliefs in a certain period cannot be fully expressed by the words required for the expression of the scientific beliefs in another period. The two sets of beliefs cannot be compared in detail.

(Cited in Ji, 1997; emphasis added)[14]

Ji (1997) makes a very good interpretation of Kuhn in terms of cognitive styles and cognitive subjects. What follows is a summary of Ji's remarks.

Semantic changes underlie worldview changes: *The change in word reference brings about the change in the way language connects nature.* According to the traditional view, language is just a tool to express thoughts and the "material shell" of thoughts, so we are used to attributing the scientific revolution to the revolution of ideas. *But as long as you think, or you rack your brains, you cannot do it without certain categories, concepts, names; that is, language operations synchronized with ideas are needed.* This is precisely the material core of ideas rather than the outer shell. Kuhn figured out this relationship. A language system is a pair of giant hands that *hold the world as a whole*, and *take charge of the world* with its own metaphor and word connotation. Therefore, the deep essence of the change in worldviews and ways of thinking is a semantic change. Language is a life style, including the way of thinking. It *conditions* people's thoughts and thus *shapes* the world in which people live. Kuhn broke the barrier between the two. Since natural science is a positive form of human understanding of nature, it is also capable of creating the world in a positive

Language: Mankind's last homestead 171

way when everyday language is refined into scientific language. Kuhn's new work in the 1980s focused on the "ontology" of linguistic connotation: *Words classify things, dissect nature*, and establish the same or different relations contained in categories, thus sketch out the whole picture of the world.

Scientific communities with different languages are like different tribes living in their own material and spiritual homes. As a cognitive subject, the scientific community is essentially a dialogue community. Through common cultivation and training, its members create a common dictionary, of which the words have the same connotation and extension, dissect the world according to the same boundary, and divide the same or different categories, so as to outline the common picture of reality. Conversely, *if different scientific communities have different languages, the "incommensurability" between them* is just like the incommensurability between the side of an isosceles triangle and its hypotenuse, or between the circumference and its radius, which can constitute an integer multiple.

3.2.4.2 Discussion on the Sapir-Whorf hypothesis

As I see, in the above-quoted preface, Kuhn does not respond directly to the Sapir-Whorf hypothesis. He points out that semantics changes after the worldview changes: The change in the word reference brings about the change in the way language connects nature. The argument that Kuhn makes in his preface is not easy to understand; in Ji's (1997) words, "the text is refined and abstruse, and unintelligible without some necessary background information" and "to translate it into Chinese is a long, hard process". However, Ji's interpretation forms a relevant response to the Sapir-Whorf hypothesis, although he does not claim so. Moreover, as a Chinese speaker dwelling in the house of Chinese, his words are more likely to bring Chinese readers closer to the Sapir-Whorf hypothesis than the words of Sapir and Whorf. Ji (1997) believes,

> A language system is a pair of giant hands that hold the world as a whole, and take charge of the world with its own metaphor and word connotation. Therefore, the deep essence of the change in worldviews and ways of thinking is a semantic change. Language is a life style with the way of thinking included. It conditions people's thoughts and thus shapes the world in which people live.

For the relationship between language and thought, Sapir uses "condition" (to determine, govern, and regulate), while Whorf uses "shaper, to shape" (to give a shape or form to). The Chinese terms 规范 ([guīfàn] "condition") and 塑造([sùzào] "shape") used by Ji are equivalents to the words used by Sapir and Whorf. However, the purpose of Ji (1997) is to introduce Kuhn's thoughts, and he does not and is not expected to provide any evidence to support that the language system conditions human thoughts.

172 *Language: Mankind's last homestead*

What I can say with certainty about the Sapir-Whorf hypothesis is that it was not put forward to grandstand. Whorf made an in-depth investigation of the Hopi Indian, and put forward the linguistic relativity principle after comparing the Hopi Indian language with English. He repeatedly demonstrated that people's views of the world are relative and based on the language they use. The key point of the Sapir-Whorf hypothesis is that "people dissect nature along lines laid down by our native languages" (Whorf, 1940; in Carroll, 1956), or that "the linguistic terms have classificatory suggestiveness" (Sapir, 1929; in Mandelbaum, 1958). "All observers are not led by the same physical evidence to the same picture of the universe" (Whorf, *ibid*.), and "the 'real world' is to a large extent unconsciously built up on the language habits of the group; and the language habits predispose certain choices of interpretation" (Sapir, *ibid*.). Here is a simple example. In Chinese, the phrase 独门独户 ([dúméndúhù] an isolated house, not a house with only one door) is from the perspective of the house itself (along lines laid down by the Chinese language). One of the equivalent expressions in English is "a house in an exclusive neighborhood", which does not focus on perspective of the house itself, but of the neighborhood. The way of dissecting is that there is a house in an exclusive neighborhood. The Chinese expression focuses on the house itself, while the English expression focuses on the neighborhood. Isn't this a manifestation of "People dissect nature along lines laid down by our native languages"? Isn't this a manifestation that "Languages dissect nature in many different ways"? Isn't this a manifestation that "All observers cannot be led by the same physical evidence (such as a separate house) to the same picture of the universe"? Isn't this a manifestation that "The language habits predispose certain choices of interpretation"?

In my opinion, the Sapir-Whorf hypothesis has not been fatally challenged so far.

First of all, this hypothesis has not been falsified, so it can be regarded as having high credibility. In order to confirm or falsify, we first sort out the two propositions (essentially the same) into universal propositions, which are exactly the same as the original proposition of the Sapir-Whorf hypothesis.

> "All languages dissect nature in many different ways" ("languages dissect nature in many different ways" is an elliptical expression). Its counter-proposition is that all languages dissect nature in the same way. (We will use this counter-propositiont below.)
>
> "All observers cannot be led by the same physical evidence to the same picture of the universe" (this is exactly the same as "the same physical evidence cannot lead all observers to the same picture of the universe").

First, it is impossible to confirm this hypothesis. The strict verification is to experiment with as many languages as there are – such as the commonly used two thousand five hundred languages, or all five thousand (?) languages– in the world to see if they dissect nature in different ways. If so, the Sapir-Whorf

Language: Mankind's last homestead 173

hypothesis holds. However, it is impossible to conduct such experiments exhaustively.

The strict adherence to the principle of verifiability will exclude the universal propositions in scientific theories from meaningful propositions. What should we do? In order to save scientific propositions, Popper (1968a, 1968b) proposed changing the principle of verification to the principle of falsification: A proposition is empirically meaningful, meaning that it is falsifiable in principle. "All swans are white" is impossible to prove but can be falsified in principle. As long as there is one experience (experiment or observation) of finding a non-white swan, this proposition is falsified. It is a clever way to falsify a proposition with limited counter-examples. As for falsification, Popper believed that it was an extremely dangerous way to infer that the hypothesis is correct from its correspondence with the fact (the so-called verification), which is likely to imply the error of confirming the result beforehand. *However, from the perspective of falsification, a hypothesis can be refuted by finding any situation where the fact is inconsistent with the hypothesis. This is the asymmetry between verification and falsification.*

Although it is impossible to prove "all languages dissect nature in many different ways" or "all observers cannot be led by the same physical evidence to the same picture of the universe", it is possible to falsify them. *If the falsification fails, their hypothesis can be assumed to be true* (G. Qian, 2002).

To falsify the above two propositions, or one of them, it takes only one experience (experiment or observation) in which it is found that all languages dissect nature in the same way, or that all observers are led by the same physical evidence to the same picture of the universe. If that happens, the Sapir-Whorf hypothesis will be overturned. For example, on March 9, 1997, the total eclipse of the sun and the Comet Hale-Bopp appeared at the same time in the sky (or other visible astronomical phenomena, terrestrial phenomena, natural phenomena, etc.). Suppose scientists using different native tongues and coming from different countries went to the same place (such as Mohe, China) to observe the phenomenon, and then they depicted it in their own native languages. If their descriptions were exactly the same or roughly the same, the Sapir-Whorf hypothesis would be overturned. If the falsification fails, this hypothesis should be deemed to have a high degree of credibility.

If the falsification method is used, it is not necessary to test speakers of all languages. Speakers of two or three languages will suffice for the test. This is the advantage of the falsification method; the minority represents the majority. This method takes advantage of the asymmetry between verification and falsification. As long as two or three persons speaking different languages dissect nature in different ways, the proposition that "All languages dissect nature in the same way" can be *directly denied (that is, be falsified)*. This is a simple truth: Now that two or three languages dissect nature in different ways, it is invalid to say that all (two thousand five hundred, or five thousand) languages dissect nature in the same way. *The falsification of the idea that "All languages dissect nature in a same way" equally supports the proposition that*

174 *Language: Mankind's last homestead*

"All languages dissect nature in different ways" (the original proposition of the Sapir-Whorf hypothesis).

Can we then find an example or experience in which two or three languages dissect nature in different ways? It is fairly easy. For example, Chinese and English have different ways to dissect kinships like 叔 ([shū] "father's younger brother") and 伯([bó] "father's elder brother"), and Chinese and Eskimo have different ways to dissect "snow". Besides, although English and Chinese share the same way to talk about hot water, they dissect "hot water" differently from Japanese (a detailed analysis is to be made later). Many more examples can be given as counter-examples to the idea that "All languages dissect nature in the same way". They were already mentioned in previous parts of this book and will not be repeated here.

Let's take a look at the following hypothesis, which refutes the Sapir-Whorf hypothesis. Greenberg holds that language cannot be said to determine worldviews and people's knowledge because if two people speaking different languages are sent to the moon, the content of the reports they make will never differ because their languages differ (cited in T. Wu, 1990, p. 39). However, Greenberg's argument cannot refute the Sapir-Whorf hypothesis. For one thing, even if the reports of the two persons speaking different languages are exactly the same in content, suggesting that they dissect nature in the same way, the conclusion cannot be drawn that "All languages dissect nature in the same way" (two thousand five hundred or five thousand cannot be replaced with two or three). For another, Greenberg's argument is not based on an experiment, but on an assumption in form of "if ... then ...". Any other person can imagine the opposite fact: The contents of the reports they made after returning to the earth are different and the images of the moon (depicted in words, not captured by photography) obtained by the two speakers of different languages are different, albeit with some identical aspects.

Therefore, the Sapir-Whorf hypothesis should be considered to have a higher degree of credibility before a real falsifying experiment succeeds. The rejection by facts put forward by some scholars in China (see T. Wu, 1990) is not based on well-designed falsifying experiments. For example, children can distinguish colors before they learn to speak; aphasics who lose the ability to speak color names can identify more colors. These facts cannot constitute a refutation to the Sapir-Whorf hypothesis, for learning languages and distinguishing colors are not governed by the same organ, and these two abilities are essentially independent. Neither can any of the following given facts (all cited in T. Wu, 1990). 1) It cannot be said that people adopting different weights and measures have different space concepts; 2) languages can be translated into each other (though a considerable number of scholars doubt the so-called translatability); 3) deaf-mutes can think (there are three forms of thinking: Pre-linguistic thinking, linguistic thinking, and supralinguistic thinking. When we say deaf-mutes can think, what kind of thinking do we mean? Can fragmented thinking be regarded as thinking?); 4) a linguist

Language: Mankind's last homestead 175

can describe the universal phenomena of many languages without being restricted by his language (however, the key is not that he "can describe", but whether what he describes are the same as or different from what another linguist describes); and 5) the Eskimo has various kinds of snow first, and then various names for snow (on the contrary, this fact just supports the Sapir-Whorf hypothesis that different languages dissect nature in different ways). Furthermore, even if the above-listed so-called facts all stand true, they may not suffice to refute the Sapir-Whorf hypothesis ("All languages dissect nature in many different ways"), because many other facts have been found to support it.

For example, many facts can verify the idea that "We dissect nature along lines laid down by our native languages". Chinese speakers refer to hot water as 热水 [rèshuǐ] along the line laid down by Chinese (热[rè]＋水[shuǐ] "hot" + "water"). Likewise, English speakers say "hot water" along the line laid down by English (hot + water). However, Japanese speakers refer to hot water as "oyu" along the line laid down by Japanese, different from that by Chinese and English (not atsu-i ("hot") + mizi (literally "water", but only referring to cold water)). In addition, Hopi Indians have different words for water in the open air and water in a bottle, but Chinese, English, or Japanese speakers do not.

The second reason why this hypothesis has not been fatally challenged is that it is difficult to overturn the fact that *at least in one's early childhood, it is the language frame that determines the thinking frame*. Because of that, even scholars who disagree with the Sapir-Whorf hypothesis believe that the hypothesis "still has its reasonable core" (see T. Wu, 1990). We can reason backwards like this: If the language pattern stipulates or determines or constrains the thinking pattern, then, among other things, we can at least find one such fact – ontogenetically, only when the language pattern is formed first and the thinking pattern is generated later, can the former regulate the latter. If the language pattern is not formed and fixed, how can it dominate, influence, and even determine thinking?

Before the 1980s, most scholars in China believed that the ability to think develops before language ability. In my view, ontogenetically speaking, *language patterns develop before our thinking patterns* (detailed discussion on this is to be made in 3.2.4.4).

Language shapes human beings before their thinking matures. *Before a child is born, the language has already been spoken by their parents, brothers, and sisters, and the structure of the world and the universe recorded by the language is already there.* Children receive the world and perceive the world. In addition to what is directly perceived by their senses, the structure of the world is perceived by children through learning to speak like the adults around them. What is perceived and felt are the relationships, frameworks, and worldviews recorded and conveyed by the language. Only when children grow up and can influence the language in turn will they interact with the language. However, childhood, especially around the age of five, is a critical period in which the

176 *Language: Mankind's last homestead*

influence children receive determines their whole life. In other words, the linguistic traces received by children during their childhood will affect them for a lifetime. *Language shapes the thinking of a child around the age of five, which means that the lifelong thinking framework of a person is defined.* This conclusion can be supported by the biological finding that at the age of five or so, the intelligence is basically molded; later growth only increases knowledge, talents, and experience, but the intelligence model will not be changed. In my opinion, the idea that "Intelligence is molded at the age of seven" is consistent with the idea that "The thinking framework is shaped at the age of seven". Language shapes everyone who is about to learn to speak. Therefore, Heidegger talks about "entering into and submitting to" language as he states,

> They [the lectures bearing the title "The Nature of Language"] are intended to bring us face to face with a possibility of undergoing an experience with language. To undergo an experience with something – be it a thing, a person, or a god – means that this something befalls us, strikes us, comes over us, *overwhelms and transforms us*. ... To undergo an experience with language, then, means to let ourselves be properly concerned by the claims of language by entering into and submitting to it. If it is true that man finds the proper abode of his existence in language – whether he is aware of it or not – then an experience we undergo with language will *touch the innermost nexus of our existence.*
>
> (Heidegger, 1982, p. 57; emphasis added)

On the part of children, *their thinking training begins with language.* It is a common fact that children's views on the objective world, thinking habits, and knowledge are trained by adults through language. Take, for example, the thinking training of children in the Chinese environment. As Xianlin Ji points out in his preface to G. Qian (1997/2002),

> The basic thinking mode of the West is analytical, while that of the East (including China, of course) is synthetic. ... Western Indo-European languages have morphological changes, and the relationship between words is expressed as clearly as possible in the form of grammatical changes. However, there is no morphological change in Chinese, and the distinction between parts of speech is often unclear. Anyway, it is a bit fuzzy.

This lays down two premises: 1) The basic thinking mode of the Chinese is synthetic; 2) there is no morphological change in Chinese, thus the linking devices between main clauses and subordinate clauses to express their relationships (i.e., the relative connectives in a compound sentence) are not necessary. Connectives can be used, but they are not required in everyday speech. The process of training children's thinking through the Chinese language may go this way: If an adult says to a child 听话，我给你糖吃 ([tīnghuà, wǒ gěinǐtángchī] "Be obedient, and I'll give you candies to eat"). What is the relationship between the main clause and the subordinate clause? There is no formal connective. However, it does not matter. Children can gradually figure out the relationship between "be obedient" and "I'll give you candies to eat" through the context and the synchronous symbol bunch (such as observing the face of the adult, that is, the facial expression and gesture) – the conditional relationship (the condition of giving candies is to be obedient), the temporal relationship (be obedient first, and then eat candies), the hypothetical relationship (if one is obedient, he will be rewarded with candies), the causal relationship (one has candies to eat because he is obedient), or the purpose relationship (to get candies, one has to be obedient). What we see is the process of a Chinese complex sentence structure without conjunctions training Chinese children to form synthetic thinking. Metaphysically, Chinese children can acquire the habit of synthetic thinking in the structural training of Chinese. In short, *at least in the early childhood, human thoughts are controlled by the language structure* (just with regard to this, the Sapir-Whorf hypothesis is not sensational at all); *one's language framework can condition one's thinking framework. As long as you acknowledge this, you will roughly draw such a conclusion that one's thinking is defined by one's language throughout his entire life.* As we have demonstrated above, the language one receives in his childhood will influence him for a lifetime. Language shapes the thinking of children around the age of five, which means that their lifelong thinking has been determined. This leads to a fact that seems strange: Language is created by mankind but in turn changes mankind who created it. What is so strange about that? Mankind created the rules of games (such as chess, martial arts tournament, football, etc.), but these rules in turn limit, guide, and improve human practice, and thus change mankind. Likewise, computers are created by us, but they also seem to have changed the way we live. For more detailed discussion on this issue, see 3.2.4.4.

Then, does that mean the Sapir-Whorf hypothesis is confirmed? My answer is that it can be finally confirmed. That is why I propose that well-designed falsification experiment should be conducted. Before it is falsified, the Sapir-Whorf hypothesis should be seen as a proposition of high credibility, though I used to be skeptical about it, believing that the hypothesis was far from being true.

Mature thoughts (not some flashes of thoughts or fragmented thoughts) depend on language, and *language is the indispensable vehicle of thought: Language and thought operate synchronously*. However, there are cases in which the carried can be separated from the carrier. For example, the wood loaded on a wagon can be separated from the wagon. If we say that A is a means to express B, we refer to the relationship between the expression, A, and the content being expressed, B. In this case, the means of expression can be separated from the expressed content, and the means of expression is selectable. For instance, sadness can be expressed in words, such as "How sad I am!" or "How painful I am!" It can also be expressed by playing a piece of music entitled

178 *Language: Mankind's last homestead*

Chants from the Sick with the erhu, a stringed Chinese musical instrument. Still, many other means can be used to express the feeling of sadness.

When we say A is the indispensable carrier of B, we mean the carried depends on the carrier and that the two cannot be separated. For example, an electric current flows on a conductor; without a conductor, the electric current cannot flow. Mature thought is to language what electric current is to a conductor, or what the oxygen in our body is to the blood. The former closely depends on the latter. *Since mature thoughts are inseparable from language, it is plausible to say that the language framework determines the thinking framework.*

When commenting on the argument that "language is a code for thought", Dummett writes,

> We have, therefore, to replace the conception of language as a code for thought by some account of the understanding of a language that makes no appeal to the prior grasp of the concepts that can be expressed in it. Such an account presents language, not just as a means of expressing thought, but as a *vehicle* for thought. The idea of a language as a code became untenable because a concept's coming to mind was not, by itself, an intelligible description of a mental event: thought *requires* a vehicle. And for this reason, the philosophical study of language assumes a far greater importance as being, not just a branch of philosophy, but the foundation of the entire subject, since it has to be, simultaneously, a study of *thought*. Only if we take language to be a code can we hope to strip off the linguistic clothing and penetrate to the pure naked thought beneath: the only effective means of studying thought is by the study of language, which is its vehicle.
>
> (Dummett, 1996, p. 99; emphasis original)

Seemingly, there is some difference between Dummet's view that "language is a vehicle for thought" and my claim that "language is the indispensable vehicle of thought". That "language is a vehicle for thought" may mean that, in some cases, language and thought are mutually separable. The idea that "language is the indispensable vehicle of thought" highlights *the inseparability between language and mature thought*. However, Dummet's view goes exactly in accordance with our claim, because, to him, "our capacity for thought is not separable from our ability to use language; that is, fully-fledged thought cannot be acquired before the acquisition of language" (Baghramian, 1999, p. 310). We cannot expect to "strip off the linguistic clothing and penetrate to the pure naked thought beneath" (Dummett, 1996, p. 99).

In addition, the Sapir-Whorf hypothesis has to answer one of the most essential questions: What kind of empirical methods can prove that after early childhood, the shaping of people's thinking patterns can exclude the cultural reality and natural reality that a nation is always exposed to and faces every day? *It is not only the language pattern but also the cultural pattern and the natural environment that shape one's thinking pattern.* It should be noted

Language: Mankind's last homestead 179

that language itself is just one of the vehicles of culture, not the only one. Although verbal behavior is an essential part of human behavior, there is also non-verbal human behavior. If cultural reality and natural reality cannot be excluded, we have to say that language patterns and cultural patterns jointly shape thinking patterns. However, even if that is true, it does not constitute an objection to the Sapir-Whorf hypothesis.

The discussion on this issue is not over yet. Regarding whether the Sapir-Whorf hypothesis is right or wrong, although there has been no heated debate in China's linguistic circle, many Chinese with established scholarly reputations have expressed their own views on this issue.

The first one that should be mentioned is Yutang Lin. Lin mentioned this issue many times in his 1936 book *My Country and My People*. In what follows, we quote some of Lin's statements in the order they appear in his book and you will see that his position is uncertain: Did he think that language patterns decided thinking patterns, or the contrary? He seems to be shifting his position between the two, just as Yinque Chen (2001) commented.

> For instance, in one place, Lin says,
> The Europeans who speak Chinese too well develop certain mental habits akin to the Chinese and are regarded by their compatriots as "queer". The Chinese who speak English too well and develop Western mental habits are "denationalized".
>
> (Lin, 1936, p. 8)

This seems to provide strong evidence for the idea that language determines thinking habits. However, even if these Europeans who speak Chinese well or Chinese who speak English well do not learn the culture of the other country (the cultural carrier not only includes language, but also art, religion, customs, habits, codes of conduct, etc.) first before they can speak the language so well, they at least develop the other party's thinking habits by simultaneously acquiring the language and culture. Lin does not explicitly point out that these people learned the thinking habits of the other country while learning the language. Therefore, according to this quotation, we can say that the language acquisition and the acquisition of cultures together with the natural environment have created these "denationalized" "queer" people.

> In another place, Lin observes,
> There are American-born Chinese, brought up in a different environment, who are totally devoid of the characteristics of the common Chinese, and who can break up a faculty meeting by the sheer force of their uncouth nasal twang and their direct forceful speech, a speech which knows no fine modulations. They lack that supreme, unique mellowness peculiar to the sons of Cathay.
>
> (Lin, 1936, p. 42)

180 *Language: Mankind's last homestead*

What is worth noting is the condition of being "American-born". There is no doubt that these Chinese people, after they were born, formed the habit of thinking and acquired American culture when they learned the English language. This example supports the idea that language patterns determine thinking patterns. However, other cultural patterns also have an impact on thought patterns.

Then, Lin seems to change his position, when he states,

> The Chinese language and grammar show this femininity exactly because the language, in its form, syntax and vocabulary, reveals an extreme simplicity of thinking, concreteness of imagery and economy of syntactical relationships.
>
> (Lin, 1936, p. 77)

This statement suggests that syntax derives from thinking, that is, thinking patterns determine language patterns.

Shortly after, to exemplify Chinese love of simplicity, Lin (1936, p. 78) points out that simply four Chinese characters, 坐吃山空 ([zuò chī shān kōng] "sit, eat, mountain, empty"), "to the Chinese clearly means that 'if you only sit and eat and do nothing, even a fortune as big as a mountain will vanish'". In my opinion, this account *interprets synthetic thinking by way of analytical thinking, just as in translating Chinese into English*. Then Lin continues to point out,

> Abstract endings like "-ness" are also unknown in Chinese, and the Chinese simply say, with Mencius, that "the white of a white horse is the same as the white of a white jade". *This has a bearing on their lack of analytic thinking.*
>
> (Lin, 1936, p. 78; emphasis added)

Apparently, he believes that thinking pattens affect language patterns.

However, just one paragraph later, Lin shifts his position to the view that language influences the style of thought, as he says,

> ... "the method of watching a fire across the river" (detachment of style), "the method of dragonflies skimming the water surface" (lightness of touch), ... This profuseness of imaginery and paucity of abstract terminology *has an influence on* the style of writing and, consequently, *on the style of thought.*
>
> (Lin, 1936, pp. 79–80; emphasis added)

With regard to a relevant topic, whether the development of a nation's natural science is determined by the nation's way of thinking, Lin, however, makes a fairly explicit statement.

Language: Mankind's last homestead   181

Sufficient discussion of the characteristics of Chinese thinking has been made to enable us to appreciate the cause of their failure to develop natural science. The Greeks laid the foundation for natural science because the Greek mind was essentially an analytical mind, a fact which is proved by the striking modernity of Aristotle. The Egyptians developed geometry and astronomy, sciences which required an analytical mind, and the Hindus developed a grammar of their own. The Chinese, with all their native intelligence, never developed a science of grammar. … The Ch'in scholars after them revived Taoism and depended on their "intuition" for the solving of the mysteries of their own bodies and the universe. Experimentation was never thought of, and no scientific method had been developed.

(Lin, 1936, pp. 80–81)

This quotation, first of all, reminds me of Shuming Liang's assertion that "Chinese culture cannot develop science by itself" (cited in Tan, 1997). Such a sharp and straightforward assertion about the relationship between context and scientific achievements is as awaking as a clap of thunder. We will come back to this later. Lin has a similar view, expressed in a milder and more specific way. Second, I am deeply impressed by Lin's words "experimentation was never thought of"! This is the most scientific and pertinent criticism made in the 1930s of the Chinese academic community, including philology. This criticism has led me to believe that the final denial of the Sapir-Whorf hypothesis relies on falsification. If the hypothesis cannot be falsified, it is highly credible.

In a section entitled "Language and Thought", Lin (1936) points out,

… the Chinese language has largely determined the peculiar development of Chinese literature. By comparison with the European languages, it is possible to trace *how much of the peculiarities of Chinese thought* and literature are *due simply to their possession of a so-called monosyllabic language*. The fact that the Chinese spoke in syllables like *ching, chong*, and *chang* was appalling in consequences. *This monosyllabism determined* the character of the Chinese writing, and the character of the Chinese writing brought about the continuity of the literary heritage, and therefore *even influenced the conservatism of Chinese thought*. … The language is characterized by a great scarcity of syllabic forms and consequently a great number of homonyms or words of the same sound.

(Lin, 1936, pp. 205–206; emphasis added)

… Moreover, the independence of character from sound greatly accelerated its monosyllabic quality.

(*Ibid.*, p. 209)

…, one sometimes wonders whether the Chinese people as a whole would be so docile and so respectful to their superiors, had they spoken

182 *Language: Mankind's last homestead*

an inflectional language and consequently used an alphabetic language. I sometimes feel that, had the Chinese managed to retain a few more final or initial consonants in their language, not only would they have shaken the authority of Confucius to its foundations, but very possibly would have long ago torn down the political structure, and, with the general spread knowledge ... would have ... given the world a few more inventions like printing and gunpowder which would have likewise affected the history of human civilization on this planet.

(Ibid., p. 210)

In the above-quoted paragraphs, there are two ideas related to the topic under discussion. First, the form of thinking is derived from the linguistic form, as directly expressed by "how much of the ... Chinese thought ... are due simply to their possession of a so-called monosyllabic language" and "this monosyllabic nature determined ... thus even contributing to the conservatism of Chinese thought". Even if you think such statements are not surprising at all, but merely reveal Lin's belief that language determines thought, you may be astonished by what is suggested in the third quoted paragraph by Lin: Language decides human destiny, which may be somewhat weird and mysterious, and a little annoying as well. Second, the characteristics of Chinese (monosyllabism) contribute to the conservatism of Chinese thinking. Following Lin's train of thought, they consequently lead to the political structure and scientific backwardness of the Chinese people. Lin's idea, though expressed in a milder manner, is in essence the same as Shuming Liang's view that "Chinese culture cannot develop science by itself".

There are two sharply opposing views on the relationship between the development of science and technology and the Chinese language and Chinese characters. One of them agrees with the above-mentioned view held by Lin and Liang. As regards this view, Tan (1997) remarks as follows.

> The contextualism opposes the traditional instrumentalism of language: Humans do not enslave language, but are enslaved by language. Humans' operational thought is not only influenced by language, but also strictly confined to the context of the language they use. Based on this view, Liang Shuming asserts that without the active invasion of Western science, Chinese culture could not develop science by itself. This is not a matter of time, but of cultural traits.

Tan holds that Liang's view is quite reasonable: The orientation of a culture depends on the desire of the cultural group to survive. According to Tan, the interest and charm of Chinese culture lie in the harmony among people, which, in Liang's words, is a culture of "inward force", while the purpose and interest of Western culture lie in the conquest of things by people, which is a culture of "outward force" (cited in Tan, 1997). The former focuses on society and

Language: Mankind's last homestead 183

ethics, while the latter is obsessed with reason and analysis. Therefore, Chinese culture cannot breed systematic science like Western cultures. Some "technologies" in ancient China were only the crystallization of some experiences, not necessary the results of theoretical research. Scientific achievements must be based on the intervention of mathematics, which was absent in Chinese thought.

However, the opposite view believes that the Chinese language should not be blamed for the backwardness of China's science and technology. Zhenning Yang observes as follows.

> There are four accepted reasons for China's backward modern science and technology. First, China had not had an independent middle class in those years, and people's thought were completely controlled by the imperial government. Second, there was no natural science in traditional Chinese thinking (positive interest in natural phenomena). Third, China's long-term imperial examination system was extremely unfavorable to the development of science and technology. Finally, there has been no rigorous logic system in China.
>
> (Z. Yang, 1998, pp. 206–207)

In explaining these four reasons, Zhenning Yang points out,

> There are some strange views or proposals, such as the view of "the ethnic degradation" of the Han nationality and the proposal for "abolishing Chinese characters and the Chinese language", which reflect the inferiority complex in face of Western science and technology.
>
> (*Ibid.*)

Zhenning Yang seems to mean that the fourth reason – "there is no rigorous logic system in China" – does not mean that the structure such as that of Chinese does not have the capacity for a rigorous logic system. Otherwise, he would not specifically point out that the proposal for "abolishing Chinese characters and the Chinese language" reflects "the inferiority complex in face of Western science and technology". I do not think that the first and the third scientists of Chinese descent who won the Nobel Prize and all the successful scientists who use Chinese have experienced the obstruction of Chinese to scientific thinking. Almost all of them have experience in using both Chinese and a foreign language (especially English). They should have a fairly authoritative voice on whether the Chinese language hinders the development of science and technology, and of course we should respect their views. Moreover, China will enjoy long-term development from the era of reform and opening up in the twentieth century if the country is prosperous and the people are at peace. Sometime in the twenty-first century, perhaps, we can draw a definite conclusion about whether science can be developed out of the Chinese language.

184   *Language: Mankind's last homestead*

Up to now, it seems clear to us that the survival desire of the Chinese-speaking cultural group is basically set by the Confucian spirit, which is an unalterable statement. It is also an indisputable fact that *the Chinese people devote too much energy to the conquest of humanity* – self cultivation, family harmony (cultivation of families), country management, and world peace (cultivation of others) – *and too little to the "bidirectional coordination with nature"*.[15] Here, I am talking about a cultural motivation, that is, the Chinese people's desire to survive is a kind of cultural spirit, not just the spirit of language as one of the vehicles of culture. We cannot equate language (one of the vehicles of culture) with culture. *Some scholars say that "language enslaves people", but what they really mean is that culture enslaves people, not language.*

To sum up, the Sapir-Whorf hypothesis is not something that a linguist can judge with one or two examples. Earlier in this section, I illustrated the process of training children's synthetic thinking through the Chinese language with the example of Chinese adults' telling children 听话，我给你糖吃 ([tīnghuà, wǒ gěinǐtángchī] "Be obedient, and I'll give you candies to eat"). However, I myself am not sure whether it is convincing enough. Many people, in their writings or speeches, claimed the Sapir-Whorf hypothesis is incorrect or idealistic, when they talked about it in passing. I always wonder: What evidence did they have to justify their conclusion? Actually, this section is written in reaction to such kind of hasty conclusions, in the hope of incurring serious debates about the hypothesis. Again, I insist that falsification experiments be conducted. Before the Sapir-Whorf hypothesis is falsified, it is highly credible.

3.2.4.3 The mechanism of language determining thought

In my view, the Sapir-Whorf hypothesis has high credibility and the following discussion is helpful in identifying the mechanism by which language determines thought.

Philosophers believe that many philosophical ideas are distorted in the linguistic mirror. After pointing out the limitations of his 1983 monograph *Pragmatics*, Levinson says,

> This book will, I hope, be of use to advanced undergraduates, as well as more advanced researchers, in linguistics, literary studies, psychology, anthropology and other disciplines with an interest in language use, as a crystallization of issues proposed, but rarely explicated in full, elsewhere. Even philosophers should find interesting the distortion of many philosophical ideas in a linguistic mirror.
>
> (Levinson, 1983, p. vii)

Levinson correctly points out that language use is the crystallization process of problems, that is, language presents problems and makes them clear. "The

Language: Mankind's last homestead 185

distortion of many philosophical ideas in a linguistic mirror" precisely proves that language conditions thought, or that thought is at the mercy of language, as stated in the Sapir-Whorf hypothesis.

> When talking about China's May 4th Movement in 1919, N. Liu (1997) states,
>> In those days, the pioneers of the May 4th Movement who chose language as a breakthrough point for literary reform had the logic that language determined the way of thinking. Classical Chinese confined the thought of the Chinese people to the old mode of perception. Then, in order to establish a new connection with the real world, the advocates of new literature promoted the use of everyday language as the literary language, and at the same time argued a full absorption of the fine structure of Western languages to convey complex ideas and intricate theories.

Given the context in which the Chinese were eager to find their way to liberation, the logic here is clear: Classical Chinese confined the thoughts of the Chinese people to the old mode of perception, so the country was backward; if we had the desire for national progress, we had to turn to a new mode of perception. Because the accurate, clear, and popular vernacular Chinese (i.e., everyday language) can train this new perception mode, it was an ideal choice. N. Liu (1997) continues to say,

> According to Ernest Cassirer, each language is an independent symbolic form, a way of integrating the world. "In a sense, language activities determine all of our other activities." Both the vernacular Chinese and the classical Chinese are the written languages of the Han people, but they respectively represent two different expression systems, which are based on different ways of thinking and life styles.

Ernest Cassirer's view is crucial. Given the idea of "language activities determining all our other activities", that "language is the last homestead of human beings" is a plausible view, about which a detailed discussion was already made in Section 3.1.1 of this book. Cassirer's main idea is two-fold: First, the way the world is integrated is determined by language; second, language activities are the basis of all other activities. What we want to emphasize here is: Even within the same language, for example, Chinese, two different sets of expression forms (vernacular Chinese as the daily language and classical Chinese as the formal language) may coexist, leading to significantly different consequences on the training of people's thinking (which is related to the imprisonment or freedom of thought, and finally to the prosperity and decline of a nation). Then, much greater differences can be expected in different modes of thought conditioned by different languages.

Reading aloud promotes the unification of thinking. C. He (1997) holds that reading aloud and reading silently not only are two necessary ways for

186 *Language: Mankind's last homestead*

human beings to acquire knowledge, but also represent different modes of human moral practices. Chinese thinkers rely to a great extent on sound and image. In our learning process from childhood to adulthood, we first learn to read aloud and then to read silently. These two ways have an incalculable effect. Reading aloud promotes the unification of thinking, and is thus favored by the authorities advocating unification. For example, children read aloud after the teacher, with accuracy of pronunciation being the primary requirement. When children do it, the relationship is established between teachers as dominators and instructors and the students as the dominated and instructed. This power relationship permeates every aspect of social life in China. When people read aloud, especially when a group of people read aloud in unison, the cadence of the voices not only conveys the secret code of identical knowledge, but also forms the common foundation of aesthetic judgement. Under the norms of reading aloud in unison, every one of the group reads with a joint pace, with no one getting ahead or lagging behind, no anomalous voice is allowed and even the leading reader has to obey the established principles. Reading poems aloud is the most powerful form of reading aloud, with the sonorous voice touching the hearts of the audience with the carried meaning. Reading aloud almost inevitably creates a glorious ritual where people express themselves in unison, which is one of the reasons why it is denounced by contemporary people. The unification of form maintains the unification of meaning, in which moral unification is entailed. In reading silently, the existence of ambiguities in words and sentences naturally challenges unification. Ambiguities and deviations can be tolerated in reading silently. However, deviations have no place in reading aloud. According to C. He (1997), reading aloud, as a verbal behavior, standardizes thoughts, standardizes customs, and promotes the unification of thinking. Every child who grows up in the Chinese environment is trained to read aloud, not only in contemporary primary and secondary schools, but also in private schools in the old times. The power relationship between the leading reader and their followers is universal, not just between teachers and students. The relationship between the person administering an admission oath for joining the Youth League or the Party and the oath-takers, that between the priest who leads the chanting and the believers who follow him in a church, and that between the abbot and the believers in a Chinese Buddhist temple ceremony are all such relationships. Chorusing is also a kind of verbal training for unifying thoughts. Religious pilgrims are also trained in this way. The best example of reading aloud in groups as a glorious ritual where people express themselves in unison is the collective reading aloud of Chairman Mao's quotations in the Cultural Revolution in China. The function of this ritual to unify and control thoughts was very powerful and perfect. Didn't people say that, in those years, one billion Chinese thought alike as if they shared only one and the same mind? Before 1949, the oral prayers 阿弥陀佛 ([ēmítuófó] "Amitabha") and 大慈大悲救苦救难观世音菩萨 ([dàcídàbēi jiùkǔjiùnàn guānshìyīn púsà] "merciful and compassionate Bodhisattva Avalokitesvara") that were popular among Chinese common people also had the function of

Language: Mankind's last homestead 187

promoting uniform thinking. The top Buddha is Amitabha. 阿 [ē] means "no, not" and 弥陀 [mítuó] refers to quantity. 阿弥陀佛 literally means "Buddha of Infiniteness or Infinite Light". It is said that when Amitabha became a Buddha, he made a promise – if a dying person keeps repeating his name, 阿弥陀佛, in his mind, he will know and come to take the dying one to the Western paradise, the heaven for resurrection. Then almost all believers do so because this is a simple and convenient way to pray to Buddha. Monks and other Buddhabelievers greet each other by saying 阿弥陀佛, and they will say it many times a day. As a result, their thoughts and ways of thinking become highly uniform. Such chanting of Amitabha makes full use of the function of reading aloud in making thinking uniform, and the chanting about Bodhisattva is a similar case. Avalokitesvara (all Bodhisattvas are male, but Avalokitesvara is often believed to appear as a female figure, showing mercy to be close to all living creatures) also comes for salvation when he hears the chanting. If anyone in danger says his name, he will come to save the person at once. Consequently, he is called "the merciful and compassionate Bodhisattva". To some extent, our discussion about mankind's living in discourse fields in 3.1.2 can also explain the view that reading aloud promotes uniform thinking.

Human beings, through leaning words, distinguish feelings, express feelings, and understand the meanings of feeling words, which also supports the view that language determines thought. A relevant observation is made by Wittgenstein.

> How do words *refer to* sensations? … But how is the connexion between the name and the thing named set up? This question is the same as: how does a human being learn the meaning of the names of sensations? – of the word "pain" for example. Here is one possibility: words are connected with the primitive, the natural, expressions of the sensation and used in their place. A child has hurt himself and he cries; and then adults talk to him and teach him exclamations and, later, sentences. They teach the child new pain-behaviour.
>
> (Wittgenstein, 1953, §244)

According to Wittgenstein, human beings distinguish feelings, express feelings, and understand the meanings of feeling words by learning the words. Under the topic of "the nature of language", Western philosophers of language have discussed private languages. Experience like the feeling of pain is purely personal, and how can they thus be known to others? Can the pain you feel be told with language? Pains are different with different people and in different situations. If the feelings expressed by you are different from those expressed by others, how can you achieve communication between subjects? However, if one person really uses his own language (the so-called private language), there would be no public rule – or it is simply called non-rule-following – and then language cannot be used for communication. Here, Wittgenstein introduces the process – "a child has hurt himself and he cries; and then adults talk to him

188 *Language: Mankind's last homestead*

and teach him exclamations and, later, sentences" – to show how people learn to distinguish feelings by learning feeling words, and how communication between subjects is realized. That is, words are taught (by adults) and learned (by children) from generation to generation. In this way, a purely personal feeling can be communicated. Personal feelings become common feelings, because there is a bridge among them, that is, one generation teaching the next. Through this process, we can see the repeated modulation of thinking by language.

Since the 1980s, linguistic researchers in China have no longer sided with their counterparts in the former Soviet Union or followed Stalin as they did, especially in the 1950s, in insisting that thought came before language; some scholars in China, more from Hong Kong than from the mainland, have begun to advocate that language drives thought. As Li (1996, p. 59) points out, "without language, there would be no thought, or most of thought would be impossible, or there would at best be only extremely primitive thought". There is a rich literature on this issue; for a review, see Li (1996).

Since I am inclined to support linguistic determinism, I have thought about the mechanism of language determining thought – hypothetically, though.

Both Heidegger and Wittgenstein hold that language dominates human beings, rather than vice versa. Likewise, language determines thought, rather than vice versa. Heidegger holds that "language gives the essence (existence) of things", and in the same sense, Wittgenstein says that "essence (existence) is expressed in grammar" (cited in Y. Xu et al., 1996, p. 286). According to Heidegger, "essence and existence speak in language" and Wittgenstein holds that "the limits of my language mean the limits of my world" (*ibid.*). Jiaying Chen makes a comment on Heidegger's and Wittgenstein's views as follows.

> What Heidegger and Wittgenstein intend to convey is not that reality takes shape in the way we speak, but that *we can only talk about reality in terms of the existence condensed in a language and a specific grammar.*
>
> (*Ibid.*; emphasis added)

In other words, when we talk about reality, we think, but our thinking is already restricted by the existence condensed in the language and the grammar. For example, there is only one moon, but Chinese poets who use Chinese and English poets who use English may describe it in different ways. You may still remember the speculation by Greenberg as we mentioned earlier in 3.2.4.2: If two people speaking different languages are sent to the moon, the content of the reports they make will never differ because their languages differ. However, my point here is: Looking at the moon from the earth, poets using different languages do make different non-scientific (emotional, of course) observations and descriptions of the moon, which are already stipulated by their own grammatical framework. In fact, the numerous Chinese lyric poems about the moon have been very different from

Language: Mankind's last homestead   189

those by British and American poets since ancient times. The differences are traditionally accounted for by the viewpoint that poets from different cultures, ethics, and countries may have different perceptions and feelings about the moon. Such an account is certainly right, but it does not tell the whole story. Obviously, it fails to take into account the existence condensed in a language and the fact that the grammar of a language shapes the reality they perceive. The essence condensed in Chinese is different from the essence condensed in English, and Chinese syntax differs greatly from English syntax. Just think about the role that a Chinese word plays in the language system, the fact that a line of a Chinese poem can be composed of only nouns (e.g., 小桥流水人家 [xiǎoqiáo liúshuǐ rénjiā] "The small bridges, the flowing river, and the houses"), the overwhelming role that vowels play in Chinese, the unique rhyming patterns, and the various types of Chinese poems in terms of their length and rhyming patterns. _Different aesthetic tastes can be revealed and different aesthetic effects can be achieved in using English and Chinese to depict a same object._ The Chinese once ridiculed their compatriots who worshiped foreign things and fawned on foreigners so much as to claim that "the moon in a foreign country is rounder". It might be disputable that the moon in another country can be rounder; however, it is indisputable that in the words of people who use different languages, the moon is not the same. In other words, _there is only one physical moon, but there are thousands of different moons as depicted in language._ This claim can be testified only by examining, comparatively, all the poems about the moon from the literatures of all countries. In our contemporary world, this job would be a piece of cake by means of computer technology.

Of course, we can still ask why it can be said that "there is only one physical moon, but there are thousands of different moons as depicted in language". As Y. Xu et al. observe,

> acquiring a language framework can be regarded as acquiring the world described by this language, but this does not mean asserting that such a world is real; it only means acquiring a language habit or a set of language rules.
>
> (1996, p. 97; emphasis added)

Thus, acquiring the framework of the Chinese language means acquiring the world described by the language, for example, the moon described in Chinese; acquiring the framework of another language (such as English) means acquiring the world described in that language, for example, the moon described in that language. Just like that, "language conditions thought" (Sapir-Whorf hypothesis: "language powerfully conditions all our thinking", "thought is, to a significant extent, determined by language", and "human beings are very much _at the mercy of_ their particular language"). How does language condition thought? _Language conditions thought with its set of rules or frameworks. We might as well consider this set_

190 *Language: Mankind's last homestead*

of rules or frameworks as part of the mechanism by which language conditions thought.

In addition, the "linguistic ontology" put forward by B. Chen (1993) is quite enlightening for understanding the mechanism by which language conditions thought. B. Chen first sketches out, drawing on the results of modern analytical philosophy, what he calls the "hierarchy of the world" and claims that as cognitive subjects, human beings cannot "directly" meet objects: Between objects and subjects lie the intermediate levels such as the world of feelings, the world of language, and the world of culture. For human beings speaking a language, the world of language is the intermediate link from the world of feelings to the world of culture. Language not only creates culture, but also conditions the feelings that make mankind human. Therefore, linguistic signs fundamentally restrict people's conception and impression of the object world. Then, B. Chen proposes a "model of language shaping thinking". The model is based on two important premises. On the one hand, thinking is divided into the ability of thinking and thinking patterns. Language cannot determine the level of thinking ability, but different languages can lead to greatly different thinking patterns. On the other hand, according to the relationship between language and thinking, human thinking can be divided into three levels: "Prelinguistic thinking", "linguistic thinking", and "supralinguistic thinking" (such as Piaget's perception-motion pattern and Zen's so-called "sudden enlightenment", which is not controlled by language). *Language determines thinking only in terms of the thinking patterns of linguistic thinking.* This is actually an important supplement to the Sapir-Whorf hypothesis. According to B. Chen (1993), there is a fundamental problem with the Sapir-Whorf hypothesis: If different languages determine the thinking patterns of different linguistic thinking, then what factors ultimately determine the differences between languages? (This is a question worthy of attention.) To answer that question, B. Chen (*ibid.*) puts forward "linguistic ontology". He believes that the initial stage of language at development is determined by arbitrariness, and the subsequent development is determined by the language's *mechanism of structural self-organization* and the *interaction* between languages. Therefore, the causes for the differences between languages as well as the *differences* in thinking patterns thus determined *should lie in languages themselves*. The phonetic, grammatical, and lexical levels of language interact with each other; the effect of each level on the other levels can only be regarded as random. In B. Chen's view, the purpose of evolution at each level is determined by structural synergy. Although the lexical system is a sensitive part of social culture, the influence of the lexical system on phonetics and grammar is random, so the influence of social changes on phonetics and grammar is also random. The purpose of language changes is not determined by social cultures, but language changes will result in changes in thinking patterns, thus affecting the spirit of a culture.

Language: Mankind's last homestead   191

In brief, now that the differences between languages are ultimately determined by each language's mechanism of structural self-organizing and by the interaction between languages, the causes for the differences between languages as well as the differences in thinking patterns thus determined should lie in languages themselves.

Then, we can ask further: How does language condition thought with its set of rules or frameworks, which are formed in the functioning of its structural self-organizing? In my 1993 monograph *Aesthetic Linguistics* (G. Qian, 1993), it is elaborated that the variation and selection of language is an important aspect of the generation mechanism of the beauty of speech and that the self-organizing movement of language promotes language variation, which works as the fundamental driving force for language variation (interested readers are referred to G. Qian, 1993, chapter 2).

What is the self-organizing movement of the language system? Both the dissipative structure theory and synergetics hold that the evolution of a system is a self-organizing process. S. Xu explains it as follows.

> The self-organizing process may be caused by the changes in the environment outside the system, or by the changes in the elements of the system, including the changes in the quantity and quality of the elements and the changes in the order in which the elements are arranged. When some changes inside and outside the system destabilize the original structure of the system, from relatively orderly to disorderly to some extent, the system will reorganize itself to restore its order and function. The evolution of a system is carried out for a reasonable self-organization. Therefore, the purpose of a system's evolution is the self-organization of the system. The self-organizing movement of a system restricts the direction and purpose of the system's evolution from the inside of the system. Thus, evolution is directional and purposeful. It is neither completely random or arbitrary nor completely determined by external factors. ... The result of variation is to *achieve a reasonable reorganization of the structure* on the basis of the original one.
>
> (S. Xu, 1991; cited in G. Qian, 1993, pp. 58–62; emphasis added)

What role does the self-organizing movement of language play in the mechanism by which language conditions thought? The self-organizing movement of language is the root of a set of *right* rules or frameworks (to perform functions) that language forms, and then, via this set of right rules or frameworks, the thinking pattern of the person who speaks the language is finally formed. Different language frames or structures will certainly lead to different thinking patterns. The latter step, the one in which a set of rules or frameworks leads to different modes of thinking, as discussed above, means that the acceptance of a language framework can be seen as the acceptance of the world described by the language. Thus, the mechanism by which

192 *Language: Mankind's last homestead*

language conditions thought can be reformulated like this: *The self-organizing movement of each language forms its unique variation and selection path, which in turn forms its own right language rules or frameworks, which ultimately determine the thinking patterns of speakers of different languages.*

3.2.4.4 Language as the pre-existing structure of human cognition of the world

At the beginning of Section 3.2.4, it was claimed that the acceptance of language as a pre-existing structure is of great importance to the understanding of linguistic determinism. By this it is meant that language is something that exists before the experience of an individual. Obviously, mankind created language, and language came after mankind. Then, in what sense can it be said that language exists before the experience of an individual? On the whole, there is no doubt that human beings collectively created language. However, after ages of development, a language has finally fallen into a pattern; when an individual is born, he is confronted with an existing language – the language that has long been in existence. In the same vein, we say that language is the pre-existing structure of people's cognition of the world.

In 3.2.4.2, we talked about the following important facts when elaborating why the Sapir-Whorf hypothesis has not been fatally challenged: At least in one's early childhood, it is the language frame that determines the thinking frame; ontogenetically speaking, language patterns develop before thinking patterns. Before a child is born, the language that the child will learn has already been spoken by their parents, brothers, and sisters, and the structure of the world and the universe recorded by the language is already there. Thus, we can say that *children's acquisition of a language framework means their acquisition of the structure of the world and the universe stored in the language framework.* Children receive the world and perceive the world; in addition to what is directly perceived by the senses, the rest are the relationships, frameworks, and worldviews recorded and conveyed by the language. When children grow up and can influence the language in turn by adding new nouns, verbs, and narrative ways to the linguistic repertoire, their relationship with language becomes interactive. A fact is that when an adult speaks, the expressions he wants to say are already in his mind before he speaks them out. Wittgenstein (1953, §337) once said, "But didn't I already intend the whole construction of the sentence at its beginning? So surely it already existed in my mind before I said it out loud!" The language frames the speaker's mind in advance.

The linguistic traces received by children during their childhood will affect them for a lifetime. Language shapes the thinking of a child around the age of five, which means that the lifelong thinking framework of a person is defined. The idea that "intelligence is modeled at the age of seven" is consistent with the idea that "the thinking framework is shaped at the age of seven". Language shapes everyone who is about to learn to speak. Therefore, Heidegger claims that "to undergo an experience with language, then, means to let ourselves be properly concerned by the claims of language by entering

Language: Mankind's last homestead   193

into and submitting to it" and "an experience we undergo with language will touch the innermost nexus of our existence" (1982, p. 57).

Thus far, it can be said that we have made it clear in what sense language is the pre-existing structure of human cognition of the world. On the one hand, ontogenetically speaking, every individual is born in a world where language has long been there, and they are born to receive the world and the universe given in the language framework, and to receive the relationships, frameworks, and worldviews recorded and conveyed by the language. *To cognize the world, one has first to perceive the world recorded and conveyed by the language structure – the relationships, frameworks, and worldviews.*

On the other hand, language is the tool for an individual to cognize the new object world. This is what we usually say: Through language, we learn knowledge, obtain information, and approach objects. However, before we do those things, we already have a pre-existing world that is recorded and conveyed by our language structure. *Human beings use such a pre-existing structure as a tool to learn and approach the current new object world.*

On the basis of what was said above, Heidegger's comments on Humboldt can be more clearly understood.

> Humboldt deals with "the diversity of the structure of human language" and deals with it in respect of "its influence on the spiritual development of mankind". Humboldt puts language into language as *one* kind and form of the worldview worked out in human subjectivity.
>
> (Heidegger, 1982, p. 119; emphasis original)

In short, according to Humboldt, the spiritual development of mankind is influenced by language, and language is one kind and form of the worldview.

Ontogenetically, people listen for a long time before they learn to speak. One begins to listen to everyone around when one is still in the mother's womb, which lays the foundation for speaking later. After birth, we listen for another period of time before we begin to speak in an incomplete sense. We start to speak in the true sense when we are about five years old. *This fact that we listen before we learn to speak is very important, for it lays the foundation for the claim that language is the pre-existing structure of human cognition of the world.* Everyone has been listening for a few years before starting to speak. The world structure is readily embedded in language, so, through listening, you receive, perceive, and store a world framework. *In this way, language imposes a world framework on you through your listening before you know it.* Heidegger makes this point clear when he says,

> Speaking is known as the articulated vocalization of thought by means of the organs of speech. But speaking is at the same time also listening. It is the custom to put speaking and listening in opposition: one man speaks, the other listens. But listening accompanies and surrounds not only speaking such as takes place in conversation. The simultaneousness

194   *Language: Mankind's last homestead*

of speaking and listening has a larger meaning. Speaking is of itself a listening. Speaking is listening to the language which we speak. Thus, *it is a listening not while but before we are speaking.*

(Heidegger, 1982, p. 123; emphasis added)

In short, language, the pre-existing structure, enters into the mind through listening.

Now, it will not be abrupt at all to make such a statement as "human beings remain committed to and within the being of language, having been dwellers in language for a quite a long time". Heidegger is right when he makes the following remarks.

In order to be who we are, *we human beings remain committed to and within the being of language*, and can never step out of it and look at it from somewhere else. ... That we cannot know the nature of language is not a defect, however, but rather an advantage by which *we are favored with a special realm* where we, who are used to speak language, *dwell as mortals.*

(*Ibid.*, p. 134; emphasis added)

3.3 Living in formulaic verbal behavior

3.3.1 *The definition and characteristics of formulaic verbal behavior*

The reader is referred to 2.2.2 for a quick review of "activity type" and "structural formula" and to 2.2.3 for a brief recall of the structural formula as demonstrated in a case of civil mediation from a countryside judicial center.

3.3.1.1 A definition

What is formulaic verbal behavior? It is an activity type or a speech event (like a deal on the cattle market, TCM inquiries, a traditional Chinese wedding) characterized by: 1) A relatively fixed set of utterances; 2) a relatively fixed set of actions in relatively fixed move orders; and 3) a relatively fixed co-occurrence of the above two. We refer to the quality consisting of these characteristics as the formulaicity of activity types or speech events. Being "formulaic" in our sense can thus be taken as a synonym, to a certain degree, for being "ritualized", "conventionalized", "routinized", or "institutionalized" in different contexts. As Levinson (1979) defines, activity type is "a fuzzy category whose focal members are goal-defined, socially constituted, bounded, events with *constraints* on participants, setting, and so on, but above all on the kinds of allowable contributions" (p. 368; emphasis original). Paradigm examples given by Levinson are teaching, a job interview, a jural interrogation, a football game, a dinner party, and so on.

Language: Mankind's last homestead 195

In formulaic verbal behavior, the relatively fixed set of utterances are repeatedly used, which may sometimes allow diachronic variations. They meet the minimal requirement of linguistic input for the communicative goal to be adequately achieved in such activity types.

A traditional Chinese wedding ceremony[16] serves as a quick example of formulaic verbal behavior. At a traditional Chinese wedding, the actions or moves performed by the bride and groom (B & G for short) are basically fixed and the same is true with the utterances produced by the master of the ceremony (M for short).

A traditional Chinese wedding ceremony

Moves	Fixed utterances	Action co-occurring with each of the utterances
Move 1	M: 一拜天地— ("First, kowtow to Heaven and Earth")	(B & G's kowtowing, with their backs facing the shrine for [Yī bài tiāndì] ancestral tablets, to pay homage to Heaven and earth)
Move 2	M: 二拜高堂— ("Second, kowtow to your parents")	(B & G's kowtowing to the groom's parents) [Èr bài gāotáng]
Move 3	M: 夫妻对拜— ("Husband and wife bow to each other")	(B & G's kowtowing to each other) [Fūqī duì bài]
Move 4	M: 送入洞房— ("Now, escort the bride and groom to the bridal bedroom")	(B & G's being escorted to the bridal bedroom, clustered [Sòngrù dòngfáng] around with their relatives and friends)

Here, M's utterances, the actions performed by B & G, the co-occurrence of the phrasing and the action at each move, and the sequence of the moves are highly formulaic and have been passed down from generation to generation for centuries. The four moves and the co-occurrence of the phrasing and the action at each move are the minimal requirement for what can be called a wedding ceremony in traditional Chinese culture. The absence of any one of them will make the event incomplete.

As noted in 1.2, throughout a formulaic speech event, there is a set of conventions, institutionalized or non-institutionalized but with socially restricting power (like verbal agreements, rules for playing a game, etc.). Conventions are what are ritualized in a culture. Ritualization, as Arndt and Richard (1987) observe, is "the way spontaneous behavior becomes standardized and integrated into collective communication systems" (p. 26). Then, how does ritualization happen? Historically, ritualization of communicative behavior arose from various cooperative activities among early

196 *Language: Mankind's last homestead*

hominids to cope with environmental and social problems, and this pressure for cooperation was finally realized selectively as conventional signals in human semiotic systems (Arndt and Richard, 1987, p. 27). Ritualization, generally speaking, is thus adaptive.

In formulaic speech events, language performs the action-guiding function; they develop in the company of language and come to an end with language. Formulaic verbal behaviors, performed by the agents through a relatively fixed set of recurrent utterances, are always situated or embedded in particular formulaic speech events.

Whether a speech event is formulaic has nothing to do with its scale. A brief speech event can be formulaic. For instance, in asking a stranger for directions or for a lighter, there goes a formulaic speech event as ritualized in the local culture or customs. If you follow the formula, you can get what you want in no time, while the defiance of the formula will lead you astray from the goal or even to a rebuke. A large-scale speech event, on the contrary, can be non-formulaic. For example, a sudden quarrel among three or more groups of people blaming each other for blocking the way will be so chaotic that no formulaicity can be talked about. The verbal exchange in that case goes nowhere and may end in a worse chaos.

On October 1, 2003, *The Interim Rules for Marriage Registration* were implemented in China. Accordingly, from that day on, in Guangzhou, Guangdong Province, a rite of issuing the marriage certificate can be held by the Civil Affairs Department of the city at the scene for the couple applying for marriage registration. With the new couple standing in front of the national emblem and the national flag, the registrar asks them the following two questions, requiring a yes/no answer. If the couple both say yes to both questions, the registrar concludes the rite with the announcement marked as 3).

1) 你们是否自愿结为夫妻？
   [Nǐmen shìfǒu zìyuàn jié wéi fūqī?]
   Do you willingly take each other to be your wedded husband or wife?

2) 你们是否了解对方没有配偶？
   [Nǐmen shìfǒu liǎojiě duìfāng méiyǒu pèi'ǒu?]
   Do you know for sure that either of you has no spouse already?

3) 我宣布你们结为夫妻。
   [Wǒ xuānbù nǐmen jiéwéi fūqī.]
   I pronounce you husband and wife.

Rites like this will become formulaic speech events; the more formal they are, the more likely they become well-established formulaic speech events. The rite of issuing marriage certificates as described above perfectly demonstrates, again, the stable co-occurrence of actions (issuing and taking the marriage certificate) and utterances (two questions and one announcement). The formulaic utterances are the utterances most relevant to the goal of the activity type (applying for the marriage certificate), and thus help attain the goal most economically in terms of time and energy (the whole event lasts less than one minute). This formulaic speech event promotes maximal efficiency of coordination (issuing and taking the marriage certificate), saving time and displaying solemnity and elegance. In a civilization that becomes more mature, formulaic verbal behavior will increase in variety and frequency of occurrence as human beings' pursuit of efficient participation in life escalates with their life becoming better-off and more secure. For instance, the welcome ceremony held recently for the first Chinese astronauts returning from space will become a formulaic verbal behavior for all astronauts in China with the boosting of aerospace engineering in this nation. And that is a safe prediction we can make.

Thus far, we have been talking about just one kind of formulaic verbal behavior, which we refer to as *formulaic verbal behavior in the strict sense*. By that, we mean those activity types or speech events where the set of actions performed by the participants are highly fixed, the move sequences are highly fixed, and particularly the concomitant linguistic contributions are restricted to a highly fixed set of recurrent utterances, the absence of which will make the speech event incomplete or invalid. The other kind of formulaic verbal behavior, that in the broad sense, is to be examined in the following section.

3.3.1.2 Formulaicity and variations

Variations may result from individualized choice-making, adapted to situational change, by the participants of an activity. As mentioned in 1.2, in some traditional Chinese wedding ceremonies, 一拜天地 ([Yī bài tiāndì] "First, kowtow to Heaven and Earth") was replaced with 一拜毛老 ([Yī bài Máolǎo] "First, bow to His Excellency Mr Mao") or 一拜邓老 ([Yī bài Dènglǎo] "First, bow to His Excellency Mr Deng"). In the above rite of issuing a marriage certificate, the couple may as well name someone else instead of the registrar to be the host. He or she can be the couple's friend or relative, only if he or she is a civil servant. In that case, more moves can be added with concomitant utterances and it is up to the couple or the host to decide what is added, and the registry office will sanction their script before the rite is performed. For example, the host may add:

4) 无论疾病贫穷，你都能对他（她）不离不弃吗？
    [Wúlùn jíbìng pínqióng, nǐ dōunéng duìtā (tā) bùlíbùqì ma?]
    Will you care for and totally give yourself to the other, for richer or for poorer, in sickness and in health?

5) 请双方交换戒指。
    [Qǐng shuāngfāng jiāohuàn jièzhǐ.]
    Please exchange your wedding rings.

198 *Language: Mankind's last homestead*

6) 现在新郎可以吻新娘。
[Xiànzài xīnláng kěyǐ wěnxīnniáng.]
Now the groom may kiss the bride.

Apparently, what is added is up to the individualized choices of the participants. Individualization is an important part of human nature. Therefore, variations are always possible in human linguistic behavior, be it formulaic or not.

Variations may also result from the change of the times and the advance of a civilization. Again, take, for example, the traditional Chinese wedding ceremony. The first move is the most vulnerable to change. In the ancient times, Chinese people believed that Heaven and Earth were the greatest gods in charge of their fate, giving them what they fed on and lived on. Heaven and Earth were thus on the top of list of things or people who they should pay homage to at such solemn and magnificent situations as wedding ceremonies. Hence 一拜天地 ([Yī bài tiāndì] "First, kowtow to Heaven and Earth") became the first move of the traditional Chinese wedding ceremony. However, with the change of the times, the awe of Heaven and Earth declined and the dependence on Heaven and Earth became gradually neglected or even denied. In the contemporary age, who still cares about Heaven and Earth in getting married? In fact, it is one of the achievements of the modern Chinese revolutionary course to free people from the shackles of gods and ghosts and other feudalist perceptions about marriage. Of course, such a freedom is attributed to the advances of science and humanism.

What is interesting is that the spirit of advancing with the times has done little change to people's homage to their parents. As you see, 二拜高堂 ([Èr bài gāotáng] "Second, kowtow to your parents") remains as it was in the traditional Chinese wedding ceremony. Why is that so? In the feudal clan times, the marriage of a person was also heavily subject to parental dominance, as reflected by the ancient saying 父母之命，媒约之言 ([Fùmǔzhīmìng, méiyuēzhīyán] "One's marriage should be decided by their parents and obliged by the agreements between their parents and the match-maker"). Many elopements took place against marriages arranged by parents and ended up in tragedies. In fact, during the modern Chinese revolutionary years, one of the motives for some people to join in the revolutionary force was to run away from the marriages arranged by their parents. However, after 1949, with the founding of the new China, parents have advanced with the times with their attitude to their children's marriage, giving them freedom of choice in marriage. And that accounts for why B & G's kowtowing to the groom's parents has remained in the traditional Chinese wedding ceremony.

The most noticeable case about variations in formulaic speech events is the diachronic changes in the speech event that takes place over the family dinner on the Lunar New Year's Eve, the most important dinner of the year for most Chinese families (for the sake of convenience, referred to as New Year Family Dinner hereafter). There was clearly identifiable formulaicity in the speech event decades ago, especially in my childhood memories.

Language: Mankind's last homestead 199

My reliable memory about the New Year Family Dinner can date back to 1945, for I still have clear memories about the brutal behavior (raping, robbing, killing, and burning things around) of the Japanese invaders in my hometown (Shahu, Mianyang, Hubei Province) around 1944. The family dinner was ritual, solemn, and full of love. It began with the table-setting and when the dishes were served and all were seated, the family paid homage to the ancestors. Then the eldest of the family, my grandmother, announced the dinner to begin, saying 一年辛苦忙到头了，都吃吧([Yīnián xīnkǔ mángdàotóule, dōuchī ba] "Each of us has been busy working hard for a whole year; let's eat now") and the dinner would witness a lot of toasts, each accompanied with formulaic utterances. In brief, there was a relatively fixed set of things to do in a relatively fixed sequence via a relatively fixed set of recurrent utterances.

During the Spring Festivals from 2001 to 2003, we collected seven cases of New Year Family Dinner talks from four provinces and two municipalities, including Jilin, Beijing, Shanxi, Henan, Hubei, and Chongqing. We planned to identify and describe its formulaicity, but contrary to our expectation, there is little trace of formulaicity. That, to some extent, is puzzling, especially in face of the fact that the New Year Family Dinner remains a custom in Chinese culture. In fact, it matters so much that people, most noticeably the rural laborers, will take all the trouble to get home from all over the country just for this family reunion dinner, which means lengthy suffering, even dangerous trips on crowded trains or jammed highways. Then what has caused the loss of formulaicity in this grand event?

It is the changes in the social and economic life of the Chinese. The once formulaic New Year Family Dinner was the crystallization of ancient agricultural Chinese civilization. In the old days, farming was the basic form of life, and all that people were busy with from daybreak to sunset was confined to the family, the basic unit of both work and life. In addition, the Confucian concepts about family and clan required the young to stay home when their parents were still alive. The lower the mode of production is, the more monotonous the form of life is. The simplicity and fixedness of life style, in turn, increased the chance that the whole family lived together. The more fixed the life style and the less mobility there is in the community, the more likely the practices of the members of the community become formulaic. All these worked together to lead to the formulaicity of the New Year Family Dinner talk, where most of the oral exchanges were noticeably oriented to eating and drinking or foods and drinks presented there.

After 1949, China started to strive for industrialization, which has been accelerated since the reform and opening-up policy was implemented. As a result, the mobility of the large population increased enormously abruptly and whether people can reach home on time for the New Year Family Dinner depends on the capacity of the transportation means. That uncertainty has become a vital strike against the maintenance of the ritual-like New Year Family Dinner. In addition, the mode and speed of industrialized production

200 *Language: Mankind's last homestead*

accelerate the pace of life, and the accelerated life pace in turn tends to make the dinner brief and convenient. The pressing need for time will make it harder to maintain the old lengthy ritual-like dinner. Besides, with the varied means of entertainment and more colorful life, nowadays, only old people enjoy sitting around the table for a lengthy dinner. Young people have little interest in the New Year Family Dinner. In most cases, they fill themselves up mindlessly and leave the table promptly with words like "Dad and Mom, we're going out". Also, the special TV programs prepared for the eve of the Chinese New Year contribute significantly to bringing the dinner to a quicker end. Usually, when the family is still at the table, the grand TV program is already on. The opening show takes people's attention away from the table, which results in the increasing non-predictability of what might come up as topics for the dinner talk, hence the loss of the formulaicity of the New Year Family Dinner talk. In brief, it is the shift from agricultural civilization to modern civilization (industrialized society in the information age) that destroyed the formulaicity of the New Year Family Dinner talk. *Changes in the forms of civilization are profound factors leading to variations in formulaic verbal behavior.*

As the reader might have noticed, our analysis of the once formulaic New Year Family Dinner talk reveals a type of formulaic verbal behavior different from what we refer to as formulaic verbal behavior in the strict sense (see 3.3.1.1). Apparently, different from the traditional Chinese wedding ceremony, formulaic New Year Family Dinner talks represent what we call the formulaic verbal behavior in the broad sense.

In the formulaic verbal behavior in the broad sense, there are a relatively fixed set of actions, but the move sequences may not be strictly followed (allowing variations), and some moves may be left out by common consent from all parties involved. Besides, the utterances concomitant with each move are highly identifiable and predictable, but the tolerance for or inclusion of variations and free-flowing conversational interaction increases, to different degrees, though, as the situation varies. That is to say, formulaic rules, or conventions in Lüger's (1983) term, can be adjusted. Conventions "play a crucial role in directing and safeguarding communication processes" and thus constitute "a reference system of patterns and types in whose framework the act of communication must take place" (Lüger, 1983, p. 695). That remark elaborates on the importance of conventions, but it should be enunciated that observing socially accepted conventions cannot ensure successful communication because "the communicating subjects must *adapt the rules according to their intentions and to the different aspects of the context*" (ibid., p. 696; emphasis original).

Variations in formulaic verbal behavior embody the adaptation of communicative rules that takes place in communication.

3.3.1.3 The tendency to formulaicity

Of course, some speech events in everyday life are neither institutional nor socially conventional, but are prompt, haphazard, or occasional (but

Language: Mankind's last homestead   201

they may, to various extents, be influenced by some formulaic ones). For instance, to a trespasser, the owner of the place may politely or sternly ask him to leave, or even furiously order him to leave. In any case, the owner may freely choose his words and he is not supposed to use any particular formulaic utterances at all. Or when you are involved in a conversation about a brand-new topic, whatever occurs to your mind seems just inappropriate; nothing formulaic is available then. Likewise, when people in a close relationship (like a couple, close friends, or working partners) are in a routine speech event, they may not use formulaic utterances even if there are such utterances. People may choose to keep room for free-flowing verbal interaction in some speech event.

However, there may be a tendency towards formulaicity in some speech events that seem to be anything but formulaic. Take, for example, the quarrelling event. "Can there be anything formulaic in a quarrel?", you may ask. In quarrelling, each party tries to gain and hold the floor to say as much as possible to increase the impression that the truth is on his side. As a result, the interaction frequently becomes a noise-making scene, as both sides talk at the same time in increasingly high and, usually, shrieking or husky voices. Quarrels happen a lot and frequently wherever there are people. There must be something reasonable in quarreling so that they are inevitable or even indispensable speech events in human life. Except the quarrels that are done just for the sake of quarrel or to drive the opponent crazy, quarreling works to solve problems that cannot be solved through normal verbal interactions. In that case, the quarrelers will try to increase the efficiency of quarreling in terms of reaching their purpose and reducing the cost of quarreling (e.g., reciprocal hurt, loss in energy, and physical well-being). A formula may thus take shape and be followed for that purpose.

As a matter of fact, in a quarrel, certain expressions are frequently and expectably heard, such as 我让你说，你也得让我说说吧 [Wǒ rang nǐshuō, nǐ yědé rang wǒshuōshuō ba] "I listened to you; you should also listen to me for a while"), 你说五分钟，我说五分钟，怎么样? ([Nǐ shuō wǔfēnzhōng, wǒ shuō wǔfēnzhōng, zěnmeyàng?] "Let's take turns to express ourselves, each for five minutes, OK?"), or 我们找一个中间人作证 ([Wǒmen zhǎoyīgè zhōngjiānrén zuòzhèng] "Let's get a third party to judge"). The use of such recurring expressions indicates the negotiation between the two parties on the rules regulating their quarrelling. The negotiation and such recurring expressions together demonstrate the inclination to formulaicity in quarrels. With such an inclination, a haphazard and irritating quarrel will somewhat turn into a "formal debate" monitored by a judge or arbiter. That is how negotiations, arbitrations, or courtroom mediations in the modern sense came into being.

Now you see, haphazard and prompt speech events, once started, tend to become formulaic with efforts made by the participants on both sides. Why? We have a good reason to believe that the emergence of formulaic speech events is nothing accidental, but something necessary and significant. To account for that, the following questions must be asked and answered.

202 *Language: Mankind's last homestead*

1) Why do formulaic utterances stably co-occur with formulaic actions? (See 3.3.2.)
2) How does formulaic verbal behavior promote human communication? (See 3.3.3.)
3) What is the pragmatic mechanism of formulaic verbal behavior? (See 3.3.4.)

3.3.2 Causes of the co-occurrence of formulaic utterances and formulaic actions

3.3.2.1 The result of human cooperation

The prerequisite for language to come into being is productive coordination, namely, cooperation, which is also the foundation for human survival and development. If the linguistic behavior in cooperative activities does not follow a certain formula, the cooperation will be frustrated. People do a lot but achieve little, and the cooperative efficiency is neither steady nor favorable. Too low an efficiency of cooperation can endanger human survival and development. Human beings tend to decide their reaction to the current situation or to predict the future event according to their experiences previously encountered. When involved in a repetitive communicative situation, the individual decides what he is supposed to do (say) and predict what is likely to come next. Through trial and error, the individual tests the suitability of different linguistic expressions. Eventually, a set of acts in particular move sequences and a set of concomitant expressions are sorted out as efficient means that enable the individual to realize his communicative ends in that communicative situation. If they follow the underlying formula of an activity type, they will see the benefit of formulaicity, that is, it helps to achieve the communicative ends and saves time, trouble, labor, and money. In brief, formulaicity in cooperative activities leads to the maximization of benefits. *To pursue the maximization of benefits in cooperation, man's linguistic behavior in some speech events will eventually become formulaic, given that the cooperation goes repeatedly and persistently enough.*

3.3.2.2 The driving force of expectations

Let's first take a look at a case of fortune-telling.[17]

> Date: July 12, 2002
> Place: The gate of Luohan Temple, Linjiangmen, Chongqing
> Participants: Fortune-teller A (a woman, about fifty years old), Teller A for short
> Fortune-teller B (a man, about fifty years old), Teller B for short
> Chu[18] (a man, thirty years old)
> Wang (Chu's wife, twenty-four years old)
> Ren (Wang's cousin, about twenty years old)

Language: Mankind's last homestead 203

(Chu, Wang, and Ren are walking to the temple gate, chatting about the history of the old Buddhist temple, located in the central downtown part of the city. Teller A approaches them and starts the conversation.)

TELLER A$_1$: 几位算不算一下嘛？[Jǐwèi suànbùsuàn yīxià ma?]
Do you want to have your fortune told?

TELLER B$_1$ (coming from another stand): 算不算？哪个算？[Suànbùsuàn? Nǎge suàn?]
Wanna have your fortune told? Which one of you wants it?

CHU$_1$: 算一下吧。[Suànyīxià ba.]
OK, we can have a try.

TELLER A$_2$ (to Chu): 哪个嘛？你呀？哟——你这个人，"印堂"[19]生的好！……你这个眉毛生得好！
[Nǎge ma? Nǐ ya? Yāo—Nǐ zhègerén,"yìntáng" shēngdehǎo!……Nǐ zhège méimáo shēngdéhǎo!]
Which one? You? Wow – your *yingtang* is great! Your eyebrows look great!
(To Wang) 他这眉毛生好了的。生得就像秦始皇那眉毛样。懂到没得嘛？
[Tā zhèméimáo shēnghǎolede. Shēngdé jiùxiàng qínshǐhuáng nà méimáoyàng. Dǒngdào méidé ma?]
His eyebrows are great. They look just like Emperor Qinshihuang's. Don't you see?

WANG$_1$ (mockingly): 他这个眉毛呀？[Tā zhège méimáo ya?]
The eyebrows of his?

(Ren bursts into laughter at Wang's words.)

TELLER A$_3$: 哎！他眉毛生得好。[Āi! Tā méimáo shēngdéhǎo.]
Yeah! His eyebrows are great.
(Turning to Ren) 你看他眉毛是不是生得好啊？
[Nǐkàn tāméimáo shìbùshì shēngdéhǎo a?]
Don't you think his eyebrows look great?
(Pointing to the part between Chu's eyebrows) 这叫做"财包"。他的"财包"是生好了的。
[Zhè jiàozuò "cáibāo". Tāde "cáibāo" shì shēnghǎolede.]
This is called "fortune container". His "fortune container" is great.
(Pointing at Chu's forehead) 看嘛，这里，田坎土厚[20]，他中间是鼓起来了的，所以"财包"是生好了的。
[Kànma, zhèlǐ, tiánkǎn tǔhòu, tā zhōngjiān shì gǔqǐláile de, suǒyǐ "cáibāo" shì shēnghǎole de.]
Look! Here, the crop-field, the ridge. The soil is rich. There is a mild bulge in the middle of his forehead; that means he has a great "fortune container".

WANG$_2$: 那个地方每个人都有得嘛！
[Nàgè dìfāng měigèrén dōuyǒudé ma!]
That part, everybody has one!

204 *Language: Mankind's last homestead*

TELLER A₄ (in raised voice): 每个人？这个兄弟"财包"生鼓起来了的。男左女右，你看左边噻！

[Měi gèrén? Zhège xiōngdì "cáibāo" shēnggǔqǐláile de. Nánzuǒ nǔyòu, nǐkàn zuǒbiānsāi!]

Everybody? This brother's "fortune container" bulges. It's the left side for men, right for women. You look at his left side!

(To Chu) 小兄弟，你晓不晓得你的时候？

[Xiǎoxiōngdì, nǐ xiǎobùxiǎodé nǐdeshíhòu?]

Young brother, do you know your birth time?

......

TELLER A₅: 你今年好多岁？[Nǐ jīnnián hǎoduōsuì?]

How old are you?

......

CHU₂ (to Teller A): 好！那……先算算嘛。你这个钱是怎么收的？

[Hǎo! Nà……xiānsuànsuàn ma. Nǐ zhègeqián shì zěnme shōude?]

OK! Well… let's do it. How much do you charge?

TELLER A₆: 我现在跟你说说，不收你的钱，帮助你。

[Wǒ xiànzài gēnnǐ shuōshuō, bùshōu nǐdeqián, bāngzhùnǐ.]

I'm just telling you something about your fortune. No charge. Just to help you.

TELLER B₂: 保证给你算准！

[Bǎozhèng gěinǐ suànzhǔn!]

I can assure you that you will know exactly what lies ahead in your future life!

......

TELLER A₇: 哎——算你啥子时候升官发财，在啥子地方发财……都给你算！

[Ai –Suàn nǐ sházǐ shíhòu shēngguān fācái, zài sházǐ dìfāng fācái…… dōugěinǐsuàn!]

Ah – I can tell you when you are to get promoted and make a fortune, where you can make your fortune… Everything!

......

TELLER B₃: 是算生辰八字²¹。实话实说，但是你不要多心哈！

[Shì suàn shēngchén bāzì. Shíhuà shíshuō, dànshì nǐ bùyào duōxīnhā!]

I will tell your fortune by the date and hour of your birth and the corresponding eight characters. I'll just tell you the truth, so don't get me wrong (if it is not good)!

......

TELLER B₄: 大方点儿嘛！拿个"月月红"²²嘛！

[Dàfāngdiǎn er ma! Nágè "yuèyuèhóng" ma!]

Be generous! Use your "good-luck notes"!

(Showing two fingers) 拿个这个数嘛！拿个"二红喜"²³嘛！

[Nágè zhègeshù ma! Nágè "èrhóngxǐ" ma!]

Give me this sum! Give me "double happiness"!

......

Language: Mankind's last homestead 205

TELLER B₅ (looking into his bag):　"二红喜"！大方点儿！

[Èrhóngxǐ, dàfāngdiǎn er!]

"Double happiness"! Be generous!

......

TELLER B₆:　我是实话实说！[Wǒ shì shíhuà shíshuō!]

I'm just telling you the truth!

......

TELLER　B₇:　"折财"是什么意思？一，你炒不得股；二，你投不得资；三，打不得大麻将。懂到没得？

["shecai" shi shenme yisi? yi, ni chao budei gu; er, ni tou budei zi; san, da budei da majiang. dongdao meidei?]

What do I mean when I talk about "loss of fortune"? First, don't buy stocks; second, don't make any investment; third, don't bet too much if you play mahjong. Got it?

一打就陷起。十打九输。

[Yīdá jiù xiànqǐ. Shídǎ jiǔshū.]

Once you do it, you'll get stuck in it. Nine out of ten times, you lose.

今年有小人儿过，你去打大麻将，你特别注意，是搞整你的。懂到没得？

[Jīnnián yǒu xiǎorén er guò, nǐ qùdǎ dàmájiàng, nǐ tèbié zhùyì, shì gǎozhěngnǐ de. Dǒngdào méidé?]

This year, some mean people will scheme against you. If you bet too much on mahjong, you must be very cautious. Got it?

但是从你信息上来看；你这个人……鼻子勾的……就是说中间拱起来一个钩钩，打不得交道！

[Dànshì cóng nǐxìnxīshàng láikàn, nǐ zhègerén......bízi gōude...... jiùshìshuō zhōngjiān gǒngqǐlái yīgè gōugōu, dǎbùdé jiāodào!]

But as your personal information shows, you... people with a hook nose... that is, the ends of their noses bulge like a small hook, don't deal with them!

......

TELLER B₈:　再往前……我要给你讲！慢慢讲起来！

[Zàiwǎngqián......wǒ yàogěinǐ jiǎng! Mànman jiǎngqǐlái!]

Look further ahead... I will tell you everything! Tell you step by step!

你这八字官运不好，但是还是挣得到钱儿，只不过说小人多了点儿。

[Nǐ zhèbāzì guānyùn bùhǎo, dànshì háishì zhēngdédào qián er, zhǐbùguòshuō xiǎorén duōlediǎn er.]

Your eight characters show your chances to be a government official or a leader are not good, but you still can make money, though quite a number of people will scheme against you.

但是之后有五年儿你走的是"颠簸运"！

[Dànshì zhīhòu yǒuwǔnián ér nǐ zǒudeshì "diānbǒyùn"!]

But, after that, the next five years will see you have "bumpy luck".

......

TELLER B₉:　嫖了的话，一切都…… [Piáoledehuà, yīqiè dōu......]

206 *Language: Mankind's last homestead*

If you use prostitute, everything will…
(Twitching his mouth) 我给你讲的是老实话。
[Wǒ gěinǐjiǎngde shì lǎoshíhuà.]
All I told you is the truth.
TELLER B$_{10}$:　八字还是不错的。[Bāzì háishì bùcuòde.]
Your eight characters are good, anyway.
(Chu, Wang, and Ren leave, putting an end to the speech event.)

As shown by the above case, there is a formula underlying fortune-telling events, based on the analysis of the ten cases of fortune-telling that we collected. It begins with the following exchange as a prelude:

FORTUNE-TELLER:　……算不算一下嘛？[……Suànbùsuàn yīxià ma?]
Do you want to have your fortune told?
CUSTOMER:　算一下吧。[Suànyīxià ba]
Ok, we can have a try.
FORTUNE-TELLER:　他/你的…… (某面相部位) 生得好。
[Tā/nǐ de……(a certain facial part) shēngdé hǎo]
His/Your … (a certain facial part) is/are great.

After the prelude, the fortune-teller will ask the potential customer for the date and hour of his birth, which is the prerequisite for the real fortune-telling deal to begin. At this time, the customer should ask about the charge. The fortune-teller usually responds with 不收钱 ([Bù shōuqián] "No charge") and then repeats such formulaic utterances as uttered at Teller B$_2$, Teller B$_6$, Teller B$_8$, and Teller B$_{10}$ to lure the potential customer into a deal. When it comes to offering the price, the fortune-teller will keep repeating the utterances at Teller B$_4$ to encourage the customer to pay as much as possible.

Then what functions do the expectations of both parties serve in the formation of the formulaic utterances? As the case of fortune-telling shows, any one (a potential customer) who approaches the fortune-teller's stand expects the fortune-teller's greeting, 算不算一下嘛？("Do you want to have your fortune told?"). And then the fortune-teller always expects a positive response in such utterances as算一下吧 ("I/we can have a try"). Given that every customer expects to hear good news from the fortune-teller, who, totally aware of this, will naturally say things like他/你的…… (某面相部位) 生得好 ("His/Your …(a certain facial part) is/are great"). Besides, he certainly knows that the potential customer will ask about the charge and has thus prepared不收钱 ("No charge") to avoid talking about the price before the real deal begins. That is because, at this stage, too high a price will drive a potential customer away while too low a price is not to the fortune-teller's favor. Of course, the customer knows that is not possible and will eventually pay for it at a negotiated price once the real deal is conducted. Likewise, knowing that the customer is most concerned with whether their fortune can be told without any mistakes or distortions, the fortune-teller keeps repeating保证给你算准

([Bǎozhèng gěinǐ suànzhǔn] "I can assure you that you will know exactly what lies ahead in your future life"), 实话实说 ([Shíhuà shíshuō] "I'll just tell you the truth"), and 我给你讲的是老实话 ([Wǒ gěinǐjiǎngde shì lǎoshíhuà] "All I told you is the truth"), which are just what the customer expects. In addition, because a person goes to fortune-telling most likely for the information about his chances for promotion or money-making, the fortune-teller will thus use such utterances as你这八字官运不好，但是还是挣得到钱儿 ([Nǐ zhè bāzì guānyùn bùhǎo, dànshì háishì zhēngdédào qián er] "Your eight characters show your chances to be a government official or a leader are not good, but you still can make money") to meet his expectation. Both chances for promotion and chances for making money are mentioned, and at least one of them happily hits the customer's expectation. Of course, it is possible that some customers may come to a fortune-teller just for fun. They may come just to make fun of the fortune-teller and may not care at all about what the latter tells. Once realizing that, the fortune-teller will just throw them a pile of cliché of fortune-telling talk, as is anticipated. In any case, the phrasing 你的八字还是不错的 ([Nǐde bāzì háishì bùcuòde] "Your eight characters are good, anyway") will be repeatedly used at the end of fortune-telling. Open to a host of interpretations, it rightly meets the customer's expectations.

Therefore, it can be said that expectations promote the formation of a set of formulaic utterances in formulaic verbal behavior, and the set of formulaic utterances, in turn, helps to have the customer's expectations satisfied within the shortest time possible, and thus at the least cost of effort. In that way, expectations in verbal interaction facilitate the formulaicity of formulaic speech events (see 3.3.1.1).

In a conversation, what is uttered at the latter turn in response to the former turn is actually a relevant response to the expectation contained or invoked in the former turn. In addition to the constraints of the dominant communicative goal of the event, the expectation contained or invoked in each turn functions as another important impetus to make a formulaic speech event formulaic as it is on the whole.

To further elaborate the impetus from expectations towards formulaicity, let us take, for another example, an excerpt of a bargaining event on the cattle market (the full event is to be presented and analyzed in 3.3.2.4). In the analysis of this case, we point out the expectation or the response to the expectation at each turn, putting it in angled brackets, < >.

BUYER (to Broker): 立叔！一会儿，给我瞅个牛？[Lì shū! Yīhuǐ'er, gěiwǒ chǒugèniú?]
  Uncle Li, can you pick one for me out of the cattle later?
  <Desiring to buy one of the cattle, expecting the broker to respond>
BROKER: 你想要个啥号的？[Nǐ xiǎngyào gè shàhàode?]
  What kind do you want?
  <Responding, meanwhile, expressing his own expectation>
BUYER: 当然是好的了。[Dāngrán shì hǎodele.]

208   *Language: Mankind's last homestead*

Of course, a good one.

<Responding, with his original expectation remaining>

BROKER (pointing at a cyan bull nearby):   你看那个牛娃儿咋样？
[Nǐkàn nàgè niúwá er zǎyàng?]
What do you think about that calf?

<Responding, expecting the buyer to take or reject it>

BUYER: 我不要这号哩。[Wǒ bùyào zhèhàolī.]
I don't want this kind.

<Rejecting, containing a new expectation, to keep looking>

BROKER: 那—   啥号哩？牤牛娃儿还是母牛娃儿？   [Nà—   shàhàolī?
Māngniúwá er háishì mǔniúwá er?]
Then – what kind? A young bull or a young cow?

<Responding, expecting the buyer to specify what he wants>

BUYER: 想买个母牛娃儿，能使能喂。[Xiǎngmǎi gè mǔniúwá er, néngshǐ
néngwèi]
I want a young cow, which can be used for both farming and breeding.

<Responding, containing a new expectation>

BROKER: 噢—，中啊。我给你看看再说。(Walking away.)
[Ō – zhōng a. Wǒ gěinǐ kànkàn zàishuō]
Oh – OK. Let me look around first and talk to you later.

<Confirming the buyer's expectation, expressing no new expectation>

The adjacent turns develop by making relevant responses to raised expectations and activating new expectations. When a turn evokes no new expectation, it works as the ending turn of a speech event or a subsection embedded within the speech event. In the above example, the last turn, with the broker's walking way, puts an end to the prelude to or the initial part of a bargaining event, where the buyer expresses his need for merchandise and the broker confirms that message and starts to look for a potential seller whose goods meet the buyer's expectations. A turn can be a negative response to the preceding turn without jeopardizing the ongoing episode on a particular topic towards to a corresponding goal. But if it goes astray from the expectations of the preceding turn, the episode gets suspended or stopped abruptly, and the participants have to work their way back to that episode and get it completed. Thus, in making a relevant response to raised expectations and activating new expectations, as long as the matrix of activity remains in progress, the set of formulaic utterances concomitant with the activity type will occur repeatedly, to meet the minimal requirement of linguistic input for the activity type to be adequately completed.

3.3.2.3 *The impetus from cultural stability*

The formulaicity of formulaic speech events (see 3.3.1.1 for review) has its root in a particular sociocultural background. If fact, it is true with language

Language: Mankind's last homestead 209

use in general, and Verschueren thus takes language use as "forms of behavior anchored in cognitive, social and cultural worlds" (1999, p. xi).

As to us, the traditional Chinese wedding ceremony serves as a most convenient and ideal example to illustrate the impetus from cultural stability to promote the formation of formulaic verbal behavior (in forms of formulaic speech events).

From the ancient times, Chinese people have referred to having a wedding ceremony as 办喜事 ([bàn xǐshì] "doing the happy thing"). They believe that in a man's life there are three happy things with the utmost gravity, namely, getting married, begetting a son, and establishing a career. Of the three, what matter more are getting married and begetting a son. Now that one cannot legitimately have a son without getting married first, getting married has thus become the foremost among all the happy things that could happen in a person's life. That accounts for why the wedding ceremony is the most complex, most magnificent, and most solemn one, with the richest customs in every ethnic group. Naturally, wedding ceremonies have attracted the greatest attention from anthropologists, sociologists, artists, and scholars in culture, literature, and folklore history. When some great ancient Chinese thinkers, for example, Zhuangzi, defined human natural death as one of the happiest things in a person's life, the term 白喜事 ([bái xǐshì] literally, "white happy things") was coined to name death from old age (for the background color is mainly white for Chinese funerals) and 红喜事 ([hóng xǐshì] literally, "red happy things") to refer to wedding ceremonies, where red is the main background color throughout the event.

On a wedding ceremony, there are a lot of things to be done and to be said by the people involved. For the purpose of this book, we focus on what people will say there. Needless to say, expressions of good wishes and congratulations are expected. From the earlier ages when wedding ceremony rituals began to take shape, various things must have been said during them, with expressions of good wishes and congratulations mingled with slips of the tongue or false moves resulting from overexcitement or anxiety on such a happy but somewhat chaotic occasion. From thousands of years of hustle and bustle, selected are a set of time-tested formulae: 一拜天地 ("First, kowtow to Heaven and Earth"), 二拜高堂 ("Second, kowtow to your parents"), 夫妻对拜 ("Third, kowtow to each other"), and 送入洞房 ("Now, escort the bride and groom to the bridal bedroom"), known as 三拜一送 [sānbài yīsòng], the Three-Kowtow-One-Escort formula. Indeed, this set of formulae is time-tested in the true sense, given that it has been repeatedly spoken in an astronomical number of wedding ceremonies throughout Chinese history. Then why have these four formulaic expressions been passed down as the most pertinent, time-saving, and effort-saving ones? This must be traced back to the stability of the Chinese cultural spirit.

Before 1949, the Chinese people generally had a spirit tablet enshrined right in the center of their household altars, which was usually a wood plaque

210 *Language: Mankind's last homestead*

bearing inscriptions honoring Heaven and Earth, the emperor, parents, and teachers. The worship of them was embodied in all aspects of people's daily life, especially in various festivals (of course, besides weddings and funerals, there are a great number of festivals counted throughout the year). The bride and groom's kowtowing to Heaven and Earth and their parents was a natural extension of that worship, which went in accordance to traditional Chinese cultural values. Heaven and Earth nourish me (giving grains and fruits for food), and have ultimate control of my life by having disasters or great fortune and happiness happen to me. The imperial power is entrusted by Heaven to be in direct control of my life and death. All I have to do is express devout worship and obedience. Who dares to show any disapproval? There actually is a further deliberation in worshiping Heaven and Earth in the wedding, that is, to have Heaven and Earth as the witness of the matrimony. This was a smart move in that you enjoyed honoring witnesses without owing them a debt of earthly interpersonal gratitude. And speaking of showing earthly interpersonal gratitude, nothing would be more natural than the bride and groom's kowtowing to their parents, who have given the man his life and are now seeing him at the start line of a new family life on his own. As a result, the Three-Kowtow-One-Escort formulae perfectly echo the values of traditional Chinese culture as demonstrated by enshrining the spirit tablet of Heaven and Earth, the emperor, parents, and teachers: To show due gratitude to those who have done you a favor and to worship the mysterious power of Heaven and Earth. In other words, *cultural stability promotes the formation of the formulaic verbal behavior in wedding ceremonies.*

Likewise, the formulaic utterances embedded within the bargaining event at the cattle market are the result of the unsound registrations of the Chinese rural market culture; due to the lack of relevant effective regulations, a successful deal depends on the mediation of the broker, which in turn relies on the broker's ingenious and intelligent, often rude and crafty, manipulation of the bargaining process. Being fully aware of this *de facto* practice, both the seller and the buyer come to the market worrying that the broker may trick them into an unfair deal. The bargaining formulae gradually came into being to lubricate the communication among the three parties, as to be seen in the analysis of a bargaining event at the cattle market in the coming section.

3.3.2.4 Human pursuit of efficiency in life

Now we come to the root cause of the co-occurrence of formulaic utterances and formulaic actions, the human pursuit of efficiency in life.

In 1.2, we mentioned in passing that in Wuhan, family members tend to say to each other, 洗了睡 ([xǐle shuì] literally, "wash and sleep") as they are turning off the TV every night. Upon a second reflection, Wuhan people can tell the charm of this formulaic phrasing as they have begun to talk about its intriguing sense to each other. It matches people's facial expressions (of satisfaction and fatigue) at that moment and the ongoing situation, usually with

Language: Mankind's last homestead 211

a woman busy in preparing hot water and urging her children and husband to get ready to wash themselves. Of course, having watched TV programs for hours, each of the family members is tired and sleepy and it is already late at night. No one would bother to make such a long speech as "Now, our favorite TV programs are all over, and each of us has had enough fun. It's bed time. Let's wash ourselves before going to bed". What people cannot wait to do then is just sleep. In terms of energy-saving and efficiency, no other expression works better than such three-character phrasing 洗了睡 ([xǐle shuì] "wash and sleep"). Now, this formulaic phrasing is being used across the country. And as can be seen in many China Central TV programs, it has even adopted a new sense, to start to do something else upon finishing something pleasant. The metaphoric usage of this expression is not just a mimic but a reflection of its popularity and people's acknowledgement of its efficiency to express themselves.

The pursuit of efficiency is natural in human life. *Efficiency in life lies in attaining the most harmonious state of life, and performing or functioning in the best possible manner with the least cost, profoundly time, money, and effort, but not confined to them.* Human beings tend to optimize their efficiency in life on all possible occasions by utilizing all possible opportunities.

If you want to make money, work to make a big fortune; the more you earn, the better. If you want to carve out a career, work as hard as possible. When you are successful, you try to go further. If you just want to live at ease, there is always a better, easier life to chase. The list may be endless, but the above three cases suffice to show what optimizing efficiency in life means.

To pursue efficiency in life on all possible occasions results from human physical and physiological needs, as well as psychological needs. For instance, when one is engaged in business negotiation, the ideal case is always the one that takes less time, but brings about greater beneficial effects. When one is surfing the Internet for data, the ideal is always to obtain the desired information within the shortest time. When one attends a concert, it is best to hear as many pieces of his favorite music as possible. When one is involved in a lawsuit, it is best to win with the fewest pieces of the most powerful evidence, the least money, and the least argument.

Likewise, to pursue efficiency in verbal communication is in essence a form of pursuing efficiency in life. Speakers try their best to realize an optimal efficiency in negotiations to achieve their communicative purposes. *Using formulaic utterances helps achieve communicative efficiency that can be best expected in particular situations. The pursuit of efficiency in life is thus at the core of an account of the stable co-occurrence of formulaic actions with formulaic utterances.*

What follows is a fairly detailed account of a bargaining case at a Chinese cattle market, known as Youtian Cattle Market in Biyang County, Henan Province, China. Reading this account, you will see that it helps not only to demonstrate how the human pursuit of efficiency in life promotes the formation of formulaic speech events, but to understand a native form of Chinese

212   *Language: Mankind's last homestead*

rural culture (including its market economy). Readers will also find that our own life can be observed as an aesthetic object, and it can be enjoyed with great interest. The ingenuity and tactfulness of human interaction are practically impossible to catch (so we call for readers' patience to finish the case study), and the philosophical and pragmatic perspectives are so close to our own lives! The analysis of the bargaining case suffices to demonstrate that formulaicity is something that is most relevant (or most directly related) to activity goals (3.3.2.4.1), that formulaicity is the most economical way to achieve activity goals (3.3.2.4.2), that formulaicity maximizes the benefits of collaboration (3.3.2.4.3), and that many other positive effects may also result from the formulaicity of speech events (3.3.2.4.4).

But before we move forward to do the case analysis, an introduction to the cattle market in Chinese rural areas is necessary to clear the ground.

A cattle market is a place that has gradually become a market as a result of the natural choices by local farmers to meet to buy or sell their cattle; it is approved by the local government, which entrusts a tax branch to supervise transactions. Usually, one or a group of farmers influential in the cattle business will volunteer and then be entrusted by the local government to serve as organizer or manager of the market. A cattle market is generally located in a remote corner of a town market.

In China's traditional agricultural society, cattle are kept by farmers as a labor force, to pull carts and other kinds of farm equipment, or as meat providers, and they may also be raised and sold for disposable cash income. A farmer may come to the cattle market as a seller, when he no longer needs a bull as his labor force, when he has more than necessary heads of cattle as his labor force, when he wants to dispose of an unwanted item, being old, weak, or in whatever way unsatisfying, when he wants to trade what he has for a different kind, or when he just needs some cash. On the other hand, a farmer may come to the market as a buyer, when he needs some cattle for a labor force (with the modernization in farming, this case is becoming increasingly rare), when he wants to breed some cattle for future sales, or when he wants to buy some cattle for meat production. In addition, there are always professional dealers of cattle at the cattle market, who make money through buying and selling cattle.

At the cattle market, there is a fundamental principle for the conduct of a deal, namely, the seller and the buyer should not directly talk to each other. Given that there are different and usually interlocked criteria for people to judge the value of a cow or bull, according to what it will be used for, it is a very intricate issue to decide the price of a cow or bull. Consequently, and normally, the seller tries to maximize the price by stressing all the possible strong points of the merchandise, while the buyer tries to minimize the price by finding as many faults as possible with it. As a matter of fact, once the buyer and the seller directly talk to each other, a quarrel will immediately arise, and may even lead to violence. That is because each side will condemn the other for lacking the ability or intelligence to tell what the fair price for

Language: Mankind's last homestead 213

the cow or bull should be. Then, as you can imagine, argument about the price will soon turn into argument about the quality of the merchandise, which will soon become a chaotic quarrel, full of contemptuous remarks about each other's lack of wise or honest judgments. Without intervention from a third party, the quarrel between the seller and buyer will immediately become intensified with verbal abuse, which will most likely be followed by physical violence. As a result, the cattle broker then comes on the stage as the professional intervener at the cattle market. Although no sources can be found to tell when the guild regulation became implemented that the seller and the buyer should not talk directly to each other, it is sure that the emergence of the cattle broker is the natural consequence of people's pursuit of efficient conduct of business at the cattle market. Acting as the professional at the cattle market, the broker is capable of judging the relatively fair price of the merchandise. It is a routine practice for the seller to ask several brokers to appraise his cow or bull and then make his own judgment. Usually, the price initially named by the seller will be higher than the highest appraisal. Likewise, the buyer will also consult several brokers about the proper price of his target merchandise, but his initial offer will be lower than the lowest appraisal. The bargaining process unfolds with the broker going between the buyer and the seller, trying his best to persuade the seller into lowering the price, and the buyer into raising his offer. When the offers on both sides come close enough to what the broker believes to be a fair or proper price, he will propose a compromise price. If the other two sides agree on it, the broker will take them to the registration desk to sign a paper record of the deal, which, in Chinese, is called 写账 ([xiězhàng] "to sign the deal"). The record will specify the major features of the merchandise and the identification information of the seller and the buyer. Once the seller and the buyer sign or press their thumbprints on the record, the deal is closed, and neither side can pull out of it. The transaction is completed when the buyer gives the money to and takes the merchandise from the broker, who immediately hands the money to the seller. It is the buyer who pays the tax and a service fee to the broker.

In the process of bargaining, before the agreement is reached to conclude the deal, the three parties involved all take their time, all acting as if they do not care so much whether a deal can be eventually reached or not. The broker keeps going back and forth between the seller and the buyer, showing his good intention to both sides and promising each side that he will make the deal go in the latter's best interests. Often, the broker will, from time to time, get himself involved in other ongoing bargaining processes that his peers are working on, or just chat with onlookers, so that both the seller and the buyer can be left alone to do their own calculation. It usually takes hours for a deal to be reached at the cattle market.

But once it comes to the point when a compromise price is likely to be agreed upon, the atmosphere abruptly becomes tense; three to five brokers rush to the seller and the buyer, pushing or pulling them and the cow or bull to the registration desk. With the brokers unintelligibly shouting and the

214 *Language: Mankind's last homestead*

onlookers crowding around making much noise, the seller and the buyer are somewhat forced to the desk. This tension is mainly due to the fact that either the buyer or the seller or both of them feel that the compromise price is not in their own favor and thus want to back off. Of course, it is possible that either the buyer or the seller or both of them are just playing a trick, by deliberately shouting 亏了 ([kuīle] "I'm losing money") and 不卖了 ([bù màile] "I won't sell it") or 不买了 ([bù mǎile] "I don't want it any more"), so that the other party will feel reassured that the deal is in his favor. Being completely aware of what is going on, the broker knows that one or both sides need a little push or pressure to agree upon the deal. Therefore, it is somewhat understandable and acceptable for them to push or even force the seller and the buyer to reach a deal at the last moment. After all, the broker's income at the cattle market depends on how many successful deals they can eventually close. Nonetheless, the extent to which the seller or buyer can be pushed or forced is something that the broker will have to decide tactfully based on his judgment of the seller's and/or the buyer's eagerness for a deal, their character, and many other factors. In view of the brokers' and the bystanders' pushing, shoving, and swearing, the cattle market is a world of men, full of craftiness, rudeness, and even a little violence mixed with witness, humor, and wisdom.

Why, then, will either the buyer or the seller or both of them feel that the compromise price is not in their favor and thus want to back off right before the deal is reached? To answer this question, we have to talk about people's attitudes towards cattle brokers. In the rural areas where cattle are used for farming, there is a saying known to almost all ages, "a cattle broker is ready to cheat even his own father". There are reasons for this stereotype about cattle brokers. Not so long ago, in China's rural areas, the concept of governing by the law was still weak and the market economy was immature. There were thus extremely strict regulations to serve as a remedy for the above two defects, with a group of tough men hired to watch the market, ready to punish those who broke the rules by whatever measures, ranging from hurling insults to violent punching and kicking. It was tacitly agreed that the seller and the buyer should not talk directly to each other and that after signing the record of the deal, no one should break the deal. Beside, in price negotiations, at least part of the bargaining was conducted not with words but by gestures. Namely, the two parties covered their hands with their jackets or something else, they made their offers known to the other by touching the different parts of their hands, each unanimously assigned a figure in tens or hundreds or thousands. The Chinese jargon for this practice is 摸价 ([mōjià] literally, "feel the price"). Once a deal was closed, the buyer gave the money to the broker at the price that the two agreed on, and then the broker gave the money to the seller at the price that they agreed on. As a result, it was impossible for the seller to know the buyer's real offer, and vice versa. Then there might be a margin between the offers on both sides, and it was quite possible for the broker to take the margin secretly. For instance, when the seller finally agreed to sell his merchandise at the price of 980 yuan, with the buyer agreeing to take it

Language: Mankind's last homestead 215

at the price of 1100 yuan, the broker could secretly put in his own pocket the margin of 120 yuan. Therefore, right before the final moment of reaching a deal, the buyer was always worried that his bid was too high, while the seller was worried that his offer was too low. Hesitation and a tendency to back off naturally emerged.

Now, with the improvement of China's legal system, such kinds of black-box operations have been forbidden by the law, and the seller and the buyer will learn from the broker or other people about each other's final offer before they agree to sign the deal. The broker keeps reassuring the seller that he will get no less than his offer, and the buyer that he will give no more than his offer. After the deal is signed, the broker immediately gives the seller all the money he takes from the buyer with all the people around as witnesses. But still, both the seller and the buyer have reasons to be worried and hesitant before the broker suggests they go to the registration desk. It is all due to the fact that no final price is unanimously agreed upon by the three parties involved until they are at the registration desk. The compromise price proposed is usually lower than the seller's final offer, but higher than the buyer's, and the broker is conventionally and tacitly endowed with the authority to announce the final price by making further adjustments ranging from 100 to 200 yuan to the compromise price. Both the seller and the buyer are afraid that the broker has made the compromise price in the other's favor and will do the same in making further adjustments to the price.

That is a very tricky and brain-racking game for the broker to play. For instance, the seller may tell the broker in private that he wants at least 2800 yuan, but claim publicly that he wants at least 3000 yuan in so loud a voice that the buyer can hear, who is always keen to overhear him. Likewise, the buyer may tell the broker in private that his highest offer is 2500 yuan, but claim publicly that it is 2300 yuan. Then, with much deliberation, the broker may come up with the compromise price, 2600 yuan, of which both the seller and the buyer will immediately express their strong disapproval. Here comes the test of the broker's professional ability in facilitating a deal. He will adopt every possible means, including tough acts like pushing and pulling and sweet talk. Making further adjustments within 100 to 200 yuan is one of them, usu-ally by tens or fifties. Generally speaking, a bargaining event that has moved this far is very much likely to reach a deal. But, when either the seller or the buyer firmly refuses to make a deal, the bargaining event will come to an end, with no deal made. The one who rejects further bargaining or negotiating will be reproached, ridiculed, and even cursed by the other two sides involved and the onlookers, for stubbornness, irrationality, greediness, or lack of respect for the broker. In brief, the seller or the buyer may show reluctance to accept the compromise price because it is hard to satisfy both parties.

Their reluctance is better justified given their reasonable doubt about the broker's credibility or fairness. Considering the broker's authority in pro-posing the compromise price and making further adjustment at the final stage of a deal, the seller tends to choose a broker that has connections with him,

216 *Language: Mankind's last homestead*

by kinship, friendship, or fellowship of any kind. So does the buyer. As a result, both the seller and the buyer will suspect that the broker is somewhat connected to both of them, but may be more closely connected to and thus more in favor of the other.

As described above, the bargaining event is a long-winded process of repeated negotiations among the seller, the buyer, and the broker, all of whom take their time and make sure they show no sign of eagerness to make a deal. Their verbal interaction embraces small talk, random chats, and jokes. Though frequently digressing, it basically revolves around the topic of price: Inquiring about the price of merchandise, naming the price, complaining about and/ or justifying the price, asking for a lower or higher price, rejecting an offer, reassuring the buyer and seller of the fairness of a price, and so forth. In the following two cases, we focus on the turns relevant to the running theme, to bring about a deal, but just mention in passing those irrelevant side talks. The formulaic utterances and their concomitant actions in the bargaining events at the cattle market are underlined for emphasis.

Case I: Bargaining event at Youtian Cattle Market

> Date of tape-recording: 9:50–11:50 a.m., July 18, 2002
> Place: Youtian Cattle Market, Biyang County, Henan Province
> Participants: Broker A, B, C, D
> The seller, a farmer around fifty years old, referred to as Seller
> The buyer, a farmer in his thirties, referred to as Buyer
> Onlooker A, B, C, D, etc., all present to learn about the market, usually planning to sell or buy a head of cattle in the near future
> (The sun is burning, and the market is noisy with cattle mooing, people shouting or murmuring. Several brokers are going back and forth between several pairs of sellers and buyers. They work independently, but some may meet to exchange a few words from time to time or get involved in others' business to help. Broker A is the one that the tape recorder follows throughout.)

BUYER (to Broker A):　立叔！一会儿，<u>给我瞅个牛</u>？
　　　　[Lì shū! Yīhuǐ'er, gěiwǒ chǒugèniú?]
　　　　Uncle Li, in a while, can you pick one for me out of the cattle?
BROKER A:　<u>你想要个啥号的？</u>
　　　　[Nǐ xiǎngyào gè shàhàode?]
　　　　What kind do you want?
BUYER:　当然是好的了。
　　　　[Dāngrán shì hǎode le.]
　　　　Of course, a good one.
BROKER A　(Pointing at a cyan bull nearby): 你看那个牛娃儿咋样？
　　　　[Nǐkàn nàgè niúwá er zǎyàng?]
　　　　What do you think about that calf?

BUYER: 我不要这号哩。

[Wǒ bùyào zhèhàolī.]

I don't want this kind.

BROKER A: 那— 啥号哩？牤牛娃儿还是母牛娃儿？

[Nà— shàhàolī? Māngniúwá er háishì mǔniúwá er?]

Then – What kind? A young bull or a young cow?

BUYER: 想买个母牛娃儿，能使能喂。

[Xiǎngmǎi gè mǔniúwá er, néngshǐ néngwèi.]

I want a young cow, which can be used both for farming and breeding.

BROKER A: 噢—，中啊。我给你看看再说。（Walking away）

[Ō—, zhōng a. Wǒ gěinǐ kànkàn zàishuō.]

Oh – OK. Let me look around first and talk to you later.

(About twenty minutes later, Broker A unties a young cow from the post and leads it to the blank space in the center of the market, pulling his whip to make the cow run quickly around him. At the same time, he tries to get attention by shouting loudly.)

BROKER A: 这个小母牛是谁的？！这个小母牛是谁的？！

[Zhège xiǎomǔniú shì shéide?! Zhège xiǎomǔniú shì shéide?!]

Whose is this young cow? Whose is this young cow?

(The owner of the cow, a slightly thin farmer around fifty years old, referred to as Seller hereafter, is squatting nearby. Now, he stands up and walks slowly and at ease towards Broker A.)

SELLER: 嗯— 我的。

[én— wǒde]

Um – mine.

BROKER A: 你这个小母牛使过没？

[Nǐ zhège xiǎomǔniú shǐguòméi?]

Was this young cow ever used to do any farming work?

SELLER: 没有。

[Méiyǒu.]

No.

Broker A (Stretching a hand to the seller): 想多少钱呀？

[Xiǎng duōshǎoqián ya?]

How much do you want for it?

(The seller holds Broker A's hand and covers the two hands with a straw hat in his other hand; by touching the Broker's hand, he names the price, 1500 yuan.[24])

SELLER: 这个,数。

[Zhège shù.]

This number.

Broker A (deliberately in a loud voice to be heard by others): 1600？！你这个卖牛的呀，晕要！

[1600?! Nǐ zhège màiniúde ya, yūnyào!]

1600? You, the seller, are charging an unreasonable price!

SELLER (smiling with no words):　…

218 *Language: Mankind's last homestead*

BROKER A: 这牛值1600？你这牛这一点儿大，你还要一千六！？

[Zhèniú zhí 1600? Nǐ zhèniú zhèyīdiǎn er dà, nǐ háiyào yīqiānliù!?]

Is this cow worth 1600? Your cow is just of this small size, but you want 1600 for it!

BROKER B: 晕要，你这是。

[Yūnyào, nǐ zhèshì.]

Definitely an unreasonable price you are charging.

ONLOOKER A: 你兔娃儿再喂一年也值不了一千六，给你说。

[Nǐ tùwá er zàiwèi yīnián yě zhíbùliǎo yīqiānliù, gěinǐshuō.]

You, old bastard, cannot make it worth 1600 even if you feed it for another year, I'm telling you.

ONLOOKER B: 一千三这个牛娃儿也卖不了！

[Yīqiānsān zhège niúwá er yě màibùliǎo!]

This little cow is not even worth 1300!

SELLER (laughing scornfully to Broker B): 我还说晌午给你个龟孙灌壶酒哩，你这个兔娃儿形，我给你灌你母的个X[25]，夜壶我都不让你喝！

[Wǒ háishuō shǎngwu gěinǐgè guīsūn guànhújiǔlī, nǐ zhège tùwá er xíng, wǒ gěinǐ guànnǐmǔdegè X, yèhú wǒ dōubù ràngnǐhē!]

I was thinking about buying you a bottle of wine for lunch, but look at you, old bastard. I may buy you your mother's X; I won't even let you drink from my urinal!

BROKER B (laughing): 我喝过你的酒没？

[Wǒ hēguò nǐdejiǔ méi?]

Did I ever drink your wine?

BROKER A (tying the cow to the post, and then walking to the buyer, Xiaofang, on the other side): 小方，你要不？

[Xiǎofāng, nǐ yàobù?]

Xiaofang, do you want this one?

BUYER: <u>不要！简直是晕要！</u>你看他那个牛娃儿是个啥东西？！

[Bùyào! Jiǎnzhíshì yūnyào! Nǐ kàn tānàgè niúwá er shìgè shàdōngxī?!]

No! He is just charging an unreasonable price! Look what kind of thing his cow is!

BROKER A (laughing scornfully, stretching out a hand to grasp the buyer's hand and cover them with his straw hat): <u>你娃子别慌，价是慢慢儿说的嘛</u>。

[Nǐ wázi biéhuāng, jià shì mànman er shuōde ma.]

Don't be mad, son. The price is always negotiable.

BUYER (communicating about the price with their hands touching): 不中，不中……中了就是这个数…… (He names 1000 yuan to the broker)

[Bùzhòng, bùzhòng……zhōngle jiùshì zhège shù …]

No, no… This is the number that works…

BROKER A: 你也晕说，是吧？中了，这个价儿，[26] 我去给你说说。 (Turning around and walking to the seller)

Language: Mankind's last homestead 219

[Nǐ yěyūnshuō, shìba? Zhōngle, zhège jià ér, wǒ qùgěinǐ shuōshuō.]

You're also giving an unreasonable price, aren't you? If you agree upon this price, I can go and talk to the seller for your sake.

BROKER C (walking to Buyer and asking Broker A when passing by him): 咋说？ (Broker A holds Broker C's hand, silently informing him of the prices he and the buyer talked about)

[Zǎshuō?]

How is it going?

BROKER A (indicating 800 yuan to the seller by gestures): 不中啊，太高了，人家只给这个价。

[Bùzhòng a, tàigāole, rénjiā zhǐgěi zhège jià.]

Your price doesn't work; it's too high. This is the highest price he can give.

SELLER (seemingly unhappy and indifferent): 那他　800百块钱都不用出了，站在大路边儿，等着捡牛吧。

[Nà tā 800 bǎi kuài qián dōubùyòng chūle, zhànzài dàlùbiān er, děngzhe jiǎnniú ba.]

Then he even doesn't have to pay 800 yuan; he may as well stand by the road, waiting to find a cow for free.

BROKER A (taking the seller's hand): 你说这个价儿中不？

[Nǐ shuō zhègejià ér zhōngbù?]

Tell me, is this the right price?

SELLER: 那不中，那根本就不沾边儿！

[Nà bùzhòng, nà gēnběn jiù bùzhānbiān er!]

No, it's far from the right price!

BROKER A: 老哥儿，你说，我跟你胡扯了吗？

[Lǎogē er, nǐ shuō, wǒ gēnnǐ húchěle ma?]

Old brother, you tell me, am I talking nonsense?

SELLER: 你叫他好好看看咱的牛，识不识货啊，他？

[Nǐ jiàotā hǎohǎo kànkàn zánde niú, shìbùshí huò a, tā?]

You tell him to take a good look at my cow. Does he have any idea about cows?

BROKER B (stretching out a hand to the seller): 你说哩再好，人家不要……来，听我说一句，　这个价儿你说我给你胡说没？

[Nǐ shuōlī zàihǎo, rénjiā bùyào……lái, tīngwǒ shuōyījù, zhège jià ér nǐshuō wǒ gěinǐ húshuō méi?]

No matter how good you say it is, he won't take it… Come on, listen to me. Does this price make sense to you?

SELLER (taking Broker B's hand, naming 1300): 这着说罢，少了这个数，您也别耽误时间了。

[Zhèzhushuō bà, shǎole zhège shù, nín yě biédānwù shíjiānle.]

Let's put it this way: If the price is less than this number, you can stop so as not to waste your time.

BROKER A (loudly): 咋？老汉儿，看见是谁在买牛没？都是这庄儿那庄儿的，低头不见抬头见，少1500还不卖牛是吧？

220   *Language: Mankind's last homestead*

[Zǎ? Lǎohàn er, kànjiàn shìshéi zàimǎiniú méi? Dōushì zhèzhuāng er nàzhuāng er de, dītóu bùjiàn táitóu jiàn, shǎo 1500 háibù mài niú shìba?]

Hey! Old man, don't you see who the buyer is? We are all from neighbouring villages, seeing each other every other day. Won't you sell the cow at any price lower than 1500?

SELLER: 你再咋说，我也不能稀乎滥贱地卖出去。

[Nǐ zàizǎshuō, wǒ yě bùnéng xīhūlànjiàn de màichūqù]

Whatever you say, I can't sell it at such a low price.

BUYER (hearing Broker A's and the seller's words, discontently): 就他那个牛，他还要1500！

[Jiù tā nàgè niú, tā háiyào 1500!]

Just for that cow of his, he wants even 1500!

ONLOOKER A (scornfully):   他要——那他要两千也中。

[Tā yào——nà tā yào liǎngqiān yězhōng]

He wants… It doesn't matter even if he wants 2000.

BROKER C: 对，对。

[Duì duì.]

Yes, yes.

ONLOOKER A: 你也可以还他—还他个五百也中！

[Nǐ yě kěyǐ huántā—huántā gè wǔbǎi yězhōng!]

You can also bargain… Say, offer him 500!

BROKER C (to the buyer):   对，对！你别怕他要。你只管说你的。(Stretching out his hand to grasp the buyer's hand) 那你这也错得太多了！

[Duì, duì! Nǐ biépà tā yào. Nǐ zhǐguǎn shuō nǐde. nà nǐ zhè yěcuòdé tàiduōle!]

That's right, that's right! Don't mind how much he wants. You just give your price. But your offer is just too far from being right!

(Broker B, at Broker C's words to the buyer, comes over to take Broker C's hand, asking about the price Broker C and the buyer just mentioned by hand-touching.)

BROKER B (to the buyer):   那说不成啊！光说。错得太多……整不到一块儿呀。

[Nà shuōbuchéng a! Guāngshuō. Cuòdé tàiduō……zhěngbùdào yīkuài er ya.]

Then we can't make it! It's all useless talk. The gap is too huge… It's impossible to bring your prices close enough to make a deal.

BROKER A (coming back to the buyer again):   光说你要， 要！要了，就正说！

[Guāngshuō nǐyào, yào! Yàole, jiù zhèngshuō!]

You just keep saying that you want the cow. If you really want it, you have to be serious about the price!

BROKER C (catching the buyer's hand to communicate about the price):   你正说，向正说！

[Nǐ zhèngshuō, xiàngzhèng shuō!]

You have to be serious. Make it higher!

BUYER: 向正说？

[Xiàngzhèng shuō?]

Make it higher?

BROKER C: 向正说！

[Xiàngzhèng shuō!]

Make it higher!

BROKER B (to the buyer and Broker C): 光说零头[27]吧！ 光摸零头就中！

[Guāngshuō língtóu ba! Guāngmō língtóu jiùzhōng!]

Just talk about the hundreds digit! Just the hundreds digit!

BROKER C: 好，光摸零头。

[Hǎo, guāngmō língtóu.]

OK, just the hundreds digit.

Buyer (finishing his hand-touching act of naming the price with Broker C, touches Broker B's hand to indicate the number 1100): 我这说的，你说咱是买家儿不？是买家儿不？！

[Wǒ zhèshuōde, nǐshuō zán shì mǎijiā er bù? Shì mǎijiā er bù?!]

This is my price. You tell me, am I a sincere buyer? Am I?!

BROKER B: 嗯，是买家儿，是买家儿！

[Ēn, shì mǎijiā er, shì mǎijiā er!]

Yeah, you are a sincere buyer, you are a sincere buyer!

BROKER C: 是买家儿。

[Shì mǎijiā er.]

You are a sincere buyer!

BROKER C (walking to the seller on the other side, grasping his hand, indicating the number 1050): 你说，这是买价不？

[Nǐshuō, zhè shì mǎijiàbù?]

You tell me, is this a fair price?

SELLER: 不卖呀，不卖！

[Bùmài ya, bùmài!]

I won't sell it, no way!

BROKER C: 唉呀！来，(Grasping the seller's hand) <u>他添着，你去着！</u>

[Āiya! Lái, tā tiānzhe, nǐ qùzhe!]

Well, Come on! His offer can go up, your charge can go down!

BROKER B: 诶，<u>就是嘛，添添去去，就是这么回事。</u>

[Éi, jiùshì ma, tiāntiān qùqù, jiùshì zhème huíshì.]

Yeah, that's right. The buyer's offer can go up, and the seller's charge can go down. That's it.

SELLER (continuing discussing price by hand touching with Broker C): 就是啊，如果一开口就说给个一千三、四，那再往上添添也能成！

[Jiùshì a, rúguǒ yīkāikǒu jiùshuō gěigè yīqiānsān, sì, nà zàiwǎngshàng tiāntiān yě néngchéng!]

Yeah, if he had begun with 1300 or 1400, we would have reached a deal with him adding a little to his offer.

222 *Language: Mankind's last homestead*

BROKER A:　你再少点儿，也没啥大不了的呀！

> [Nǐ zàishǎodiǎn er, yě méishà dàbùliǎode ya!]

> You may as well reduce your charge by a little more; it's no big deal!

SELLER (scornfully, to the onlookers):　哼！　他净想那美事儿！　<u>啥货卖啥价儿！</u>

> [Hēng! Tā jìngxiǎng nàměishì er! Shàhuò màishàjià ér!]

> Humph! He is just daydreaming! The quality of the goods decides their prices!

BROKER C (releasing the seller's hand, loudly to the people around):　那弄不成，你非要一千五，他只给一千，那说到明天也弄不成！

> [Nà nòngbùchéng, nǐ fēiyào yīqiānwǔ, tā zhǐgěi yīqiān, nà shuōdào míngtiān yě nòngbùchéng!]

> Then we can't make it. You insist on 1500, he gives only 1000. We can't make it even if we keep bargaining till tomorrow!

BROKER B:　相成 (The seller's first name)，给他吧！

> [Xiāngchéng, gěitā ba!]

> Xiangcheng, just sell it to him!

SELLER (smiling):　我也想给他呀！你总得先把价说好吧？

> [Wǒ yěxiǎng gěitā ya! Nǐ zǒngdé xiānbǎ jià shuōhǎo ba?]

> I want to sell it to him, too! But you have to fix the price first, right?

ONLOOKER:　卖了吧！卖了，马上就是钱！

> [Màile ba! Màile, mǎshàng jiùshì qián!]

> Sell it! Once you sell it, you will have money in hand!

BROKER B:　<u>就是，走，写帐去！</u> (Pulling the seller to the registration desk)

> [Jiùshì, zǒu, xiězhàngqù!]

> That's right! Now, let's go and sign the deal!

SELLER:　少了这个数，我可不卖啊！

> [Shǎole zhège shù, wǒ kěbùmài a!]

> If it's less than this number, I won't sell it!

BROKER B:　中，中。

> [Zhōng, zhōng.]

> OK, OK.

> (Meanwhile, Broker C is also pulling the buyer to the registration desk.)

BUYER:　咱可说好，多一分我都不要！

> [Zán kěshuōhǎo, duō yīfēn wǒ dōu bùyào!]

> Let me be clear, I won't take it if the price is higher even by just one cent!

BROKER C:　<u>好，好，不叫你多一分！</u>

> [Hǎo, hǎo, bù jiàonǐ duōyīfēn!]

> OK, OK, we'll not let you spend one more cent than what you offer!

BROKER A (grabbing a pen and pushing it into the seller's hand):　来，老汉儿，签个名儿。

> [Lái, lǎohàn er, qiāngèmíng er.]

> Come on, old man, sign your name here.

SELLER (holding the pen, puzzled): 这到底是多少钱呀？

[Zhè dàodǐ shì duōshǎoqián ya?]

What on earth is the price?

BROKER A: 你来写吧！落一千二百块钱！

[Nǐ láixiě ba! Luò yīqiān èrbǎi kuàiqián!]

You just sign it! You're gonna have 1200 yuan!

SELLER: 不卖，不卖！瞎捣哩，你！

[Bùmài, bùmài! Xiādǎolī, nǐ!]

I won't sell it, I won't sell it! You are just fooling me!

BUYER: 不要，多一分不要！

[Bùyào, duō yīfēn bùyào!]

I won't take it, not even if the price is higher by just one cent!

BROKER B (grabbing the seller, who is struggling to free himself, in a low voice): 你鳖子别挣了，比比刚才人家卖的那头牛你自己说这个价亏你没？！

[Nǐ biēzi bié zhēngle, bǐbǐ gāngcái rénjiā màidì nàtóu niú nǐ zìjǐ shuō zhège jià kuīnǐméi?!]

You bastard, stop struggling. Don't you yourself know it? Compared with the price of the cow that was just sold over there, this price is by no means lower than just what your cow is worth, is it?

SELLER: 没亏，没亏，我不卖了总中吧！

[Méikuī, méikuī, wǒ bùmàile zǒngzhōng ba!]

It is not, it is not. But I can decide not to sell it now, can't I?

BROKER C: 老汉儿，你亏不了，回家合计合计，要是亏了，你见我一次骂一次！

[Lǎohàn er, nǐ kuībùliǎo, huíjiā héjì héjì, yàoshi kuīle, nǐ jiàn wǒ yīcì mà yīcì!]

Old man, the price is no less than what your cow is worth. You can do the calculation back home. If it is, you can spit on me each time you see me!

BROKER A (grabbing the buyer, who is struggling to free himself): 小方，你娃子识不识货？！你说我给你瞎说没？！

[Xiǎofāng, nǐ wázi shìbùshíhuò?! Nǐ shuō wǒgěinǐ xiāshuō méi?!]

Xiaofang, son, can't you tell good from bad? You tell me, am I talking nonsense?

BUYER: 你没瞎说，我瞎说了，中吧？我不要，清不要！

[Nǐ méi iāshuō, wǒ xiāshuōle, zhōng ba? Wǒ bùyào, qīngbùyào!]

You're not talking nonsense, I am, OK? I don't want it; no way!

BROKER A (in a low voice): 你娃子只管牵回家，要真是嫌贵了下集再牵来。我保证最少还给你卖这个数！

[Nǐ wázi zhǐguǎn qiānhuíjiā, yào zhēnshi xiánguìle xiàjí zài qiānlái. Wǒ bǎozhèng zuìshǎo háigěi nǐ mài zhège shù!]

Son, you just take the cow home. If you really think the price is more than it's worth, then bring it back next time. I promise to sell it for you at least at the same price!

224 *Language: Mankind's last homestead*

(At this moment, the seller, half-willingly and half-forced with Broker A and C's pulling and pushing, presses his thumbprint on the record of the deal)

Seller (shouting) <u>我这个牛最少也少卖一两百，您这……这……这样整，那—会中？</u>

[Wǒ zhège niú zuìshǎo yě shǎomài yīliǎngbǎi, nín zhè……zhè……zhèyàngzhěng, nà—huìzhōng?]

The selling price for my cow must be at least one or two hundred (yuan) less than it's worth. You… make me do this. Is this fair?

(Seeing that the seller has agreed, the buyer also presses his thumbprint on the record of the deal, half-willingly and half-forced by Broker A)

BUYER (to Broker A): <u>你说的啊，这要是太贵了，我下集还拉来你给我卖了！</u>

[Nǐ shuōde a, zhè yàoshi tàiguìle, wǒ xiàjí háilālái nǐ gěiwǒ màile!]

You just said it. If I've paid more than it's worth, I'll bring it back next time and you help me sell it.

BROKER A: <u>中，中！</u>

[Zhōng, zhōng!]

OK, OK!

BROKER C (to the buyer): <u>贵不了，就这个价，你娃子心里还没 数儿？</u>

[Guìbùliǎo, jiù zhège jià, nǐ wázi xīnlǐ hái méishù er?]

You've paid no more than it's worth. About this price, son, don't you have any idea?

(The buyer counts the money and hands it over to Broker A, who counts it and gives it to the seller. The seller counts the money and puts it in his bag, and then leaves, mumbling; the buyer also leaves with the cow)

As was pointed out earlier, formulaic verbal behavior consists of a relatively fixed set of utterances and a relatively fixed set of actions in relatively fixed move orders. The co-occurrence of the two is relatively fixed and highly repetitive. In other words, when such actions take place, the corresponding linguistic expressions will be uttered. Take the cattle market, for instance. When a bargaining event takes place, the underlined utterances occur as shown in the above case. In what follows, we elaborate on how the human pursuit of efficiency in life promotes the formulaicity of formulaic verbal behavior.

3.3.2.4.1 FORMULAICITY IS THE MOST RELEVANT TO ACTIVITY GOALS

Now, let's see if the formulaic utterances underlined in the above case of a bargaining event at the cattle market are of greatest relevance to the goals of the activity.

Formulaic utterances at the initial stage

BUYER: <u>……给我瞅个牛？</u> [28]

… can you pick one for me out of the cattle later?

Language: Mankind's last homestead 225

BROKER A:　你想要个啥号的？
　　What kind do you want?
　　我给你看看再说。
　　Let me look around first and talk to you later.

Formulaic utterances at the primary bargaining stage
BROKER A (stretching a hand to the seller): 想多少钱呀？
　　How much do you want for it?
SELLER (holding the broker's hand and indicating a price):　这个数。
　　This number.
BUYER:　不要！简直是晕要！
　　No! He is just charging an unreasonable price!
BROKER　A　(laughing　scornfully):　你娃子别慌，　　　价是慢慢儿说
的嘛。
　　Don't be mad, son. The price is always negotiable.
BROKER A:　中了，这个价儿，我去给你说说。
　　If you agree upon this price, I can go to bargain with the seller for
　　your sake.
BROKER A (taking the seller's hand):　你说这个价儿中不？
　　Tell me, is this the right price?
BROKER C (grasping the seller's hand):　他添着，你去着！
　　His offer can go up, and your charge can go down!
BROKER B:　就是嘛，添添去去，就是这么回事。
　　That's right. The buyer's offer can go up, and the seller's charge can go
　　down. That's it.
　Seller, Buyer, and Broker all may say the formulaic utterance:
啥货卖啥价儿！
　　The quality of the goods decides their prices!

Formulaic utterances at the stage of the broker's announcing a compromise
price
BROKER　B:　就是，走，写帐去！　(Pulling the seller to the registration
desk)
　　That's right! Now, let's go and sign the deal!
SELLER:　少了这个数，我可不卖啊！
　　If it's less than this number, I won't sell it!
BROKER B:　中，中。
　　OK, OK.
BUYER:　咱可说好，多一分我都不要！
　　Let me be clear, I won't take it if the price is higher by just one cent!
BROKER C:　好，好，不叫你多一分！
　　OK, OK, we'll not let you spend one more cent than what you offer!
BROKER A:　你来写吧！落一千二百块钱！
　　You just sign it! You're gonna have 1200 yuan! (The number may vary
　　from case to case)

226 *Language: Mankind's last homestead*

Formulaic utterances at the secondary bargaining stage (after the broker's announcing a compromise price)

SELLER: 不卖，不卖！瞎捣哩，你！

I won't sell it, I won't sell it! You are just fooling me!

BUYER: 不要，多一分不要！

I won't take it, not even if the price is higher by just one cent!

BROKER A (to the buyer): ……只管牵回家，要真是嫌贵了下集再牵来。我保证最少还给你卖这个数！

…you just take the cow home. If you really think the price is more than it's worth, then bring it back next time. I promise to sell it for you at least at the same price!

BROKER C (to the seller): ……你亏不了，回家合计合计，要是亏了，你见我一次骂一次！

…the price is no less than what your cow is worth. You can do the calculation back home. If it is, you can spit on me each time you see me!

Formulaic utterances at the concluding stage

SELLER (half-willingly and half-forced by the brokers, pressing his thumbprint on the record of the deal and shouting): 我这个牛最少也少卖一两百，您这……这……这样整，那—会中？

The selling price for my cow must be at least one or two hundred (yuan) less than it's worth. You… make me do this. Is this fair?

BUYER (seeing that the seller has agreed, also pressing his thumbprint on the record of the deal, half-willingly and half-forced, shouting to the broker): 你说的啊，这要是太贵了，我下集还拉来你给我卖了！

You just said it. If I've paid more than it's worth, I'll bring it back next time and you help me sell it.

Another case of a bargaining event at the cattle market can further demonstrate how such formulaic utterances work as they always do. Likewise, the formulaic utterances in this case are also underlined.

Case II: Bargaining event at Youtian Cattle Market

Date of tape-recording: 9:50–11:50 a.m., July 24, 2002
Place: Youtian Cattle Market, Biyang County, Henan Province, China
Participants: Broker A, B, C

The seller, a farmer around fifty years old, referred to as Seller
The buyer, a farmer around forty years old, referred to as Buyer
Onlooker A, B, C, D, etc., all present to learn about the market, usually planning to sell or buy a head of cattle in the near future

Language: Mankind's last homestead 227

SELLER (to Broker A):　龙啊，龙！瞅瞅有人要没，把我那个牛给卖了。

[Lóng a, lóng! Chǒuchǒu yǒurén yàoméi, bǎ wǒnàgè niú gěimàile.]

Long, Long! Help me sell my cow. Look around and see if anyone wants it.

BROKER A:　哪个？

[Nǎge?]

Which one?

SELLER:　这边最前面的那个。

[Zhèbiān zuìqiánmiàndì nàgè.]

The first one in the front of this line.

BROKER A:　中啊。这阵子没人买大家伙了，这阵子。

[Zhōng a. Zhèzhènzi méirén mǎi dàjiāhuo le, zhèzhènzi.]

OK. No one wants such a big one these days.

BROKER B (approaching the seller):　老汉儿，想多钱呀？

[Lǎohàn er, xiǎng duōqián ya?]

Old man, how much do you want?

SELLER:　你看看能换几个钱儿？

[Nǐ kànkàn nénghuàn jǐgèqián er?]

How much do you think it's worth?

BROKER B:　俩钱，中吧？

[Liǎqián, zhōng ba?]

Two grand, OK?

SELLER:　俩钱？！你给我不好好整，我光给你灌酒喝哩，是吧？

[Liǎqián?! Nǐ gěiwǒ bùhǎohǎo zhěng, wǒ guānggěinǐ guànjiǔhēlī, shì ba?]

Two grand?! You are not doing anything good for me even though I keep treating you with wines, are you?

BROKER B:　灌酒喝？你给我灌过一回儿没？自打那次我给你买那头牛回家后，你给我灌过一次没？

[Guànjiǔhē? Nǐ gěiwǒ guànguò yīhuí er méi? Zìdǎ nàcì wǒ gěinǐ mǎi nàtóuniú huíjiā hòu, nǐ gěiwǒ guànguò yīcì méi?]

Treating me with wines? Did you ever treat me once? Have you ever treated me with wine since I helped you buy the cow last time?

SELLER:　那，你不上我家，怪谁？

[Nà, nǐ bùshàng wǒjiā, guàishéi?]

Well, you never came to my house. Who is to blame?

BROKER B:　我走到你家门口，老是找不着你！

[Wǒ zǒudào nǐjiā ménkǒu, lǎoshì zhǎobùzháo nǐ!]

I passed by your home many times, but you were never home.

SELLER:　那你要是死了，永远都不喝了！

[Nà nǐ yàoshi sǐle, yǒngyuǎn dōu bùhēle!]

Well, once you die, you can never drink my wine!

BROKER B:　那死了，还喝啥哩？光说点子不沾边儿的话！

[Nà sǐle, hái hēshà lī? Guāng shuōdiǎnzi bùzhānbiān er de huà!]

Of course, no one drinks any more once he is dead. What you said just makes no sense here!

228 *Language: Mankind's last homestead*

BROKER A (smiling): 说正经的哟。(Stretching out a hand to hold the seller's hand) 表叔你想多少钱吧？

[Shuōzhèngjīng de yāo. Biǎoshū nǐ xiǎng duōshǎoqián ba?]

Let's talk business. Uncle, how much do you want?

BROKER B (watching the seller and Broker A negotiating the price through hand-touching): 三千三？！ 就这一个？带牛娃儿没？

[Sānqiānsān?! Jiù zhèyīgè? Dài niúwá er méi?]

3300 yuan? Just for this one? Without a calf?

SELLER (indifferently): 牛娃儿刚摘开。

[Niúwá er gāng zhāikāi.]

The calf has just been weaned.

BROKER B: 瞅着也够呛了，老变牙口了吧？(Approaching the cow and starting to check its teeth)

[Chǒuzhe yěgòuqiàng le, lǎobiànyákou le ba?]

It looks quite old. Has it shed its primary teeth long before?

SELLER: 没有，没有，刚变牙！

[Méiyǒu, méiyǒu, gāngbiànyá!]

No, no. It's just shed its primary teeth.

BROKER A: 那— 正当年呐。

[Nà— zhèngdàngnián nà.]

Then – it's just of the fine age.

SELLER: 咱这牛没啥缺陷。能吃好喂，使起来顺当；下牛娃儿漂亮！

[Zán zhèniú méi shàquēxiàn. Néngchī hǎowèi, shǐqǐlái shùndang; xiàniúwá er piàoliang.]

There is nothing wrong with my cow. It eats everything you give it, and works well for farming. It also gives birth to wonderful calves.

BROKER A: 这牛看着是不赖。可是…… 我给你看看再说吧。 (Walking away)

[Zhèniú kànzhe shìbùlài. Kěshì…… wǒ gěinǐ kànkàn zàishuō ba.]

This cow looks great. But… Let me look around first and talk to you later.

(Ten minutes later)

BUYER (to Broker C): 老表啊，老表！给看看那个老母牛咋卖。

[Lǎobiǎo a, lǎobiǎo! Gěi kànkàn nàgè lǎomǔniú zǎmài]

Cousin, cousin! Please go to check for me how much that cow is.

BROKER C: 哪个？

[Nǎge?]

Which one?

BUYER: 那边儿拴的第一个。

[Nàbiān er shuānde dìyīgè.]

The first one in that line over there.

BROKER A (hearing the buyer's words): 看中那个啦？那牛不赖！敢打保票，好喂好使，下牛娃儿漂亮。

[Kànzhòng nàgè la? Nàniú bùlài! Gǎndǎbǎopiào, hǎowèi hǎoshǐ, xiàniúwá er piàoliang.]

Language: Mankind's last homestead 229

Which one do you like? That cow is great! I can absolutely guarantee that
it's not picky about food, and works well for farming. It also gives birth
to wonderful calves.

BUYER:　多钱?
[Duōqián?]
How much?

BROKER A:　他说三千五。我给他说，让二百，他总得让。
[Tā shuō sānqiānwǔ. Wǒ gěi tā shuō, ràng èrbǎi, tā zǒngdé ràng.]
He wants 3500 yuan. If I ask him to lower the price by 200 yuan, he will
surely do so.

BUYER:　你别那着说，整谁哩呀？！
[Nǐ bié nàzhe shuō, zhěng shéi lī ya?!]
Don't put it that way. Who are you trying to fool here?

BROKER A:　那你说能给多少儿?
[Nà nǐshuō nénggěi duōshào er?]
Then, tell me, how much will you pay?

BUYER:　两千块钱到顶!
[Liǎngqiān kuàiqián dàodǐng!]
2000 yuan at most!

BROKER A:　你是不是买牛的?
[Nǐ shìbùshì mǎiniúde?]
Are you here to buy a cow?

BUYER:　不买，我问它干啥哩？！
[Búmǎi, wǒ wèntā gànshà lī?!]
If not to buy one, why am I asking you about it?!

BROKER A:　好货卖好钱，你两千……
[Hǎohuò màihǎoqián, nǐ liǎngqiān……]
Good goods deserve good prices. You, only 2000…

BUYER:　好货也得好价钱才能卖嘛!
[Hǎohuò yědé hǎojiàqián cáinéng mài ma!]
It's also true that good goods can be sold only at good prices!

BROKER A:　我给你说三千三，中不?
[Wǒ gěinǐ shuō sānqiānsān, zhōngbù?]
Let me bargain with the seller for you. Make it 3300 (yuan). Is that OK?

BUYER:　要说的话，你就照两千给我说。
[Yàoshuō de huà, nǐ jiùzhào liǎngqiān gěiwǒshuō.]
If you're going to do it, make it 2000 (yuan).

BROKER A:　两千也太……
[Liǎngqiān yě tài……]
2000 is too…

BROKER C:　走，过去先说说再说也中啊。
[Zǒu, guòqù xiānshuōshuō zàishuō yězhōng a.]
Come on, let's go over and talk to the seller first and see what might
happen next.

230   *Language: Mankind's last homestead*

BROKER A: 中，中，先说说再说。 (Broker A and C walk away to the seller)
[Zhōng, zhōng, xiānshuōshuō zàishuō.]
OK, OK. Let's talk to the seller first and see what might happen next.

BROKER A (smiling helplessly to the seller):   不中啊，表叔。只有一个要家儿，人家只出俩数儿。
[Bùzhòng a, biǎoshū. Zhǐyǒu yīgè yàojiā er, rénjiā zhǐchū liǎshù er.]
Your price doesn't work, uncle. Only one man is interested in your cow, and he offers only two grand.

SELLER: 那就不用说了。
[Nà jiù bùyòng shuōle.]
Then no more talk is needed.

BROKER C: 老汉儿，你是卖的不？
[Lǎohàn er, nǐ shì màide bù?]
Old man, aren't you to sell the cow?

SELLER: 牵来了就是卖的！
[Qiānláile jiùshì màide!]
Of course, I have brought it here just to sell it!

BROKER C: 那就落实说说，中吧？
[Nà jiùluòshí shuōshuō, zhōng ba?]
Then name a fair price, OK?

SELLER: 是真买家儿的话，仨数儿给他。
[Shì zhēnmǎijiā er de huà, sāshù er gěitā.]
If he is a sincere buyer, I'll give it to him for three grand.

BROKER B: 你这个老母牛，要能卖三千块钱，你叫我头朝下走路我都走。
[Nǐ zhège lǎomǔniú, yào néng mài sānqiān kuài qián, nǐ jiào wǒ tóucháoxià zǒulù wǒ dū zǒu.]
Just this cow, if you can sell it for 3000, I will walk on my hands if you order me to.
打意卖了唻，咱就好好说；不打意卖了就算了。
[Dǎyì màile lài, zán jiù hǎohǎo shuō; bù dǎyì màile jiù suànle.]
If you really want to sell it, let's be serious about the price talk. If not, let's just stop here.

SELLER: 卖不了，我还拉回家，怕啥？！
[Mài bùliǎo, wǒ hái lāhuíjiā, pàshà?!]
If I can't sell it (for 3000), I'll just take it back home. Why should I be worried?!

BROKER A: 表叔啊，你这仨钱，现在这行势，它真是不好卖。
[Biǎoshū a, nǐ zhè sāqián, xiànzài zhèhángshì, tā zhēnshi bùhǎomài.]
Uncle, for three grand, on the cattle market this time of the year, you really can hardly sell it.

BROKER B: 仨钱打烂，俩半不散，咋样儿？
[Sāqián dǎlàn, liǎbàn búsàn, zǎyàng er?]
Make the price lower than three grand and you get exactly two and a half grand. It that OK?

Language: Mankind's last homestead   231

SELLER: 你说那话，不沾边儿！

[Nǐ shuō nàhuà, bù zhānbiān er!]

What you said is far from being the right price!

BROKER C: 你不比那几天，那几天，牵来的牛都有人要。

[Nǐ bùbǐ nàjǐtiān, nàjǐtiān, qiānláide niú dōu yǒurényào.]

The market is different these days from those days. Those days, each head of the cattle on the market was wanted.

有天上午，牵来十一头牛，卖了十个。剩下一个，还是个母牛娃儿。

[Yǒutiān shàngwǔ, qiānlái shíyītóu niú, màile shígè. Shèngxià yīgè, háishìgè mǔniúwá er.]

One morning, there were eleven heads of cattle; ten were sold. Only one was left unsold, a young cow though.

这几天，日他奶奶，贵贱没人要！

[Zhèjǐtiān, rì tānǎinai, guìjiàn méirén yào!]

These days, damn it! No one wants to buy anything, be it cheap or expensive!

你要是在三月三庙会上，你这老母牛咋会才卖这点儿钱？

[Nǐ yàoshi zài sānyuèsān miàohuìshàng, nǐ zhè lǎomǔniú zǎhuì cáimài zhèdiǎn er qián?]

If you had brought your cow to the temple fair on March 3, it couldn't have been sold just for this amount of money.

SELLER: 唉呀，不说那话！刚才那老母牛是啥样子？人家还买三千二哩！

[Āiya, bùshuō nàhuà! Gāngcái nà lǎomǔniú shì shàyàngzi? Rénjiā háimǎi sānqiānèr lī!]

Oh, don't say that! What is that old cow like, the one that was sold just now? It was sold for 3200!

BROKER B: 你比人家那头牛，人家那是一对子；你说你这个能值恁些儿钱不？

[Nǐ bǐ rénjiā nàtóu niú, rénjiā nà shì yīduìzi; nǐ shuō nǐ zhège néngzhí nènxiē er qián bù?]

You compare your cow with that one? That one was sold with its baby cow, and the price was for both of them. You tell me, is it possible for your cow to be worth that much?

你这个要能卖恁些儿钱，日他奶奶，我就，我就不再卖牛了。

[Nǐ zhège yào néngmài nènxiē er qián, rì tānǎinai, wǒ jiù, wǒ jiù bùzài mài niúle.]

If you can sell your cow for that much, damn it, I will quit this job as a broker.

SELLER: 你不卖算了。

[Nǐ bùmài suànle.]

I don't care whether you'll quit the job or not.

BROKER   C: 不卖，咱干脆就说不卖；你要卖了咪，咱就落实说！别光在这儿胡白。

232 *Language: Mankind's last homestead*

[Bùmài, zán gāncuì jiùshuō bùmài; nǐ yàomàile lài, zán jiùluòshí shuō! Bié guāng zàizhè'er húbái.]

If you are not selling it, just tell us straightforwardly that you are not selling it. If you really want to sell it, just name a fair price! Stop talking nonsense here!

SELLER: 对，咱都别胡白！

[Duì, zán dōubié húbái!]

Alright, let's all stop talking nonsense.

BROKER A: 表叔，咱这都不是外人，你落实说个价儿！

[Biǎoshū, zán zhè dōu bùshì wàirén, nǐ luòshí shuōgèjià ér!]

Uncle, we are all relatives to each other. You just name a fair price.

SELLER: 中！落实说罢。都是明眼人，好货卖好钱。

[Zhōng! Luòshí shuō bà. Dōushì míngyǎnrén, hǎohuò mài hǎoqián.]

OK! Let's name a fair price. We can all make good judgments and good goods deserve good prices.

两千八！你们觉得能说的话，就去说说。

[Liǎngqiānbā! Nǐmen juédé néngshuō dehuà, jiùqù shuōshuō.]

2800! If you think it's a fair price, then go and talk to the buyer.

要，他要；不要，这牛还是咱的！

[Yào, tāyào; bùyào, zhèniú háishì zánde!]

If he takes it at that price, he has it. If he doesn't want it, the cow is still mine!

BROKER A: 中，走，咱再去说说看！ (Broker B and C walk away to the buyer; Broker A leaves on request to attend another ongoing deal)

[Zhōng, zǒu, zán zàiqù shuōshuōkàn!]

OK. Let's go and talk to the buyer and see what might happen.

BROKER C (to the buyer): 老表，不中啊，你说俩数儿根本就不沾！

[Lǎobiǎo, bùzhòng a, nǐ shuō liǎshù er gēnběn jiù bùzhān!]

Cousin, your offer doesn't work. Two grand is too far from the right price.

Buyer (laughing): 不沾—，咱再添添嘛。

[Bùzhān—, zán zài tiāntiān ma.]

Too far from the right price – then I can make my offer go up a little.

BROKER B: 对，这才是买家儿！看货给钱，没行势有比势……

[Duì, zhè cáishì mǎijiā er! Kànhuò gěiqián, méihángshì yǒubǐshì……]

Great! This is a sincere buyer! You decide your offer according to the quality of the goods; although there is no reliable market trend to decide the right price, but the right price can always be made by comparison…

BUYER: 他多少能给呀？

[Tā duōshǎo nénggěi ya?]

How much will he sell it for?

BROKER C: 仨数儿。

[Sāshù er.]

Three grand.

BUYER: 仨数儿？我日，他这不是晕要吗？！

[Sāshù er? Wǒrì, tā zhè bùshì yūnyào ma?!]

Three grand? Damn it! Isn't he charging an unreasonable price?!

BROKER C (stretching out a hand to grasp the buyer's hand): <u>老表你落实说，能出多少？</u>

[Lǎobiǎo nǐ luòshíshuō, néngchū duōshǎo?]

Cousin, be serious about your offer; how much can you offer?

......

(Broker B and C bargain with the buyer, through words and hand-touching; ten minutes later)

BROKER B (to the buyer): <u>两千六……这钱你说能要不？</u>

[Liǎngqiānliù……zhèqián nǐshuō néngyàobù?]

2600... Just think about it. Isn't the cow worth the money?

BUYER: 太多了！

[Tài duōle!]

Too much!

BROKER C: <u>两千六，这你还说不了？！</u>

[Liǎngqiānliù, zhè nǐ hái shuōbule?!]

2600, you still say no to it?!

......

(Broker B and C continue trying to persuade the buyer to accept the price; a few minutes later)

BROKER C: 老表，就这着说，<u>两千六，我再去跟他说，卖了他卖，不卖算了！</u>

[Lǎobiǎo, jiù zhèzhe shuō, liǎngqiānliù, wǒ zàiqù gēntāshuō, màile tā mài, bùmài suànle!]

Cousin, let's put it this way: Your offer is now 2600; I'm now going to speak to him. If he sells it at this price, it's OK; if he doesn't, we just put an end to this deal.

BUYER: <u>中，中！两千六，多一分我都不要！</u>

[Zhōng, zhōng! Liǎngqiānliù, duōyīfēn wǒ dōubùyào!]

OK, OK! Just 2600. I won't take it if the price is higher by just one cent!

BROKER C: 行，行！(walking with Broker B back to the seller)

[Xíng, xíng!]

OK, OK!

BROKER B: 老汉儿，再落实落实！人家最多只出两千五。

[Lǎohàn er, zài luòshí luoshí! Rénjiā zuìduō zhǐchū liǎngqiānwǔ.]

Old man, lower your price a little further! The buyer's highest offer is only 2500.

SELLER: 那，你就别说了！<u>两千八，少一分都不卖！</u>

[Nà, nǐ jiù biéshuō le! Liǎngqiānbā, shǎoyīfēn dōu bùmài!]

Well, you can save your words then! 2800. If it's less by a cent, I won't sell it!

BROKER B: 麦前头，大李庄儿的有你这样一个牛，那真是卖了这个数。

[Màiqiántou, dàlǐzhuāng er de yǒu nǐzhèyàng yīgè niú, nà zhēnshi màile zhège shù.]

Before the wheat harvest time, there was a cow just like yours, owned by a man from Dali Village. It was really sold at the price you named.

234 *Language: Mankind's last homestead*

BROKER C: 那时候，高；那时候，价就高！
 [Nàshíhòu, gāo; nàshíhòu, jià jiùgāo!]
 Those days, the price was high; those days, the price was really high.
SELLER: 我不管是啥时候，就这个价！
 [Wǒ bùguǎn shì shàshíhòu, jiù zhègejià!]
 I don't care what time it is; this is exactly the price I want!
BROKER B: 你还这着说，那不是还治不成事儿？
 [Nǐ hái zhèzhu shuō, nà bùshì huán zhìbùchéng shì er?]
 Now that you're still talking like that, doesn't it mean that we can't make
 a deal?
SELLER: 治不成算了。
 [Zhìbùchéng suànle.]
 It doesn't matter at all if we can't make a deal.
BROKER C: 老汉儿，你看看，这牛是给谁的，你说？
 [Lǎohàn er, nǐ kànkàn, zhèniú shì gěishéi de, nǐ shuō?]
 Old man, just have a look. Who is the buyer? You tell me.
SELLER: 给谁的都不中。不管给谁，这日他奶奶……
 [Gěishéide dōu bùzhòng. Bùguǎn gěishéi, zhè rì tā nǎinai……]
 Whoever the buyer is, his price isn't right. Whoever the buyer is, the damn
 price should be…
BROKER B: 一分都不少？
 [Yīfēn dōu bùshǎo?]
 Not a cent less than your price?
SELLER: 不少！
 [Bùshǎo!]
 No!
BROKER B: 那中，<u>走！写帐去！</u>
 [Nàzhōng, zǒu! Xiězhàng qù!]
 That's OK. Now, let's go and sign the deal!
SELLER: 两千八啊！
 [Liǎngqiānbā a!]
 2800!
BROKER B: 两千八！ (To the buyer) 走，大张沟的！<u>走，写个帐儿去！</u>
 [Liǎngqiānbā! Zǒu, dàzhānggōu de! Zǒu, xiěgèzhàng er qù!]
 2800! Now, the man from Dazhanggou Village! Now, let's go and sign
 the deal!
 (Broker A, at Broker B's yelling, runs over to push the buyer to the regis-
 tration desk; Broker C walks over to untie the cow from the post and
 joins Broker B in pushing the seller to the registration desk. In no time,
 Broker A and C write down the seller's and the buyer's addresses and
 other relevant information on the record of the deal)
BROKER B (to the seller): 来，老汉儿，<u>按个手印儿</u>。
 [Lái, lǎohàn er, àn gè shǒuyìn er.]
 Come on, old man, press your thumbprint here.

SELLER: 先说好，两千八，<u>少一分我可不卖！</u>

[Xiān shuōhǎo, liǎngqiānbā, shǎoyīfēn wǒ kě bùmài!]

Let me be clear, 2800. I won't sell it if the price is lower by just one cent!

BROKER B: 好，你放心，<u>少一分不卖</u>。

[Hǎo, nǐ fàngxīn, shǎoyīfēn bùmài.]

OK, don't worry; you won't sell it if the price is lower even by just one cent.

(The seller presses his thumbprint on the record of the deal)

BROKER B (to the buyer): 来，大张沟的，<u>你也按个印儿</u>！

[Lái, dàzhānggōu de, nǐ yě àngèyìn er!]

Here, man from Dazhanggou Village, you press your thumbprint, too!

BUYER: <u>咱可是说好了的，多一分我不要</u>！

[Zán kěshì shuōhǎole de, duōyīfēn wǒ bùyào!]

We both agree: I won't take it if the price is higher even by just one cent!

BROKER B: 好，多一分你不要！

[Hǎo, duōyīfēn nǐ bùyào!]

OK, you don't take it if the price is higher even by just one cent!

BROKER C: 老表，你只管放心！

[Lǎobiǎo, nǐ zhǐguǎn fàngxīn!]

Cousin, you don't have to worry at all!

(The buyer presses his thumbprint on the record of the deal)

BROKER B (having handed the record of the deal to the one in charge, announcing loudly): 好，这牛是好牛，咱这买家儿卖家儿也都不是外人；

[Hǎo, zhèniú shì hǎoniú, zánzhè mǎijiā er màijiā er yě dōubùshì wàirén;]

OK, this cow is a good one, and the buyer and the seller are relatives to each other;

<u>你说两千五，他说两千八，我来当个家儿，两千七买了！</u>

[Nǐ shuō liǎngqiānwǔ, tā shuō liǎngqiānbā, wǒ lái dānggèjiā er, liǎngqiānqī mǎile!]

Your offer is 2500, his charge is 2800; let me make a compromise price: You buy the cow for 2700!

SELLER (fuming with rage): <u>不中，不中！少一分不卖</u>！

[Bùzhōng, bùzhōng! Shǎoyīfēn bùmài!]

No, No! I won't sell it if the price is lower by just one cent!

BUYER: <u>不要，不要！我不要</u>！

[Bùyào, bùyào! Wǒ bùyào!]

No, no! I won't take it!

BROKER A (to the seller): 诶，表叔，卖了算了。<u>恁大个牛，少一百多一百也都是那个样儿</u>！

[Éi, biǎoshū, màile suànle. Nèndàgè niú, shǎoyībǎi duōyībǎi yě dōushì nàgèyàng er!]

Hey, uncle, just sell it. For such a big cow, 100 yuan more or less makes little difference!

236 *Language: Mankind's last homestead*

有你大侄子在，能会亏了你？！

[Yǒu nǐdàzhízi zài, nénghuì kuīle nǐ?!]

Now you have me, your nephew, with you; how could you suffer a loss of money?

ONLOOKER A: 卖了吧，老汉儿！你上午卖，下午就不用再喂它了！

[Màile ba, lǎohàn er! Nǐ shàngwǔ mài, xiàwǔ jiùbùyòng zàiwèi tā le!]

Sell it, old man! If you sell it in the morning, you can save the trouble of feeding it this afternoon!

(Meanwhile, Broker B and C are trying to persuade the buyer)

BROKER B (giving the buyer a meaningful wink): 唉呀，你看看这牛，多加两百你也不会亏呀！

[Āiya, nǐ kànkàn zhèniú, duōjiā liǎngbǎi nǐ yě bùhuìkuī ya!]

Come on, look at the cow. The price is still in your favor even if you add 200 more!

我给你打保票：好吃家儿，好使，下好牛娃儿！

[Wǒ gěinǐ dǎbǎopiào: Hàochījiā er, hǎoshǐ, xià hǎoniúwá er!]

I can guarantee: It's not picky about food, works well for farming, and gives birth to wonderful calves.

BROKER C: 老表，我给你说—，牵住算了。亏了你找我！

[Lǎobiǎo, wǒ gěinǐ shuō—, qiānzhù suànle. Kuīle nǐ zhǎo wǒ!]

Cousin, let me tell you: Just take it. If you suffer a loss of money, I will take the responsibility for it!

(Just like that, persuaded by the brokers with words and through pushing around, the buyer counts and hands the money (2700 yuan) to Broker B, who counts the money and hands it to the seller. The seller, half-willingly, half-forced, takes the money. He counts it and puts it in his bag. The crowd disperses.)

Comparing the underlined parts in the above case with the formulaic utterances we listed at the beginning of this section, you will see that most of them are repeatedly used ones, with slight variations in only some of them. The point is: Once involved in the context of a cattle market, the buyer, the seller, and the broker each work towards their respective goals, namely, to buy or to sell a head of cattle at a favorable price, or to help make a deal so as to earn a service fee. To reach their goals, they must produce those formulaic utterances. Of course, the participants of a bargaining event on the cattle market will say other things, like doing small talk, telling jokes, and talking about things that are relevant to the cattle market. On the one hand, these kinds of things may be increased. On the other hand, they may be reduced or refined or may even not be spoken. However, these formulaic utterances selected over a long period of time must be spoken, because these words are those that are most relevant to the respective goals of the three parties. The most relevant words are the bottom line of the communication in such a context and are the most preferred choices of the speakers.

Language: Mankind's last homestead 237

G. Qian (1997/2002, p. 152) puts forward the Goal-Intention principle of conversation.

> When there is a general communication goal for a conversation, the goal will be decomposed into a series of relevant intentions conveyed and reached by individual utterances, so that the communication can proceed smoothly. However, if there is no general communication goal for a conversation, it is impossible for the intentions of each turn to develop around a central goal so that communication in the real sense cannot start or will break down halfway. Therefore, it must be observed as a principle: There is a general communication goal for a conversation, the goal is decomposed into a series of relevant intentions conveyed and reached by individual utterances so that the communication can proceed smoothly. This is the Goal-Intention principle of conversation.

Formulaic speech events provide direct means to achieve communication goals and intentions. In formulaic speech events, the participants can, by using the formulaic utterances, achieve the general communication goal without beating around the bush. In short, the formulaicity of speech events goes most prudently in accord with the Goal-Intention principle.

3.3.2.4.2 FORMULAICITY PROVIDES THE MOST ECONOMICAL MEANS TO ATTAIN
ACTIVITY GOALS

To be economic in language use is to save time and effort. Saving time means doing something more quickly so that it will not take as much time, and saying the least to achieve the most is one way to save time. Saving effort means saying less but with an equal or greater effect in achieving the goal. For example, at the cattle market, using formulaic utterances that are selected over time can save time and effort. Of course, a deal can also be made successfully even if the participants choose not to use the time-tested formulaic utterances but to generate novel or creative utterances inpromptu, which goes against the principle of economy of time and effort. If it takes more novel utterances than the set of formulaic utterances to make a deal, there will be a waste of time and effort. However, if the novel utterances can not cover all the functions that the formulaic utterances serve, then communicative failure happens. That goes against the Goal-Intention principle, and is detrimental to the maximization of efficiency in collaboration (to be discussed in detail in 3.3.2.4.3) and efficiency in performing rites (to be discussed in detail in 3.3.2.4.4).

Nonetheless, there are costs for the most economical means, including communication frustration. As a compensation, there is the strategy of redundancy.

238 *Language: Mankind's last homestead*

> Tolerance of linguistic redundancy refers to language users' employment and manipulation of semantic redundancy in communication. The strategy of redundancy is an effective tool for language users to facilitate smooth communication by employing or manipulating a proper amount of redundant information.
>
> (G. Qian, 1997/2002, p. 190)

The strategy of redundancy accounts for the fact that a bargaining event at the cattle market is abundant in small talk, jokes, and other verbal exchanges about things that are not so relevant to the ongoing bargaining. Take, for instance, that stretch of conversation between the seller and Broker B in the second bargaining event, from the seller's turn: 俩钱？！你给我不好好整，我光给你灌酒喝哩，是吧？ ("Two grand?! You are not doing anything good for me even though I keep treating you with wines, are you?") to Broker B's turn: 那死了，还喝啥哩？光说点子不沾边儿的话！ ("Of course, no one drinks any more once he is dead. What you said just makes no sense here!"). This stretch of small talk seemingly makes no sense with regard to the matrix bargaining event, as one of the participants himself is fully aware (this is what we call metalinguistic awareness). However, it is such small talk, which seemingly makes no sense with regard to the matrix speech event, that helps establish a close relationship between the seller and the broker, and the seller therefore can expect the broker to do him a favor when bargaining with a potential buyer. This, in turn, is in accordance with the Goal-Intention principle. *The Goal-Intention principle keeps a proper tension between the most economical means and the strategy of redundancy.*

3.3.2.4.3 FORMULAICITY HELPS MAXIMIZE EFFICIENCY IN COOPERATION

The maximization of efficiency in cooperation means that when the whole speech event comes to an end, the goals and intentions of the parties involved in the collaborative communication are all achieved as satisfactorily as possible, with as little setback as possible. The maximum efficiency in cooperation can only be achieved through formulaic utterances that have been repeated thousands of times. Transactions on the cattle market are collaborative activities. Neither the buyer nor the seller comes here for the sake of nothing. The seller wants to get the money he expects, while the buyer desires to bring home a head of cattle. Then there is the pressure for cooperation. According to Arndt and Richard (1987, p. 27), "historically, ritualization of communicative behavior arose from various cooperative activities among early hominids, and this pressure for cooperation was finally realized selectively as conventional signals in human semiotic systems". In other words, conventional signals, that is, *formulaic utterances, result from pressures for cooperation. Pressures for cooperation, ultimately, result from the human pursuit of efficiency.*

The pressure for cooperation gives the parties involved the desire and foundation to collaborate, and the cooperative activity can be completed

Language: Mankind's last homestead 239

through the use of formulaic utterances. That is why the broker at the cattle market keeps repeating such formulaic utterances as 我给你看看再说 ([Wǒ gěinǐ kànkàn zàishuō] "Let me look around first and talk to you later"), 中了，这个价儿，我去给你说说 ([Zhōngle, zhège jià ér, wǒ qùgěinǐ shuōshuō] "If you agree upon this price, I can go and talk to the seller for your sake"), and 你说这个价儿中不? ([Nǐ shuō zhègejià ér zhōngbù?] "Tell me, is this the right price?"). The three parties involved can all say repeatedly such formulaic utterances as 啥货卖啥价儿! ([Shàhuò màishàjià ér!] "The quality of the goods decides their prices!"), 好货卖好钱 ([Hǎohuò màihǎoqián] "Good goods deserve good prices") or 好货也得好价钱才能卖嘛! ([Hǎohuò yědé hǎojiàqián cáinéng mài ma!] "It's also true that good goods can be sold only at good prices!"). In addition, the broker is always saying 他添着，你去着! ([Tā tiānzhe, nǐ qùzhe!] "His offer can go up, and your charge can go down!") and 就是嘛，添添去去，就是这么回事 ([Jiùshì ma, tiāntiān qùqù, jiùshì zhème huíshì] "That's right. The buyer's offer can go up, and the seller's charge can go down. That's it"). However, the most frequently used formulaic utterance by the broker is the positive response to the seller's or the buyer's request regarding the price, 中，中 ([Zhōng, zhōng] "OK, OK"). In most cases, the broker, by saying 中，中, promises to both the seller and the buyer that the final price will be exactly what each of them insists, but in the end, neither of them will get completely satisfied or thoroughly dissatisfied. Therefore, 中 ("OK") actually means 不中 ("Not OK"). However, neither the seller nor the buyer feels deceived, for they have come to the cattle market knowing that the broker is entitled with the authority to propose a compromise price in the final stage so that a deal can be made, with both of their goals achieved. This is a lively picture, which shows that formulaic utterances are efficient and that language plays an indispensable part in human collaboration. Just as Malinowski (1923, p. 316) observes, "language in its primitive function and original form has an essentially pragmatic character" and "it is a mode of behaviour, an indispensable element of concerted human action".

3.3.2.4.4 FORMULAICITY BOOSTS EFFICIENCY IN THE PERFORMANCE OF RITES

In a rite, formulaic utterances and concomitant formulaic actions go hand in hand. The formulaicity not only enables the performers to smoothly go through the ritual with ease but also helps formulaic utterances and actions enhance each other's appeal to the audience. As described in Z. Liu's study, on a sacred platform, the astrologer leads his students to look up, observing the celestial phenomena, and then to take a bird's-eye view of the land, studying its geographic features; in the meanwhile, he teaches them to sing Butian Song and Jia Zi Table.[29] Likewise, at the religious ceremony, the priest and his assistants chant the divine epic while they are performing worship actions so that the people of the clan not only hear about but also witness the images and merits of their gods, ancestors, and late kings. In such activities where formulaic utterances and formulaic actions co-occur, teaching through words

240 *Language: Mankind's last homestead*

and teaching by actions are inseparable. The ritualized context is repeated year after year along with the formulaic utterances, and they are engraved in people's memory and passed on from generation to generation. In addition, oral discourses with fixed rhetorical formulas, such as myths, legends, epics, etc., often leave faintly discernible traces in the written text when they are written down. *The formulaic utterances are easy to remember and recite due to the concomitant ritual actions; in turn, the ritual actions become more lively and lovely due to the rendering of the utterances. This is a complementary relationship.*

Bamo (2003, pp. 10–16) points out that *specific and dynamic ritual situations enhance people's understanding and memory of the concomitant texts.* To exemplify this point, she mentions the fact that at all kinds of rites of the Yi people in China, teaching through words co-occurs with teaching by actions. When the chief priest (called "Bimo" in the Yi language) chants scriptures, he is often surrounded by several students (called "Bija" in the Yi language), only six or seven years old, who follow the priest to recite the scriptures word by word. There, the teacher performs as a model reciter of scriptures, with words accompanied by corresponding actions. According to Bamo (*ibid.*), the acceptance of scripture texts, from the perspective of cultural dissemination and social communication, is not constituted by individual reading activities, but by collective listening and recitation activities, and is completed in various religious ceremonies and folk rituals. People as recipients can only listen to, recite, and comprehend scriptures through ritual activities, instead of reading them. Oral narration of a written text is another form of linguistic aesthetic activity, and the text gains new life when presented through the medium of sound. The poeticization of Yi-language scriptures is based on the special requirements of memorization and oral transmission. Yi literature is in the style of verse, which shows that the application of the Yi language has not been separated from specific real communication and contexts (rites). Bamo (*ibid.*) observes that *ritual life acts as a kind of social glue: The presentation of texts at the rite activates ethnic memory, dynamically disseminates knowledge, enlivens community communication, and strengthens cultural identity.* The functions that ritual life serves, in my view, best demonstrate how the co-occurrence of formulaic utterances and formulaic actions promotes the human pursuit of efficiency in life. Until now, as Bamo states, in the Yi communities of the mountainous areas of China, writing is not divorced from the communication context of its oral culture. The ancient epic tradition of the Yi people in Liangshan, "Le'e" (meaning the ethnic narrative passed down by word of mouth), is regarded by the Yi people of the Nuosu branch as a historical "root genealogy" and a cultural treasure. It has been developing for a long time in the interplay of diachronic writing and the simultaneous oral performances with concomitant actions, and has been widely spread and accepted through oral debates (called "Kezhi" in the Yi language) in the folk ritual life. From this, it can be told that ritual life brings about ritual discourse, with the latter depending on the former.

Language: Mankind's last homestead 241

3.3.3 *How formulaic verbal behaviors promote human communication*

3.3.3.1 *Positive effects of following formulaicity*

To be brief, once the formulaicity is followed, there will be positive effects, for formulaicity is something that is the most relevant (or most directly related) to activity goals, provides the most economical means to attain activity goals, and helps maximize efficiency in cooperation, as was elaborated on in the previous sections. What should be emphasized here is that the positive effects of following formulaicity enable us to better live in humanistic networks. Interested readers are referred to *Pragmatics in Chinese Culture* (G. Qian, 1997/2002, pp. 285–291) regarding the idea that pragmatics is speechology in humanistic networks. The main points are as follows. The social humanistic network always "speaks" and "has the final say" when you speak; human freedom is not what you are born with, and does not mean doing what you want to, but doing what you should do; it can even be said that pragmatics is not about the semiotic system, but about the context system (i.e., the social humanistic network); the strategy of pragmatic appropriateness is about how we human beings behave appropriately, not about the appropriateness of language itself. *With the help of utterances that are formulaic to a certain degree, we can live in a relatively simple and economical way when facing the complicated humanistic network, and can, to a certain extent, feel at ease in dealing with it.* Here, by emphasizing the positive effects of following formulaicity, we are actually foregrounding that non-compliance will bring about negative effects.

3.3.3.2 *Negative effects of violating formulaicity*

Then, what will happen if formulaicity is not complied with? For example, if one goes to the cattle market, deciding to reject what is near at hand and seek what is far away, that is, to say some novel phrasings impromptu instead of using the ready-made formulae that have been used for a long time, we should expect this: Novel phrasings are not necessarily the most relevant to the activity, nor the most economical means to fulfill the activity goals, and they do not necessarily help maximize the benefits of collaboration. (Of course, novel utterances may work as well. We will come back to this topic in the following section.) Take, for instance, the moment when the broker urges the seller and the buyer to go the registration desk to sign the deal. If the seller, instead of using the most frequently used formulaic utterance, 少了这个数，我可不卖啊！([Shǎole zhège shù, wǒ kěbùmài a!] "If it's less than this number, I won't sell it!") or its variant, another equally frequently heard formulaic utterance, 少一分我可不卖！([Shǎoyīfēn wǒ kě bùmài!] "I won't sell it if the price is lower by just one cent!"), chooses to say some other utterances, he may get his meaning or intention delivered, but no other utterances can hit the nail on the head more efficiently and effectively than the two formulaic utterances at such a critical point of the bargaining event.

242   *Language: Mankind's last homestead*

The two formulaic utterances can best show the seller's strong-willedness not to give in by any chance. Likewise, If the buyer, instead of using the most frequently used formulaic utterance, 咱可是说好了的，多一分我不要！([Zán kěshì shuōhǎole de, duōyīfēn wǒ bùyào!] "We both agree: I won't take it if the price is higher even by just one cent!") or its equally frequently used variant, 多一分我不买！([Duōyīfēn wǒ bùmǎi!] "I won't take it if the price is higher even by just one cent!"), chooses to say some other utterances impromptu, he may also get his meaning expressed, but no other utterances can go right to the point as the above two formulaic utterances do just before a deal is to be made. The two formulaic utterances can best show the buyer's determination not to give in by any chance. In the same vein, if the broker, going between the seller and the buyer, chooses not to use the formulaic utterance, 中，中 ([Zhōng, zhōng] "OK, OK") in responding to the seller's or the buyer's request regarding the price, but tries to say something else impromptu, it will be hard for him to think of anything else that can work more efficiently than the one-character formulaic utterance 中. It seems to be a confirmative response, but can reasonably be interpreted or explained in many different ways, due to its ambiguity. In commenting on a price under discussion, the broker may as well say something else, but nothing else can work better than the formulaic utterance 啥货卖啥价儿！([Shàhuò màishàjià ér!] "The quality of the goods decides their prices!"), or its frequently heard variants, 好货卖好钱 ([Hǎohuò màihǎoqián "Good goods deserve good prices") and 好货也得好价钱才能卖嘛！([Hǎohuò yědé hǎojiàqián cáinéng mài ma!] "It's also true that good goods can be sold only at good prices!"). Resorting to people's common sense, the three formulaic utterances can best win all parties' approval, including the onlookers, who are potential sellers or buyers at the cattle market. Finally, in announcing that it is time for the seller and the buyer to go the registration desk and sign the deal, if the broker chooses not to say the formulaic utterance 走，写帐去！([Zǒu, xiězhàngqù!] "Now, let's go and sign the deal!"), but says something like 走，我们最后拍板 ([Zǒu, wǒmen zuìhòu pāibǎn] "Now, let's make the final decision"), he may be seen as lacking the authority and self-confidence that a broker is expected to show at the cattle market, and the people around may even doubt his professionalism as a broker on the cattle market.

3.3.3.3 Positive and negative effects of variations in formulaicity

Formulaic utterances are always in the process of changing, which may go in two possible ways. The effects of variations in formulaicity may be told along three dimensions: Whether the variation is the most relevant to activity goals, provides the most economical means to attain activity goals, or helps maximize the efficiency of cooperation.

In one way, the variation is even more relevant to activity goals than the old formula; at the same time, it, to a greater extent, provides the most economical means to attain activity goals and helps maximize the efficiency of

Language: Mankind's last homestead 243

cooperation. Take, for instance, the bargaining event at the cattle market. One of the formulaic utterances that all the three parties involved can say is 啥货卖啥价儿! ([Shàhuò màishàjià ér!] "The quality of the goods decides their prices!"). Its variant, 好货卖好钱 ([Hǎohuò màihǎoqián] "Good goods deserve good prices"), is equally good, close in meaning. Another variant, 好货也得好价钱才能卖嘛! ([Hǎohuò yědé hǎojiàqián cáinéng mài ma!] "It's also true that good goods can be sold only at good prices!"), entails the former two utterances and moves further to remind the seller of the possibility that the price is too high to be good, for no one will buy the goods at an unreasonably high price no matter how good the goods are. Variations like this may work better than the original formulaic utterance in practice, in that it may sound more acceptable and persuasive to both the seller and the buyer. As to the formulaic utterance少了这个数，我可不卖啊! ([Shǎole zhège shù, wǒ kěbùmài a!] "If it's less than this number, I won't sell it!"), its variant 少一分我可不卖! ([Shǎoyīfēn wǒ kě bùmài!] "I won't sell it if the price is lower by just one cent!") is shorter but more efficient in expressing the speaker's determination to insist his charge. The same is true with the seller's formulaic utterance, 多一分我不买! ([Duōyīfēn wǒ bùmǎi!] "I won't take it if the price is higher even by just one cent!"), as a variant of 咱可是说好了的，多一分我不要! ([Zán kěshì shuōhǎole de, duōyīfēn wǒ bùyào!] "We both agree: I won't take it if the price is higher even by just one cent!"). In some other cases, the variations may convey the same meaning as the other formulaic utterances but are more personalized and of greater rhetorical effect so as to be more successful in reaching the communicative purposes. For example, in reassuring the buyer or the seller that the price is to his favor, the broker may use the formulaic utterance, 你亏不了，……要是亏了，你见我一次骂一次! [Nǐ kuībùliǎo, …… yàoshi kuīle, nǐ jiàn wǒ yīcì mà yīcì!] "The price is no less/more than what the cow is worth. ... If it is, you can spit on me each time you see me!"), its variation 你亏不了，……要是亏了，你叫我头朝下走路我都走 ([Nǐ kuībùliǎo, …… yàoshi kuīle, nǐ jiào wǒ tóucháoxià zǒulù wǒ dū zǒu] "The price is no less/more than what the cow is worth. ... If it is, I will walk on my hands if you order me to") means exactly the same, but is more personalized and humorous.

In the other way, the variation does not work as well as the original formulaic utterance. That is to say, the variation is not so relevant to the activity goals as the original formulaic utterance, or it is less economical as a means to attain the activity goals or less effective in helping maximize the efficiency of cooperation than the original formulaic utterance. Take, for example, the formulaic utterance 走，写帐去! ([Zǒu, xiězhàngqù!] "Now, let's go and sign the deal!"), which the broker uses to announce that it is time for the seller and the buyer to go the registration desk and sign the deal. Possible variations that we may think of might be 走，我们最后拍板 ([Zǒu, wǒmen zuìhòu pāibǎn] "Now, let's make the final decision") or 走，我们最后把这事儿办了 ([Zǒu, wǒmen zuìhòu bā zhèshì er bànle] "Now, let's put an end to this") or 走，我们进行下一个程序 ([Zǒu, wǒmen jìnxíng xiàyīge chéngxù] "Now, let's move on

244   *Language: Mankind's last homestead*

to the next stage"). None of them sounds as good as the original one, just told from our mother-tongue intuition. Therefore, in a particular activity type, the participants generally tend to observe its formulaicity, using the time-tested set of utterances and following the relatively fixed move order of actions that co-occur with respective formulaic utterances.

3.3.4   The pragmatic mechanism of formulaic verbal behavior

As described in Section 3.3.1.1, the set of formulaic utterances will remain relatively fixed as long as the activity type remains unchanged. As a result, in formulaic verbal behavior, the relatively fixed set of utterances are repeatedly used (which may sometimes allow diachronic variations). They meet the minimal requirement of linguistic input for the communicative goal to be adequately achieved in the activity type.

Then, what leads to the formulaicity of formulaic verbal behaviors? Or, more specifically, why is the relatively fixed set of utterances repeatedly used, and why is the set of formulaic utterances the minimum linguistic input that a formulaic activity type requires? Generally speaking, to answer these two questions, we should take into consideration the constraints of discourse fields, the action-guiding function of language, the nature of language use as a game (i.e., a process of decision-making), the restrictions of expectations as well as communicative goals and intentions, etc., which all contribute to the formation of the formulaicity of formulaic verbal behavior.

3.3.4.1   The constraints of discourse fields

All the utterances that are produced in a speech event and the interrelationships among them form a discourse field and the discourse field, in turn, imposes constraints on what can be uttered in the speech event. Take, for instance, the bargaining event at the cattle market.

Due to the practical need in life to buy and to sell cattle, there is the discourse field of a bargaining event of selling and buying cattle, where the initial stage must include the following formulaic utterances.

BUYER: ……给我瞅个牛？ [30]
    … can you pick one for me out of the cattle later?
BROKER A: 你想要个啥号的？
    What kind do you want?
    我给你看看再说。
    Let me look around first and talk to you later.

Then, the broker's utterance 我给你看看再说 ("Let me look around first and talk to you later") activate the series of formulaic utterances repeated in the bargaining stage, including the following.

Language: Mankind's last homestead 245

BROKER A (stretching a hand to the seller):　想多少钱呀？
　　How much do you want for it?
SELLER (holding the broker's hand and indicating a price): 这个数。
　　This number.
BUYER:　不要！简直是晕要！
　　No! He is just charging an unreasonable price!
BROKER A (laughing scornfully):　你娃子别慌，价是慢慢儿说的嘛。
　　Don't be mad, son. The price is always negotiable.
BROKER A:　中了，这个价儿，我去给你说说。
　　If you agree upon this price, I can go to bargain with the seller for
　　your sake.
BROKER A (taking the seller's hand):　你说这个价儿中不？
　　Tell me, is this the right price?
BROKER C (grasping the seller's hand):　他添着，你去着！
　　His offer can go up, and your charge can go down!
BROKER B:　就是嘛，添添去去，就是这么回事。
　　That's right. The buyer's offer can go up, and the seller's charge can go
　　down. That's it.
Seller, Buyer, and Broker all may say the formulaic utterance: 啥货卖
啥价儿！
　　The quality of the goods decides their prices!

The formulaic utterances at the bargaining stage prepare the ground for
and lead to the production of formulaic utterances at the stage of the broker's
announcing a compromise price.

BROKER B:　就是，走，写帐去！　(Pulling the seller to the registration
　　desk)
　　That's right! Now, let's go and sign the deal!
SELLER:　少了这个数，我可不卖啊！
　　If it's less than this number, I won't sell it!
BROKER B:　中，中。
　　OK, OK.
BUYER:　咱可说好，多一分我都不要！
　　Let me be clear, I won't take it if the price is higher by just one cent!
BROKER C:　好，好，不叫你多一分！
　　OK, OK, we'll not let you spend one more cent than what you offer!
BROKER A:　你来写吧！落一千二百块钱！
　　You just sign it! You're gonna have 1200 yuan! (The number may vary
　　from case to case)

With the broker announcing a compromise price, new conflicts among
the three parties arise and there will be new doubts about the fairness of the
price on either the seller's part or the buyer's part. Therefore, the three parties

246   *Language: Mankind's last homestead*

will go into a secondary bargaining stage and formulaic utterances like the following are to be heard.

SELLER: 不卖，不卖！瞎捣哩，你！
　　I won't sell it, I won't sell it! You are just fooling me!
BUYER: 不要，多一分不要！
　　I won't take it, not even if the price is higher by just one cent!
SELLER: 那不中，那根本就不沾边儿！
　　No, it's far from the right price!
BROKER C: ……你亏不了，回家合计合计，要是亏了，你见我一　次骂一次！
　　… the price is no less than what your cow is worth. You can do the calculation back home. If it is, you can spit on me each time you see me!

If the secondary bargaining stage works in the right way, it will lead to the concluding stage where a deal is made with both the buyer and the seller signing the record of the deal. Given that a deal is made, it can be said that both the seller and the buyer are satisfied, for they have reached their purposes, to sell or to buy a cow. However, due to the lack of an objective or scientific measure to decide the price on the cattle market, either the seller or the buyer will leave the market with some doubt about the fairness of the final price (and is thus not fully satisfied), as the following formulaic utterances show.

SELLER (half-willingly and half-forced by the brokers, pressing his thumbprint on the record of the deal and shouting): 我这个牛最少也少卖一两百，您这……这……这样整，那—会中？
　　The selling price for my cow must be at least one or two hundred (yuan) less than it's worth. You … make me do this. Is this fair?
BUYER (seeing that the seller has agreed, also pressing his thumbprint on the record of the deal, half-willingly and half-forced, shouting to the broker): 你说的啊，这要是太贵了，我下集还拉来你给我卖了！
　　You just said it. If I've paid more than it's worth, I'll bring it back next time and you help me sell it.

The stages of a bargaining event on the cattle market are strongly interrelated with one another. The previous stages constrain and activate the next stage, which develops in reaction and adapts to the previous ones. The lack of any of the stages, together with the corresponding formulaic utterances, will lead to the incompleteness of a bargaining event at the cattle market. As long as the bargaining event at the cattle market remains unchanged, the relatively fixed set of utterances will be repeatedly used, and function as the minimum linguistic input that a formulaic activity type requires for it to be successfully conducted.

3.3.4.2 *The action-guiding function of language*

The action-guiding function of language means: 1) That action and language are embedded in each other; and 2) that language directs action, rather than vice versa. These two points are well demonstrated in formulaic speech events. Take, for instance, an excerpt from Case II: Bargaining event at Youtian Cattle Market.

BROKER B: 那死了，还喝啥哩？光说点子不沾边儿的话！
　　[Nà sǐle, hái hēshà lī? Guāng shuōdiǎnzi bùzhānbiān er de huà!]
　　Of course, no one drinks any more once he is dead. What you said just makes no sense here!
BROKER A (smiling): 说正经的哟。(Stretching out a hand to hold the seller's hand) 表叔你想多少钱吧？
　　[Shuōzhèngjīng de yāo. Biǎoshū nǐ xiǎng duōshǎoqián ba?]
　　Let's talk business. Uncle, how much do you want?
BROKER B (watching the seller and Broker A negotiating the price through hand-touching): 三千三？！就这一个？带牛娃儿没？
　　[Sānqiānsān?! Jiù zhèyīgè? Dài niúwá er méi?]
　　3300 yuan? Just for this one? Without a calf?
SELLER (indifferently): 牛娃儿刚摘开。
　　[Niúwá er gāng zhāikāi.]
　　The calf has just been weaned.
BROKER B: 瞅着也够呛了，老变牙口了吧？(Approaching the cow and starting to check its teeth)
　　[Chǒuzhe yěgòuqiàng le, lǎobiànyákou le ba?]
　　It looks quite old. Has it shed its primary teeth long before?

Broker B's utterance, 那死了，还喝啥哩？光说点子不沾边儿的话！("Of course, no one drinks any more once he is dead. What you said just makes no sense here!"), implies that what the seller says has nothing to do with the business (selling his cow), and naturally brings about the action on Broker A's part, stretching out a hand to hold the seller's hand (to negotiate the price through hand-touching).

BROKER A (smiling): 说正经的哟。(Stretching out a hand to hold the seller's hand) 表叔你想多少钱吧？
　　Let's talk business. Uncle, how much do you want?

The formulaic utterance by Broker A, 表叔你想多少钱吧？, brings about the action of negotiating the price through hand-touching. Then, Broker B's utterance, 三千三？！就这一个？带牛娃儿没？("3300 yuan? Just for this one? Without a calf?"), implying that a calf should be included for the named price, leads to the seller's action to express his unhappiness, for he thinks that Broker B's request is too much.

248 *Language: Mankind's last homestead*

SELLER (indifferently): 牛娃儿刚摘开。

    The calf has just been weaned.

In addition, by saying 瞅着也够呛了，老变牙口了吧？("It looks quite old. Has it shed its primary teeth long before?"), Broker B's utterance brings about his own action, approaching the cow and starting to check its teeth.

For another example, let us take another look at an excerpt from the case of fortune-telling we examined in Section 3.3.2.2.

CHU$_1$: 算一下吧。

    [Suànyīxià ba.]

    Ok, we can have a try.

TELLER A$_2$ (to Chu): 哪个嘛？你呀？哟——你这个人，" 印堂"[31]生的好！……你这个眉毛生得好！

    [Năge ma? Nĭ ya? Yāo—Nĭ zhègerén,"yìntáng" shēngdehăo!……Nĭ zhège méimáo shēngdéhăo]

    Which one? You? Wow – your *yingtang* is great! Your eyebrows look great!

    (To Wang) 他这眉毛生好了的。生得就像秦始皇那眉毛样。 懂到没得嘛？

    [Tā zhèméimáo shēnghăolede. Shēngdé jiùxiàng qínshĭhuáng nà méimáoyàng. Dŏngdào méidé ma?]

    His eyebrows are great. They look just like Emperor Qinshihuang's. Don't you see?

…

WANG$_2$: 那个地方每个人都有得嘛！

    [Nàgè dìfāng měigèrén dōuyŏudé ma!]

    That part, everybody has one!

TELLER A$_4$ (in raised voice): 每个人？这个兄弟"财包"生鼓起来了的。男左女右，你看左边嗖！

    [Měi gèrén? Zhège xiōngdì "cáibāo" shēnggŭĭláile de. Nánzuŏ nŭyòu, nĭkàn zuŏbiānsāi!]

    Everybody? This brother's "fortune container" bulges. It's the left side for men, right for women. You look at his left side!

The customer, Chu, agrees to have his fortune told by giving the utterance at Chu$_1$, which serves as a direction leading to a series of actions and utterances by the fortune-teller at Teller A$_2$, complimenting Chu on his looks and trying to convince Wang to believe him. Wang's utterance at Wang$_2$ poses a challenge to the fortune-teller, expressing doubt about his point: That kind of eyebrow looks very common; how do you know it looks just like Emperor Qinshihuang's? As a result, Wang's utterance leads the fortune-teller to the act of refuting at Teller A$_4$.

In the traditional Chinese wedding ceremony, each utterance guides a corresponding action, the bride and groom's kowtowing to Heaven and Earth (or bowing to the portrait of Zedong Mao, or Xiaoping Deng in a particular period of time), to the groom's parents, to each other, and then being escorted to the bridal bedroom.

If a formulaic activity type (e.g., a wedding ceremony, a funeral, or a civil mediation, etc.) remains unchanged, a set of action-guiding utterances are expected to appear repeatedly, with one at a certain stage brought about by the ones at previous stages. The repeated utterances tend to remain relatively fixed, rejecting the addition of other utterances (which will go against the principle of least effort or the economy principle in language), and they are thus the minimum linguistic input that a formulaic activity type requires.

Then, which one came first, the formulaic utterance or the formulaic action? Given that the formulaicity of a formulaic activity type is the result of choice-making by trial and error over a long time, it is hard to tell whether the formulaic utterance came prior to the formulaic action or vice versa; besides, speaking itself is also a kind of behavior. Nonetheless, with the creation of writing, actions have been explained in words, and this makes utterances appear to be prior to actions. In fact, the action-guiding function of language should be talked about with respect to particular cases.

As to the action-guiding function of language, some argue that it does not come from the speakers' intentions but from certain conventions of use, as Marcondes de Souza puts in the following remarks.

> ... it can be said that the force of these speech acts, the action-guiding elements, i.e. the elements which guarantee their effectiveness, are derived not from the speakers' intentions but from the conventional character of the formulae, and from the more general conventions governing the language games (e.g. trials, religious ceremonies, and other institutional practices).
>
> (1983, p. 50)

In other words, once a formulaic activity type is activated, what happens will be governed by "the conventional character of the formulae" and "the more general conventions governing the language games", but not by the speakers' intentions. Marcondes de Souza's observation might be surprising, but it is insightful, which, in a way, is in agreement with our observation on the constraints that the social humanistic network imposes on speaking (G. Qian, 1997/2002).

3.3.4.3 The game theory of language use

There are existing efforts applying game theory to the study of language use. However, we are not making any reference to them. Instead, we choose to put forward our version of the game theory of language use by combining the essence of the theory of games with the pragmatics in Chinese culture, in the hope of complementing Western scholars' applications of game theory to language use. Let us begin with what game theory is:

250   *Language: Mankind's last homestead*

Approach to the study of decision-making that models situations of competition, cooperation, and conflict in terms of the rules, strategies, risks, and variable outcomes of games. It was founded by the Hungarian-American mathematician John von Neumann and amplified in his and Oskar Morgenstern's *Theory of Games and Economic Behavior* (1944). Game theory studies the ways in which people make decisions in circumstances where the outcome depends on others' as well as one's own strategic choices and resulting "moves", and is therefore concerned with players' assumptions and expectations about each other in interactive situations. Unlike real life, game theory assumes that all the players will act rationally and, generally, that they have complete information about the projected "payoff" of any given course of action.

Games can be *two-person* – a one-to-one confrontation – or *n-person*, in which coalitions are often necessary for success. They are *cooperative* or *noncooperative* depending on whether or not the players can profit from collaboration. *Zero-sum* games are those in which one player's gain is another's loss – the net gains and losses add up to zero. In *non-zero-sum* (or *mixed-motive*) games, both sides can benefit, or benefit to differing degrees. Non-zero-sum games are most interesting to game theorists, who are concerned with applying theoretical principles to real-world socio-logical, economic, and political relationships in which outcomes are usually the result of bargaining and compromises, not winner-take-all victories. Game theory has been applied, for example, to the study of MARKET behavior, DETERRENCE and arms control, and legislative strategy. It has also been criticized, however, as dependent on unrealistic assumptions and artificial models.

(Rohmann, 1999, p. 156; emphasis original)

The following is a much briefer introduction of game theory.

The mathematical theory of situations in which two or more players have a choice of decisions (strategies); where the outcome depends on all the strategies and where each player has a set of preferences defined over the outcomes.

(Blackburn, 1994, p.153)

The essential points of game theory can be summarized as follows.

1) It is about decision-making, and the use of strategies.
2) It models situations of competition, cooperation, and conflict in terms of variable outcomes of games.
3) The outcome depends on others' as well as one's own strategic choices and resulting "moves".
4) The outcome is also concerned with players' assumptions and expectations about each other in interactive situations.

Language: Mankind's last homestead   251

5) Games are cooperative or noncooperative depending on whether or not the players can profit from collaboration.
6) Outcomes are usually the result of bargaining and compromises, and each player has a set of preferences defined over the outcomes.

Hopefully, the above summary rightly covers all the most essential elements of game theory. On the basis of these essential points, a game theory of language use, from my point of view, should go along the following line of thinking. I will elaborate my points with cases of language use in the bargaining event at the cattle market.

Verbal communication is about decision-making and choice of strategies. Language use, especially dialogue, is a process in which language users make strategy choices. In the bargaining event at the cattle market, each of the three parties involved make choices, at each step, about what to say and what strategies to use, depending on what the other party or the other two parties have said and will say.

Verbal communications are situations involving competition, cooperation, and conflict in terms of the rules, strategies, risks, and variable outcomes of games. This view of verbal communication is more scientific than those that emphasize only the cooperative principle (Grice, 1975) and it supports the idea that it is not necessarily a principle to cooperate in verbal communication (G. Qian, 1997/2002, p. 151). Conversations can be conflictive and the outcomes may be nothing but failure to the participants. For example, in the bargaining event at the cattle market, the outcome can be that no deal is reached or signed.

The outcome of a conversation depends on other participants' as well as one's own strategic choices and resulting "moves". In the bargaining event at the cattle market, for instance, the critical resulting move for the three parties involved is to give or accept a price, which is to their own respective benefit.

The outcome of a conversation is also concerned with participants' assumptions and expectations about each other in the interactive situation. For example, the buyer, the seller, and the broker each come to the cattle market with particular assumptions and expectations. When they say something, they expect another participant to say something that goes in agreement with their expectation; otherwise, the negotiation has to go on.

Conversations can be cooperative or noncooperative, depending on whether or not the participants can profit from collaboration. If all the participants want to benefit, the conversation is a hopeful one. However, if any one of the participants want to take all the benefit and to make the other participant(s) suffer from a complete loss, the conversation will go nowhere. This is vividly shown by the bargaining event at the cattle market.

Moreover, the outcomes of conversation are usually the result of bargaining and compromises, with each player having a set of preferences defined over the outcomes. At the cattle market, the critical resulting move for the three parties involved is to give or accept a price, which is to their own respective

252 *Language: Mankind's last homestead*

benefit. When each of them is trying to fix a price in their own favor, compromise is the only choice to reach a deal, if all the parties want to profit from the conversation. However, if any one of them wants to win a winner-take-all victory, the conversation will fail or go nowhere. A conversation that goes nowhere is not desirable to any one of the three parties involved; therefore, they tend to compromise, satisfied with limited benefit, so that each side can benefit, or benefit to differing degrees. That is how the bargaining event at the cattle market ends successfully with a deal signed. The set of preferences of each participant, namely, the set of utterances that they may say respectively to get what they want, will be defined over the outcomes of the conversation, the communicative purposes they want to achieve respectively. Specifically, the buyer can obtain what he wants at a price as low as possible, the seller can get as much as possible for what he sells, and the broker can get the service fee for helping them make a deal.

That is how language functions in formulaic verbal behavior, a special form of language game. Within this mechanism, language use proceeds in spontaneity combined with necessity, and under willingness and coerciveness. Driven by their assumptions and expectations, the participants make strategic choices from a set of preferences defined over the outcomes and take resulting moves to deal with the competition, cooperation, and conflict that develop in the activity, by bargaining and compromising. To achieve their respective goals and purposes, participants tend to use a set of formulaic utterances, which co-occurs with a set of actions, as long as the activity type remains unchanged. Moreover, the set of utterances functions as the minimum linguistic input that a formulaic activity type requires for it to be successfully conducted.

In fact, the game theory of language use sheds insight into the mechanism of language use in general, not just the pragmatic mechanism of formulaic verbal behavior. As Rohmann (1999, p. 156) observes, game theory can be applied to "real-world sociological, economic, and political relationships" and has been applied to "the study of market behavior, deterrence and arms control, and legislative strategy". Then, the game theory-based mechanism of language use is not just about verbal communication, nor just about formulaic verbal behavior. It is also one of sociological, economic, and political relationships. In other words, the pragmatic mechanism of formulaic verbal behavior is deeply embedded in sociological, economic, and political relationships. This viewpoint is in agreement with the observations I made in *Pragmatics in Chinese Culture* (G. Qian, 1997/2002): 1) The social humanistic network "speaks" and "has the final say" whenever we speak; 2) pragmatic principles and strategies are not so much a means for language users to achieve communicative success as a means for them to deal with the interference into their using linguistic signs from the social humanistic network; and 3) all the important theories in pragmatics are developed by taking into account human beings or society composed of human beings.

Language: Mankind's last homestead   253

3.3.4.4 *The restrictions of goals and intentions*

What role do goals and intentions play in the formation of the formulaicity of formulaic verbal behavior? Simply put, when you become involved in a particular activity type with a particular goal, you are naturally supposed to say the repeatedly used expressions to achieve your goal (only if the activity type remains unchanged). Besides, those expressions are the minimum linguistic input that the activity type requires for it to be successfully conducted. Anything other than the time-test utterances may lead to unexpected troubles that may jeopardize the development and the desired outcomes of the activity type.

As the game theory of language use reveals, in verbal communication, each participant has a set of preferences defined over the outcomes. Take, for example, the bargaining event at the cattle market. The buyer's goal is to buy what he wants at as low a price as possible; the seller's is to get as much as possible for what he sells; the broker's is to earn some service fee for helping them make a deal. The set of formulaic utterances for each of the three parties is defined over the their respectively desired outcomes. The repeatedly used time-test utterances meet the minimum requirement for language use at each stage of the event. If a participant says more than what is expected at a particular stage, a new problem may arise. For instance, at the stage of signing the deal, the buyer or the seller should sign on the record of the deal and then leave the market immediately if they are satisfied with the outcome. Anything more than the formulaic utterances they say about the deal may lead to unexpected consequences, which may eventually go against their respectively desired goals.

3.4 Chapter summary

3.4.1 *Human beings making themselves present by speaking*

In the introduction to this chapter, when we answered the question as to why the present research is a philosophical study, we mentioned two arguments. On the one hand, "Being" draws mankind into language (see 2.1.2). On the other, human beings make themselves present by speaking. Chapter 3 is entirely devoted to elaborating the latter proposition. Without this chapter, readers may feel uncertain about whether the present research can be taken as a philosophical endeavor. Just as the poet Stefan Georg repeatedly chants that "where word breaks off, no thing may be", Chapter 3 reiterates the claim that *there is no presence of mankind where the word is lacking.*

It may be asked: What is the relationship between the two propositions "There is no presence of mankind where the word is lacking" and "Human beings make themselves present by speaking"? Obviously, they are fully consistent with each other. If there is no presence of mankind in the absence of words, then it is logical to say that mankind can make himself present only

254 *Language: Mankind's last homestead*

when he speaks. As a reminder, let's recall the main arguments made in this chapter.

To begin with, mankind lives in language. This is the case because major forms of human behavior are parasitic on speaking and human beings live in discourse fields. Here, the following points are presented: That listening and speaking constitute a primary form of human life, that a super discourse field already exists even before one speaks, that one or two sayings may control our entire life, and that the inheritance of a discourse field is the inheritance of history.

Second, mankind has to live in language. This is because language itself is a kind of human life activity, and language is the last fingerprint and heritage of an ethnic group. Language, rather than religion, is the primary marker of ethnic identity, and a language community functions like a fingerprint. Moreover, people who identify with their hometown accent when they are away are seeking for a psychological homestead. Language plays a great role in the falling or lasting of a civilization, and the most effective way to conquer and assimilate a people is by means of language. The mother tongue as well as mother culture is the warmest cradle of a civilization. In addition, the incommensurability between languages helps to stabilize civilizations. The stability of a language and its writing system safeguard a civilization. While the "septum" between languages safeguards a civilization, the communication between languages increases the vitality of a civilization. Finally, in examining the theory of linguistic determinism and its mechanism, we made a critical review of the Sapir-Whorf Hypothesis, and argued that language is the pre-existing structure of human cognition of the world.

Last, mankind lives in formulaic verbal behaviors. A formulaic verbal behavior is characterized by: 1) A relatively fixed set of utterances; 2) a relatively fixed set of actions in relatively fixed move orders; and 3) a relatively fixed co-occurrence of the above two, although variations may take place. The relatively fixed co-occurrence of formulaic utterances and formulaic action is the result of human cooperation, prompted by expectations, cultural stability, and the human pursuit of efficiency in life. Formulaicity is the most relevant (or most directly related) to activity goals, provides the most economical means to attain activity goals, and helps maximize efficiency in cooperation. There are thus positive effects of following formulaicity and negative effects of violating formulaicity; however, there are both positive and negative effects of variations in formulaicity. The pragmatic mechanism of formulaic verbal behaviors involves the constraints of discourse fields, the action-guiding function of language, the nature of language use as a game (i.e., a process of decision-making), the restrictions of communicative goals and intentions.

In a nutshell, the three livings are roughly the basic state of human existence. It is in such a basic state of being that we live as we do and we are as we are. Especially when we, by speaking, make a thing (actual or virtual) in the world present, we also make ourselves present in the world. Hopefully, this chapter has succeeded in leading readers to that conclusion.

Language: Mankind's last homestead   255

Now that "Being" draws human beings into language (see 2.1.2), it is natural to say that language is the last homestead of human beings.

Louis Hjelmslev, a representative figure of the Copenhagen School, has given us a seemingly romantic but actually vivid description of the functions and properties of language in his masterpiece *Prolegomena to a Theory of Language*. He argues,

> Language is inseparable from man and *follows him in all his works.* Language is the instrument with which man forms thought and feeling, mood, aspiration, will and act, the instrument by whose means he influences and is influenced, *the ultimate and deepest foundation of human society.* But it is also the ultimate, indispensable sustainer of the human individual, his refuge in hours of loneliness, when the mind wrestles with existence and *the conflict is resolved in the monologue of the poet and the thinker. Before the first awakening of our consciousness language was echoing about us, ready to close around our first tender seed of thought* and to accompany us inseparably through life, from the simple activities of everyday living to our most sublime and intimate moments – those moments from which we borrow warmth and strength for our daily life through that hold of *memory that language itself gives us.* But language is no external accompaniment. *It lies deep in the mind of man,* a wealth of memories inherited by the individual and the tribe a vigilant conscience that reminds and warns. And speech is *the distinctive mark of the personality,* for good and ill, *the distinctive mark of home and of nation,* mankind's patent of nobility. So inextricably has language grown inside personality, home, nation, mankind, and life itself that we may sometimes be tempted to ask whether language is a mere reflexion of, or simply is not all those things – *the very seed leaf of their growth.*
>
> (1943/1961, p. 3; emphasis added)

The following of Hjelmslev's arguments are noteworthy.

1) Language follows man in all his works. This resonates with the view of language game and fits well with the main thesis of this book, that is, a study of the basic state of human existence involves pragmatics and other disciplines (see 2.2).
2) Language is the ultimate and deepest foundation of human society. This is tantamount to saying that language is the last homestead of human beings.
3) The conflict (between mind and existence) is resolved in the monologue of the thinker. This suggests that it is language (monologue) that expresses, silently, thoughts (ideas or abstract entities that only exist in consciousness but are substantial and mankind's spiritual phenomena are a kind of abstract entity) and make them manifested beings (see 2.1.1).

256   *Language: Mankind's last homestead*

4) Before the first awakening of our consciousness, language was echoing about us. This opinion coincides with the important idea that the world structure underlying language determines, stereotypes, and formulates human thoughts, as argued in 3.2.4.
5) Language itself gives us memory. To put it differently, language anchors our memories.
6) Language lies deep in the mind of mankind. This answers the question of where language is preserved.
7) Speech is the distinctive mark of the personality. This is another way of saying that speech production itself is a dynamic human activity, as argued in 3.2.1.
8) Speech is the distinctive mark of home and of nation. This is in perfect agreement with what we argued in 3.2.2 – that language is the last fingerprint and heritage of a people.
9) Language is the very seed leaf of the growth of personality, home, nation, mankind, and life itself. This, on the whole, supports our argument that language is the last homestead of human beings.

As we acquire our mother language as a kid, we also acquire the culture we live in as well as the rationality we need to get along with other people and the traditional wisdom of the home nation. In this sense, language has become the carrier of culture, rationality, and wisdom. Once aware that we inhabit the secure house of language, we are already living in a place mixed with culture, rationality, and wisdom.

What Hjelmslev argues above contributes to our understanding of the basic state of human existence, that is, mankind lives in language, mankind has to live in language, and mankind lives in formulaic verbal behaviors. This state of existence reveals the great extent to which mankind relies on language.

To demonstrate why this research is philosophical, we recall some important arguments Heidegger made about his statement that "language is the house of Being" (see 2.1.1.1).

His first argument goes like this.

> … with that expression ["house of Being"], I do not mean the Being of beings represented metaphysically, but the presence of the two-fold [or *Zwiefalt*], Being and beings – but this two-fold understood in respect of its importance for thinking them.
>
> (1982, pp. 26–27)

Here, special attention should be drawn to Heidegger's identification of "house of Being" with "the presence of the two-fold or *Zwiefalt*".

In a second instance, Heidegger argues:

> Something *is* only where the appropriate and therefore competent word names a thing as being, and so establishes the given being as a being.

Language: Mankind's last homestead 257

Does this mean, also, that there is being only where the appropriate word is speaking?

(1982, p. 63; emphasis original)

He also keeps reminding the reader of Stefan George's lines in *The Word* (*Das Wort*), "Where word breaks off no thing may be" (*Kein ding sei wo das wort gebricht*) (*ibid.*, p. 60). In so doing, Heidegger is opining that things come into existence only when they are successfully expressed by words. This opinion, which bestows a profundity on Heidegger's thoughts, stands in stark contrast to the traditional materialist view that a thing or entity is there even in the absence of the designating word. Why does Heidegger repeatedly cite the line "Where word breaks off no thing may be"? As I see it, what Heidegger really intends to express is that "if the word does not have this bearing, the whole of things, the 'world', would sink into obscurity" (*ibid.*, p. 73). This suggests that it is words that hold all things in reserve and make them present in the Being. In other words, words make "the world" clear.

In a third place, Heidegger claims that "to say means to show, to make appear, the lighting-concealing-releasing offer of world" (*ibid.*, p. 107). Obviously, he is trying to tell us that saying makes the world appear, or, rather, that mankind is the subject while the world is the object.

In Heidegger's eyes, "thing" means "anything that in any way *is*" (*ibid.*, p. 62; emphasis original).

Under what circumstances does a thing exist but not be present? A thing, be it tangible or intangible, actual or virtual, may exist, but it cannot be said to be "present" if it is not designated by words, even if it is there. Suppose there is a rock on the hill, and the shape of the rock looks like something but somehow it cannot exactly be said what it is like. In this case, it is safe to say that the rock is there, but is still not present.

Then, under what circumstances does a thing exist and in the meantime be present? A thing can be considered "present" if and only if it is not only there but also has been named by words. Take again, for example, the rock on the hill. Suppose it has a certain shape (that already exists), and suppose it is like a monkey reaching out for the sea. Then, by trial and error, someone suddenly cries out, "Look! It's a monkey reaching out for the sea!" When and *only when* it is labeled as such with these words, the monkey-like rock comes to be "present" or is made to "appear".

Mankind makes a thing (actual or virtual) present by virtue of language. This is a view proposed by Heidegger, and it can be represented in the following illustration.

$$☺ → ⊙ / ※ → Ω$$

(In the above illustration, ☺ represents an individual, ⊙ an actual entity, ※ a virtual entity, Ω the resulting presence of an entity, and → the process of "making present by virtue of language".)

258   *Language: Mankind's last homestead*

For the sake of survival and development, mankind has to do a lot of things and take part in all kinds of activities, doing things with words. *Mankind makes himself present by virtue of language.* This is the theme of the present book, which can be graphically represented as follows.

☺ → ☺

(In this illustration, the first ☺ represents an individual, the second ☺ the resulting presence of the individual, and → the process of "present by virtue of language".)

As the second illustration shows, mankind is not facing the world, but himself. He makes himself present by speaking or through language.

If someone never speaks all his life, then we may say that he has never been present although he lives in the world. In the sense that language makes mankind present, *an individual who never utters a word in his life has not made himself present.* Of course, this would never happen in real life. That is to say, speaking, as evidenced in the three livings (to which this entire chapter is devoted), makes mankind present. However, *it is possible that an individual is unwilling to speak on a particular occasion, when he chooses not to be present.*

3.4.2 *The core of the view of language as mankind's last homestead*

The thrust of the view of language as mankind's last homestead can be summarized as follows.

As one of the basic facets of human existence, mankind has to depend on language for every single moment of existence; we live in language, we have to live in language, and we live in formulaic verbal behavior. It is in such a basic state of Being that we live as we do and we are as we are. Especially when we, by speaking, make a thing (actual or virtual) in the world present, we also make ourselves present in the world. There is no presence of mankind where the word is lacking. The presence of human beings in the world is of greater significance than that of things, for it is human presence that makes possible the presence of things.

As summed up above, it is obvious that my statement that mankind makes things in the world present by speaking is derived from Stefan George and Heidegger's claim that "where word breaks off no thing may be". However, there are three important distinctions between my view of language as mankind's last homestead and Heidegger's view of language as the house of Being.

To begin with, in our claim that mankind makes himself present by speaking, *mankind is both the subject and the object, that is to say, the subject acts upon himself.* It is completely different from the argument made by Heidegger, "to say means to show, to make appear, the lightening-concealing-releasing offer of world" (1982, p. 107). In Heidegger's view, *man is the subject while the world is the object*, and the world reveals itself in mankind's speaking, so a boundary can be drawn between the subject and the object.

Second, we distinguish two types of "presence" and make a sharp contrast between them. It is one thing that mankind makes things (actual or virtual) in the world present by speaking, and it is quite another thing that mankind makes himself present by speaking. The presence of things becomes possible and makes sense only after mankind makes himself present with his words. Heidegger emphasizes in more than one place that mankind's speaking makes things present; however, what seems more important to me is that *mankind makes himself present through his words*. I would not like to say that Heidegger has pitifully failed to stress this point, or that he just did not see it. In any case, by distinguishing and paralleling the two types of "presence", we not only lend support to Heidegger's idea, but move further ahead to some extent.

Last but not least, the two theories are also different in perspective, approach, and commitment. Heidegger's proposition that language is the house of Being focuses on the relation between language and existence, and Stefan Georg and Heidegger's claim that "where word breaks off no thing may be" targets the relation between words and objects. However, our view of language as mankind's last homestead focuses on and is based on one of humans' basic behaviors or one of the basic facets of human existence, namely, the three livings. We examine one of the basic facets of human existence from both philosophical and pragmatic perspectives. However, Heidegger tries to solve an age-old problem in Western philosophy: What is there? (Or: What exists? What is this? What is that?) In other words, Heidegger makes his arguments with an ontological commitment, while we do not; we have only tried to reveal mankind's being in the world, both philosophically and pragmatically.

3.4.3 Involvement of the spirit of Chinese philosophy

The spirit of Chinese philosophy is embedded in the verbal behavior of the Chinese and it is a spontaneous process. Naturally, the verbal behavior of the Chinese reflects the spirit of Chinese philosophy (i.e., the Chinese cultural spirit) from stem to stern. Of all the issues discussed in this chapter, those relating to the Chinese all involve the spirit of Chinese philosophy.

To approach the verbal behavior of the Chinese only from the perspective of Chinese philosophy will be nothing but another ordinary endeavor, given that there is already an immense quantity of writings of that kind. However, it is fresh to argue that "Being" draws mankind into language and that mankind makes himself present by speaking. It is a novel attempt from the perspective of Western philosophy, and the pursuit of "novelty" is exactly what the present study strives for.

Notes

1 An ordinary logical fallacy in which *a*, which is observed to occur after *b*, is regarded as *b*'s consequence.
2 From a night show on CCTV 2 dated November 21, 1998.

260 *Language: Mankind's last homestead*

3 Form a news report of Guangdong TV Station Pearl River Channel in mid-November 1998.

4 This and the following ballads are provided and explained by Guanzhi Qian, a high-school teacher born in 1945 and a long-time resident in Xiantao. He also revised the interpretations and explanations of the above ballad.

5 The chronicles of new words, such as that edited by the China Social Science Academy and *Chinese Word Database Construction* (Hong Kong Association for the Chinese Language) are important programs. In each issue (one issue a year), they record new words without unduly comments on whether they are acceptable by the language norm or not, just giving them a "snapshot". As time elapses, one can see from these "fossils" very vivid pictures of China's economic, political, social, and cultural conditions in those years. However, it is not enough to have one issue each year. It would be even better that there be a collection every decade. The decade collection issue can be optimized. Such decade collections will be increasingly more useful as time passes. Some European and American countries have their own new-word chronicles, but they may not yet have a decade collection. We can overtake them in doing this work. The workload for compiling a decade collection is heavy indeed, but it is worth doing, for the great social and cultural benefits it brings to the Chinese in the future can never be overestimated.

6 Yusheng Luo, a well-known performer of Jingyun Dagu, a kind of story-telling in the Beijing dialect with drum accompaniment.

7 Ancient Roman general Caesar the Great, *veni, vidi, vici* ("I came, I saw, I conquered") (cited in Ding, 1996, p. 115).

8 Han is the name of the majority ethnicity of the Chinese; Hu is an old umbrella term referring to the northern non-Han ethnic groups. (The translator's note.)

9 *Sachima*, also called *shaqima*, is a common Chinese pastry, originated among Manchus in Northeast China. It is made of fluffy strands of fried batter bound together with stiff sugar syrup.

10 The Baishou dance, literally "hand-waving dance", is a 500-year-old historic group dance of the Tujia in China.

11 The Wuling, literally "Five Mountains", is a mountain range in South China separating the Pearl River Basin from the Yangtze Valley and the dividing line between south and central subtropical zones. (The translator's note.)

12 What is the cultural common core? All human cultures share a common core. In other words, the cultural common core is the cultural consensus in all mankind cultures (G. Qian, 1994).

13 In the 1980s, a Chinese philosopher, Shuli Ji, planned to edit a Chinese symposium entitled *Kuhn's Selected Works of Philosophy of Science*. In 1988, Kuhn wrote a preface for this planned symposium. For reasons that Ji never made clear, this symposium never came into being. A decade later, Ji translated and introduced Kuhn's preface to Chinese readers in his 1997 article. (The translator's note.)

14 Given there is no way for us to find the English version of Kuhn's preface, we translate Ji's Chinese translation of it back into English. (The translator's note.)

15 This is obviously different from "conquering nature". The idea of "bidirectional coordination with nature" means that we should overcome disasters without destroying nature, and study and utilize nature without abusing it. If human beings were compelled to "conquer nature" in the prehistoric era, up to now, sticking to this slogan and action is tantamount to actually continuing to perform the slogan and action that undermine nature. As early as before the fear of SARS, we had

Language: Mankind's last homestead 261

already "conquered" "nature" to a horrible extent. It seems that we have to go through several "super-SARS fears" to remember this lesson: To destroy nature and to "conquer" "nature" equal to destroy human beings.

16 In its general sense, a traditional Chinese wedding ceremony consists of a set of rites, of which what we present as an example is only a part, called in Chinese 拜堂 ([bàitáng] "kowtowing to the parents") or 拜天地 ([bài tiāndì] "kowtowing to Heaven and Earth"). But the present part is the central and indispensable part, which is functionally equivalent to a Christian wedding. It is after this part that the bride and groom will be socially taken as husband and wife, although there afterwards will be some other rites taken as parts of the wedding like 喜宴 ([xǐyàn] "the wedding banquet"), where the newly wedded couple ceremonially present wine or other drinks to guests (Qu, 2000, p. 83). In view of that and for the sake of convenience, we just call this part "the traditional Chinese wedding ceremony". In fact, the other rites that happen on the wedding day are also formulaic speech events in our sense. (The translator's note.)

17 In transcription, subscript numbers indicate the turns taken by the respective participant; "–" indicates a lingering voice; "…" within turns indicates a pause or an unfinished utterance. A double-ellipsis (six dots) indicates turns left out. (The translator's note.)

18 Chu, Wang, and Ren are family names. This case is taken from the transcript of Side A of the tape Fortune-Telling 1. Due to the limit of space, only the formulaic parts of the fortune-telling event are presented here.

19 The part right between the two eyebrows.

20 Jargon used by fortune-tellers to name the different facial parts.

21 生辰 [shēngchén] refers to the date and hour of one's birth; 八字 [bāzì] are the corresponding eight Chinese characters to express times and seasons. It is said that from the combinations of these characters, one's fortune or fate can be told. (The translator's note.)

22 月月红 ([yuèyuèhóng] literally, "red for every month") refers to the 100-yuan note in Chinese currency, which is reddish; red is a symbol of happiness, good luck. (The translator's note.)

23 二红喜 ([Èrhóngxǐ] literally, "double red happiness") means two 100-yuan notes. Fortune-tellers use jargon to express their charges, all carrying special meanings with reference to good or bad luck, happiness or sorrow, success or failure, etc. (The translator's note.)

24 As we once mentioned, price negotiation at the cattle market usually goes in secret, just between the two parties involved, and they often name their desired price by touching different parts of their hidden hands. The real prices they name are not known to a third party. However, in order to know each specific detail of the bargaining process, the recorder had talked in advance with the broker (who was a distant relative of the recorder) so that he allowed the recorder to follow him closely and was willing to tell the recorder the real prices he and the seller (and later the buyer) gave to each other. The broker at that time had no idea about our research and he was told about the recording only afterwards and happily gave us the permission to use the transcripts of the tapes for our case study.

25 X is used to indicate a Chinese curse, equivalent to an English four-letter word.

26 The broker suggested a price to the buyer by hand-touching, but he didn't tell the recorder what exactly it was. It could have been about 1100 yuan, according to the final price they agreed upon. (The translator's note.)

262 *Language: Mankind's last homestead*

27 In the Chinese way of talking about numbers, 零头([língtóu] roughly, "digits of lesser place value") may refer to any (group) of the digits after the leftmost digit of a number. For example, for a four-digit whole number, the hundreds digit together with the tens digit and the ones digit can be referred to as 零头, as can the tens digit together with the ones digit. Of course, the ones digit can also be referred to as 零头 on its own. In this case, according to the final price, 零头 must mean the hundreds digit. (The translator's note.)

28 For the sake of brevity, in repeating the formulaic utterances, we leave out the Chinese pinyin.

29 Butian Song is an ancient Chinese song of the astrological systems. Jia Zi Table refers to the Chinese 60-year calendar cycle, which is also named the Sexagenary Cycle. The Year of Jia Zi is the beginning of the Sexagenary Cycle. (The translator's note.)

30 For the sake of brevity, in repeating the formulaic utterances, we leave out the Chinese pinyin.

31 The part right between the two eyebrows.

4 Language betraying human beings

The paradox of "language being mankind's last homestead"

To cast light on the basic state of human existence, we put forward the proposition that "language is the last homestead of human beings". Hopefully, we have successfully elaborated on the three key points: 1) Mankind lives in language (most human behaviors are parasitic on verbal behaviors; human beings live in discourse fields); 2) mankind has to live in language (language itself is a kind of life activity; language is the last fingerprint and bequest of an ethnic group; language is of vital importance to the fall or lasting of a civilization; language shapes thought); and 3) mankind lives in formulaic verbal behavior. We have used quite warm phrases like "the last homestead", "psychological homestead", "the warmest cradle" to describe the positive relation between language and human beings and the dependence of the latter on the former. This chapter, however, does an about-face turn as it talks about how language betrays human beings. Such a seemingly self-contradicting U-turn forms a paradox, but it is a paradox of great importance. A paradox arises when a set of apparently incontrovertible premises leads to unacceptable or contradictory conclusions[1] (Blackbum, 1994, p. 276). The two contradictory statements we have here – that "language is mankind last homestead" and that "language betrays human beings" – can both be asserted (evidenced sufficiently). It is a typical case of paradox indeed.

Nonetheless, being paradoxical is true of the basic state of human existence. Only when we have described, in an open and frank manner, the situations in which language betrays human beings can we approximate the truth of the last homestead of human beings.

When we say "language betrays human beings", we are only applying a rhetorical device, for the truth is: In most cases, *it is not language that betrays human beings, but human beings who betray themselves; and it is not that language is at odds with human beings, but that human beings are at odds with themselves. On the other hand, linguistic signs do have their own limitations.* Whatever the case is, the betrayal manifests itself in linguistic signs.

4.1 Harmful false information

Rather detailed studies on the spread of harmful false information among human beings have been done by Gilsenan (1976), Aitchison (1996), G. Qian (1997/2002), and Campbell (2001).

G. Qian (2002, pp. 183–189) defines false information in speech as untruthful information given and received in verbal communication (both oral and in writing). There are two types of false information. The first is intended to hoodwink and deceive the receiving party, usually known as "lies", which can be referred to as interest-related false information. We call the false information "harmful false information" when the speaker, fully aware that the information is false, deliberately gives it out to the hearer for the purpose of causing adverse consequences for the hearer. On the other hand, we call the false information "beneficial false information" when the speaker deliberately gives it out to yield beneficial or at least harmless results for the hearer. Instances of the latter include telling a lie to keep a fatally ill patient from despair, or using soothingly sweet lies to those who are frustrated. With this understanding, we would not feel astonished at all when coming across Gilsenan's (1976) idea that lying is vital to the existence of social code and indeed makes social life possible or easier. To make social life possible or easier, then, so many people are glad to adopt the pragmatic strategies of irony, joke, teasing, etc., and take delight in doing so. Harmful false information and beneficial false information share one thing in common: The hearer is in the dark about the falsity of the information (G. Qian, 1997/2002). In this case, *the release of harmful false information is one of the instances of language betraying human beings*. On the other hand, to Aitchison (1996), fictitious and non-backed messages or "little white lies" are normal and constitute an ingrained part of everyday life.

The second type of false information is called functional false information (G. Qian, 1997/2002). The speaker knows that the information to be released is false and the hearer can detect the falsity from some clues, but the speaker goes on to deliver it, while the hearer does not care about the falsity, or is not aware of the falsity, or may even be glad to accept the falsity, considering it better than truth. Functional false information is an untruthful message relayed against a certain confirmatory background and leads to special communicative effects (*ibid.*). Viewed from this angle, Campbell's (2001) research on how falsity plays its historical role in human civilization and social progress bears great importance. Considering the role that falsity plays in human civilization, we hold that delivering functional false information should not be viewed as a betrayal of human beings. Case studies in this respect can make a lively part of research in pragmatics. For example, suppose a speaker jeers at a hearer, saying: "You are surely omniscient, Buddy." With just a slight hint (against certain contexts), such as phonetic stress, tone, timbre, sound imitation, sigh, speed, intensity, pause or silence, etc., the hearer who was jeered at would soon decode the true message the speaker intended to convey, which is "You know nothing. Quit your nonsense with me."

Language betraying human beings   265

In *Pragmatics in Chinese Culture*, I pointed out that the criterion for distinguishing functional false information and interest-related false information is whether it is possible for the hearer to detect the true message implicit in the false information he or she receives. The identification of false information is context-based. A given context is composed of non-linguistic media, common sense, logic, convention, principle, the consistency of the participants' behaviors, who they are, the mismatch between the phonetic features of the utterance and its literal sentence meaning, the already-existing relationships between the participants, and so on.

A study of functional false information should focus on who talks falsely to whom, on what occasion, at what time, and how. We use language for communication, and the information a communicator intends to convey is, above all, either true or false. For this reason, the assertion of some pragmaticians that verbal communication follows the maxim of "truthfulness" is in fact a misinterpretation of the actual state of language use. Does verbal communication violate the maxim when an untruthful message is conveyed? The answer is negative. *People cannot do without talking falsely and this is true of life in reality.*

False information is ubiquitous in verbal exchanges. False information features falsity, but it should not be equated with badness. Employment of functional false information is one means of interpersonal communication, and works as a pragmatic strategy, which vitalizes or vivifies verbal exchanges. Without this pragmatic strategy, verbal communication would appear imperfect, incomplete, and unattractive. For special communicative effects, sometimes it may even be better to release false information than to release true information.

4.2 Language distorting the world

The limits of language are talked about in G. Qian (2002, pp. 83–96) along four dimensions. First, *the objective world is reduced when it enters the world of language*. The objective world exists in a synchronic and multi-dimensional mode, but can be linguistically presented only in a diachronic and one-dimensional way. This is the first distortion of the world by language, and the most substantial distortion. However, we can do nothing but "generously forgive" this distortion. Second, *linguistic signs are finite in number and unable to form a one-for-one relationship with the infinite abundance of the world*. Of course, we cannot accuse language of distorting the world on purpose, but feel pity about the limitedness of language or its inadequacy. Signs for representing the world are limited in many aspects. Once again, we must "understand" and excuse language. Third, *language always lags behind reality. Fourth, the world of human feelings and emotions suffers an even greater loss when it enters the world of language.* In short, we must forgive language for its "breach of duty". To forgive language for its breach of duty is to treat ourselves leniently. After all, none of us is able to describe in an exact, thorough,

266 *Language betraying human beings*

and exhaustively detailed manner the taste of preserved bean-curd, the scene of a child acting up in tantrum, or the beauty of a melody, etc.

Naming is one of the most typical occasions where language distorts the world and human beings. About language betraying the original intention of its user, Hegel pointed out in his *Phäenomenologie des Geistes* that *it is the nature of language to subvert truth* (cited in D. Wang, 2002, pp. 112–116). A speaker can tell others what he means only by dint of "concepts" (names), and concepts (names) are always abstract, unable to represent the rich "primarily real" content of what the speaker perceives. However, all of us have to "name" the world we perceive in order to talk about the world as we perceive it, thus letting "naming" distort our world. As to how much the "concepts" enable our listeners to associate with what and how we perceive, it must depend on the game of social interaction (D. Wang, 2002, pp. 112–116). In 2003, Xiaoyan Zhang, son of Jingguo Jiang, late head of the Taiwan administrative authority, proposed direct flights between Taiwan and the mainland of China by charter airplanes on both sides of the Taiwan Strait during the Spring Festival. The then-Taiwan authorities finally decided on a plan by which the planes could fly to the mainland via Hong Kong and Macao. The authority named the flights 间接直航 ([jiànjiē zhíháng] "indirect direct flight"). What is an "indirect direct flight"? Such a naming distorted, beyond doubt, the fact (it was an indirect flight). However, in this instance of distortion, the language form *per se* should not be blamed for being inept, because there are adequate signs available for the situation, such as 非直航 ([fēi zhíháng] "non-direct flight" (to mainland) or 间接飞航 ([jiànjiē fēiháng] "indirect flight"). No one knows for sure how many cases of naming distortions, such as "indirect direct flight", have been produced in the world so far. Likewise, any attempt to define or to name the taste of preserved bean-curd is bound to distort the taste of preserved bean-curd. Such labels as "professor", "PhD candiate supervisor", "market", "superstar", and so on are quite familiar to us, and we rarely feel uneasy in using them. However, once they are put to serious scrutiny, we find that in many cases they are not applied exactly or appropriately to the entities they are attached to. Facts are distorted by language. Some of them are even distorted beyond recognition.

4.3 We have to live in lies and fallacies

Lies are meant to cheat, though good-willed in some cases. Fallacies may be produced by honest speakers, but they are false, mistaken, or unscientific.

It goes without saying that we live in lies and fallacies. But the point is, we have no choice but to live in lies and fallacies. For instance, there are discourses containing certain empty names with no bearer or reference (such as "Santa Claus", "Bodhisattva Guanyin", etc.), which speak about non-existent facts or about the existence of an entity that does not exist at all (once you utter or write down the phrase "gold mountain", you acknowledge that the non-existing thing exists). However, such discourses are not instances of language betraying human beings. Ordinary people seldom ponder over, nor are they bothered by, lies or fallacies. However, lies and fallacies pose vexing entanglement that philosophers cannot dismiss easily. Rather, philosophers enjoy inquiring into them. Parents in Western cultures tell their children, "Santa Claus has a white beard", and Chinese people, especially before 1949, used to say "Bodhisattva Guanyin relieves all creatures of their misery and delivers them from torment." If we say that "Santa Claus" and "Bodhisattva Guanyin", as empty names, are meaningless, then we simply cannot make sense of the utterances "Santa Claus has a white beard" and "Bodhisattva Guanyin relieves all creatures of their misery and delivers them from torment." However, it is true that "Santa Claus" and "Bodhisattva Guanyin" are proper names with no bearer or reference, but they are meaningful and we understand these utterances with no difficulty. For this reason, the referential theory developed by Western philosopher John Stuart Mill appears to be rather simplistic in claiming that every name must have a corresponding reference, or that a reference fixes the meaning of a name. Further, Mill's referential theory is unable to justify negative existential statements, such as "Santa Claus does not exist" or "Bodhisattva Guanyin does not exist." If we are necessarily committed to the existence of Santa Claus and Bodhisattva Guanyin, so long as we use (utter or write down) the names of "Santa Claus" and "Bodhisattva Guanyin", then isn't it self-contradictory that we deny at once their existence (as in the above negative existential statements)? How can one negate the existence of the very things that one uses words to name at the same time? Ideally, a theory of meaning and reference should be able to explain how it is possible to *speak about the non-existent things meaningfully* and how we can *meaningfully talk about the entity whose existence we are obliged to be committed to*. What we need is a referential theory that allows assertive sentences, e.g., "Polar bears are white", to be meaningful and true, but also permits such sentences as "Unicorns are black" or "The Monkey King (one of the leading character in the Chinese classic *Journey to the West*) covers a distance of one hundred and eighty thousand miles by a single somersault" to be meaningful, though false, without committing us to the existence of unicorns and the Monkey King. We refer to this issue for inquiry as "the problem of existence" with referential theories. The problem of existence was later resolved successfully by Frege (1892/1999), according to whom different names refer to the same object, that is, have the same reference, but have different senses. For example, in Chinese, 马铃薯 ([mǎlíngshǔ] "potato"), 土豆 ([tǔdòu] "potato"), and 洋芋 ([yángyù] "potato") have the same reference, potato, but each of the names has a different sense. The literal sense of 马铃薯is "potato in the shape of a 马铃([mǎlíng] 'horse bell')"; the literal sense of 土豆 is "a soya-like bean that grows in the soil"; and the literal sense of 洋芋 is "a yam introduced from foreign lands". By distinguishing sense and reference, the problem of empty names, such as "Santa Claus", "Bodhisattva Guanyin", "unicorn", and so on, can be resolved theoretically. The use of an empty name is meaningful because the name has a sense (believers of

268 *Language betraying human beings*

Buddhism can talk about the sense of "Bodhisattva Guanyin" or those who tell unicorn stories can tell the sense of "unicorn"), but does not have a reference. Once sense and reference are separated, all these empty names become justifiable, since it is not compulsory that every name be connected with a reference. The rational, emotional, and esthetical life of human beings is in need of a large number of empty names that have a sense but do not refer to any entity in the world. According to Frege's theory of sense and reference, a negative existential statement does not necessarily commit us to the existence of a thing whose very existence is denied by the statement. On the one hand, you do not need to accept that there exists Santa Claus or Bodhisattva Guanyin whose existence you deny (if you take it seriously and say that there is no Santa Claus or Bodhisattva Guanyin in the world). On the other hand, you can go on talking about them, because even if they do not exist (with no reference), they have a sense, are cognitively meaningful, and can be used in different statements (Baghramian, 1999, pp. xxxviii–xxxix).

To talk about things that do not exist in the world, we are in serious need of these "lies". Hamlet and the castle he stayed in, Ah-Q and the small town he lived in, Baoyu Jia, Daiyu Lin and Jia's Mansions they resided in – none of these persons or places ever existed, but these individuals and the non-existent castle, small town, and Jia's Mansions are much talked about and appreciated by us. They are the esthetic objects. Aitchison (1996, p. 23) even holds that the skill of lying is the "ultimate goal of language learning", as *it involves displacement (reference to absent or non-existent events), which is an "important characteristic of language"* (emphasis added). We have invented entities such as Hamlet and the castle he stayed in, Ah-Q and the small town he lived in, Baoyu Jia, Daiyu Lin and Jia's Mansions they resided in, etc., to bring to life certain kinds of people or places so that we can get to know, understand, and appreciate them.

What we shall talk about next are benignant and (especially) malignant lies, motivated respectively either by a good will or (especially) an evil will that hatches a sinister plot from the start.

We live not only in sayings and aphorisms (Cf. 3.1.2) but also in lies. Commenting on Campbell's *The Liar's Tale: A History of Falsehood*, D. Wang (2002, pp. 115–116) says,

> Flattery is nearly all lies. Eighty-five percent of the speeches of a civilized people is composed probably of lies, or constructed for the purpose of lying ... In the speech of a civilized people, lying is sincere hypocrisy, polite rudeness, and enthusiastic callousness. We need speech of this nature just because of our "civilization", for such speech is as "useful" to civilization as the "*yin-yang* candle atlas" is to shareholders.

Power, in all forms, reshapes in a subtle way the meaning of our language, through which the world we understand is reshaped. We simply cannot count clearly how many lies are being churned out in this world every day. For

Language betraying human beings 269

example, the insanity of shareholders is instigated by the lies by which the liar pumps up the stock market. The ecstasy of fraudsters and the misery of the cheated are but the continuation of some prior deceptive speech. During the 1950s, we lived in the fable of "the arrival of communism" and in the 1960s and later we lived in the admonition that "class struggle has been and will always be existing". On those occasions, not everyone was there to cheat on purpose, but those who taught us made some mistakes. Things like this happen throughout the world. Those statements are more fallacies than lies. Great figures may utter both fallacies and truths. The same is true with ordinary people. During "the Great Proletarian Cultural Revolution", carried out from 1966 to 1976 in China, some people were told that their actions were "in defense of the correct political line" or "in defense of the triumphant fruit of the Great Proletarian Cultural Revolution", when they were cruelly persecuting their own good friends. Meanwhile, many of those who died in the armed fights believed at the last moment of their lives that they sacrificed themselves "in defense of the correct political line" or "in defense of the triumphant fruit of the Great Proletarian Cultural Revolution". Quite a lot of people criticized and denounced, without feeling guilty, their former good comrades on a trumped-up charge, and this was said by the then-prevalent slogans to be "eradicating what is bourgeois and cultivating what is proletarian", "combating selfishness and repudiating revisionism", and "wiping out the last exploiting class in human history". Meanwhile, those who were criticized and denounced would be warning themselves repeatedly, after being wrongly criticized and denounced, that they should not resist the violent actions of the revolutionary masses. Instead, they should convince themselves that those were the actions of "eradicating what is bourgeois and cultivating what is proletarian", "combating selfishness and repudiating revisionism", and "wiping out the last exploiting class in human history" and that they were to have a new life after the pain and suffering, a process of rising like a phoenix from the ashes. Many individuals felt deeply proud of their behaviors of beating, smashing, looting, and destroying the treasures of traditional Chinese culture, and the editorials of newspapers appraised their behaviors as "revolutionary actions" of "attacking on the Four Olds: Old thoughts, old culture, old habits, and old customs, and building the Four News: New thoughts, new culture, new habits, and new customs". Aren't these the instances of living in lies or fallacies? In addition, lies often go together with hegemony, invasion, and plunder in international relationships. Take, for example, the Iraq war in 2003. The American administration used so-called "solid evidence" as an excuse for its aggressive actions, and claimed that taking military actions in Iraq was simply to "free its people". Likewise, in World War II, fascists led by Hitler fabricated packs of lies every day.

Fallacies violate the conversational "maxim of quality" (Grice, 1957), but are not necessarily intended to cheat. In the realm of scientific studies, there is a proliferation of fallacies. However, scientific conjectures or predictions are not fallacies, because they are announced publicly for future falsification.

270 *Language betraying human beings*

Things may even go as far as to the extreme: When a whole society is willing to believe lies and fallacies, those who tell truth are doomed to be forsaken. History has witnessed this in different cultures.

In the world as it is, myths, literature, religion (not including evil cults), and white lies will continue to entertain, please, and fascinate people, and lies and fallacies may as well continue to hoodwink and harm people. The latter is the cost we have to pay for life. In the face of lies and fallacies, no individual can always be entertained, pleased, and fascinated, praying not to be hoodwinked or harmed. That is just a wishful request, which life will not grant us. Heaven simply ignores such an undue request, and it is wise for us to be ready to live with both kinds of consequences of lies.

But the probability of being harmed by lies and fallacies is higher in a country where philosophical thoughts do not sell well (philosophers can pride on themselves only in their studies without their ideas being known by the general public and graduates with a degree in philosophy can hardly make a living by doing philosophy) and the way of thinking is ossified. Russell (1945, p. xxiii) makes this point clear when he makes the following statement.

> Every community is exposed to two opposite dangers: ossification through too much discipline and reverence for tradition, on the one hand; on the other hand, dissolution, or subjection to foreign conquest, through the growth of an individualism and personal independence that makes cooperation impossible.

Throughout history, Chinese people have more than once been hoodwinked by lies and fallacies because of ideological ossification. The Confucianist tradition of thinking, keen on "state-running craft and practical application", does not encourage an abstract and analytical way of thinking and much less does it encourage, or it even fears, independent and initiative thoughts on the part of the whole nation. That has provided a thick and solid hotbed for breeding and unchecked spreading of lies and fallacies. Russell (*ibid.*) makes a profound point when he continues to say,

> In general, important civilizations start with a rigid and superstitious system, gradually relaxed, and leading, at a certain stage, to a period of brilliant genius, while the good of the old tradition remains and the evil inherent in its dissolution has not yet developed. But as the evil unfolds, it leads to anarchy, thence, inevitably, to a new tyranny, producing a new synthesis secured by a new system of dogma.

When lies and fallacies ooze out like a trickle, they trap only a few persons; but once they collude with political power to form a huge tide, the whole nation may not be able to ward it off and is destined to be thrown into endless chaos and various disasters, such as a collapse of the national economy, moral bankruptcy, and the proliferation of anarchism, etc. Though "a new

Language betraying human beings   271

synthesis" can be produced, a long-lasting unendurable trauma is, after all, unfortunate for a nation.

A study by Lippard (1988) shows that deception is a normal part of interpersonal communication rather than a form of social or moral deviance, since deception can be used for being polite, attracting attention from others, or requesting others to do things. According to Goffman (1969), cheating, whether concealment or omission, plays an important role in avoiding hurting others, maintaining face and self-image, and alleviating awkwardness. It is thus a realistic means of building and keeping the favorable position the speaker is in.

4.4 "Philosophical problems arise when language goes on holiday"

Now let us focus on the language problems in the eyes of philosophers. Not all philosophers blame language for various problems, but some of them do, especially those after the "linguistic turn" in Western philosophy that began around the end of the nineteenth century, i.e., those of the ideal language school. To them, the ordinary language is problematic in many ways, which is the cause of the conundrums in philosophy.

In the very beginning of her book *Modern Philosophy of Language*, Baghramian (1999, p. xxix) lists 14 questions that philosophers of language ask and attempt to answer. The eighth one is: "Does language distort reality or does it enable us to give accurate accounts of what there is?" This question postulates that language might have gone wrong in fulfilling philosophical tasks, running into the trouble of "distorting reality". Baghramian then makes the following observation.

> Frege and Russell revolutionized logic by inventing new ways of representing the logical form of language in formal notations. These innovations led to the hope that logically perfect or ideal languages could be constructed, *free of the ambiguities of ordinary languages, able to express scientific truths clearly and precisely.*
>
> (1999, p. xxxi; emphasis added)

Why should Frege and Russell invent a "logically perfect or ideal language"? For they believed that ordinary languages are defective: full of ambiguities, unclear, and imprecise. Baghramian continues to point out:

> A common feature of early analytic philosophy of language was a mistrust of ordinary languages. Frege, for instance, had argued that "someone who wants to learn logic from language is like an adult who wants to learn how to think from a child. When men created language, they were at a stage of childish pictorial thinking. *Languages are not made to logic's ruler*." ... One of the many problems with ordinary languages, according to Frege, is that *they are vague and contain predicates whose boundaries*

272 *Language betraying human beings*

are not clearly drawn (e.g., is tall, is bald), and hence fail to refer. Frege hoped that, eventually, a perfect or ideal language would be devised, with the help of his logical notation, which would be capable of expressing thoughts in an accurate way.

(*Ibid.*, p. xxxii; emphasis added)

To put it in another way, for Frege, language is intractable to the discipline of logic, and ordinary languages are unable to express thoughts with clarity and exactness. Philosophy is a propositional activity, and propositions are in turn brought forward by language. Consequently, *a language that does not obey logic's discipline would certainly cause difficulties in the propositional enterprise.* Russell agrees with Frege, as Baghramian (*ibid.*) points out in the following remarks.

Russell, in a similar vein, *dismissed the relevance of ordinary languages to the correct logical and scientific understanding of thought and the world.* According to him, ordinary languages such as English can *give rise to erroneous metaphysical beliefs and encourage a false view of the world,* by giving "metaphysical importance to the accidents of our own speech".

(Emphasis added)

To Russell, the problem appears to be even more serious. Not only is language incapable of a "correct logical and scientific understanding of thought and the world", but also it "gives rise to erroneous metaphysical beliefs and encourages a false view of the world". Of course, ordinary people in their use of ordinary languages will not give this issue much thought. Language just gives philosophy a hard time in the eyes of some Western philosophers. According to Baghramian (*ibid.*), "Russell was interested in analyzing components of ordinary languages only to unmask the true *logical form of language expressions that had been distorted by their misleading grammatical form*" (emphasis added).

It would be interesting for us to take a look at Russell's analysis in some details (Russell, 1956). He started with the following sentence.

The present king of France is bald.

(Emphasis added)

This sentence is an assertion, which, apparently, has to be either true or false. Then is it true or false? According to Russell, a correct analysis of this sentence should go in this way.

1) There is at least one king of France.
2) There is at most one king of France.
3) That man (the king of France) is bald.

Language betraying human beings 273

In light of this analysis, the correct answer to the above question is: It is false. Because condition (1) is not satisfied – there is no present king of France – with France being a republic, "there is at least one king of France" does not hold. Since the first condition is nullified, why bother talking about the other two? The king does not exist, and speaking of his baldness is out of the question. Russell continues to say that his description theory shows that the grammatical form of a sentence may mislead us, because the logical form of the proposition the sentence expresses is hidden by its surface grammar. He solves this problem with his description theory. However, we are not to go on discussing his theory. What interests us is the question: Why is the grammatical form of a sentence possibly misleading? A proposition such as "The present king of France is bald" commits you to the existence of an entity (the present king of France) that you deny, whether you assert that the proposition is true or that it is false. How does the grammatical form of a sentence "mislead" people? In Russell's view, that is because the logical form of the proposition the sentence expresses is hidden by its surface grammatical form. What philosophers must do then is to make explicit the hidden logical form, as Russell did in the above analysis in three steps.

What Russell endeavored to do could explain why philosophers of the ideal language school were deeply indulged in creating a system of formal logic notation. The logical form of a language expression can be distorted by its surface grammar. That was, of course, the viewpoint of some Western philosophers, which underwent tit-for-tat refutations from the philosophers of the ordinary language school that was formed later on (after the 1930s).

When recollecting what analytic philosophy was and how it arose, Martinich points out,

> What had already begun to take the place of logical positivism in the 1940s was ordinary-language philosophy, one strand of which emanated from Cambridge in the later philosophy of Wittgenstein, the other from Oxford. One of Wittgenstein's motivating beliefs was that philosophy creates its own problems and that means that they are not genuine problems at all. *The confusion arises from philosophers' misuse of ordinary words.* They take words out of their ordinary context, the only context in which they have meaning, use them philosophically, and thereby discover anomalies with the displaced concepts expressed by these words: "For philosophical problems arise when language goes on holiday".
>
> (Martinich and Sosa, 2001, pp. 2–3; emphasis added)

Martinich correctly points out that philosophical confusions arise because philosophers misuse ordinary words. However, he claimed at the same time that *philosophical problems occur when language is not doing its duty.* But what we want to stress is that *it was not the various problems of language that turned Western philosophy to language study and that the linguistic turn in Western*

274　*Language betraying human beings*

philosophy happened for some other reasons. From a general perspective, the reason why Western philosophy came to its linguistic turn (a turn of philosophical study and not one of language study itself) is that the study on the understanding of language is an inquiry into the relationship between speakers, their thoughts, and the world. Obviously, language itself is not what interests them. Just as Baghramian (1999, p. xxviii) states, "Philosophy of language is an attempt to understand the nature of language and its relationship with speakers, their thoughts, and the world." Western philosophy is marked by its preference to delving into the issue of "existence", which has been going on for over two thousand years (the age-old problem). The typical question is: "What is this?" (What is that? What exists here?, i.e., What is there?). When philosophers realize that language is related to the other three and that to study language is a direct way to study speakers' thoughts and the world, they grasp language rightfully. To grasp language is to hold the key to speakers' thoughts and to the world. This "world" is the "existence" that rivets their attention. This explains why phrases like "the relationship between language and the world" and "the connection between language and the world" appear in high frequency in the literature of the Western philosophy of language. "Philosophers of language are also concerned with questions about the relationship between language and the world" (Baghramian, 1999, p. xxviii). That means that *they are concerned with language, not in the same way as linguists are for finding the rules and patterns of language per se, but for observing the world in the perspective of language in order to uncover the laws of the world.* Please note that in the eyes of Western philosophers, the words of "world", "reality", "Being", "existence", and "entity" are very close in meaning and are highly frequently used. Baghramian makes clearer the cause of the linguistic turn in philosophy (please note the use of "entity" and "reality") when she says,

> They [philosophers of langauge] also believed that reality cannot be studied directly without also studying the main medium for thinking about it and describing it, i.e., language. Their concern was with language as an abstract entity that expresses thought and whose structure, if analyzed correctly, can reveal the structure of reality and they had no, or very little, interest in the actual use of language in its social context.
>
> (*Ibid.*, p. xxxi)

Language is the main medium for thinking about and describing reality. Do you attempt to study reality? Then you cannot start directly from reality (entity) (at the ontology stage, the inquiry did begin directly from reality but was nowhere near any solution. If the answers to questions about reality or entity could be found directly in reality or entity, why should there have been the epistemological turn and the linguistic turn?), nor can you bypass language and study reality directly (analytic philosophers or philosophers of language think this way). Things such as gold, wood, water, earth, and so on are entities

Language betraying human beings 275

and so is language, an abstract entity for expressing thoughts. If language structure is correctly analyzed, then the structure of reality can be laid bare. To rephrase this idea in a compact way, *"language structure reveals the structure of reality"*. All right, the structure of reality, i.e., the structure of Being, is exactly what Western philosophers seek. For this reason, the ninth question listed by Baghramian (1999, p. xxix) is of far-reaching importance, "Are the truth and falsehood of our statements determined by the world or by our linguistic conventions?" From the point of view of materialist philosophers, the truth or falsity of a statement is of course determined by the material world; "Man's social being determines his consciousness", and how can this be questioned? However, as the twentieth-century analytic philosophy of language holds it, what a statement talks about is indeed the world, but it is human beings that make the statement, presented by the propositional activity. Moreover, in the eyes of Western philosophers of language, language structure can illustrate the structure of reality, i.e., the structure of the world. Consequently, the truth or falsity of a statement is of course determined by language conventions.

Thus far, we see clearly that it was not the various problems of language that turned Western philosophy to language analysis. The linguistic turn in Western philosophy happened due to this motivation; to grasp language is to hold the key to speakers' thoughts and especially to the world. Because language structure reveals the structure of reality, philosophers set out to resolve age-old philosophical problems by means of language analysis. Baghramian (1999, p. xxxi) makes a revealing point about what analytic philosophy is and why philosophers turn to language analysis when she says, "Analysis of language would reveal hidden logical structures and, in the process, help us solve age-old philosophical problems, hence the term 'analytic philosophy'." *Language is not cast aside for having various problems; on the contrary*, Western philosophers place their great hope on language, which gave rise to the trend of analytic philosophy or the philosophy of language between the end of the nineteenth century and the 1970s.

The philosophy of language has developed from (the ideal language school's) mistrust of language for undertaking philosophical tasks to the (ordinary language school's) concentration on natural-language analysis. That is because the improper use of language does result in the obscurity of concepts and, therefore, philosophical arguments have to start from the clarification of language meaning. A well-known saying by Wittgenstein (1958, §109) hits the nail on the head: "Philosophy is a battle against the bewitchment of our intelligence by means of language."

When language does not allow human beings to enter its "homestead", philosophers become busy. This particular period of history of Western philosophy, i.e., the period of analytic philosophy or the philosophy of language, witnessed how busy philosophers were. There has been a rich literature, including many classic works, on the philosophy of language, and especially in recent years there have been quite a few publications in China on the linguistic

276 *Language betraying human beings*

turn, to which interested readers have easy access. We thus leave this topic aside here.

Note

1 According to this definition, it appears improper to understand "paradox" as "error" or "absurdity", as some authors did. Though the thesis and its contradictory antithesis are mutually exclusive, both are nevertheless arguable – for example, the thesis "The world has a beginning in time and is limited in space" and its antithesis "The world has neither a beginning in time nor is it limited in space."

5 Choosing not to speak

It has been argued throughout the whole book that language is the last home-stead of human beings, for mankind lives in language, mankind has to live in language, and mankind lives in formulaic verbal behavior. Why, then, do we make an abrupt turn to discuss the case in which human beings choose not to speak?

Choosing what to say and choosing what not to say are two alternatives always standing side by side. When people choose what to say, they simultaneously make the choice of what not to say.

Speaking is the most important part of human basic behaviors. *Deprived of the ability to speak, mankind, as a whole, would not be able to exist or develop effectively.*

In order to live and develop effectively, individuals often have to decide whether to speak or not before speaking becomes a *de facto* behavior. Once they make the decision to speak, there are two possibilities for them to face (or there are two issues for them to deal with). On the one hand, they have to further decide: 1) What to say and what not to say because not all things need to be spoken out; and 2) what can be said and what cannot be said because not all things can be said given various contextual factors. On the other hand, after he decides to speak, he may find himself somehow unable to speak.

In the first case, the decision about what to say and what not to say is basically a matter of pragmatic strategies, while the decision about what can be said and what cannot be said has something to do with the social humanistic network, as described in G. Qian (1997/2002, p. 285).

> In short, the social humanistic network interferes with our discourse. It is mere wishful thinking that we can say whatever we want to say. We cannot say whatever we want to say, nor can we speak however, wherever, or whenever we want to. Still, we have to make the decision about what to say according to whom we are talking with. In speaking, we have to take into consideration this or that factor so that our original intention may keep changing. We are, literally, slaves to the linguistic context. Moreover, we are subject to the non-linguistic context. We are just like birds, seemingly free, caged in a vast net, which is composed of various

278 *Choosing not to speak*

social relations, cultural traditions, moral standards, codes of conduct, physical environments, and natural forces. This vast net is nothing but the social humanistic network ... *which "speaks" and "has the final say" whenever we speak.*

(Emphasis original.)

About what cannot be said, can we have a specific list? Any attempt to give such a list will be in vain. There is no such a list at all, and no one can give one. It is impossible to find a solution to this problem even if you grill life or history.

There are cases where one decides to speak but finds himself somehow unable to speak. Under what circumstances will this happen? For instance, when we recommend a piece of music or a book to others, we, more often than not, hear ourselves saying something like "I cannot tell why, but I just think that the book is so great and you must read it", or "I really can't tell you why for this moment, but I just feel the music is so wonderful...". This is actually what Zhuangzi says, "Once you get the fish, you forget the net. ... Once you get the meaning, you forget the words". Suppose someone is impressed by a novel, say, *A Dream of Red Mansions*, it can be said that he has got its general meaning. What he remembers is its main content, not all its words or sentences. He might remember some individual sentences, but would not be able to recite all the sentences in the whole book. Just as the famous poet Yuanming Tao wrote, "I get some true vision from it, but I am at a loss for words when I try to tell". At a loss for words, one is unable to speak. What the reader faces is a book itself, and what the listener faces is a piece of music itself, and in both cases, they "face the things themselves" (*Zu den Sachen selbst*[1]). Furthermore, even if the one who recommends the book has grasped its general "meaning", he will have to undergo a process of careful thinking and straighten up his ideas before he is able to say the "meaning" clearly and completely. Therefore, he tends to begin with something like "For this moment, I just can't tell...".

Nonetheless, before speaking becomes a *de facto* behavior, one may choose not to speak. This is the major concern of this chapter: Why may an individual choose not to speak?

From the perspective of the speaker, the following may be possible reasons.

1) The speaker feels it unnecessary to say anything because what he wants to say is self-evident to the hearer.
2) The speaker is unable to say it (for lack of knowledge, facts, or appropriate conditions) even if he wants to.
3) The speaker is unwilling to say it.
4) The speaker cannot say it because there may be negative consequences if he says it.

Moreover, the reasons might be approached from the perspective of cultural-social interaction.

First, choosing not to speak is a matter of pragmatic strategy, but this by no means tells the whole story.

Second, choosing not to speak is a matter of wisdom. Therefore, it has something to do with the speaker's subjectivity, but has more to do with the social culture he lives in. Sometimes, not to speak is a wiser, safer, and more efficient choice than to speak. A case in point is Xiaoping Deng's request in the 1990s to suspend the disputes in government-directed newspapers and magazines over whether socialism is better than capitalism. In fact, Deng was an expert in "choosing not to speak". In February 1973, after Deng's return to Beijing from exile in Jiangxi Province, Chairman Mao asked him at their first meeting, "What have you been doing in Jiangxi these years?" Deng replied, "Waiting". It was perhaps the best and wisest answer given the political environment at the time. Under the historical conditions of his time, was it appropriate for him to carp at the Cultural Revolution, or question the legitimacy of cracking down on a large number of people like him, or request that someone redress the wrongdoings? Under such a circumstance, saying just one word, "Waiting", amounts to saying nothing. It can be interpreted as "I have been waiting for a decision from you", which was a matter of fact and would cause no unwanted consequences. In another case, when Maomao, Deng's daughter, planned to write a book (i.e., *My Father, Deng Xiaoping*, published later) after his retirement, she asked him, "What did you do during the Long March?" He replied, "Just followed the lead".[2] It is hard to tell whether this is humor, wit, modesty, or his practical style of doing things.

In our daily lives, this kind of wisdom finds expression in many good-will warnings and criticisms as well as self-protecting and positive comments, like "Better not to speak than to confuse", "Don't inquire about what you are not supposed to know", "I said nothing", "Pretty women are silly while smart women talk too much", and "He looks dull but is actually quick in mind".

Third, choosing not to speak can have something to do with the special culture of a particular profession or institution. A typical example is the ancient Chinese Chan masters' advocacy for silence (G. Qian, 1997/2002, pp. 265–276), which is a special profound form of culture and has been recorded in various koans (*gong'an*, in Chinese). Silence in speaking and speaking in silence are both embodiments of this culture. According to Chan masters, silence can be interpreted in myriads of ways, while any saying can only be interpreted in a definite way. This is the prevailing philosophy of Chan Buddhism, because Chan is open to various interpretations only when definiteness is suspended. Given that the subject matter of the present book is verbal behavior and "choosing not to speak" is only an exception to verbal practices, it suffices to illustrate the Chan Buddhist philosophy of silence with just one example. As Ouyang (2001, p. 38) argues, among all Mahayana sutras, the doctrine of nonduality finds best expression in "The Dharma-Door of Nonduality" of *The Teaching of Vimalakirti*. There, to the question of how bodhisattvas enter the Dharma-Door of Nonduality raised by the Licchavi Vimalakirti, thirty-one bodhisattvas gave their answers from different perspectives, and finally

280 *Choosing not to speak*

the Bodhisattva Manjusri summarized, "To know no teaching, to express nothing, to say nothing, to explain nothing, to announce nothing, to indicate nothing, and to designate nothing, that is the entrance into nonduality". Then, Manjusri turned to Vimalakirti for an explanation; the latter kept his silence, whereupon Manjusri applauded, "Excellent! Excellent! This is indeed the entrance into the nonduality of the bodhisattvas, without using any words" (cited in Ouyang, 2001, p. 38). Silence itself was the right answer. Generally speaking, the principle of nonduality advocates remaining neutral instead of going to extremes. This is exactly what Huineng, the sixth patriarch of Chan Buddhism, taught his disciples, as documented in *Platform Sutra* (*tanjing*, in Chinese), "Whenever a man puts a question to you, answer him in antonyms, so that a 'pair of opposites' will be formed. For example, 'coming' and 'going' are the reciprocal cause of each other; when the interdependence of the two is entirely done away with, there would be, in the absolute sense, neither 'coming' nor 'going'" (*ibid.*, pp. 39–40). Silence is in complete conformity with the doctrine of nonduality.

Fourth, choosing not to speak is also an old topic in philosophy. The wisdom of choosing not to speak is well articulated in the early Wittgenstein's philosophy, more specifically by the last statement of his *Tractatus Logico-Philosophicus*, "Whereof one cannot speak, thereof one must be silent" (1922/1983, p. 189). In earlier parts of the said book, he argues, "There is indeed the inexpressible. This *shows* itself; it is the mystical" (*ibid.*, p. 187; emphasis original) and "What *can* be shown *cannot* be said" (*ibid.*, p. 79; emphasis original).

To be more exact, Wittgenstein believes that the logic form cannot be said. In order for a proposition to depict a state of affairs, it must share a logical form with that state of affairs, but the logical form itself does not depict the state of affairs. The inexpressibility of the logical form results from his dichotomy between saying and showing ("What *can* be shown *cannot* be said"). Second, science depicts the world while philosophy does not. Philosophy does not provide a picture of reality, and neither can it confirm nor refute scientific findings (Wittgenstein, 1922/1983, p. 75, 4.111). If philosophy does not depict the world, what does philosophy do? In a letter to Russell, Wittgenstein called the boundary between the expressible and the inexpressible "the fundamental issue of philosophy" (cited in J. Chen, 2003, p. 150) To sum up, the task of philosophy is to clear the ground for speaking meaningful propositions. In a third place, "It is clear that ethics cannot be expressed. Ethics is transcendental. (Ethics and aesthetics are one.)" (Wittgenstein, 1922/1983, p. 183). Finally, Wittgenstein argues that everything in the mystical is inevitable, and language can only tell the accidental facts. However, he sometimes argues that language can only tell what is isomorphic to language and what can be analyzed, while everything in the mystical including metaphysical entities cannot be analyzed. In brief, Wittgenstein's argument goes roughly as follows.

1) To some extent, there *exist* metaphysical entities.
2) These "things" cannot exist in the real world.
3) We can only talk about the real world.

Choosing not to speak 281

In the mystical region, there is one thing special, that is, the existence of the world. We can comprehend how the world exists, but can hardly explain why some objects exist while other objects do not exist in the world. In addition, since the central subject matter of *Tractatus* is that propositions depict the states of affairs, anything that does not depict the states of affairs cannot be said. This suggests that the limits of facts are the limits of what language can express, or put differently, what is beyond the boundary of facts cannot be said, including the boundary itself. So, I (the subject) and language, etc. are all deemed by Wittgenstein as the limits of the expressible.

The research object of Western philosophy is the universe or the world, while Chinese philosophy focuses more on society and life. As an important by-product, philosophical research makes us become clearer in both thinking and speaking. Heidegger reminds us to face language, because "Only where the word for the thing has been found is the thing a thing" (1982, p. 62). He adds, "The word alone gives Being to the thing; ... if the word ... had not spoken, then there would be no sputnik" (*ibid.*). This, I think, is a case in which the thing exists but is not yet present because words are absent. Simply speaking, *the existence of a thing does not necessarily entail its presence.* On the contrary, only if proper words are found to express the thing can it be a thing. Then, we can say that *a thing not only exists but also is present.* The usage of "present" and "presence" as they are used here, of course, is not my own coinage, but is derived from Heidegger's use in "the presence of Being" and "the presence of the two-fold" (1982, pp. 26–27). Here is my interpretation of the Wittgensteinian mystical inexpressibility: Making human beings become clearer in both thinking and speaking is not the purpose but the benefit of philosophy. What is inexpressible in philosophy has little to do with philosophy, but has much to do with language barriers. It is for this reason that this chapter is not entitled "Ineffability" or "Inexpressiblity" but "Choosing not to speak", which helps to lift the mystical veil of the inexpressible. In the same vein, as I see it, the Wittgensteinian mystical inexpressibility is not a matter of "choosing not to speak", but a result of language barriers. When words are found by trial and error that can express a thing, the thing will come not only into existence but also into presence, and of course can be spoken about.

Notes

1 This is Husserl's slogan in his criticism of traditional logical speculations, which, as Yi Jiang argues, represents "the fundamental spirit of Husserlian phenomenology" (cited in Su, 2004, p. 56).
2 I came across these two anecdotes about Deng in several different sources, one of which is an issue of *Old Pictures* published in November 2003.

Postscript
Picking the grapes within my reach

The period from the publication of my first journal article, "The Tolerance of Redundant Information of Language", in 1986 to the publication of the four monographs, *Aesthetic Linguistics* (1993), *Pragmatics in Chinese Culture* (1997), *The Theory of Language Holography* (2003), and this book, *Language: The Last Homestead of Human Beings* (2005), has lasted for eighteen years or so. But the time I first gained access to the literature of linguistics started earlier, approximately in 1982, i.e., three to four years before 1986. In other words, I have studied linguistics for about twenty-two years. As a researcher of linguistics, my work, I have to admit, has been a process with Heaven's help and self-help as well. A scholar is similar to a pilgrim in that both of them are and have to be pious enough, but they are meanwhile different from each other in that a pilgrim had a sacred place as his destination before he started on the journey, while a scholar has to search again and again on the way before he finally comes to and identifies an object of research.

Therefore, in what follows, my narration and reminiscences cannot be a real "paradigm example" in any sense but just one of the many possible ways for a scholar of foreign languages in China.

My education and development can be summarized as a process in which I have developed a gradual access to linguistics, an unconscious but reasonable process developing from a wide interest or involvement in a special field of study (i.e., linguistics of foreign languages). Looking back on this process, I find that the profession that one has chosen for his life is determined by such factors as a running-in combination of his own quality and the requirements the society makes for him, a relation between contingency and necessity, and a match between his input and output. If we say that this process has been determined by some Heavenly will, then one's own quality/cultivation and the needs of the society, contingency and necessity, and the way his input and output work can be a kind of Heavenly will.

I was born in 1939 in a water-bound area in the Jianghan Plain of Hubei Province: Shahu Town of Xiantao City (also known as Mianyang County in the old days). As a network of lakes and rivers connecting each other in various ways, Shahu, my hometown, was a land of mystery because of its

Postscript 283

wilderness and an abundant place because of its ecological diversity. My father was a businessman, but he was not a true man of business. He was not a successful merchant, but he liked reading and developed a long-lasting interest in all kinds of books. His familiarity with poetry of the Tang Dynasty and *ci* of the Song Dynasty, and novels like *Romance of the Three Kingdoms* and *Outlaws of the Marsh*, benefited me a lot when I was a child. More fortunately, the people of my hometown were enthusiastically engaged in all kinds of cultural activities all year round: Drama shows, delicate and enormous performances of all kinds, and splendid street performances accompanied me through my intoxicating childhood. In the heated, deceitful, and fanatic street fights, I was usually commander of one of the sides, which helped me acquire the rules of life games. Indeed, the five major elements of childhood, eating, drinking, playing, recreating, and sleeping, were all completed in such an atmosphere. Needless to say, every cultural activity has become the origin of my aspiration. In my monographs or even purely deductive theoretical works, there have arisen, from time to time and unconsciously, some anecdotes of my life (as have been found by many of my readers), which might be subconscious releases of the only aspirations from my hometown. This is, perhaps, why up till now I have been yearning for my hometown and cherishing the memory of my parents.

I finished my complete primary school in the town (six years for a complete primary school system and four years for an initial primary school system). My record of mathematics was not good enough; at the end of one of the terms, I received a score of only 62 out of 100. But I had a good record in essay-writing; many of my essays were commented on by the teacher as model essays. Once a land reform mobilization meeting was held by the township government and I was urged by my teacher to give a speech on behalf of all the primary school students of my school. Without a prepared script, I finished the speech with success. Up till now my teaching can still attract students perhaps because I was urged to "deliver a speech" in public at the age of six. In my primary school years, I liked the course Chinese, but I liked even more courses such as nature, geography, history, and music. Ever since my fourth grade, the total score of my courses always ranked third, but I never ranked first, because I did not have a good memory. Many of my primary school teachers impressed me greatly, including my teachers of Chinese, Yuqing Wu (whose husband was surnamed Yang, and who was good at teaching students of grade one, speaking mandarin Chinese with a beautiful Beijing accent and telling stories about Niulang and Zhinü), Shouxi Xiao, and Yuangong Yang, teacher of nature Mingru Qi, and music teacher Songyun Yue. The bell for the course of nature was a call of great enjoyment. Mr Qi encouraged all of us to ask questions or speak in class, saying: "A student who cannot ask questions is not a good student". I asked then: "Why does a small piece of tile fall to the ground of a river when thrown into it while a large boat[1] does not?" My question was followed by a heated argument after which the teacher came to a summary. What I learned from his classes was quite similar to what Karl

284   *Postscript*

Marx uttered: "I am interested in all human knowledge". Due to the guidance by my primary teachers, readers today can often find in my works knowledge beyond linguistics. Such was my primary school education before 1953.

From 1953 to 1955, I received my junior high-school education in the seat of the county. My school was the Mianyang Middle School, ranking today among the best middle schools in terms of the national university matriculation test results (although it is a wrong idea to assess schools in terms of the examination scores). In this school, I, due to my family's increasing poverty, was often informed that my meals were going to be terminated, but I worked very hard at my lessons. I had an average school record and was not excellent in my grade. I was not tall and did not have stamina. I became horrified as soon as I ascended a height and, therefore, I could not participate in physical education activities. I could produce excellent musical notes but did not have a good voice, so I could not play any role in school music activities. But I kept a very good record in Chinese. Once a little classmate asked: "Hey, you guy, why on earth do you always get scores of 90 or more?" My Chinese essays were often praised and I could expect which essay of mine would be praised. In an unguided composition-writing exercise, I described scenes of desolation in my hometown after floods, and in the comments made by Mr Liu, my teacher of Chinese, there was a sentence which I can still remember now: "The language is like honey". As a young child, I did not know that this was the teacher's encouragement, but understood its literal meaning and thus enjoyed myself alone for a long time. Later, Mr Daxun Zhu came to teach us Chinese, and his mysterious and attractive way of teaching was so fascinating. I decided to become a writer, a dream which lasted for a long time. First, I became the course representative of Chinese, and then of Russian. Our teacher of Russian had an enormous body. During his first class, he wrote three characters, 周斯宁 [Zhou Sining], on the blackboard, and said in his Sichuan Mandarin Chinese and with a little coarse voice: "the 周 of 周恩来 (Zhou Enlai), the 斯 of 斯大林 (Stalin), and the 宁 of 列宁 (Lenin)". Because of him, I started to become fascinated by foreign languages, the starting point for me to be a teacher and scholar of foreign languages. His assistant was a Russian lady (also called a Russian woman by the local people) stranded in my hometown. In her class, we were asked to recite texts until we became extremely hungry. In this case, we learned Russian with a real Russian accent, and later in my college years, and perhaps because of this, I ranked second in the recitation contest of the department. In my class, I was always the one to communicate with Russian teachers on behalf of my class. In Mr Zhou's class, he started by teaching us texts with nothing about theories of pronunciation, but in the second semester he turned back to teach rules of pronunciation with great success. In the first session of one semester, he started by asking me to pronounce the word "ПИСЬМО", and I unexpectedly finished the job correctly. This was not strange because he had helped us develop our sense of pronunciation and because of this we were able to know some rules of pronunciation.

Postscript 285

During my three junior high-school years, I still did not have a good record in mathematics, but I liked physics and other courses more. Once during the comment after the mid-term examination, Mr Luo, when talking about how to increase friction force, commented,

> This item was assigned a full score of five points, and you should have got all the five points because you had offered the two methods introduced in the coursebook, but Guanlian Qian offered one more method: Increasing the friction force of something by increasing its weight, and hence you were given only four of the five points.

Another interesting thing that I have remembered and taken pride in is as follows. In 1954, there was a flood. Led by the local government, we moved to Yanglin Township, Tianmen County. Once my younger brother and I went to buy rice, but on the way back, we, in order to shorten the way, went astray down to a gulf beside the Hanshui River. Without knowing that the place before us was a marsh, we fell more and more deeply in it, and finally became horrified. But then I remembered what I had learned about the inverse proportion of pressure and contact area in physics, i.e., the bigger the contact area becomes, the smaller the pressure is on an area unit. In this case, my younger brother and I started to stretch ourselves and crawled forward so as to reduce our pressure, and finally we moved out of the marsh safely. This experience reminded me that knowledge is not only power but also a necessary guarantee for survival. Ever since then, my longing for knowledge, my thinking about learning, and my eagerness to solve difficult problems have been a great pleasure in my life. And later in 1993, when I wandered along streets in Antwerp (where I had been invited to do a cooperative research project by the International Association of Pragmatics), looking at the proud and self-confident passers-by in suits who worked for enterprises or universities, it occurred to me that people are not equal in this world because high-paying jobs and comfortable offices and working conditions are prepared only for intelligent or better-educated people. This strong yearning for knowledge, learning, and difficulty resulted in my adventurous turn to the Western philosophy of language after I turned fifty-five, as if I believed that "one can live a life of two hundred years and thus can swim three thousand *li*".

From 1955 to 1958, I was educated as a senior high-school student at the Jingzhou Middle School (formerly known as the Jiangling Middle School) of Hubei for three years, a period of happy time for me after my childhood. As an ancient city, Jingzhou was famous for its old walls, battements, and setting sun, all constituting a "poem". No sighing was needed: The setting sun, which was as red as blood, was submerged in the sky of red clouds and became flat, and then at dusk it went down into a sea of clouds, leaving a beautiful exclamation mark. It was greatly fortunate for a boy at an age of becoming strong and knowledgeable to attend a good school, and to come across a good headmaster and some good teachers. And I was such a lucky boy. Feeling

286   *Postscript*

almost no pressure from the national university entrance examination, we were fortunate and lucky enough to escape the examination-oriented education (but were informed by the school at the end of the third year to get prepared for entering universities or becoming workers, as the then-popular slogan said: A red mind, two choices). In this school, we were able plan our studies and develop ourselves on the basis of our interests and aspirations. While developing a balanced knowledge structure, we were also able to spend more time on topics in which we were interested. In fact, we started our "research-based studies" even when we were senior high-school students. Our awareness of "research" started with a lecture delivered by the school dean of students, Mr Fu Yuanyuan, who taught us to think associatively while reading (during the "Anti-Rightist" movement days, he was not brave enough to ask us young students to "do academic study", three taboo words at that time). Later, I found that it was this "associative thinking" that provided me with an alternative way of thinking when I was doing my original thinking. When one is attempting merely to interpret others' ideas, no associative thinking is needed. Only when he attempts to find a new way out does he need to think associatively. Associative thinking results in comprehension, enlightenment, and breakthroughs. In what sense can we say that one has a good comprehension? One who can find the relation between two things in a short period of time can be said to have a good comprehension. A good comprehension, however, has to base itself on a good theoretical knowledge of both China and the West as well as relations of different kinds.

In a writing contest, my essay "Summer Diary" and a poem by one of my school mates "How I Want to Become a White Pigeon" both ranked first. My study of Russian was going smoothly and at the end of the third year, I finished an exercise of academic research in some sense: I came up with a table of the adessive relations of Russian verbs, but did not present it to the teacher. Accidentally, my teacher of Russian was again Mr Sining Zhou (who transferred to Jingzhou Middle School from Mianyang Middle School when I entered Jingzhou Middle School). He placed much emphasis on our spoken-language training. I was a student he often questioned in class, although I could not say that I was his favorite student. Later, during one of my visits to Mr Zhou in the 1990s, he asked frankly: "You did not have a good record in foreign languages in your junior and senior high-school years, but why have you made such great achievements now?" I answered: I dare not say that I have made "great achievements", but in my school years I worked hard at all my lessons and thus had a good record in all my courses, perhaps a quality of my potential ability. Today senior high-school students are working to pass the university entrance examinations, forgetting that their most basic ability is creativity. Indeed, in my senior high-school years, I practiced a research-based method in the study of all my courses. Once Mr Xiong, our teacher of history, found that my notes of history clarified all the clues of history and told the whole class that "Guanlian Qian's method of study is worth summarizing and promoting". In my answer to a question concerning the formation of insect

Postscript 287

protective coloration, I collected some specimens of insects and attached to them a comment that was a little bit research-based. My record in mathematics was, however, in jeopardy: I failed twice in the formative assessment of trigonometry, a purely deductive course. I became nervous and thought: Do I have to take a make-up examination before I graduate? Calming down, I started early and became well prepared before the final examination. I did one math problem after another and when I worked out all the problems, I finally grasped the law of deducing trigonometrical formulas. In the graduation examination, in which even the top students of mathematics in my class did not attain a full score, I earned the full score of 5. Meanwhile, I was also one of the top students in Chinese in my class. Before I finished my senior high-school education, I finished reading almost all the classical Chinese literary works. When we finally came to fill in university application forms, a number of my schoolmates refused to choose liberal arts. When mobilizing the students to choose liberal arts, our class advisor said: "It is not right to think that those who will choose liberal arts do not have a good school record. Guanlian Qian has unexpectedly squeezed into the ten top students in the school". The word "squeeze" he used indicated his unexpectedness and surprise. I know that his judgment was based on the statistics of the school office of teaching affairs; all of the other nine top students had applied for universities of science and engineering. I was able to squeeze into the list because I had a reasonable knowledge structure, which had benefited me all my life. But I had not intended to enter the list, for it was a common belief then that if a student placed his emphasis on the pursuit of a high-class ranking, he would make all the efforts to use his memory rather than his creativity. In this case, he would finally fall into the trap of rigidity. The only barrier that prevented me from applying for a university department of philosophy was that I did not have a good record in mathematics. If I had applied for philosophy, I could have been accepted to study Chinese philosophy, and would not have turned to the Western philosophy of language as my major research interest after I was fifty-five years old.

As far as my present study of language is concerned, what I did with the most "hindsight" during my senior high-school days was my careful study of classical Chinese. Mr Shouxian Zhang, our teacher of Chinese and class advisor, was always telling us the importance of memorizing classical Chinese texts. Often in his class, Mr Zhang, who frequently took off and put on his thick glasses, said: "Be sure to memorize excellent classical Chinese texts while you're young and have a good memory. Just do it, and it'll benefit you for all your life. Otherwise, you'll be regretful". I took his word and even today I can still recite many classical Chinese texts from my memory. In fact, my command of classical Chinese was established at that time. From my four monographs, readers will find that I have quoted a lot from Confucius, Zhuangzi, Laozi, Xie Liu, Zen Buddhist encounter dialogues, and Zhongshu Qian's *The Pipe and Awl Collection* and *Notes on Literature and Art*, and that my *Pragmatics in Chinese Culture* has involved Chinese syntax. My courage for this has come

288 *Postscript*

partly from the idea that "I have done a good job even if I have made a mistake in the use of classical Chinese and been criticized", and partly from the fact that I have a good command of classical Chinese. Here a sore spot of foreign languages is touched: A scholar of foreign languages who does not have a good command of his native language is usually inclined to interpret literature from foreign countries and does not have the courage to go into the "backland" or origins of Chinese (even one who has regarded Chinese as his data does not dare to quote or take examples from Chinese classics) and therefore cannot make important findings about laws of language. The reason for this is quite simple: On the one hand our sense of foreign languages is naturally not as sensitive as that of foreign linguists, so our study of foreign languages has to be copied and transported little by little from foreign scholars, but finally will not be accepted as a study of the language by them. On the other hand, our sense of our native language Chinese is not as sensitive as that of local Chinese linguists, and therefore our study of Chinese will not be accepted by the native Chinese linguists either. Such "half-cooked rice" between foreign and native Chinese scholars is the situation confronting scholars of foreign languages today. Of course, wise masters like Li Wang and Shuxiang Lü were not limited by languages: They had a good command of both Chinese and English but regarded Chinese as their main object of research, and therefore were able to naturally make great achievements. Yuanren Zhao was another example of excellent linguistic scholars. As a Chinese, he first of all achieved a good command of Chinese, and then, studying abroad, grasped English (later his working language) and learned many other European languages. Based on his own theoretical achievements and contributions, he became chairman of the American Society of Linguistics. What the three predecessors showed for us is that in order to liberate ourselves from the dilemma of being "half-cooked rice" between foreign and native Chinese scholars, scholars of foreign languages in China have to develop a good command of their native language while doing research in foreign languages. At no time and in no case can "scholars of foreign languages" view a poor command of their mother tongue as a matter of course.

From 1958 to 1962, I studied at the Department of Foreign Languages, Central China Normal University as a major of Russian. During those four years, I took courses in Russian literature, Russian grammar, phonetics, lexicology, historical grammar, and teaching methodology. My teacher of lexicology was Mr Bingrang Jie (who later became dean of the department), whose teaching was delicate and detailed. Prepared by Mr Jie himself, his teaching materials were imbued with his own insights, insights into how to do academic research. My teacher of historical grammar was Mr Juan Yang. Mr Yang's teaching was a travel through words of English, German, Russian, and French, and based on his analysis of the phonetic changes of these words, he helped us to identify the origins and developments of the words, a mind-blowing and interesting journey indeed. In his class, I made all my efforts to record whatever I had heard in a fascinating course. The courses offered by

Postscript 289

Mr Jie and Mr Yang lasted for merely one semester, but they served as a real introduction to linguistics for me. For average people, linguistics is indeed a boring subject, but for me it is such a course of ever-lasting interest. Why? The answer is the introduction by Mr Jie and Mr Yang, an introduction that has given me a taste of its interest and flavor. In fact, my unintended interest in linguistics was started at this time. Soon after my second year of college began, I started my reading of Russian literature works, first *How the Steel Was Tempered*, a Russian novel that I did not need to consult dictionaries much to understand. Then *War and Peace*, which I had to give up later because, although I did not have to consult dictionaries for Russian words, I came across many paragraphs of French that I could not read or understand. As far as the Russian readings translated from Chinese were concerned, I was able to read them smoothly without having to consult dictionaries, a result from my study of Russian in my junior and senior high-school days. At the time of my graduation (i.e., 1962), however, I was not able to pursue MA and PhD degrees, and therefore I did not have the chance to be trained in the profession of linguistics at all. This was a delay in my study of linguistics. Thus, courses in Russian grammar, lexicology, phonetics, historical grammar, and teaching methodology could be regarded as the primary preparation for my learning and study of linguistics afterwards.

Also during my university days, I finished a job of far-reaching significance for myself: I accumulated a long list of translated readings in world literature, mainly in Russian, English, and French. The library of Central China Normal University boasted a lot of the books found on the list, but I managed to finish reading them one by one. Thus, at the time of my graduation, I had achieved a basic understanding of literature of the major countries in the world. Although the English and French translations served to "skim the surface" of the works only (because expressed in different media, the original and translated versions of the works often resulted in a world of differences in the readers' understanding of the works), yet I had a better understanding of the three Russian masters (L. Tolstoy, A. Pushkin, and A. Chekhov) and a celebrity (M. Gorky). At that time, doing reading like this was a risk. Expectedly, I was soon officially regarded as a student of the expert road (though up to now I still have not come to know how to take the politics-oriented road) and I'd been so fearful of this when the CPC secretary of the department announced my rehabilitation at a students' conference in the third year. Indeed, at the beginning of this, I started to feel the critical eye cast on me, but I did not have the time to worry about this. The library of world literature was so fascinating that any student who liked this type of human wisdom would have to be attracted by it. As far as my university life is concerned, a warm and moving story still often occurs in my memory. As my professor of lexicology and supervisor for my educational practice, Mr Bingrang Jie, when summarizing our achievements as dean of the department, spoke highly of me, and asked (behind my back, i.e., without me knowing) the secretary of the Communist Youth League: "Has Guanlian

290 *Postscript*

Qian joined the Communist Youth League? Have you talked about this with him?" Looking back at this, I know that he was attempting to share a warm concern. Later, when I was sent to work in the "Siberia" of Hubei in the 1970s, he came to see me twice on his business trips, a student who was still visiting "purgatory". In 2002 when we students got together to celebrate the fortieth anniversary of our graduation, a group of us went to visit Mr Jie. In front of my classmates, in a consultative tone I raised the question: Why has Mr Jie been respected by so many students and colleagues? Then I tried an answer: In those years when ultra-leftist ideas were praised as progress, Mr Jie was trying to look for truths from facts and in his hidden way give us his own human and humanist concern. This hidden concern did not show publicly but it contained deep warmth of its own. All my classmates nodded their heads, agreeing and sighing.

As soon as the third year began, I started to take an immediate measure that turned out to have saved me for my work now: I paid my attention mostly to the optional course of English. I took this action at that time not because I predicted that the relation between China and the USSR would change and deteriorate (although there were signs of this breaking then), or because I dreamed that there would be a day of opening to the outside world in the future and that English would be of more use (moreover, at that time, both the British and American empires were still regarded as our first enemies). Of course, I did this not because I was farsighted enough to know in advance that literature of linguistics would be searched and retrieved mainly in English. The reason for me to have concentrated on English at that time was my persistent belief that a real foreign-language learner could not learn and have a command of only one foreign language. I had to study a second (and moreover a common) foreign language, and best a third foreign language. But unfortunately, perhaps for all my life, I did not make use of the time of the Great Cultural Revolution to study German. If I had studied German at that time, then today I would be able to read Heidegger directly, rather than by means of English. Furthermore, I was able to start to learn English at that time also because all conditions for the study of English were satisfied: From the second year on I attained a score of five for each of my Russian courses and won a place in all the study contests of the department, e.g., first place in the writing contest, and second place in the recitation and the handwriting contests. However, during my college years, there were no recorded audios to listen to, videos to watch, teaching by native teachers from the UK or the USA, studying of British literature, or training in English listening, speaking, and writing. In such a situation, I could not expect to achieve very great results in my study of English! Nonetheless, what mattered was that I continued the habit of reciting English in the morning every day (until I was fifty years old) and because of this I made two achievements from the two years (1961–1962). First, I remembered the sentence "We must learn from Wenxue Liu", and second, I developed a very good command of the IPA of English. Later I forgot all about the young hero Wenxue Liu, but kept in

Postscript 291

my mind the alphabet, which was of great use in my study of English after I became a teacher.

All this can be the academic preparation I made during my childhood and school days. Yet in terms of my study of linguistics, such preparation was just a beginning. One can find that in my above-mentioned development, I have accorded more attention to subjects other than English, especially my native language, Chinese. Overall, I have taken an academic path going from a wider and more general perspective to a narrower and more professional one. This, needless to say, is a possible way, as has been verified. I do not believe that one who has concentrated himself on foreign languages without learning anything else could become a real scholar of foreign languages. The first difficulty for a scholar of foreign languages is that he cannot go from professional knowledge to professional knowledge but has to go from general knowledge to professional knowledge. In this case, he has to spend time reading and studying extensively and if he is not patient enough, he will retreat. The second difficulty for a scholar of foreign languages is that he who has completed his university education is still unable to write essays in his target language fluently. Therefore, he still has to spend a relatively long period of time practicing writing his target language while a student of the department of Chinese can write very good Chinese at the time he graduates. Thus, a student of foreign languages loses out to a student of Chinese even at the time of their graduation, and those who are not patient enough but need to spend more time improving their target language have to retreat. This is mainly why scholars of Chinese look down upon scholars of foreign languages because "the latter know nothing except their target foreign languages". Is there any shortcut to the fluent use of the target language? No, or at least the answer seems to be no to me. The third difficulty for a scholar of foreign languages will be discussed below.

In 1962, I was assigned to a post in Enshi, the "Siberia of Hubei", and worked in the First Senior High School, a provincial key senior high school of Hubei. There I taught Russian as well as English, but after class I spent all my spare time teaching myself English with the textbooks compiled by Prof. Guozhang Xu. Before the Great Cultural Revolution, the *Journal of Foreign Language Teaching and Research* was still in publication and I tried to read all the papers in it. My extensive reading involved *Beijing Review*, *China Construction*, and then English novels (first detective novels and then novels by Mark Twain). Also worth mentioning is an event that I have kept in my mind: Before the Great Cultural Revolution, I was asked to teach open class (demonstration lessons) when visitors from other schools came to observe lessons in my school, and of the first graduates I taught in that school, fourteen were admitted to universities or colleges of foreign languages in Beijing and Wuhan, an unprecedented record in a school in such a mountainous area. At the time when the Great Cultural Revolution started, however, I began to be criticized. The night before I was criticized, I spent the whole night reading the English version of *On the Long March with Chairman Mao* by Changfeng

292 *Postscript*

Chen. I do not know why I became so powerful and so brave when confronted by such an insult of criticism, a fact to show how one can be more courageous when placed in an extremely difficult situation.

In 1973, when the Great Cultural Revolution was still going on, and the policy of reformation and opening had a few years to come, I was further assigned (of course as a punishment, I know) to a teaching post in the Xianfeng Normal School, a school located in a more frigid alpine area. In this school, however, I unexpectedly found 38 English carbon records and a hand-operated gramophone. An amazing chance of survival from desperation. The fact was that the Ministry of Education had equipped all the key normal schools all over the country with records for all their English textbooks. Equipped with these records, I started to listen to each of them at least ten to twenty times. Based on my experience of learning my first foreign language (Russian), I made conscientious efforts to develop my sense of sound in that I strongly believed that with a clearer, more correct, and richer sense of sound, I could come to listen to and speak the language itself more accurately and fluently. Yet in an environment where "a student who did no reading could become a hero of rebellion" or "a student who did not study ABC could be a revolutionary", how could one like me listen to records of English in public like this? I had a legitimated identity for doing so: I was a teacher of English; how could anybody else criticize me when I listened to records of English? Another good way to practice was appearing to be reading English versions of *Selected Works of Mao Zedong*. Thus, before I started to study English, I closed the door, and whenever there were knocks at the door, I covered my English textbooks with *Selected Works of Mao Zedong*, and then rose up to greet the guests.

At the beginning of 1978, I was transferred to West Hubei University (later the Hubei Minzu College) and worked there as a teacher of English. With the beginning of reformation and opening, my study of English started to change from being an "underground" activity to an "above-ground" one. I still spent a lot of time listening to and speaking English. As usual, as soon as I finished my class of English, I switched my role and became a college student practicing my aural and oral English. In my own view, I was a student of English who resumed my college education. As my wife put it, "Look, in this university, you are the only person who is working as hard as a college student". Of course, I was surely not the only one "who worked so hard", but I was surely working "as hard as a college student".

This is how I became prepared for my study of linguistics, a process that was indeed unbelievably long. The longest delay during this process resulted from the fact that after my graduation from college (1962) I did not have a chance to continue my studies to pursue MA and PhD degrees as well as the waste of time brought about by the Great Cultural Revolution.

It was not until the beginning of the 1980s, approximately 1982, that I started my real study of and research in linguistics. I obtained a chance for a two-year in-service training, first at Wuhan University and then at Fudan

University. At Wuhan University, I attended a one-year course in American literature and culture offered by two teachers from the USA. Yet this was not my greatest benefit because without the in-service training I could have learned the knowledge from other sources. My greatest benefit was rather that I really practiced my English writing with one of the two American teachers, a responsible lady, checking and correcting my essays with great care. At Fudan University, I spent another year studying American literature, which has a history of not more than two hundred years, but to my great pleasure I gained access to and managed to read some literature of linguistics. While excellent and of course lucky scholars of foreign languages from universities located in big cities, such as the Beijing Institute of Foreign Languages, the Shanghai Institute of Foreign Languages, and the Guangzhou Institute of Foreign Languages, went abroad for further studies, I was still struggling in West Hubei University (presently Hubei Minzu University), located in a small city in a mountainous area. There, I, from 1978 to 1989, taught *Advanced English* (a textbook compiled by Prof. Hanxi Zhang), listening to English recordings ascetically and reading literature of English linguistics introduced and compiled by my country scholars. My first endeavor was to read (of course uncritically) all the papers published in the three journals sponsored respectively by the Beijing Institute of Foreign Languages, the Shanghai Institute of Foreign Languages, and the Guangzhou Institute of Foreign Languages, all the papers introducing and reviewing linguistics abroad. Second, I tried to find English books on linguistics, one of which was a small English book called *General Linguistics* compiled on the basis of linguistic references from abroad by a professor from Shanghai Institute of Foreign Languages. What impressed me most was that approximately in 1984 I acquired from the Beijing Institute of Foreign Languages a copy of *Principles of Pragmatics* by Geoffrey N. Leech, which was the earliest literature I had access to in linguistics and the first book I read on pragmatics. I read this book sentence by sentence, chewing every word over and over again, with difficulty and hardship that, looking back on it, still excite me nowadays. The greatest difficulty for me was the terminology. Terms are the crystals of a discipline and one who knows the major terms of a discipline can enter its field successfully. In the warm winter sunlight of a mountain area, a reader was reading on the balcony of a house. Feeling drowsy, he fell asleep, and coming to, he resumed his reading. To offer a linguistics course in English in a mountain university (also called a "third world university"), I played a small trick: When presenting the necessity for this to the university office of teaching affairs, I said: "As stipulated in a document, an associate professor has to offer new courses, and otherwise you cannot punish me in the future because I have not fulfilled my responsibility". This worked well and I received the permission from my open-minded leaders to offer a course in linguistics to an in-service training class of English teachers. I therefore became the first teacher in the university to offer a linguistics course in English. Yet I do not know whether the course continued after the

294   *Postscript*

graduation of the teacher training class because later in 1989 I transferred to the Guangzhou Institute of Foreign Languages.

After a preparation of four to five years I decided to write my own papers. In 1986, I finished my first paper on linguistics, "Tolerance of Language for its Redundant Information", and submitted it to a journal for the first time, but it was rejected. Then I submitted it to *Modern Foreign Languages*. During my wait for the response, I told my wife: "If this paper is rejected this time, I'll enjoy myself with you for the rest of our life". This sounded like a tone of anger, but actually one indicating my self-ridicule and self-confidence. If whatever I do, I do it with no self-confidence, what's the use of it? My anger was real anger, not a joke, because my paper was real research work. I had a strong belief that I could bear to be criticized as being immature in this or that respect, but I could not bear to produce a study that was a useless repetition of some existing study. An immature study can be judged some day in the future with a score of 60 while a useless repetition will always be given a score of zero. I highly respect high-quality introductions and reviews of theories from abroad, for without introductions and reviews of this type, I could not have had access to what I have today, but I myself would rather cultivate a real wasteland of my own. I believed that "Tolerance of Language for its Redundant Information" was not a useless repetition of previous works but a paper with its own new ideas. If such a groundbreaking paper were not accepted by the academic circle, what hope would I have in front of me? Or, how could I like and respect an academic circle that had no interest in a groundbreaking work? My paper was published as a lead article in *Modern Foreign Languages* (with Prof. Dasan Zhang as its editor-in-chief). Yet this did not give me enough self-confidence, for a single success could be an accident. I must have another chance to have myself tested. My second paper "Functional False Information of Speech: Saving Grice's Co-operative Principle" (opposing Grice's ideas) was published in *Journal of Foreign Languages* (without the names of the editorial members) in 1987. Clearly the publication of the two papers really "saved" me. Otherwise I would have amused myself to the old. First of all, the social assessment system told me that I could do linguistics. Second, the social assessment system recognized and respected creative work. These two beliefs have influenced my research for the past twenty-two years. As a result, of the sixty-eight papers I have published up till now, two-thirds of them are characterized by new and original ideas while one third of them are interpretations of existing ideas. My four monographs, however, are all my own theoretical attempts and explorations, although they still suffer from weaknesses of different types.

Looking back on my writing of the four monographs, I can see how the running between my personal quality and the needs of the society, the relation between my contingency and necessity, and the pairing between my input and output all have performed their decisive functions therein.

Inspired by *A History of Scientific Aesthetic Thought* by Jimin Xu, my first book *Aesthetic Linguistics* was conceived when I was living in a mountain

Postscript 295

area (thanks to Prof. Shenghuan Xu for his revision). The conception of this book was an accident, but whether I could be inspired and then produce a book like *Aesthetic Linguistics* was a necessity in that it was determined by my own knowledge structure (my early input). In the writing of this book, I mobilized my knowledge of different subjects such as physics, mathematics, chemistry, biology, astronomy, literature, aesthetics, art, and system theory. Of course, here all these types of knowledge are parasitic on the tree of linguistics. After its publication, the book gradually aroused many echoes: Soon after its publication in 1993, the *Digest News* edited by the *Guangming Daily* published the news of its publication with a comment on it; *Foreign Language Teaching and Research* (1994, 2) published a short review of it by Prof. Herman Parrat (consultant of the IPrA Research Center, and professor of philosophy and linguistics, at the University of Leuven and Universiteit Brussel, Belgium); *Pragmatics* (1993, 12) published a survey of the major points of this book with a short comment by Yan Nuyts (professor of the IPrA Research Center); *Yangcheng Evening News* (July 31, 1994) published an introduction to it; the column "A Book A Week" (December 31, 1994) of Lingnan TV, Guangdong TV introduced this book; the GDZJ once more introduced this book on January 1, 1995; *Book Extract* (1994, 2) sponsored by the *Guangming Daily* published an extract of the third chapter of the book "Aesthetic Choices in the Channels of Verbal Communication"; *Word Construction News Letter* (1993, 2), a journal of the Chinese Language Society of Hong Kong, reprinted one of its chapters " 'Dyeing' of Borrowed Words by the National Aesthetic Ideas"; The Library of Congress housed the book; On August 8, 1994, it won the first prize (the highest prize) of the 7th Chinese City Press Excellent Book Award; the authoritative *Xinhua Digest* (1994, 10) published the abstract of "The Influence of National Aesthetic Ideas on the Structure of Sentences"; On December 5, 1995, at the closing ceremony of the first annual conference (Changsha) of the China Association for Comparative Studies of English and Chinese, I, invited by the participants and executive chairman of the conference, introduced the design of my aesthetic linguistics and answered questions raised thereupon; the *Nanjing Service Herald* published an excerpt of this book, "Aesthetic Choices in Verbal Communication", on June 4, 1994; *Journal of Foreign Languages* (1995, 2) published a review article of it; my paper "Outline of Aesthetic Linguistics" was published first in *Foreign Languages and Their Teaching* (1996, 3) and then included in *Collection of Papers* published in 1997 by the Shanghai Foreign Language Press. The fact that a book published a decade ago is still popular today can be regarded in a sense as the author's luck. In fact, over the past ten-plus years, readers have contacted me for copies of this book and it is actually through this book that I have become known to many scholars of Chinese linguistics. Recently, in the writing of this Postscript, I have been informed that a new revised edition of this book will be published by the Higher Education Press, another luck of mine, though a small luck.

296   *Postscript*

My second book *Pragmatics in Chinese Culture* is more an echo of my personal quality with a need of society as well as a result of the adjustment between contingency and necessity. During 1992 and 1993 when I worked as a co-investigator at the International Pragmatics Association, I consulted numerous publications of pragmatics in English but failed to find any based on Chinese data. This was an accidental, but shameful, stimulus, a shame experienced by a Chinese scholar summoned by Heaven from afar. Yet but for my idea of writing (because not everybody likes or is able to cultivate a wasteland), I would not have taken this challenge. In addition, when Tsinghua University Press agreed to publish a book of mine on pragmatics, I was just planning to base the book on my previous papers. Yet as soon as I started the plan, I remembered the regret I experienced abroad when I failed to find books on pragmatics by Chinese scholars. The uncontrollable idea of writing such a book dawned on me: It was time for me to write a book on an independent theoretical framework of pragmatics in Chinese culture. After my study and thinking of ten years (my input), I finished the book (my output) in seven months. Of course, this was due to the convenience of computer use. Yet the world needed to listen to the voice of Chinese scholars and China at the same time also needed to be heard – the need of society. This social need coincided with my accumulated knowledge and my idea developed over the following decades, and a result of this was my output, *Pragmatics in Chinese Culture*. The book gradually aroused heated echoes both at home and abroad: It was recommended by the Graduate Students' Office of the Ministry of Education as a coursebook for graduate students' teaching and soon its second edition was published; it was widely introduced in Japan, South Korea, and Taiwan and Hong Kong of China, where its CD-ROM version was published; it was housed by the Library of Congress. When Mr Jiehua Chen, a professor of pragmatics from the National Chung Hsing University of Taiwan, called to invite me to Taiwan for an academic visit, he told me on the phone that Prof. Zhuanglin Hu, a leading figure in China's linguistics circle, had recommended this book to him and spoken highly of it. During a period of time (about 2002) in the recommended readings in online libraries in China, *Pragmatics in Chinese Culture* ranked always first or at least second; in the bibliography for Chinese linguistics recommended by the Department of Chinese, Peking University, it ranks 617; in the *New Explorations in Chinese Pragmatics*, Chenfeng Shi and Jianxin Cui referred to and commented on the book as "Qian's pragmatics", including statements such as "the three and one theoretical system of pragmatics is a new and creative system of pragmatics" and the like.[2] All of this indicates that the needs of a society are the driving force for the emergence of a theory. For me, this book is just the beginning of the localization of Western pragmatics in China. Here I have to acknowledge Prof. Xianlin Ji and Prof. Zongyan Wang for their direct encouragement for me, and Prof. Shuxiang Lü and Prof. Guozhang Xu for the influence they exerted on me by virtue of their views on the unification of the "two pieces of skin" as one.

Postscript 297

The writing of *The Theory of Language Holography* was largely an accidental event. One day during the Spring Festival of 1998 (after I finished *Pragmatics in Chinese Culture*), when I was writing *Language: The Last Homestead of Human Beings*, I, while searching books in a bookstore in a lane near the Guiyuan Temple of Wuhan, found a monograph on the law of biological holography. Before I finished reading the book, another hypothetical proposition came to my mind: The structure of language is also holographic. Thus, I suspended *Language: The Last Homestead of Human Beings*, finished *The Theory of Language Holography* instead, and had the latter published before the former. Moreover, the entire book of *The Theory of Language Holography* was logically based on deductive inference, i.e., the logic of conjecture and refutation advocated by the method of falsification, an attempt which is somewhat not so familiar to Chinese scholars of linguistics. After it was published by the Commercial Press, all the copies printed were sold out within one year and it was reprinted quite soon. That a purely theoretical work became so popular among so many readers was a great luck and comfort to me and a great joy to the Commercial Press as well. In this book, I mobilized knowledge from a larger number of subjects than I did in *Aesthetic Linguistics* and drew on more literature from Western linguistics. Since the editor in charge of the book, Dr Huaying Feng, worked with great diligence and care, readers up till now have not found in this book any printing or editing errors (though different ideas or views are available everywhere). If I had not managed to strike a balance between the types or subjects of knowledge I had pursued since my school days (my input), I could not have been able to accomplish the work (my output). I have always preferred a cultivation of the theoretical wasteland, but do not expect to be accepted and appreciated "with applause" by others. All will be left to history: The views of an individual are trivial indeed.

As far as the present book, *Language: The Last Homestead of Human Beings*, is concerned, I have in its Preface offered details of the origin, experience, pause, and completion of its writing and will thus say no more about it.

The achievements one has made in different periods of his life may differ greatly in the details of their content. Yet it might be the case that the style, characteristics, and ideas of his research are inherent and consistent. It is, therefore, necessary to clarify the style, the characteristics, and the ideas of his academic research so that he can keep critically examining himself from time to time. The major point here is that the style, the characteristics, and the ideas of one's academic research have to do with the man himself.

First, the style. "The style", as the French literary theorist G. L. L. Buffon (1707–1788) put it, "is the writer".[3] The way one behaves on the whole determines the way he writes. It is quite insightful for us Chinese to regard a man as his writing. To clarify the relations between these three features of a scholar and the way he behaves, let us examine two example masters in China: Yinque Chen and Zhongshu Qian. As far as the two scholars are concerned, we believe that some of their features can be learned, some are

298 *Postscript*

difficult to learn (almost impossible), and others do not have to be learned. If we reverse the order and talk about "what does not have to be learned", we will find that if one compares himself with them in terms of the academic heights they have achieved (because he wants to learn from them), he will find himself so disheartened that he finally cannot live in this world but rather must withdraw and settle down to do whatever he can. Second, "what is difficult to learn" about them is, e.g., the depth, the thickness, and the width of the knowledge they have mastered, and the number of the foreign languages they have learned and mastered with exactitude and flexibility. There is one more feature of them that might be the most difficult to learn: On March 24, 1940, Prof. Yinque Chen, who had showed no interest in politics, made a special trip to Chongqing to vote for the new director of Academia Sinica. When Chiang Kai-shek appointed his secretary Mengyu Gu as the director of Academia Sinica, scholars including Prof. Yinque Chen became dissatisfied with this and decided not to vote for Gu.[4] Their unyielding spirit for academic freedom, their courage to believe that "you can give up your original style of calligraphy, but I would work for my freedom even though I have to give up the flower"[5] is perhaps what we cannot achieve or learn. No great inventions have come without free explorations. Struggling for academic freedom does not by nature mean to struggle for freedom just for the sake of freedom itself, because "a university cannot strive for the maximization of its freedom, but a maximization of its knowledge creation and its contribution to society".[6] Besides, after the Anti-Japanese War, Zhongshu Qian was required each month to go to Nanjing for a report on his work. One day he said after going back home: "At the dinner party this evening, the 'summit' (Chiang Kai-shek) was going to shake hands with us, but I came back home earlier".[7] In 1974, when Zhongshu Qian was a member of the group of five in charge of translating Zedong Mao's poems, Qing Jiang twice passed on messages inviting Qian and his wife, Jiang Yang, to stay at the Diaoyutai State Guesthouse. Their response was for both them to stare, dazed, without a word. On the National Day of 1975, Zhongshu Qian received a card inviting him to the state banquet, but he asked for a sick leave. At night when Qing Jiang sent a car to take him and Jiang Yang for a garden party, he responded: "I even didn't attend the state banquet".[8] Traditionally, scholars in China have generally developed a psychological need to attach themselves to people of power and wealth. When they find favor in the eyes of these people, they feel greatly flattered. Of course, this is quite different from patriotism. Patriotism of intellectuals and their attachment to the country are a bright state of mind, because it is clear that they can enjoy and obtain more opportunities to develop themselves so long as their country has developed and become rich and powerful. Attaching oneself to people of power and wealth indicates that one has no confidence at all in himself; he is on the one hand afraid that his scholarship will not be established or accepted, and on the other he wishes to be promoted, have vanity, and be given a golden chair; it is therefore a shame, a boneless shame. "One who has made no contribution to society has to live on his title".[9] Also a person of this kind is always trying to offer different types of excuses like "for academic purposes", looking as if he cannot accomplish his scholarship if he is not attached to people of power or wealth. Such a lack of self-confidence will psychologically help to develop a worship of and a blind faith in foreign scholarship due to the fact that both power attachment and worship for foreign scholarship are derived from the same mentality. Over the past years, scholars of foreign languages in China have depended too heavily on theories from abroad. This is a fact that can be easily understood and positively accepted in the sense that the introduction of excellent foreign theories can greatly benefit us (I myself have benefited from this introduction and have written reviews of linguistic theories from abroad). Yet, as has been proven time and again in history, if we depend on foreign theories for our own dignity or even depend on foreigners for our own dignity, we will not have any "self-dignity" but merely "self-contempt". In comparison, the way Yinque Chen and Zhongshu Qian stayed away from people of power and wealth as one stays away from a plague is evidence of an amazing and even unique self-dignity and self-love among modern Chinese intellectuals, a self-dignity and self-love that is also a nobility highly and extremely needed by intellectuals of the Chinese nation. One who enjoys such self-dignity and self-love will develop a settling and unyielding state of mind. One who does not have such a settling and unyielding state of mind will never achieve a mastery of great scholarship. One who has developed a settling state of mind will develop wisdom of his own; one with a quiet, pious, kind, and simple mind will surely become strong-minded and, of course, wise as well. From this has come the wisdom of Yinque Chen and Zhongshu Qian indeed. One who enjoys such a pure state of mind will find it easy to receive information from different sources. A hollow valley will surely sound far away, but a high unity of moral quality and academic quality... Finally, their features that "can be learned". Yinque Chen's profound knowledge accumulation and his "spirit of independence and freedom of thinking", for instance, can be learned. As far as Zhongshu Qian is concerned, his thorough knowledge of both Chinese and Western studies can more or less be learned as well.

Now back to our original topic: One's academic style, the characteristics of his research, and his academic ideas are inseparable from the way he behaves as a moral being in his life. In other words, since he behaves morally like this, he will develop an academic style, characteristics of research, and academic ideas of that kind. When we write papers, for instance, for a chance of promotion two months later, can we behave as Yinque Chen did (i.e., "gradually developing a profound knowledge and calmly producing and presenting it")? Or if we endeavor to complete a project just for a specific and practical purpose, can we still work as Zhongshu Qian did when he, based on an enormous body of data of foreign languages, and modern as well as classical Chinese from different dynasties, came to do a detailed comparative study between China and the West? Or if we are really trying to work out the number of papers for a coming evaluation, can we still be patient enough and settle down to do work of originality and creativity? Driven by such practical purposes

300 *Postscript*

and interests, can we still attempt to maintain our styles, characteristics, and ideas? These questions have, over the past twenty-two years, tortured (sometimes obliquely) and impacted me. Over the past years, there has been a war in my mind, a war between inordinate gains, vanity, and the understandable desire to survive on the one hand and the truth of life and truth of scholarship on the other. When the latter defeated the former, or a step forward was taken in the latter, I made a little progress in my learning. When the former defeated the latter, or when it prevailed, I would undergo an adulteration in my academic work. What has amazed me from time to time in the past twenty-two years is that when I found my path of life cramped, expected no favor for me from Heaven, I thus had to settle down to read and write. I made a down-to-earth progress in my work since at this time what I wrote was more likely to stand up to the scrutiny and polish of time.

If I could have a doctrine for my research, then what I have been doing is to avoid repeating what previous scholars have done, that is, I have been attempting to do creative work. By creation is meant the creation of (new) ideas, (new) concepts, (new) categories, (new) propositions and values. I strongly believe that knowledge can be created, and that creation is of course not an easy job. Don't we enjoy knowledge created by previous scholars every day? If we just repeat what has been done, then what will our later generations learn from us?

The creative ability is thus the ability to create new things from nothing. By "nothing" here we mean that "this or that thing" does not exist before it is created and therefore comes into being. Of course, during the process of creating something from nothing, one has to draw upon the work of previous researchers, so as to create what does not exist in this world. Yuanren Zhao, Changpei Luo, Shuxiang Lü, and Li Wang all wrote what had not existed before them, things that had come from nothing. Besides, "the creation of new things from what has existed" is creative work as well. John Langshaw Austin, for instance, proposed the speech act theory, an example of creating something from nothing; John Searle, his student, improved his theory by successfully classifying speech acts into five types, an example of creating new things from what has existed.

If asked about my idea of doing research, I would put forward "one emphasis and three basings" as the basic principles to follow: Emphasizing learning theories of linguistics from the West, basing myself on the construction of my own theories, basing myself on the data of my native language, and basing myself on the originality of my work. The above-mentioned four monographs are in fact experiments of this persuasion, and of course most of my papers are attempts of this kind. It is here that lies the third difficulty confronting scholars of foreign languages. But how to borrow excellent ideas from abroad and yet manage to avoid basing our own self-dignity on theories or even scholars from abroad? If, I think, we believe in and practice the idea of "basing ourselves on the construction of our own theories, basing ourselves on the data of our native language, and basing ourselves on the originality of

Postscript 301

our work", we will proceed to localize our research. And once we localize our research, we scholars of foreign languages will manage to liberate ourselves from the fate of "followers" and become real and independent researchers. This is a difficult task for us, but it is a task that we can manage to accomplish and must accomplish. The reason for this is that "it is impossible for a country which is powerful to be a parasite which has no academic tradition of its own and thus has to depend on others for its spirit".[10] Only when no scholar would like to be a parasite depending on others for his spirit can we have a country that would not be a parasite depending on others for its spirit. The problem, no matter who has raised it, has to do with whether a nation or a country can become really powerful in spirit. A scholar of foreign languages who has to introduce ideas from abroad and meanwhile do his own independent research has therefore to make double efforts. Yet once he manages to overcome this difficulty of double efforts, he will come to make great findings. For it is almost impossible to study just one language and come up with great findings. "There exists in any isolated system a tendency of kinetic energy decrease, an irreversible process which will further lead to the final death of the universe".

> A dissipative structure has a special resistance against death. Where does this resisting energy come from? First it gets its energy from the outside world, and second, the structure itself can produce energy by itself, and thereby it finishes its energy exchange with the outside world.[11]

A system (a language) has to cross another system (another language) in order that the two systems can both survive or remain alive. As the best examples of this kind, Yuanren Zhao, Shuxiang Lü, and Li Wang developed a good command of foreign languages, then turned to study Chinese and thereby made the greatest contributions. They are examples of localizations of Western scholarship in China, examples of overcoming the difficulty of double efforts, and of course examples of "one emphasis" and "three bases".

The difficulties confronting a scholar of foreign languages can thus be summarized as follows. First, it takes a long time for him to go from the study of general knowledge to that of specialized knowledge (foreign languages). Second, after he graduates from college, he has to spend another long period of time practicing his foreign language writing ability, without which all his ideas will have no basic means to be expressed. Further, it takes another longer period of time for him to go from pure introduction and interpretation to the "three basings".

I am often asked: Writing and doing research like this, do you feel tired? If I had to give a false answer, I would say "Yes", while pretending that it is not easy to do so. If I were required, however, to give a true answer, I would like to say "Not always". If one writes by copying and making extracts, and thus by repeating all the time what others have said, he will regard writing as a burden and will have no interest in it. In this case, he will feel tired. If he, however, starts out on a journey of discovery, to find a new proposition, to create a new

302 *Postscript*

concept, to find a new category, then he will have a constant series of joys. In this way, he will have pleasures, and he, I think, will not feel tired. Up till now (the same henceforth), I have never worked far into the night on a monograph or a paper. On the contrary, I have been working and living in an unhurried and regular way, and even the time and route of my walk remain the same every day. Furthermore, if I need to work harder one day, I will increase my frequency of walk instead. For my doctrine of life is: In this life of mine, I will merely do what I can. I will try to go beyond myself, but I will not risk my life, or tiptoe to pretend that I am taller. If the grapes above me are too high and beyond my reach, I will walk away and leave them, and while leaving them, I will not say that the grapes are sour. My philosophy of life is: Pick the grapes in my reach, and take time to taste them no matter whether they are sweet or sour.

True, I have accomplished one or two tasks due to some Heaven's help. As I stated at the outset of this Postscript, one's own quality/cultivation and the needs of society, contingency and necessity, and the way his input and output work can be a kind of Heaven's help. This is my first Heaven's help.

My second Heaven's help is the aforementioned precious instruction and training I have received from my primary school, middle school, and university teachers. They are valuable gifts sent to me by Heaven.

The third Heaven's help I have received is the people who have given me help in my life. The first person is Prof. Dasan Zhang, who, as editor-in-chief of *Modern Foreign Languages*, accepted my first paper and had it published as the lead article of one of the issues of the journal. This made me know what I could do, an important help for me. Further, he wrote and invited me to join Guangdong University of Foreign Studies, an important event that helped to significantly improve my living and research conditions for the first time. Another favor that helped me over a turn in my life came from Prof. Zhenhua Xu (PhD) and my colleague Prof. Chuming Wang (PhD). At the age of sixty (1999), when I was prepared for my coming retirement, Prof. Zhenhua Xu, president of GDUFS, resolutely retained me, thus paving the way for my later unexpected development. At this time, the university successfully applied for the National Center for Linguistics and Applied Linguistics and Prof. Chuming Wang, director of the Center, offered to invite me to join them. Later, without my knowledge, he prepared and paved the way for me to become a supervisor of PhD candidates. When he told me that my application had passed the evaluation of all the five external examiners, he breathed a sigh of relief in front of me. From then on, my research conditions were further improved. More importantly, my students will continue my work, and they will, and they should, do better than I. In my fifties, when I was confronted with difficulties, those who gave me warm-hearted help, support, and concern included my seniors Prof. Chuxiang Chen and Prof. Houchen Zhang, and my peer Prof. Zijian Yang. I also owe my sincere gratitude to the Haitian Press, the publisher of *Aesthetic Linguistics*, and its editor, Mr Cheng Song; the Higher Education Press, the publisher of *Aesthetic Linguistics* (2nd edn), and its editor, Mr Wei Jia; Tsinghua University Press, the publisher of *Pragmatics in Chinese Culture*, and its editor, Mr Youquan Ning; and the Commercial Press, the publisher of *The Theory of Language Holography* and *Language: The Last Homestead of Human Beings*, and its editor, Dr Huaying Feng, for their cultivation and hard work, which have made my work a contribution to our society. Also worth mentioning are especially Mr Dasan Zhang, Mr Cheng Song, Mr Wei Jia, Mr Youquan Ning, and Dr Huaying Feng, who knew nothing about and had no contact with me before they came to help me. Likewise, all the other people who did not have any benefit exchange relationships with me except normal contacts before they came to help me. As Prof. Chuxiang Chen put it, "If this was a help for you, I'd like to say that I'd have offered the help even if it had not been for you". When I was in the mountainous area of West Hubei, I often had academic discussions with and received help from my friends, such as Mr Zuohuan Liu, Mr Guangyao Sun, Mr Xianjun Tang, Mr Guofu Zhang, and Mr Zhiyu Li, whose support helped me pass the unforgettable years. It is the truth, goodness, and beauty I received from them that constitute such a memorable world.

The fourth Heaven's help I have been given is from the present time. This, I think, can be understood in two ways. First, it refers to the trials and tribulations one has to go through and even suffer from when he is trying to survive a situation, a necessary "lesson" in the whole process of his development. When talking about the church reforms of the eleventh century, Bertrand Russell said: "Before going to heaven, however, he would have to spend some time – perhaps, a very long time – suffering the pains of the purgatory".[12] As it often happens, theoretically we know that undergoing pains is a necessary experience in our life. Were pains really to happen to us, however, nobody would accept them with serenity but always complain that Heaven is unfair to us. Second, Heaven's help for me refers to the numerous good opportunities from the time of reformation and opening. It is, for example, the constant deepening of the reform that has made it necessary and possible for the one hundred national key research centers to have been established. Improvement in the living and research conditions of scholars is by nature the benefit brought to us by the development of the society. It is often heard nowadays that a scholar from this or that university has been awarded a research project and thus obtained the corresponding financial support, a favor that has finally come to intellectuals of China, and, one cannot but say, a great progress in our society has been made. Whomever it occurs to, such an opportunity comes first from Heaven's help, but basically it comes more from one's own self-help.

As is always the case, one has to suffer from his weaknesses. I know where my weaknesses lie. Of course, we do not have to talk about our failures and setbacks all the time, but we cannot forget them.

Whatever we do, we do it first for practical purposes, second for the significance of it, and third – but implicitly – for our memory after we leave this world. Yet there will come the doomsday, when the earth will stop its turning

304   *Postscript*

and everything will end and be buried in oblivion. However, one with such a view of the universe will not become a pessimist because the "meaning" of living and enjoying the process of doing something itself is in itself of significance. We could not say for sure that one who is walking on the path of science will surely succeed in the end, but we could say for sure that one who has made efforts will surely experience and enjoy the meaning of life.

So, picking the grapes within my reach and tasting them is by nature perhaps experiencing the meaning of the act of picking itself. For others, this is not a summary of a wonderful period or a coming goal, but for me, this could be a summary of a period that is neither too ambitious nor too starry-eyed, or the aim of a new period.

Midnight, January 10, 2004
Revised on the morning of January 21, 2004
Guangzhou, China

Notes

1 In my hometown there was is a river called the Tongshun River. During the yearly flood season, traveling between Hankou and the Shahu Township was a very small steam ship called "the straw sandal heel" by the local people. This was the observation from which my question came.
2 Shi, C. and Cui, J. (2002). *New Explorations in Chinese Pragmatics*. Tianjin: The Tianjin Ancient Books Publishing House, p. 9.
3 From Wu, D. (1997). *The Soul of Scholars: A Biography of Chen Yinque* (2nd edn). Shanghai: Shanghai Literature & Art Publishing House, p. 172.
4 *Ibid.*, p. 131.
5 Chen, Y. (2001). *Selected Poems by Chen Yinque: An Answer to a Guest from the North*. Beijing: The SDX Joint Publishing Company, p. 100.
6 Zhang, W. (2004). "Academic Freedom, 'Official Standards' and Academic Norms", *Reading*, 1: 91.
7 Yang, J. (2003). *We Three*. Beijing: SDX Joint Publishing Company, p. 121.
8 *Ibid.*, pp. 152–153.
9 Zhang, W. (2004). "Academic Freedom, 'Official Standards' and Academic Norms", *Reading*, 1: 93.
10 Li, M. (2004). "University Reforms and Academic Traditions", *Reading*, 1: 101.
11 Qian, G. (1993). *Aesthetic Linguistics*. Shenzhen: Haitian Press, p. 52.
12 Russell, B. (1972). *A History of Western Philosophy*. New York: Simon and Schuster, p. 408.

References

Aitchison, J. (1996). *The Seeds of Speech: Language Origin and Evolution.* Cambridge: Cambridge University Press.

Arndt, H. & Richard, W. J. (1987). The Biological and Cultural Evolution of Human Communication. In W. Lorscher & R. Shulze (Eds.), *Perspectives on Language and Performance: Studies in Linguistics, Literary Criticism and Language Teaching and Learning* (Vol. 1, pp. 19–45). Tübingen: Gunter Narr Verlag.

Austin, J. L. (1962). *How to Do Things with Words.* London: Oxford University Press.

Austin, J. L. (1970). Performative Utterances. In J. O. Urmson & G. J. Warnock (Eds.), *Philosophical Papers* (2nd edn, pp. 233–252). Oxford: Oxford University Press.

Ayer, A. J. & Rhees, R. (1954). Symposium: Can There Be a Private Language? *Proceedings of the Aristotelian Society, Supplementary Volumes*, 28, 63–94.

Baghramian, M. (Ed.). (1999). *Modern Philosophy of Language.* Washington, DC: Counterpoint.

Bajin. (1989). Shìjièyǔ (Esperanto). In Suíxiǎng lù (*Random Thoughts*) (Vol. 2, Tànsuǒ jí (*Explorations*), pp. 82–86). Beijing: People's Literature Publishing House.

Bamo, Q. (2003). Kǒutóu chuántǒng yǔ shūxiě chuántǒng (The Traditions of Speech and the Traditions of Writing). Dúshū (*Reading*), 10.

Blackburn, S. (1994). *Oxford Dictionary of Philosophy.* Oxford: Oxford University Press.

Brown, P. & Levinson, S. C. (1978/1987). *Politeness: Some Universals in Language Usage.* Cambridge: Cambridge University Press.

Cai, Y. (2002). Měiguó tǔzhù yǔyán fǎ'àn (The Native American Language Act). Dúshū (*Reading*), 10, 115–122.

Cameron, D., McAlinden, F., & O'Leary, K. (1988). Lakoff in Context: The Social and Linguistic Functions of Tag Questions. In J. Coates & D. Cameron (Eds.), *Women in Their Speech Communities: New Perspectives on Language and Sex* (pp. 74–93). London/New York: Longman.

Campbell, J. (2001). *The Liar's Tale: A History of Falsehood.* New York: W. W. Norton and Company.

Canfield, J. & Hansen, M. V. A. (1996). *A 3rd Serving of Chicken Soup for the Soul.* Deerfield Beach: Health Communications.

Carroll, J. B. (Ed.). (1956). *Language, Thought and Reality: Selecting Writings of Benjamin Lee Whorf.* Cambridge, MA: The MIT Press.

Chao, G. (2003). Kǒutóu·wúxíng·fēiwùzhí yíchǎn mànyì (On Oral Intangible Heritage). Dúshū (*Reading*), 10, 17–21,

306   *References*

Chen, B. (1993). Yǔyán wénhuà lùn (*On Language and Culture*). Kunming: Yunnan University Press.

Chen, J. (2003). Yǔyán zhéxué (*Philosophy of Language*). Beijing: Peking University Press.

Chen, R. (2001). Yǔyán kēxué yánjiū xué (*Ethics of Language*). Beijing: Peking University Press.

Chen, Y. (2001). Féngyǒulán "zhōngguó zhéxué shǐ" shěnchá bàogào (A Review Report on Feng Youlan's *History of Chinese Philosophy*). In Jīnmíng guǎn cónggǎo èrbiān (*The Second Volume of Manuscripts from Jinming Library*) (pp. 247–252). Beijing: SDX Joint Publishing Company.

Chen, Y. (2002). Qíng·lǐ·fǎ: Lǐzhì zhìxù (Compassion, Rites and Law: The Order of Rites). Dúshū (*Reading*), 1, 69.

Cheng, Y. (1994). "Gé" zhī yīlì (An Example of "Septum"). Dúshū (*Reading*), 10.

Cheng, Z. & Jiang, Y. (2003). Zhéxué xīn cídiǎn (*A New Dictionary of Philosophy*). Changchun: Jilin People's Press.

Clark, H. H. (1996). *Using Language*. Cambridge: Cambridge University Press.

Dai, Y. (1996). Zhōngguó rén zěnyàng shuōhuà (How the Chinese Talk). Dúshū (*Reading*), 2, 108.

Derrida, J. (2005). *The Politics of Friendship* (G. Collins, Trans.). London: Verso.

Ding, Z. (1996). Méiyǒu míng de ēnshī: Gǔ luómǎ dàjiàng kǎisǎ fāchū de háo yán: veni, vidi, vici (Mentor Without a Title: Ancient Roman General Caesar's Heroic Saying: *Veni, vidi, vici*). Dúshū (*Reading*), 3, 115.

Dong, L. (1993). Zhǔyì èr tí (On -Isms). Dúshū (*Reading*), 11.

Dong, L. (1994). Dōngfāng zhǔyì dàhéchàng ma? (Chorus of Orientalism?). Dúshū (*Reading*), 5, 103.

Du, N. (1998). Xiàndài yǔyán xiéhuì huìkān": Zúyìxìng yǔ wénxué (*Journal of Modern Language Association*: Ethnicity and Literature). Dúshū (Reading), 12.

Du, W. (1998). Rénwén jīngshén yǔ quánqiú lúnlǐ (Humanistic Spirit and Global Ethics). In Zhōngguó dàxué rénwén qǐsīlù (*Humanistic Thoughts in Chinese Universities*) (Vol. 2, pp. 88–99). Wuhan: Huazhong University of Science and Technology Press.

Duan, B. (1998). Mínjiān de jīngyīng (Folk Elite). Dúshū (*Reading*), 10.

Dummett, M. (1975). What is a Theory of Meaning? (Part 1). In S. Guttenplan (Ed.), *Mind and Language* (pp. 97–138). Oxford: Oxford University Press.

Dummett, M. (1976). What is a Theory of Meaning? (Part 2). In G. Evans & J. McDowell (Eds.), *Truth and Meaning* (pp. 67–137). Oxford: Oxford University Press.

Dummett, M. (1996). *The Seas of Language*. Oxford: Clarendon Press.

Duranti, A. (1997). *Linguistic Anthropology*. Cambridge: Cambridge University Press.

Eco, U. (1984). *Semiotics and the Philosophy of Language*. Bloomington & Indianapolis, IN: Indiana University Press.

Fang, Q. (1996). Rénshēng chán (*Zen of Life*) (Vol. 1). Beijing: China Youth Press.

Fei, X. (1998). Cóng fǎnsī dào wénhuà zìjué hé jiāoliú (From Reflection to Cultural Self-Awareness and Communication). Dúshū (*Reading*), 11.

Feng, Y. (1996). Zhōngguó zhéxué jiǎnshǐ (*A Short History of Chinese Philosophy*) (2nd edn). Beijing: Peking University Press.

Feng, Y. (1998). Zhōngguó zhéxué de jīngshén: Féng Yǒulán wénxuǎn (*The Spirit of Chinese Philosophy: Selected Writings by Youlan Feng*) (H. Zhang, Ed.) Beijing: International Culture Press.

References 307

Frege, G. (1892/1999). On Sense and Reference. In M. Baghramian (Ed.), *Modern Philosophy of Language* (pp. 6–25). Washington, DC: Counterpoint.

Ge, J. (1996). Gàishì yīngxióng háishì qiāngǔ zuìrén (A Hero or a Traitor?). Dúshū (*Reading*), 5.

Gilsenan, M. (1976). Lying, Honor and Contradiction. In B. Kapferer (Ed.), *Transaction and Meaning* (pp. 191–219). Philadelphia, PA: Institute for the Study of Human Issues.

Goffman, E. (1969). *Strategic Interaction*. Philadelphia, PA: University of Pennsylvania Press.

Grice, H. P. (1975). Logic and Conversation. In P. Cole and J. Morgan (Eds.), *Syntax and Semantics* (pp. 41–58). New York: Academic Press.

Grice, H. P. (1957/1989). Meaning. In *Studies in the Way of Words*. Cambridge, MA: Harvard University Press.

Guo, Y. (2003). Kǒushù lìshǐ: Yǒuguān jìyì yǔ wàngquè (Oral History: About Memory and Forgetting). Dúshū (*Reading*), 10, 62–68.

Habermas, J. (1979). *Communication and the Evolution of Society* (T. McCarthy, Trans.). Boston, MA: Beacon Press.

Han, S. (1994). Shìjiè (The World). Huāchéng (*Huacheng*), 6.

He, C. (1997). Lǎngdú yǔ mòdú (Reading Aloud and Reading Silently). Dúshū (*Reading*), 11.

He, Q. (1999). Wénhuà gèxìng yǔ "wénhuà rèntóng" (Cultural Individuality and "Cultural Identity"). Dúshū (*Reading*), 9, 100–105.

Heidegger, M. (1950). *Der ursprung des kunstwerks, holzwege*. Frankfurt: Klostermann.

Heidegger, M. (1953). *Einfuehrung in die metaphysik*. Tübingen: Niemeyer.

Heidegger, M. (1975). *Poetry, Language, Thought* (A. Hofstadter, Trans.). New York: Harper & Row.

Heidegger, M. (1978). *Brief über humanismus, wegmarken*. Frankfurt: Klostermann.

Heidegger, M. (1959/1982). *On the Way to Language* (P. Hertz, Trans.). New York: Harper & Row.

Heidegger, M. (1993). Letter on Humanism (F. A. Capuzzi & J. G. Gray, Trans.). In D. F. Krell (Ed.), *Basic Writings* (p. 217). San Francisco, CA: Harper San Francisco.

Heidegger, M. (1996). *Being and Time: A Translation of Sein und Zeit* (J. Stambaugh, Trans.). New York: SUNY Press.

Heidegger, M. (1959/1999). Zài tōng xiàng yǔyán de túzhōng (*On the Way to Language*, Z. Sun, Trans.). Beijing: The Commercial Press.

Heidegger, M. (2000). *An Introduction to Metaphysics* (G. Fried & R. Polt, Trans.). New Haven, CT: Yale University Press.

Hjelmslev, L. (1943/1961). *Prolegomena to a Theory of Language* (F. J. Whitfield, Trans.). Madison, WI: The University of Wisconsin Press.

Hou, L. (2001). Shíjiān fúhào yǔ mínzú rèntóng (Symbols of Time and Ethnic Identity). Dúshū (*Reading*), 10, 95.

Hu, S. (1997). Zhōngguó zhéxuéshǐ dàgāng (*Outline of the History of Chinese Philosophy*). Shanghai: Shanghai Classics Publishing House.

Huang, C. (1996). Yīngyǔ wéntǐ de biànqiān (The Change of English Styles). Dúshū (*Reading*), 7.

Huang, P. & Wang, D. (1998). Xuéshù fēnkē jí qí chāoyuè (Academic Division and the Transcendence of It). Dúshū (*Reading*), 7.

Huang, Y. (1999). Lìshǐ de chǐdù (The Yardstick of History). Dúshū (*Reading*), 11, 38–43.

308 *References*

Huo, Y. (2006). *Mitigation and Pragmatics as a Linguistic Regulation Theory: The Case of TCM Clinical Interviews.* Kunming: Yunnan University Press.

Hymes, D. (1972). Models of the Interaction of Language and Social Life. In J. J. Gumperz and D. Hymes (Eds.), *Directions in Sociolinguistics: The Ethnography of Communication* (pp. 35–71). New York: Holt, Rinehart, & Winston.

Jaspers, K. (1954). *Way to Wisdom: An Introduction to Philosophy* (R. Manheim, Trans.). New Haven, CT: Yale University Press.

Ji, S. (1997). Liǎoquè yīzhuāng xīnshì (A Worry Relieved). Dúshū (*Reading*), 1.

Jin, K. (1995). Lìshǐ bìng wèi guòqù (History is Not Past). Dúshū (*Reading*), 2, 34–39.

Jin, K. (1997). Wénhuà lièyí (*Controversial Issues about Culture*). Shanghai: SDX Joint Publishing Company.

Jin, K. (1998). Táofàn de tìdāo (The Razor of a Fugitive). Dúshū (*Reading*), 12.

Kachru, B. B. (1985). Institutionalized Second-Language Varieties. In S. Greenbaum (Ed.), *The English Language Today* (pp. 211–226). Oxford: Pergamon Press.

Kasher, A. (1995). Philosophy of Language. In J. Verschuren & J. O. Östman (Eds.), *Handbook of Pragmatics Manual.* Amsterdam/Philadelphia, PA: John Benjamins.

Lakoff, G. (1975). Pragmatics in Natural Logic. In E. Keenan (Ed.), *Formal Semantics of Natural Language* (pp. 253–286). Cambridge: Cambridge University Press.

Leech, G. N. (1983). *Principles of Pragmatics.* London: Longman.

Levinson, S. C. (1979). Activity Types. *Linguistics*, 17 (5/6), 365–399.

Levinson, S. C. (1983). *Pragmatics.* Cambridge: Cambridge University Press.

Lewis, D. (1972). General Semantics. In D. Davidson & G. Harman (Eds.), *Semantics for Natural Language* (pp. 169–218). Dordrecht: Reidel.

Li, T. (1996). Lǐ Tiānmìng de sīkǎo yìshù (*Tianming Li's Art of Thinking*). Beijing: SDX Joint Publishing Company.

Li, X. (1998). Shìgé yǔ jùyì (Event Case and the Meaning of Sentences). Wàiyǔ yǔ wàiyǔ jiàoxué (*Foreign Languages and Foreign Language Teaching*), 7, 4–9.

Lin, S. (1998). Xīng": Duì zhuānzhèng zhéxué de cháofèng (*Star*: Dictatorship Philosophy as a Joke). Dúshū (*Reading*), 9, 45.

Lin, Y. (1936). *My Country and My People.* London: William Heinemann Ltd.

Lippard, P. V. (1988). "Ask Me No Questions. I'll Tell You No Lies": Situational Exigencies for Interpersonal Deception. *Western Journal of Speech Communication*, 52, 91–103.

Liu, N. (1997). "Yǎowénjiáozì" liùshí nián (The 60 Years of *Being Particular about Wording*), Dúshū (*Reading*), 7.

Liu, Z. (2003). Wénzì yuán shì yī zhāng pí (Words are Actually a Piece of Skin). Dúshū (*Reading*), 10, 3–9.

Long, Y. (1996). Gānbēi ba, Thomas Mann (Cheers, Thomas Mann). Dúshū (*Reading*), 2, 53.

Lu, S. (1998). Fùzá de zú chēng yǔ qítè de yǔyán,"yuè hǎi tóngxīn (Complex Names of Ethnic Groups and Particularities of Languages). Yuè hǎi tóngxīn (*Unity of Cantonese*), 12, 6.

Lu, Y. (1998). Zhèngzhì yǔ jiěgòu (Politics and Destruction). Dúshū (*Reading*), 12.

Lu, Y. P. (2002). Bù miè de shū (An Immortal Book). Dúshū (*Reading*), 9, 65–69.

Lüger, H. (1983). Some Aspects of Ritual Communication. *Journal of Pragmatics*, 6, 695–711.

Malinowski, B. (1923). The Problem of Meaning in Primitive Languages. In C. K. Ogden & I. A. Richards (Eds.), *The Meaning of Meaning* (pp. 296–336). New York: Harcourt, Brace & World.

References 309

Malinowski, B. (1935/1978). *Coral Gardens and Their Magic* (Vol. 2). London: Allan & Unwin.

Mandelbaum, D. G. (Ed.). (1958). *The Selected Writings of Edward Sapir in Language, Culture, and Personality*. Berkeley, CA: University of California Press.

Marcondes de Souza, D. (1983). Action-Guiding Language. *Journal of Pragmatics*, 7(1), 49–62.

Martinich, A. P. & Sosa, D. (2001). *A Companion to Analytic Philosophy*. London: Blackwell Publishers.

Mey, J. L. (2001). *Pragmatics: An Introduction*. London: Blackwell Publishers.

Morris, C. (1938). Foundations of the Theory of Signs. In *Foundations of the Unity of Science: Towards an International Encyclopedia of Unified Science* (Vol. 1, 2). Chicago, IL: University of Chicago Press.

Morris, C. (1946). *Signs, Language and Behavior*. Englewood Cliffs, NJ: Prentice Hall.

Nan, F. (1998). Chǎnshì yǔ duìhuà (Interpretation and Dialogue). Wénlùn Bào (*Literary Review*), March 12.

Ni, L. (1996). Yì, háishì bù yì (To Translate or Not to Translate). Dúshū (*Reading*), 4.

Ouyang, Y. (2001). Zhàozhōu gōng'àn yǔyán de móléngxìng yánjiū (*A Study of the Ambiguity of Zhaozhou's Koans*) (Unpublished doctoral dissertation). National Chengchi University, Taiwan, China.

Popper, K. R (1968b). *Conjectures and Refutations: The Growth of Scientific Knowledge*. New York, Evanston, IL: Harper & Row.

Popper, K. R. (1968a). *The Logic of Scientific Discovery*. London: Hutchinson & Co.

Qi, G. (1997). Hànyǔ xiànxiàng lùn cóng (*Collection of Theses on the Chinese Language*). Beijing: China Books Company.

Qi, L. (1998). Qǐ Liáng jí (*Collection of Writings by Liang Qǐ*). Shanghai: Shanghai Xuelin Publishing House.

Qian, G. (1986). Cíyǔ de huàshí gōngnéng (The Fossil Function of Words). Cí kù jiànshè tōngxùn (*Newsletter of Chinese Word Database Construction*) (Hong Kong Association for the Chinese Language), 8.

Qian, G. (1990). Yīn'gán zhàohuàn (The Calling of the Sense of Sound). Wàiyú xuékān (*Journal of Foreign Languages*), 5.

Qian, G. (1993). Měixué yǔyánxué (*Aesthetic Linguistics*). Shenzhen: Haitian Publishing House.

Qian, G. (1994). Cóng wénhuà gònghé kàn fānyì děngzhílùn (On the Theory of Equivalent Translation from the Perspective of Cultural Consensus). Zhōngguó fānyì (*Chinese Translators Journal*), 4.

Qian, G. (1995). Zhìhuì de sǐwáng (To Die Wisely). Jiēdào (*The Street*), 7.

Qian, G. (1997/2002). Hànyǔ wénhuà yǔyòngxué (*Pragmatics in Chinese Culture*) (2nd edn). Beijing: Tsinghua University Press.

Qian, G. (2002). Yǔyán quánxílùn (*The Theory of Language Holography*). Beijing: The Commercial Press.

Qian, G. & Xie, D. (Eds.) (1998). Yǔyánxué lùnwén jí (*Collection of Linguistic Papers*) (Vol. 5). Guangzhou: South China University of Technology Press.

Qian, Z. (1997). Qián Zhōngshū sǎnwén (*Essays by Zhongshu Qian*). Hangzhou: Zhejiang Literature & Art Press.

Qu, Y. (2000). Zhōngguó hūnlǐ yíshì shǐlüè (A Brief History of Chinese Wedding Ceremonies). Mínsú yánjiū (*Folklore Studies*), 2, 75–88.

Robins, R. H. (1969). *A Short History of Linguistics* (2nd edn). London: Longmans.

310 *References*

Rohmann, C. (1999). *A World of Ideas: A Dictionary of Important Theories, Concepts, Beliefs, and Thinkers*. New York: Ballantine Books.

Rorty, M. R. (1967). *The Linguistic Turn*. Chicago, IL: University of Chicago Press.

Russell, B. (1956). "Descriptions and Incomplete Symbols" from "The Philosophy of Logical Atomism". In *Logic and Knowledge: Essays* (1901–1950) (pp.175–282). London: Allen & Unwin.

Russell, B. (1945). *A History of Western Philosophy*. New York: Simon and Schuster.

Sadock, J. (1974). *Toward a Linguistic Theory of Speech Acts*. New York: Academic Press.

Sanmu. (2003). Yīgè kòngbái de xuǎntí (A Proposal to Fill Up a Research Gap). Dúshū (*Reading*), 9, 67–74.

Sapir, E. (1929). The Status of Linguistics as a Science. *Language*, 5, 207–214. Reprinted in D. G. Mandelbaum (Ed.) (1958), *The Selected Writings of Edward Sapir in Language, Culture, and Personality* (pp. 160–166). Berkeley, CA: University of California Press.

Sbisà, M. (1995). Analytical Philosophy. In J. Verschuren & Jan-Ola Östman (Eds.), *Handbook of Pragmatics Manual* (pp. 28–36). Amsterdam/Philadelphia, PA: John Benjamins.

Schopenhauer, A. (2010) *The World as Will and Representation* (Vol. 1) (J. Norman, A. Welchaman, & C. Janaway, Trans.). Cambridge: Cambridge University Press.

Searle, J. R. (1965). What is a Speech Act? In M. Black (Ed.), *Philosophy in America* (pp. 221–239). Ithaca, NY: Cornell University Press.

Searle, J. R. (1969). *Speech Acts: An Essay in the Philosophy of Language*. Cambridge: Cambridge University Press.

Sheng, X. (2000). Huàyǔ guīzé yǔ zhīshì jīchǔ (*Discourse Rules and the Basis of Knowledge*). Shanghai: Xuelin Publishing House.

Shi, C. & Cui, J. (2002). Hànyǔ yǔyòngxué xīntàn (*A New Approach of Chinese Pragmatics*). Tianjin: Tianjin Classics Publishing House.

Stenius, E. (1972). Mood and Language Game. In D. Hockney (Ed.), *Essays in Philosophical Logic* (pp. 251–271). Dortrecht: Reidel.

Su, W. (2004). Lìshǐ de ròushēn (The Flesh of History). Dúshū (*Reading*), 2, 56.

Sun, G. (1995). Zuòwéi fāngfǎ de rìběn (Japan as a Method). Dúshū (*Reading*), 3.

Sun, Y. (1999). Bèiqiè de yídài suànjiùzhàng (The Stolen Generations Demand Compensation). Yángchéng wǎnbào (*Yangcheng Evening*), March 4, A10.

Suo, S. (1999a). Dàoqí máolǘ de āfántí yǔ xìnxī shídài (Afanti's Back-facing Ride on a Donkey and the Information Age). Dúshū (*Reading*), 1.

Suo, S. (1999b). Yǔyán, zǒuguò lìshǐ de cāngsāng (Language and its Vicissitudes through History). Dúshū (*Reading*), 7.

Suo, S. (2000). Yǔyán de qínggǎn jiàzhí yǔ yìzhě de juésè (The Emotional Value of Language and the Role of Translators). Dúshū (*Reading*), 2, 24–29.

Tan, L. (1997). Cóng jīdūjiào de hànhuà shuōkāiqù (Sinicization of Christianity and Other Notes). Dúshū (*Reading*), 6.

Thompson, J. B. (1982). Universal Pragmatics. In J. B. Thompson & D. Held (Eds.), *Habermas: Critical Debates* (pp. 116–133). London: Macmillan Press.

van Peurson, C. A. (1970). *Ludwig Wittgenstein: An Introduction to His Philosophy* (R. Ambler, Trans.). New York: E. P. Dutton and Co.

Verschueren, J. (1999). *Understanding Pragmatics*. London: Edward Arnold.

Wang, C. & Yan, C. (1995). Yǔzhòu quánxí tǒngyī lùn (*The Theory of Universal Holographic Law*). Jinan: Shandong People's Publishing House.

References   311

Wang, D. (1997). Jiǎng gùshì de luójí (The Logic of Storytelling). Dúshū (*Reading*), 10, 138–141.

Wang, D. (2002). Yǔyán de bēijùxìng (The Tragedy of Language). Dúshū (*Reading*), 7, 112–116.

Wang, M. (1997). Jiāyán yǔ jǐngjù (Dictums and Aphorisms). Dúshū (*Reading*), 7, 117.

Wang, Z. & Wang, T. (2002). Guānyú "cúnzài" hé "shì" (About "Existence" and "Being"). In J. Song (Ed.), BEING yǔ xīfāng zhéxué chuántǒng (*BEING and the Traditions of Western Philosophy*) (Vol. 1). Baoding: Hebei University Press.

Whorf, B. L. (1940/1956). Science and Linguistics. In J. B. Carroll (Ed.), *Language, Thought and Reality: Selecting Writings of Benjamin Lee Whorf* (pp. 207–219). Cambridge, MA: The MIT Press.

Wittgenstein, L. (1953). *Philosophical Investigations* (G. E. M. Anscombe, Trans.). London: Macmillan Press.

Wittgenstein, L. (1958). *The Blue and Brown Books* (R. Rhees, Ed.). Oxford: Blackwell.

Wittgenstein, L. (1922/1983). *Tractatus Logico-Philosophicus* (C. K. Ogden, Trans.). London: Routledge & Kegan Paul Ltd.

Wu, T. (1990). Yǔyán juédìng rénde sīxiǎng ma? (Does Language Determine Human Thoughts?). In Yǔyán yǔ sīwéi guānxì xīntàn (*A New Exploration of the Relationship between Language and Thinking*) (pp. 32–41). Shanghai: Shanghai Educational Publishing House.

Wu, X. (1999). Yānyuán shīzōng (Poetic Traces of Yanyuan). Dúshū (*Reading*), 9, 136.

Wunderlich, D. (1972). Sprechakte. In U. Maas & D. Wunderlich (Eds.), *Pragmatik und Sprachliches Handeln* (pp. 69–188). Frankfurt: Main.

Wunderlich, D. (1976). *Studien zur Sprechakttheorie*. Frankfurt: Suhrkamp.

Xiaoxiao (2002). Lìshǐ shàng de shìshì fēifēi (The Rights and Wrongs in History). Dúshū (*Reading*), 5, 130–139.

Xie, D. (1997). Kèjiāhuà qiánzhān (The Prospect of Hakka Chinese). In Y. Huang (Ed.), Kèjiārén cóng nǎlǐ lái (*Where Are the Hakka From?*) (pp. 383–391). Guangzhou: Guangdong Economics Press.

Xu, J. (1987). Kēxué měixué shǐ (*A History of Scientific Aesthetics*). Changsha: Hunan People's Press.

Xu, S. (1991). Yǔyán biànyì yǔ yǔyán xìtǒng (Language Variation and Language System). Xiàndài wàiyǔ (*Modern Foreign Languages*), 1.

Xu, Y., Zhou, G., Chen, J., & Shang, J. (1996). Yǔyán yǔ zhéxué (*Language and Philosophy*). Beijing: SDX Joint Publishing Company.

Yang, S. (1996). Chōngtú yǔ xuǎnzé: Xiàndài zhéxué zhuǎnxiàng wèntí yánjiū (*Conflicts and Choice: A Study of Turns in Modern Philosophy*). Beijing: Beijing Normal University Press.

Yang, Z. (1998). Jìndài kējì jìnrù zhōngguó de lìshǐ huígù yǔ qiánzhān (Historical Review and Prospect of the Entry of Modern Science and Technology into China). In Zhōngguó dàxué rénwén qǐsīlù (*Humanistic Thoughts in Chinese Universities*) (Vol. 2) (pp. 206–207). Wuhan: Huazhong University of Science and Technology Press.

Yu, Q. (1998). Huáyǔ qíngjié (The Chinese Complex). In Qiūyǔ sǎnwén (*Collection of Proses by Qiuyu*) (pp. 486–506). Hangzhou: Zhejiang Literature & Arts Press.

Yuan, J. (1989). Liánbāng déguó yǔyán xué jiā D. Wunderlich de yányǔ xíngwéi lǐlùn (The Speech Act Theory of the German Linguist D. Wunderlich). Guówài yǔyánxué (*Linguistics Abroad*), 4, 185.

312   *References*

Zhang, Q. (1998). Xūwù zhǔdǎo xìng yǔ wéiwùlùn dì sì xíngtài tàntǎo (Probe into the Dominance of Virtual Matter and the Fourth Form of Materialism). Lǐlùn tàntǎo (*Probe Into Theories*), 3, 41–44.

Zhang, R. (1998). Lǐjiě Yánfù (Understanding Fu Yan). Dúshū (*Reading*), 11.

Zhang, S. (1998). Zhéxué de xīn fāngxiàng (The New Directions of Philosophy). Běijīng dàxué xuébào (*Journal of Peking University*), 2.

Zhang, X. (1996). Xiě xiǎoshuō de fúhàoxué jiā (The Semiologist Who Writes Novels). Dúshū (*Reading*), 11, 92–94.

Zhao, N. (1994). Rènzhī kēxué yǔ guǎngyì jìnhuàlùn (*Cognitive Science and General Evolutionism*). Beijing: Tsinghua University Press.

Zhao, Y. (1994). Lākāng yǔ zhǔtǐ de xiāojiě (Lacan and the Dissolution of the Subject). Dúshū (*Reading*), 10, 25–33.

Zhou, Z. (2004). Táiwān yǔwén fāzhǎn de qílù: Shì "mǔyǔ huà", háishì "gūdǎo huà"? (The Chinese Education in Taiwan Gone Astray: Nativization or Isolation?). Dúshū (*Reading*), 2, 41–46.

Index

Abbasid Dynasty 126
Abdullah, King 126
Aboriginal identity 115, 134
abstraction 23–24
accent identity 139–140
action-guiding function of language
247–249
activity structure 45–46
activity-type-based pragmatic analytical
framework 57
aesthetic activities 9, 240
Aesthetic Linguistics (G. Qian) 10, 165,
191, 282, 294–295
aesthetic process of choice making
73
Age of Civilization 93
agricultural society 212
Aitchison, J. 264, 268
alignment of sense of sound 122
American Academy of Humanities and
Sciences 134
American Society of Linguistics 288
Amitabha 187
Analects, The 97, 125
analytical philosophy 30–32, 62
Ancient Songs of the Miao People
97
Anglo-American pragmatics 11
announcements 8
anti-Spanish-colonialism 135
anti-this or *anti-that* 136
aphorisms 81–82
Aristotle 21–22
Arndt, H. 195, 238
Ashima 63n6
associative thinking 286
Atkin 144
Austin, John Langshaw 4, 32, 40–41, 57,
67, 69, 73, 97

Australian Human Rights Committee 134
Avalokitesvara 187
Aztec civilization 142

Bacon's philosophy 89
Baghramian, M. 271–272, 274
Baishou dance 119, 260n10
báishuàishuài 133
Bamo, Q. 240
bargaining event at Youtian Cattle
Market 216–224, 226–236; on
markets 9
behaviors 4; mental behaviors 4; speech
acts 4; spontaneous physiological
behaviors 4; with words or without
words 4
Being 65; to be 26; clarification 13–14;
expression 14; manifestation of 2, 8;
presence and present 33; resides in the
word 15; saying 17
Being drawing human beings into
language 32–34
Being–language–human beings 33
Being of beings 17–19
Bija 240
bilingual education 130
Bimo 240
bio-holographic law 18
blackbox operations 215
Bodhisattva Guanyin 187, 266–268
brain-racking game 215
Brodsky, Joseph 163
B-type languages 143
Buddha of Infiniteness or Infinite
Light 187
Buddhism 114
Bullock, Alan 156
business talks 8
Butian Song 239

314 *Index*

Cai, Y. 143–144
Campbell, J. 264
capitalism 146
capitalism and liberalism 145
Cassirer, Ernest 185
categorization 23
categorizing 4
Catholicism 136, 151
cattle markets 6, 216–236, 246
causal relationship 177
Chao, G. 94
Chen, B. 190
Chen, Chuxiang 302
Chen, Jiaying 26
Chen, Yinque 50, 117–118, 179
Cheng, Y. 155
China Central TV programs 211
China's legal system 215
China's May 4th Movement in 1919 185
China Social Science Academy 260n5
Chinese civilization 80
Chinese dinner talks 44
Chinese funerals 209
Chinese grammar 150
Chinese-language education, Taiwan 133
Chinese Loulan culture 141
Chinese Lunar New Year 106
Chinese philosophy of language 34–35
Chinese sayings and aphorisms 89–92
Chinese-speaking community in
    Singapore 120
Chinese Spring Festival 114
Chinese wedding ceremonies 6–7, 194,
    195, 197–198, 209, 248, 261n16
*Chinese Word Database
    Construction* 260n5
choosing not to speak 277–281
Christianity 152
cí (words) 93
civilizations 141, 163, 166; Aztec 142;
    Chinese 80; Confucian 146; cultural
    patterns of 167; human 67; Indian
    142; Mayan 142; modern 115; Olmec
    142; Teotihuacan 142; Toltec 142;
    Western 147
civil mediation 48–58
Civil War 144
Clark, H. H. 44
Clash of Civilizations, The
    (Huntington) 149
cognitive-psychological constraints
    43, 47, 56
cognitive style 160

colonization 136
communication 38; human
    communication 241–244; between
    languages 163–164; linguistic 40;
    social 67; verbal 211; verbal networks
    72; violent 157
communism 269
Communist Manifesto 145
*Compendium of the Languages of the
    Turks* 125–126
computer software 76
conceiving 4
conceptualizing 4
conceptual virtual entity 14
concerted human action 37
conditional relationship 177
Confucian civilization 146
Confucianism 126
Confucius 67, 97, 125, 140
Confucius moves 161
conservatism of Chinese thinking 182
contemplating 4
contextualism 11, 182
contractual relationship 68
conventionality 45
conversations 251
co-occurrence of formulaic utterances
    and formulaic actions: cultural
    stability 208–210; driving force
    of expectations 202–208; human
    cooperation 202; human pursuit of
    efficiency in life 210–216
cooperativeness 44
cosmos 120–121
court debates 8
court investigations 8
creativity 73, 300
criminal punishments 140
cross-cultural sensitivity 122
crystallization process 184–185
C-type languages 143
Cui, J. 11
cultural activities 9
cultural common core 260n12
cultural community 120
cultural conquests 137
cultural dominance 82
cultural group 120
cultural organization 120
Cultural Revolution in China 77, 79,
    112–113, 115, 166, 186, 279
cultural septum 157
cultural stability, impetus 208–210

Index 315

cultural tradition 160
cultural untranslatability 157
cultural validity 121
culture, orientation of 182
cúnzaì *see* to exist
curse of Babel 159
cyberspace 157

Daming Palace 138
Dan Li 17
Dao 24
das Sein 24–30; Chen 26;
    Heidegger 24–26
decision making 251
declarative sentences 72
default practices 6
defending oneself 9
de Gourmont, R. 109
democratization 149
Deng, Shaomang 22
Deng, Xiaoping 248, 279
Derrida, J. 129
diagnosing 9
Dialogue on Language, A (Heidegger) 2
dictums and aphorisms 81–82
diplomatic protests 9
discourse fields 72–108; as checking
    mechanism 81–82; constraints of
    244–246; crystallization of 104;
    defined 78; dialect chunks 78–79;
    formulaic verbal behavior 244–246;
    history, transmission 96–107; human
    being 72–108; inheritance of 92–107;
    listening and speaking 73–78; phonetic
    chunks 78–79; preexistence of 78–87;
    rectification mechanism for society 81;
    sayings 88–92
discourse hegemony 132
discourse segments 82–86
dominance 82
dominant discourse system 82
Dong, Leshan 110
Dragon Boat Festival 114
Dream of Red Mansions, A 278
drug trafficking 115
D-type languages 143
Du, Weiming 130, 134
Duan, B. 97
Dummett, M. 31, 88, 178
Duranti, Alessandro 37

Earth Charter, The 132
East Asian languages 153

Eco, Umberto 14
economic development 133
economic politics 75
effective expressions 165
enculturation 128
English, spread of 120
Enshi in Hubei province 125
environmental pollution 115
epistemology 164
Erfolgreich- Sein 41
Esthetic Linguistics (Qian) 108–110
ethnic assimilation 115
ethnic clothing 119
ethnic group's identity 119
ethnic identity, religion and language in
    113–120
existence 25
existence, language and human beings 34
existentialism 164
extralinguistic interaction 41
$E_{сть}$ 27

facial expressions and postures 109
fallacies 269–270
false democracy 77
falsification 165, 173
Fei, Xiaotong 120
Feng, Youlan 35, 74, 148, 158–159
folk ballads 97–100
foreign-language learning 121–122
forgiveness 156
formality 42, 44
formulaicity 45–46, 207–210, 212;
    activity goals 224–237; economical
    means 227–238; effects of 241;
    efficiency in cooperation 238–239;
    negative effects of violating 241–242;
    performance of rites 239–240; positive
    and negative effects of variations
    242–244; of speech 5, 8; tendency to
    200–202
formulaic phrasing 211
formulaic speech 7, 208–210
formulaic utterances 224–226, 241–242
formulaic verbal behavior 1–2, 5, 7–8,
    197, 254; action-guiding function
    of language 247–249; constraints
    of discourse fields 244–246; co-
    occurrence of formulaic utterances
    and formulaic actions 202–216;
    cultural stability 208–210; definition
    and characteristics 194–197;
    expectations 202–208; fixed move

316 *Index*

orders 254; fixed set of utterances 254; formulaicity 224–226, 237–240; formulaicity and variations 197–200; game theory of language use 249–252; goals and intentions 253; human communication 241–244; human cooperation 202; human pursuit of efficiency in life 210–216; pragmatic mechanism 244–254; tendency to formulaicity 200–202
fortune-telling 202–207
fossils 125
Foundations of the Theory of Signs (Morris) 37
four-move ritual 6
Frege, Gottlob 31–32, 62, 271–272
Frege's theory of sense and reference 268
friction 62
Fujian dialect 154
functional false information 264–265
Future Problems with Chinese Characters, The (Xuantong Qian) 154

Gadamer, Hans-Georg 17
game rules 6
game theory of language use 249–253
Ge, J. 128
General Linguistics 293
George, Stefan 63n3, 65, 257–259
Gilsenan, M. 264
globalization 114, 131
goal-intention principle of conversation 237–238
Golden Rules for Living 4–5
Gongshu, Ban 70
governance 44
Great Cultural Revolution 291–292
Great Proletarian Cultural Revolution 269
Greenberg, 188
Grice, Paul 32
Guangdong 104
Guangzhou 104, 196
guildhalls 139
Guo, Y. 94

Han, Shaogong 125
Han Chinese culture 116, 127, 141
Han Dynasty 128
hànzì táiyǔhuà 133
harmful false information 264–265
He, C. 185–186

Hegel, Georg Wilhelm Friedrich 22, 97, 266
hegemony 130
Heidegger, Martin 1–4, 14–17, 33, 65–66, 130, 152–153, 164, 176, 188, 193; *see also* language is the house of being
Heidegger's philosophy 3, 255–258
Heidegger's quotations 19
Herman, Robert S. 89
history, inheritance of 92–107
history, transmission of: speech 94–96; writing 93–94
History as a Mirror (Guang) 93
History of Scientific Aesthetic Thought, A (Xu) 294
Hjelmslev, Louis 254
Hong Kong 104
Hopi Indian language 172
Hopi Indians 175
Hou, L. 113–120
household-responsibility system 49
Hu, Shi 140, 147
Huang, C. 163–164
Huang, P. 22, 142
Hui people in China 113, 138
human beings 33–34, 74, 78
human civilizations 67, 77, 133
human cooperation 202
human existence, philosophical perspective 13–14; being drawing human beings into language 32–34; language is the house of being 14–32; spirit of Chinese philosophy 34–35
human existence, pragmatics perspective: activity constraints and constraint conditions 46–48; activity goals and activity types 44; activity structure and structural formula 45–46; activity types 42–48; civil mediation 48–58; language use 36–42; pragmatic analyses of ordinary language 58–62; variations 44–45
humanism 156
humanistic network 153
human natural death 209
human nature 33
human productive activities 67
human pursuit of efficiency in life 210–216
human skulls 125
human social behavior 42
human society 74
human sounds 74

Index   317

human-specific attributes 9
human spirit 14
Humboldt 193
Huo, Y. 64n14
hypothetical relationship 177

ideal language 62
ideological dominance 82
illocutionary acts 40
imperative sentences 72
implicit charm of *qi* (air, vitality)
    movement 109
impotence 124
incommensurability 150–152
Indian civilizations 142
Indian languages 143
innate limitation 93
institutionalized conventions 6–7,
    9
intellectual reasoning 11
intention- motivated activity 47
Interim Rules for Marriage Registration,
    The 196
interlocutors 40
international corporation 115
interpersonalcultural (social)
    constraints 43
interpretation 158–159
interrogative sentences 72
intersubjectivity, linguistic
    relationships 68–69
interviewing 9, 27–28
introducing people 9

Jewish people 113
Ji, Xianlin 170–171
Jia, Baoyu 268
Jiang, Jingguo 266
Jianghan Plain in Hubei Province 101
Jiangxi Province 279
Jia Zi Table 239
Jin, K. 25
Jin Dynasty 129
Jingyun Dagu 260n6
Judaism 113

Kachru 120
Kai-shek, Chiang 148–149
Kakuzo, Okakura 146
Karakhanid dynasty 125–126
Kasher, A. 69
Kashgari, Mahmud 125
Kezhi 240

Kinte, Kunta 127
Klaus, Michelle 143
knowledge alignment 122
kowtow (four-move ritual) 6–7
Kuhn, Thomas S. 166, 169–171
Kuhn's Selected Works of Philosophy of
    Science 169

Lacan, Jacques 68–69
Lakoff, G. 41
language 33, 39; action-guiding function
    of 247–249; analysis 30–32; anti-
    hegemony 137; betraying 266; betrays
    human beings 263; bred by human
    minds 125; Chinese philosophy
    34–35; Chinese to English 155;
    communication between 163–164;
    community 120–124; concealing of
    22; defined 66, 139, 159, 175–176,
    255–256; destroying 4; discrimination
    130; equality 132; expression 17;
    framework 189, 191; functions
    of 10, 22, 72; game 10, 18; habits
    167; hegemony 137; heritage 129;
    heritage from forefathers 124–125;
    incommensurability 150–152; issues
    136–137; and mature thought 178;
    pragmatics 11; primitive function and
    original form 239; property of 21–22;
    reality, thinking about and describing
    274; scientific study of culture 166;
    social problems and processes 167;
    social reality, guide to 167; strategy,
    United States 142; superiority 143;
    system 171; thinking of children 177;
    and thought 171; unity 144; use, game
    theory 249–250; Western philosophy
    34–35; *see also* language and human
    beings; language is the house of being;
    living in language
language-and-culture assimilation 144
language and human beings 263;
    distorting the world 265–266; harmful
    false information 264–265; language
    problems 271–276; lies and fallacies
    266–271
language games 38–41, 46, 57–58
language is the house of Being 14–15;
    Being of beings resides in the word
    17–19; Being to beings, word gives
    19–21; functions of language,
    inverting and concealing 21–24;
    Heidegger's idea of proposition

318   *Index*

15–17; language, analysis of 30–32;
proposition 15–17; statements 15–16;
word *das Sein* 24–30
Lantern Festival 114
Laozi's philosophy 22, 24
Laplanders 129
Latin American Radio Stations
Association of Education 132
"leaving Asia" frenzy 146
lecturing 9
Letter on Humanism (Heidegger) 1–2, 15
Levinson, S. C. 41–42, 44, 46–47, 57, 72,
184, 194
Lewis, D. 41
Li, Dan 63n4
Li, Liqun 140
Li, Si 20, 22
Li, T. 188
Li, Xiyin 27
Liang, Shuming 181–182
Liar's Tale: A History of Falsehood, The
(Campbell) 268
liberalism 146
lies and fallacies 266–271
life, form of 39
Lin, Daiyu 63n5, 268
Lin, Yutang 179–180, 182
linguistic communication 40, 73
linguistic determinism and mechanism
164–167; language determining
thought 184–192; pre-existing
structure of human cognition 192–194;
Sapir–Whorf hypothesis 165–184
linguistic heritage 132
Linguistic Holographic Law 75
linguistic ontology 190
linguistic phenomena 60
linguistic regulation theory (LRT) 61
linguistic relativity 168–169
linguistic signs 265
linguistic thinking 190
linguists 70
linking verbs 28
Lippard, P.V. 271
Liu, N. 185
Liu, Z. 239
live in language, having to 108; accent
identity 139–140; civilization,
language and lasting of 140–164;
communication between languages
163–164; conquest and assimilation
141–145; ethnic group, fingerprint
and heritage 113–140; ethnic identity,

religion and language in 113–120;
heritage of people 124–138; language
community, fingerprint value 120–124;
language determining thought 184–192;
language incommensurability 150–153;
life activity 108–113; linguistic
determinism 164–194; mother tongue/
mother culture 145–150; pre-existing
structure of human cognition 192–194;
Sapir-Whorf hypothesis 165–184;
septum between languages 155–163;
stability of language 154–155
living-fossil function of words 106
living in language 66–67; discourse
fields, human being 72–108; human
behavior 67–72; inheritance of history
92–107; listening and speaking 73–78;
preexistence of discourse fields 78–87;
sayings control life 88–92
locutionary acts 40
logical thinking 18
Long, Yingtai 110
Lu, S. 119, 130
Lü, Shuxiang 288, 301
Lu, Xun 77, 93
Lüger, H. 200
Lugu Lake 116
Lunar New Year 101
Luo, Yusheng 110, 260n6
Luoyang 128, 136

Macao 104
Malinowski, Bronislaw 10, 37, 40, 239
Manchu ethnic group 118
Manjusri, Bodhisattva 280
mankind 21
mankind, behavior: discourse fields
72–108; forms 68; formulaic verbal
behavior 263; language 263; language
to perform some behavior 68, 254;
mental behavior 68; metabolism
68; produce 68; virtue of language
257–259
man speaks 3
Mao, Zedong 248
market economy 18
Martinich, A. P. 273
maxim of quality 269
Mayan civilization 142
Mayan culture 141
meditating 4
Meiji Restoration 137
mental behaviors 4, 74

Index 319

metabolism 4
metaphysics 14
metapragmatic awareness of language
  users 61
Mid-autumn Festival 114
Mill, John Stuart 267
Ming Dynasty 74, 93
Miyako, Hashikawa 146
modern civilization 115
modernization, Japan 146
modern linguistics 94
Modern Philosophy of Language
  (Baghramian) 15, 271
Monkey King 267
Monks 187
monosyllabic language 182
Moore, George Edward 32
Morgenstern, Oskar 250
Morris, Charles 37–38
Mosuo ethnic distinction and language
  115–117
mother tongue 113, 127, 138, 256;
  accumulation 150; mother culture
  145–150
Mozi 70
My Country and My People (Lin) 179

naming 266
Nan, F. 81–82
Nanyang accent 155
National Center for Linguistics and
  Applied Linguistics 302
National Revolution 138
national sentiments 136
Native American Language Act 144
natural disasters 115
negotiations 9
Nestorianism 150
New Approach of Chinese Pragmatics, A
  (Shi and Cui) 11
New Culture movement 137
New Year Family Dinner talk 200
Ni, L. 159
noise-making scene 201
nominalism 19–20
nominalists 20
non- formulaic speech events 7–8
non-formulaic verbal behaviors 7
non-Han ethnic groups 260n8
noninstitutionalized conventions 6–7,
  9
nonnative varieties of English 28
nonverbal behaviors 5

non-zero-sum (or mixed-motive)
  games 250
Northern Expedition Memorial 138
Northern Wei Dynasty 125, 127
Nuo god 119
Nuo opera 119

Olmec civilization 142
one-character formulaic utterance 242
one-to-one confrontation 250
On the Equality of Things (Feng) 74
On the Long March with Chairman Mao
  (Changfeng) 291–292
On the Way to Language (Heidegger) 3
oral agreements 6
oral data collection 94
Orthodox Church 149
Outlaws of the Marsh 138

parasitic behaviors 69
Paris Peace Treaty 136
Peace Plan 144
perlocutionary acts 40
Peurson, Van 39
Philippine Independence Movement 136
Philippines 136
Philosophical Investigations
  (Wittgenstein) 32
phonetic system 133
physiological attributes 9
physiological behaviors 74
physiological disharmony 109
Plato 17, 22, 67
poetic imagination 3
poetic language 3
Poetry, Language, Thought
  (Heidegger) 2–3
poets 2–3
political hegemony 130
political jokes 87
Politics of Friendship, The (Derrida) 129
Popper, K. R. 173
post-modern age 131
pragmatic mechanism of formulaic
  verbal behaviors 254
pragmatics 60; as discipline with
  specific linguistic units of analysis 58;
  narrow sense against the background
  of Chinese culture 58; perspective
  with no specific linguistic units of
  analysis 58
Pragmatics in Chinese Culture (Qian) 11,
  241, 265, 282

320   *Index*

pragmatists 76
precept 77
predicate verbs 28–29
prelinguistic thinking 190
presence of Being 16
price negotiation 216–224, 226–236
Principles of Pragmatics (Leech) 293
private languages 122–124, 187
producing 4
production activities 74
Prolegomena to a Theory of Language (Hjelmslev) 255
pronunciation 186
psychological homestead 139–140, 263
purpose relationship 177
pursuit of efficiency 211

Qi, Gong 141
Qian, Guanlian 237–238, 264–265, 277; *Aesthetic Linguistics* 294–295; associative thinking 286; Chinese philosophy 287; course in American literature 293; Department of Foreign Languages 288; early life 282–283, 285; education and development 282–287, 289; familiarity with poetry 283; First Senior High School 291; foreign languages 287–288; open class teaching 291; *Pragmatics in Chinese Culture* 295–296; *Principles of Pragmatics* (Leech) 293; research-based studies 286; study of linguistics 292; Summer Diary 286; *Theory of Language Holography, The* 297; "Tolerance of Language for its Redundant Information" 294; university life 289–291; West Hubei University 292; Xianfeng Normal School 292
Qian, Xuantong 154
Qian, Zhongshu 66, 76, 94, 109–110, 159
qiángqiánggǔn 133
Qianlong (emperor) 151
queer people 179

rational thinking 9
reading poems aloud 186
realism 19
recommending oneself 9
Records of the Grand, The (Qian) 93
reflecting 4
Reform Movement of 1898 137
region-based guildhalls 139
reincarnation of pragmatics in China 10–12

relatively speaking 69
relatives, classification of 160–161
renaissance 156
Revolution of 1911 137
rewrite history 93
Ricci, Matteo 151
Richard, W. J. 195, 238
ritual and music 140
ritualization 195–196
ritualization of communicative behavior 195, 238
Rizal, Jose 135
Romance of the Three Kingdoms 138, 282
root genealogy 240
Roots: The Saga of an American Family (Haley) 127
Rorty, M. R. 31
ruling thoughts discourse 87
rural discourse in Shahu Town 100–107
rural mediating activities 51–55
Russell, Bertrand 32, 62, 270, 272–273
ruthlessness 88
Ryle, Gilbert 32

sachima 118, 260n9
Sadock, J. 41
salvation 187
Santa Claus 266–267
Sapir, E. 159
Sapir's linguistic determinism 167–168
Sapir-Whorf hypothesis 165–185, 189, 192, 254
Sbisà, M. 31
scriptedness 42, 44
Searle, John 32, 40–41
Selective Series of Guizhou Folk Literature and *Research Series of Guizhou Folk Culture* 97
self-organizing movement 191–192
Senior's Day 114
sentence types 72
septum between languages 155–162
Shahu Town in Xiantao City 114
Shahu Town Mianyang County 101, 103
Shakespeare 17
Shanghai 104
Shannxi Province 94
shaqima 260n9
Shen, Jiaben 50
Sheng, X. 39
Shenzhen 104
shì 25, 29
Shi, C. 11
shūbùjìnyán 93
silence in speaking 279

Sinicization 127–129, 141, 152
sinologists 160
situational-physical activities 47
situational-physical constraints 43, 57
Slavism 149
social behavior in society 71
social communication 67
social conflict mediation 49
social habitat 48
social humanistic network 249, 277
social information, material- based
  signs 14
social process 57
societal modernization 119
sociocultural (interpersonal)
  activities 47, 55
sociocultural attributes 9–10
Socrates 17, 67
Song, Ziwen 148–149
Song Dynasty 79, 281
Southern Song Dynasty 140
speaking 68
speaking in silence 279
speaking of language 3, 253
*Specters of Marx: The State of the Debt,
  the Work of Mourning and the New
  International* (Derrida) 130
speech acts 4, 41, 68, 70, 74;
  crystallization by 78; events
  6–7; history, transmission of 94–96;
  illocutionary 40; locutionary 40;
  perlocutionary 40
speech act theory 38, 40–41
spirit of Chinese philosophy 32–34
spiritual activities 9
spiritual baptism 80
spiritual creative activities 69
spiritual development of mankind
  193
spiritual pleasure 80
spiritual pursuits 89
spontaneous physiological behaviors 4
Spring Festival couplets 81
sputnik 19
stable match between actions and
  utterances 6
standard English 28
Status of Linguistics as a Science, The
  (Sapir) 166
Stenius, E. 41
Stolen Generations 134
Strawson, Peter Frederick 32
Stress of Thinking (Deng) 22
structural constraints 47
structural formula 45–46

*Structure of Scientific Revolutions,
  The* 170
subjectivity of human beings 69
sudden enlightenment 190
súgēdàwǎn 133
Sun, Yat-sen 138
Suo, S. 136
super-computers 76
super-SARS fears 261n15
superstructure activities 9
supralinguistic thinking 190
súsúmài 133
symbolic activities 9
syntactic fluency 122
systemic Chinese literary criticism 125

Taiwanese language 133
táiyǔ hànzìhuà 133
Tan, L. 182
Tang Dynasty 93, 150, 281
Tao, Yuanming 278
tendency to formulaicity 200–202
Teotihuacan civilization 142
Tezuka, Tomio 33
Theory of Games 18
Theory of Games and Economic Behavior
  (Morgenstern) 250
Theory of Language Holography, The
  (G. Qian) 120, 282
thing 19–20
thinkers 2–3
thinking habit 160
Three Bar Drums 101
Three-Kowtow-One-Escort formula
  209–210
three livings 1–2, 8, 11; human existence
  9–10, 65
three togethers 117
three-to-one theory 11, 61
to be 25
to exist 25
tolerance 155–156
Toltec civilization 142
Tomb-sweeping Day 114
Tomio, Tezuka 130–131, 152–153
tongue-twisters 87
Touch Me Not, The Reign of the Greed
  (Rizal) 135
traditional Chinese medicine (TCM) 6,
  9, 44, 46, 194
traditional Chinese weddings 6
translatability 174
translation 158–159
Triple Flame, The 29
Tujia autonomous prefecture 118

322   *Index*

Tujia language 119
Tuoba, Hong 127
two-fold (èrchóngxìng) 63n2
type variation 44–45

unilingualism 143
Universal Holographic Law 75
untranslatability 157
urbanization of rural areas 104

variability of speech 8
variation parameters 44–45
verbal behaviors 1, 5, 8, 48, 71, 108
verbal communication 211, 251, 265
verbal communication networks 72
verbalness 42, 44
Verschueren, J. 60
Vimalakirti, Licchavi 279–280
violent communication 157
virtual entity 14
virtual physical entities 14
virtual social entities 14
virtue-story-telling 103
vocabulary size 122
voicing pattern 109
von Neumann, John 250

Walcott, Derek 163
Wang, Chuming 302
Wang, D. 22, 75
Wang, Li 288
Wang, M. 82, 89
Wang, T. 63n1
Wang, Z. 63n1
Warring States 93–94
wash and sleep (xǐle shuì) 5–6
waves, material-based signs 14
wedding ceremonies 8
Wei Dynasty 136
Wen, Tianxiang 140
Western civilizations 147
Western English 28
Westernization 145–149
Western languages 157
Western philosophy of language 34–35
wholeness 21
Whorf, B. L. 160
Whorf's principle of linguistic relativity
    168–169
Wittgenstein, Ludwig 31–32, 39–40, 46,
    57, 62, 157, 188, 192, 280
Wittgenstein's theory of language 71
Word, The (George) 65

World Guide, The 131–132
writing, transmission of history
    93–94
writing letters 9
writing style 110
Wu, Ningkun 67
Wuhan, China 5
Wuling 260n11
Wunderlich, D. 40–41, 46, 57

Xianbei culture 128
Xianbei language 127–128
Xianbei people 128
Xiaowen (emperor) 125, 127–129,
    136, 141
Xinhua News Digest 28
Xinjiang 126
Xu, Guozhang 291
Xu, Y. 189
Xu, Zhenhua 302

yán (speech) 93
Yan, Fu 147
Yang, Lixin 115–116
Yang, Zhenning 183
Yang, Zijian 302
Yangtze River 80
Yi language 240
Youtian Cattle Market in Biyang County
    211–212
Yu, Qiuyu 125, 139–140
Yuan, Xun 127
Yuan Dynasty 151
Yukichi, Fukuzawa 146

Zen Buddhism 140, 152
Zen Buddhist 70
zero-sum games 250
Zhang, Houchen 302
Zhang, Q. 14
Zhang, R. 148
Zhang, San 20–22
Zhang, Shouxian 287
Zhang, Xiaoyan 266
Zhao, N. 162
Zhao, Yuanren 288, 301
Zhenguan 150
Zhuang people 119
Zhuangzi 93, 278
Zhuge, Liang 138, 144
Ziwen Song 148–149
zoon logon echon 74
Zwiefalt 256